ETHICAL THEORY AND BUSINESS DECISIONS

James Owens, Professor of Management
American University
College of Business
Washington, D.C. 20016

Copyright © 1982 by James Owens. All rights reserved. No part of this publication may be reproduced, stored in a retrieval system, or transmitted, in any form or by any means without the prior written permission of the author.

Library of Congress Number 82-90137
ISBN 0-943170-02-8

MANAGEMENT EDUCATION LTD.
12326 Riverview Rd.
TANTALLON, MARYLAND 20744

In summary, a new age of instant information and public insistence on ethical behavior has transformed business ethics from an ideal condition to a reality, from a luxury to a practical necessity for the survival and success of organizations. The central instrument for making ethics operational and real in an organization is a written code of ethics which is specific, is both positive and negative in its ethical content, is based upon general ethical standards, and is enforceable by appropriate sanctions.

James Owens
BUSINESS HORIZONS
February 1978

CONTENTS

CASE INDICENTS

Preface

The Liberty Bell on the cover strikes the major theme of this book: American freedom can be sustained only by voluntary self-regulation (i.e. ethics rather than law) on the part of most citizens and businesses. True and free democracies appear rarely in human history and have never endured for long; because freedom, if abused, is expendable whereas social order is not, and usually, as in South America or Russia, a strong central government (always dictatorial) is needed to maintain the essential order. Thus, business ethics, the main scope of this book, is not a mere sentimental ideal but a real and practical necessity if America's business system is to remain basically free instead of an arm of central government regulated by a growing maze of laws.

The purpose of the book is twofold: to present a rigorous theoretical foundation of ethical concepts and method, drawn mainly from the field of philosophy; and to apply ethical theory to a large sample of contemporary American business decision-situations. In most books on business ethics (many excellent and included in the bibliography), one or the other of these goals is the intent, but not both. The reason is that business ethics involves two major disciplines (philosophy and business management), each of which is very complex as a field of knowledge and experience in itself and both are radically different from (many would say opposed to) each other, in ends, methodology, history and the training required for professional practitioners in the fields. Thus the typical book in business ethics is written by a philosopher and is strong on ethical theory (while light on experienced application to business) or by a business specialist and is strong on the realities of the marketplace and the workplace (while light on theoretical foundations for ethical analysis). The author of this book, for a variety of life circumstances, has traveled through both fields (doctorate degree and university teaching in philosophy and, later, and now, a professor of business management along with a heavy business consulting practice) and hopes his combined backgrounds will contribute to a useful book in business ethics, balancing ethical theory with business practice.

This book, therefore, is about half theory and half application to the realities of business. Both are necessary - and in the same book. Ethical theory alone is inadequate to the tasks of business ethics: sound theory applied to the poorly understood realities of the actual world of business. But genuine understanding of business ethics cannot be gained without the sound foundation in ethical theory along with experienced appreciation of the realities of the business world. Both are necessary. And the effort in this book has been to combine sound ethical theory with realistic application to the business world -in approximately equal proportions throughout the book. Hopefully, the book begins to approach the requirements of a combined treatment of business ethics, building upon both sound philosophical theory as well as sound experience and understanding of the real business world.

The purposes above dictate the book's structure. Chapters 1 and 2 describe briefly the history of business practices and explore the urgent practical necessity of business ethics in modern America (if the business system is to remain free, with free markets prevailing rather than central dictator-like government). Chapters 3 and 4 lay the theoretical foundations of basic ethical concepts and their philosophical sources, the only intellectually solid grounds for serious ethical analysis and applications whether to business or any other field of human life. Chapter 5 explains the systematic methods of ethical analysis, these skills far more critical for a manager's lifetime career than specific conclusions about current issues (whether drawn today by this or any other author). Chapter 6 is an examination, both historical and analytical, of the nature of business, its purposes and varieties under different economic systems (capitalism vs socialism) and different political systems (democracy vs dictatorships). Chapters 7 through 12 apply ethical theory and methods to business's relationships with consumers, employees, stockholders, the general public and foreign nations. A section of 52 cases provides further opportunity for application of ethical concepts to current business issues.

The book is intended for senior-level college students, graduate students and practicing managers to improve on-the-job skills in ethical analysis of business situations, most of which today (and more so in the future) involve ethical dimensions as part of daily business decisions. Its intent is practical, for now or future practicing managers; not typical academic fare for university professors. Thus explicit effort has been made to present complex concepts in the clearest English, with as little use of either philosophical or business jargon as possible and with consistent use of examples throughout - examples being surely the best way to make an idea clear, as well as interesting reading, and drive it deep and forever into the mind of a reader. This does not mean that the book is quick and easy reading; that would be impossible, considering the rich and technical literature comprising both the fields of philosophy and business (economic) theory. But, to the extent possible, the book introduces and deals with difficult concepts (and technical terms) clearly, always with clarifying and current examples, so as to be easily understood by a careful reader concentrating on and analyzing each sentence, paragraph, section and chapter of the book.

Thus, the book, in addition to its intended clear and relatively simple explanation of complicated concepts, must be studied -not merely read or scanned- to be properly understood by the reader. It is a book to be used as a tool rather than read for enjoyment or amusement (although many of the examples used will provide much of the latter). Conceived as an intellectual tool, the book will be easily handled as such: the Contents, at the front of the book, is detailed and provides page numbers for every detailed concept (for easy reference); the Index, at the back of the book, is even more detailed for quick references; and, throughout the book, parenthetical references are consistently made to concepts or historical events discussed earlier in the text. As a tool for improving the needed skills of ethical analysis, the book is easily used and useful. The Bibliography at the end of the book, although selective, provides about 200 of the best, recent works in the rapidly emerging field of business ethics - so that readers can easily pursue further specific areas that spark special interest. The Bibliography is not a routine one; it is limited to only those works the author has found genuinely useful either in whole or in part (most of the books are in his personal library for re-reading and reference).

The title of the book includes the words "business decisions." It is important to note that, for our purposes and within our scope, "business" is not limited to profit-oriented corporations but explicitly includes the activities of all organizations, government, education, voluntary, medical, and so on. Except where otherwise noted or implied by the context, the discussion is confined mainly to American organizations. Thus, here, business ethics includes the activities of corporation directors and managers, mayors and congressmen, doctors and professors, salesmen and one-man stores or shops, the names in each case indicating the "business" each is in.

Few subjects strike raw nerves and elicit strong emotions more than the subject of ethics, touching as it does our deepest values and lifelong attitudes about what is right vs wrong, good vs evil. So it is inevitable that many specific moral positions appearing in the book, especially the author's examples and interpretations of history, might oppose the reader's -and even be irritating. Insofar as virtually every specific topic dealt with is controversial (the essence of a free America means we can disagree and freely debate our differences), differences in views between the reader and the author are not alarming, but healthy rational exercise in man's search for truth and the best methods for finding it. An essential point throughout the book will be the proper methods of ethical analysis, not the specific conclusions you or I or someone else might happen to arrive at in a field laden with honest differences in human values.

Controversy can be removed from a book on ethics only by careful and comfortable abstractions and avoiding specifics and examples, resulting in anemic fare for the reader. The choice taken in this book is just the opposite: that controversy is free and healthy debate, part of any true intellectual education, and a continuing opportunity to review critically the views of another (especially the rational case made) as well as one's own. (The Introduction to Case Analysis, p.269 below, explains this rationale in detail, and should be read carefully.)

Despite the above cautions about controversy and how it upsets some readers, objectivity in treatment of material has been an explicit intent, more often achieved, it is hoped, than not. In many instances, the author has tried to provide the best case for and then against certain positions in the effort to be objective. To the extent possible, the book is never used as a vehicle for promotion of his personal positions on most issues (this belongs in journal and magazine articles, not a text).

But several convictions of the author openly pervade this book as essential to its major themes and purposes. They are as follows:

(1) A free market (capitalistic and profit-oriented) economic system, even if necessarily modified by minimum government regulation in order to work, has proved to be -and remains- man's best hope for life of high human quality. And, all efforts should be made to sustain it.

(2) For over fifty years, despite good initial reasons for it (the "robber barons" and other unethical business actions), government regulations and laws have mushroomed excessively until, today, both the freedom and the international competitive power (productivity) of all Americans and their businesses are weak and in serious jeopardy.

(3) The spirit of Americans, over the past fifty years, is gravitating away from the traditional American values of free enterprise, individual pride, self-reliance and voluntary mutual human help, as well as the old "work ethic," and moving by increasing momentum toward government control of business, socialist government-run "welfare" arrangements, "cradle-to-grave" government-guaranteed security for all (whether productive or not) and national costs that are bankrupting the nation - and making it a soft opponent in the eyes of a stronger aggressor (Russia).

(4) The work ethic is a sound American value, to be restored.

(5) Voluntary ethical sensitivity and action, by both citizens and businesses, at least by most (as distinct from laws enforced by central government power), constitute the practical foundations for a sustainable free America. If ethics and freedom fail, then, by long-tested historical patterns, freedom becomes expendable and social order (not achieved by voluntary and ethical action) is simply imposed dictatorially. This iron pattern of history abounds in most of today's world and is clearly closing

in on current America. The American experiment in human freedom was launched three (not two) centuries ago by people risking all personal security to fight, slowly but determinedly, for both political and economic (business) freedom. They achieved the toe-hold on a free nation, in 1776, based mainly upon a spirit of self-reliance and strong ethical principles (not government-guaranteed security for life or government laws controlling every detail of life - indeed, that was exactly what they were fighting against). The choices for business today are clear: either pursue the route of voluntary ethical action, armed with skills of ethical analysis, and self-regulation -or- submit increasingly to growing laws and government regulations demanded by the public (in lieu of voluntary action by business).

Thus, ethics in business, as advocated in this book, is far from the stereotype (one might expect) of sentimental or religious moralizing in the abstract; rather, it is proposed and, I think, fully justified as a hard practical necessity, if American business is to remain self-regulated and free as opposed to government-regulated and a slave to government. As will be detailed in the book, new and higher standards of business ethics are advocated - but mainly for practical and realistic business reasons.

It is obvious that readers of general socialist leanings and values (I hope few) will find this book uncomfortable - or intolerable. So be it. The above convictions of the author, as clearly stated, pervade the book.

Some suggestions for professors and other insturctors using this text:

(1) The book has been designed as essentially a self-teaching text in its basic format. Easy and logical reference mechanisms (Contents, Index, parenthetical references, etc.) guide the reader always to review and renew understandings of key concepts. At the end of each chapter, a series of questions, problems and exercises, short but carefully chosen, structures a comprehensive review of the central material in the chapter. Given the book's dedication to clear and understandable English in the handling of ideas -and with pointed examples, the instructor is spared the waste of valuable classroom time "explaining the explanations" in a text and is free to get on with his own special efforts to expand, enliven, amplify and apply the ideas to the current real world of business. In short, the book aims to be a help, rather than a hindrance, for the creative teacher of business ethics.

(2) Chapter 4 (my favorite from either a theoretical or historical viewpoint) can be deleted from the instruction plan, if time restraints demand it, without critically affecting the essential flow and purposes of the book. Chapter 4 (Historical Development of Ethical Theories) explains the historical and philosophical sources of the basic ethical concepts organized logically, rather than historically, in Chapter 3 (Ethical Theories and Concepts). But, Chapter 3 can stand alone.

(3) Footnotes and end-of-chapter numbered references have been kept to an absolute minimum, used only when documentation of a stated fact or quotation was essential (this policy in line with the practical, rather than acacemic, objectives of the book). The instructor will wish, of course, to add his own material, with his own documentation, in order to "flesh out" chapter topics with his own experience and news of recent and current events. For example, serious students of our subject here in this book should be reading regularly The Wall Street Journal (for daily business information) and/or Business Week (for weekly information) as well as consulting key "thought" journals in the library such as The Conference Board's Across the Board, Harper's, special reports in the Atlantic, monthly issues of the Business and Professional Ethics Journal, Business and Policy Journal, and other similar sources of information. Other institutional sources of ideas and serious work in the field of business ethics are, of course, Hastings Center in New York, the Ethics Resource Center in Washington, the Center for Applied Ethics at the University of Virginia, Maryland University's and American University's similar centers for the study of business ethics and business-government relations.

(4) Based on the author's experience, the 52 cases at the back of the book are an essential teaching aid. Although theory is a major part of the book, our purpose here is practical: the reader's improved skills in applying theory soundly in ethical analysis, not merely an abstract knowledge of theory. For our purposes, theory is not an end in itself, but a means to the practical goal of proper use of it. The cases are an ideal vehicle for this. They can be assigned for analysis and discussion in a variety of ways to suit particular instructors' approaches (key issues in each case are listed in the Contents).

Finally, given the goals and themes of this book, it is worth noting a portion of the 1977-78 Harvard University Annual Report (pp. 15-18), prepared by university president Derek C. Bok, which was devoted to a comprehensive review and critique of its prestigious business school:

> "Many executives spend up to half their time on government, regulatory, and community affairs. And yet, most business curricula pay little attention to these issues but still concern themselves primarily with matters of marketing, finance, etc. ...Most classroom discussions still proceed on the unexamined assumption that growth and profits are the only serious concerns of the corporate manager. The study of ethics has fared no better."

James Owens
Washington, D.C.

1 The Practical Aspects of Business Ethics

Business ethics, like medical ethics or ethics applied to any field of life, concerns and in many cases controls human decision making - and is therefore practical.*

For example, what is more practical than deciding who will live or die, or who will retain their jobs or be fired, or who will keep their homes or lose them? As a matter of daily routine, doctors and managers make final decisions on such issues and thereby determine how, and even whether, people will live; and the course and conditions of their lives - issues that are very practical indeed.

Hasting's Center's Institute of Society and Ethics presented a seminar of teachers and medical students with a case involving allocation of scarce medical resources among an excessive number of patients who would die without access to these resources. This is a common situation with newly developed drugs, equipment and surgical procedures such as kidney machines and cardiac bypass surgery. In the Hasting's case, seven patients needed a life support system when only one such was available. Members of the seminar were given fact sheets on the seven patients (age, number of dependent children, marital status, sex, etc.) and asked to decide which patient should live - and to explain which ethical standards and value preferences they used in making their final decisions. Some seminar members were unable to make such a decision, some avoided it by refusing to "play God" and resorting instead to a choice by lottery, some chose a widow who was the sole guardian of

---

* "Ethics" is both a singular and a plural noun depending upon use. Ethics, as a field of study or body of theory, is singular as in the text above; ethics, as particular standards or practices, are plural as, for example, in saying "your ethics are obviously opposed to mine."

small children, others chose the youngest patient. In most cases, the decision makers were very vague as to the ethical analysis and standards leading them to their decisions; improved skills in such ethical analysis are the objective of the Hasting's seminars.[1]

Ethical knowledge, understanding and sensitivity as well as skills for sound ethical analysis are also the objective of this book.

An S & L's Lesson About Ethics

In 1981 Savings and Loan banks were hurt by sky-high interest rates driving mortgage rates and the cost of money to a near-20% level while the S & L's still were stuck with earlier unprofitable mortgage loans to homeowners at 9% and even 6%. S & L managers naturally smiled with joy whenever a 9% mortgage became paid in full by a house sale permitting them to loan that money in new and profitable 16% mortgages. Some aggressive S & L managers began to look for opportunities to force such home sales and mortgage "rollovers" by foreclosing (demanding full repayment of the mortgage loan from a homeowner which usually meant selling the home and evicting its former owners). Foreclosing is a legal option all S & L's possess if a homeowner is even one month late in making his monthly mortgage payment, although no major S & L ever resorts to this extreme punishment unless a homeowner exhibits persistent failure and irresponsibility about his mortgage over many months.

Technically within their legal rights, late in 1981 a few S & L's began to foreclose on low interest mortgages about a month delinquent and with no prior notice to permit the homeowner to pay arrears; one S & L refused a late but certified check and proceeded with an eviction notice effective December 23, 1981.

The Washington Post carried the story in mid-December, the general public was outraged at the S & L's behavior and timing, threats of boycott and other public action abounded, and the S & L's reputation was critically damaged. Although technically legal, its action was judged unethical by the moral standards of the general public.* All practical consequences of a decision perceived to be unethical.[2]

Ivan Hill on the Importance of Ethics

In the early 1970s, Ivan Hill left a top position in industry to begin an unpaid career as president of The Ethics Resource Center in Washing-

---

* In free nations, the Law typically follows and reflects the ethical values of the general public. Currently, by law, mortgages contain the requirement that foreclosure cannot be executed until a homeowner is given in writing five days' prior notice and the opportunity during that period to pay arrears, avoiding foreclosure.

ton, D.C. working for honesty and social responsibility in government and business. When he retired in 1981, Marvin Stone, editor of U.S. News & World Report, interviewed Hill whose views are paraphrased as follows.[3]

Based on years of practical experience in industry and with the Ethics Resource Center, Hill declared explicitly that "the most urgent task in the country was being neglected - that of trying to strengthen our ethical underpinnings." Defining Ethics as an "obligation to consider not only our personal well-being but also that of others and of human society as a whole," he rated ethical sensitivity and behavior as the nation's highest priority in the sophisticated social environment of today's businesses and governments. Ethical sense was an essential condition at mankind's beginnings; recent books on anthropology, such as People of the Lake,[4] attribute man's early survival to his ability to identify one's own personal survival and welfare with that of others, to share and cooperate; honesty, ethics and fair dealing with others are basic conditions for human survival, not just sentimental moralizing or religious rhetoric. This is even more true in today's electronic and nuclear age. If man ends in destroying himself, his technological advances will be the means but the basic reason will be ethical failure.

Ethical failure could first wipe out the systems of freedom (in markets, politics and business) and convert America into a closed, tightly controlled society. "When trust in one another diminishes to a point where we can no longer do business without pervasive dishonesty and corruption, an open society cannot function and will become unmanageable,...severely undermining the private enterprise system itself. A change in the system will then become inevitable."A change to what? If most people are not (voluntarily) ethical and honest most of the time, peoples' freedoms would be restricted, possibly eliminated as in Soviet bloc countries, by national leaders restoring order and essential stability at the expense of freedoms. Historian Arnold Toynbee traced the struggle for human freedom in conflict with the absolute need for order in human societies, and summed it up: "Freedom is expendable, stability is indispensable."[5] Order and stability in a society have always taken precedence over the human and risky desire for freedom (which is more often abused than used constructively and ethically). If self-control, whether by individuals or organizations in a society, is not sufficient to preserve order and stability, increasingly authoritarian acts of the national government remove the freedoms and enforce dictatorial control in the ultimate interests of essential order in society. Hill concludes, I hope wrongly:"I think this is the probable outlook for the U.S. in the foreseeable future."

Without ethics, a nation is doomed to chaos or dictatorship.

Ideas Have Consequences

In the cases above and throughout this book, the generic theme is that ideas (theory), developed and accepted by humans, control human lives in every practical detail; and ethical ideas specifically more than any others. Ethical theories and ideas constitute the deepest values rooted in people and guide every detail of how they live, work, love, eat, clothe and shelter themselves, raise children, build societies and laws, and even how they fight and die.

Religions and their ideas have molded the daily lives of billions of people throughout the centuries. Each of these people lived fulfilling or miserable lives based mainly on the religious beliefs inculcated in his time and place of birth, dominated by Hinduism, Buddhism, Taoism, Judaism, Christianity, Islam, tribal faith and rites or any of the many thousands of versions of these and other religions. The practical consequences of these ideas pervaded everyone's life from birth to death, requiring or prohibiting in various periods and places such profoundly important details of life such as: eating meat or other foods; sleeping beyond sunrise; selling goods or services for a profit; charging interest on money loaned; working at particular times and days; marrying; when (or usually not) to engage in sexual intercourse, and even how (or not); what, or whether, one could read, write and say; execution by hanging or burning for heresy or witchcraft; trial by ordeal; and so on. What could be more practical than life issues such as these? All of them and many others were determined by the ethical values and ideas of the regional religion one happened to be born in.

Thus a society's dominant value system molds the thinking which sets the directions of its people, drives their human energies and controls their daily living. Entire nations and generations of people live by the ideas of religious, philosophical, political and other thinkers and even die in wars for these ideas. Friedrich Nietzsche's super-race ideas led generations later to Nazism in Germany and the holocaust of World War II. Darwin (with species) and Adam Smith and Herbert Spencer (with economies and human societies) elaborated the idea of evolutionism and competitive "survival of the fittest" which molded nineteenth-century Europe and America into industrial giants. The ideas developed by John Locke of England and the founding fathers of America (in the American Declaration of Independence and Constitution) set the course and future achievement of this nation -its ideas of human rights and freedom, individual worth and dignity, due process under fair laws for all, political democracy and economic opportunity have been the driving forces creating the greatest nation in history. The ethereal and almost unintelligible philosophical theories of George Hegel led soon to Marx and dialectical materialism which, in the form of dogma called Communism, controls minutely half of the earth's present population. The "brain-trust" (economists and other intellectuals), advising President Roosevelt in the 1930s, imbedded into American economics and national policy the deficit spending ideas of John Maynard Keynes and America's free-enterprise system eroded into the current socialistic system of ever-rising government spending, tax rates and central control of every American. Keynes himself was keenly aware of the overwhelming consequences of ideas; his classic observation was:

> "The ideas of economists and political philosophers, both when they are right and when they are wrong, are more powerful than is commonly understood. Indeed, the world is ruled by little else. Practical men, who believe themselves to be quite exempt from any intellectual influence, are usually the slaves of some defunct economist. Madmen in history, who hear voices in the air, are distilling their frenzy from some academic scribbler of a few years back.[6]"

When considered in terms of their practical consequences for millions of people, I think it can be said that theoretical ideas are the most practical things in the world.

Ethics and the Chief Justice

We referred above to a businessman (Ivan Hill) and his practical views on the importance of ethics; let's listen to a top representative of another very practical and pervasive arena in American life, the legal system and its courts. On November 11, 1962, Earl Warren, then Chief Justice of the United States, gave a remarkably insightful address at the Louis Marshall Award Dinner of The Jewish Theological Seminary of America. Some of its highlights, concerning the necessity of ethics, are quoted or paraphrased as follows.[7]

"In civilized life, Law floats in a sea of Ethics. Each is indispensable to civilization. Without Law, we would be at the mercy of the least scrupulous; without Ethics, Law could not exist. Without ethical consciousness in most people, lawlessness would be rampant."

The Chief Justice sketched man's growing experience with ethics. Before men knew the word or its principles, they learned early of its importance to survival. Material goods are finite but human desire for them is infinite, which creates conflict within societies, tribes and even families. Only Law, which in primitive times was identical with ethics, could resolve these conflicts without mutual destruction of all. Man's invention of Law and ethics saved him from early extinction.

Without ethics (voluntary compliance with socially constructive norms of behavior) and a general ethical commitment to observe the Law, judicial and police systems are helpless in controlling the mass chaos of jungle-like lawlessness and mutual injuring of people -except in tightly controlled societal systems (often called "police states") such as dictatorships which enforce necessary order and stability at the expense of all human freedoms. Many societies survived (for a while!) this way: the Roman Empire, the Christian empire of medieval Europe, South American "strong man" dictatorships and, recently, the totalitarian nations of Nazi Germany, Cuba, Soviet Russia, Communist China and most Soviet bloc countries in Eastern Europe. As Toynbee noted, freedom is expendable, stability is indispensable -this theme runs through human history. It is obvious, from historical experience, that free democracies like America can survive as free democracies only by the voluntary practice of ethics. "Therefore, the genius of the civilized world, particularly of the English-speaking peoples, has made obedience to Law and acceptance of decisions of duly authorized agents of the community mandatory as an ethical principle."

Voluntary ethical behavior, in a free society, must control far more of human behavior than Law can, except, as noted, in dictatorships where Laws come to control every facet of behavior and Law becomes identical with ethics (as the State perceives them). We learned, from bitter experience, in America, the dangers of confusing the Law with ethics: the era of Prohibition (prohibiting alcohol by federal laws) was generally resented as government invasion of personal conscience, the laws were almost universally ignored and the lawlessness spawned organized crime that, even today, we cannot eradicate.

"Under our Constitution, with its system of checks and balances, the three great departments of government, the Legislative, the Executive and the Judiciary, are each bound by oath to support the basic law of the land and to avoid encroachment on the prerogatives of one another. Such restraint could not be enforced in the absence of Ethics." The personal and voluntary oath of all concerned, an ethical or moral kind of obligation, must be held sacred and constitutes the roots sustaining the American system; a system unique in history.

But, because of the unparalleled freedoms Americans enjoy, their system is uniquely vulnerable to deterioration, and ultimate collapse, unless most of them are voluntarily ethical most of the time. Otherwise anarchy and chaos, which, being intolerable, lead rapidly to an all-controlling central government or even dictatorship. In Warren's words:

"Society would come to grief without Ethics, which is unenforceable in the courts and cannot be made part of Law. If there were no sense of love in families, if there were no sense of loyalty, if friendship meant nothing, if we all, or any large proportion of us, were motivated only by avarice and greed, Society would collapse almost as completely as though it lacked Law. Not only does Law in civilized society presuppose ethical commitment; it presupposes the existence of a broad area of human conduct controlled only by ethical norms and not subject to Law at all." (Emphasis added.)

"There is thus a Law beyond the Law, as binding on those of us who cherish our institutions as the Law itself, although there is no human power to enforce it. Our economy rests to a great extent on the mutual faith of seller and buyer, which implies far more than the courts could possibly enforce." The same can be said for all business relationships as agreements and promises, by giving one's word only, often by phone, become firm and established daily in the millions of transactions among buyers, sellers, brokers, lawyers, doctors, suppliers, manufacturers, dealers and so on. When I phone my stock broker and ask him to sell a stock at $16 or not at all, there are no signed legal contracts to enforce my wish, only my trust in my broker's word and ethics that, in my interests, he will forego a large sales commission on a sale lower than the agreed upon $16. Without ethical practice, most of the time and by most people, the daily business of Americans would grind to a halt. This necessity of (voluntary) ethical behavior "places heavy responsibilities on every individual. It is he who has to apply it (ethics) in difficult and perplexing situations. This necessity requires him to be trained in the discernment of right from wrong and in the will to accept the right without the slightest duress. His problem is the more complicated because the issues presented by life are rarely simple."

"This ability properly to appraise different values in their relevance to specific issues, we call character. A person able to discern the right in the midst of great confusion and to pursue it, is a person of character. ....The man of character, sensitive to the meaning of what he is doing, will know how to discover the ethical path in the maze of possible action --thus the importance of educating men of character..."

Such education is also a major purpose of this book.

Ethics and a Democratic (Free) Society

Let's analyze further the dynamics of the American democratic system and why voluntary ethical behavior is so critical to its survival. Especially ethical behavior by businesses and their managers.

Business decisions are not made in a vacuum but in a democratic system with political, economic and legal components, all influenced ultimately by general public opinion (the public's ethical beliefs). In such a system, majority vote in Congress and throughout the nation's state polling places and legislatures determines by law what businesses can and cannot do, quite apart from whether such voting by the people seems rational or not to business owners and managers (who, of course, also have a vote but a minority one). And, as depicted in the diagram below, the majority will vote as influenced by their deep-down ethical

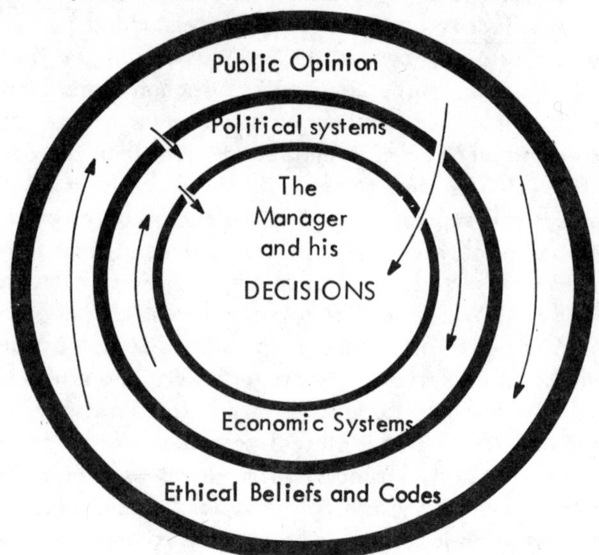

beliefs and feelings. Thus, again, ethics (general public opinion about right versus wrong and good versus evil) are the ultimate determinants underlying the entire political, economic and business system called "America." In a well-informed and free democracy, the decisions of business managers are ultimately subject to the general acceptance of the voting public (or its rejection). In the slow "due process of law" in America, this can take time but the democratic process grinds on until laws and regulatory agencies are voted into existence to crush business or other practices unacceptable to the public ethics. The practical consequences of ethics in America pervade its business history. For example, in the late 19th century, business decisions resulting in huge, wildly profitable but unfair "trusts" (essentially holding companies, with interlocking boards of directors, monopolizing entire industries such as oil, steel, railroads and meat and thus setting prices at will and against the public interest) caused such a public outcry that antitrust, antimonopoly and "fair business practices" laws were finally enacted outlawing all such decisions and practices. As usual, the public reaction was excessive, laws passed over the decades were too restrictive (including the FTC and its excessive, if not absurd, regulations) but all this wild anti-business legislation was invited by unethical business decisions.

Many believe (I among them) that, unfortunately, too many such government regulatory agencies have been established ; that many of them, created under public pressure to curb short-sighted and unethical business practices, have gone too far (an "overkill") and now strangle the free market system rather than promoting its vitality. In a free political system, however, it becomes obvious that the practical consequences of unethical business decisions are to unleash public condemnation and votes against business and to transform voluntary business ethics into coercive laws (which usually end up hurting both business, its employees and its customers). Again, ethics emerge as very practical and important in the daily lives of Americans.

The New Social and Technological Environment of Business

It would probably be naive to expect most people most of the time to behave ethically if there were no external pressure to do so. Or to obey the law if there were no fines or jails. This is especially true of the minority who seem to be amoral, explicitly unconcerned about ethics or even laws so long as "they don't get caught."

The pressure upon people to obey the laws of the land is the set and known penalties (such as imprisonment) and the determination of every society to enforce the law fully and systematically by means of police, courts and prison systems. The pressure upon people to behave ethically, in the majority of matters not covered by explicit laws, is much more subtle, unsystematic but still powerful: public opinion in the forms of approval and praise or disapproval and condemnation of a person's actions, no matter what the person's age, sex, trade, position or role. We all judge each others' actions and peer pressure is a powerful agent encouraging compliance with acceptable norms within the family, the local community and the society at large. Such pressure toward ethical behavior presumes, of course, that a person's actions are observable and out in the open rather than secret and concealed. The child who sneaks into the cookie jar while no one is around, the woman who returns for full credit used dresses to her department store as unused and useless, the man who cheats on his wife with other women while traveling on business, the manufacturer who profits by building products 5% below stated specifications, the builder who "shorts" the quantity or quality of materials in a construction project, the retailer who deceives his customer or the salesman who "cons" his prospect, or the customer who shoplifts, all presume that their unethical -or illegal- actions will go unnoticed and never known or condemned by friends, peers or authorities whose respect they cherish. Otherwise they would probably restrain themselves from such unethical behavior which, if known, would cost them the peer respect they need and damage their reputations. Few people can tolerate being known as merely a liar, cheat or characterless or unreliable about promises, trustworthiness and personal honesty. Fortunately, most of us can't even tolerate such knowledge about ourselves, quite apart from "who else knows," and thus restrain ourselves from actions in our personal histories which would damage our inner character and cause the loss of self-respect, quite apart from losing the respect of others. Such a loss can be worse than death - or cause it. Discredited military officers, business executives and others, with their reputations and self-respect gone, often retire to a quiet office, position a loaded pistol against the head and end the agony of personal worthlessness.

But, still, public knowledge of personal or business actions is the supreme sanction and human pressure for generally ethical behavior.

Consider the example of grossly unethical business practices in 19th and early 20th century America. This was the age of the "robber barons", miracle cure salesmen, boiler room stock brokers, take-it-and-run bankers, speculators on other peoples' money and a host of other con artists. The barons who created the giant industries of America (oil, steel, railroads, etc.) did it mostly by secret deals behind closed doors and no one knew for years about them; the drummers (salesmen) who travelled and "worked" the expanding territories of America promised much and deceived more with products whose failure to provide the services as advertised could seldom be traced (drummers often chose never to return to the same territory twice); stock brokers, bankers and speculators ran to parts unknown where they were unknown after each business venture. These Americans were no worse (or better) than the businessmen who preceded them by centuries (British trading companies, German lords, Italian bankers, Oriental merchants, etc.). Hence the bad reputation of business (see Chapter 2 below). For the most part, this history of unethical business behavior prevailed because it could be easily hidden for years or forever. Given the primitive information facilities of these centuries (virtually none but word of mouth and few records), business was done in secret, hidden from the world and even local communities, unethical actions easily denied or usually never known. Unethical action obviously thrives when no one will or can know much about it or link it to particular persons; their reputations remain safe in the darkness of non-information.

Today's Age of Instant Information

Scientific and technological advances in the communications field, now operating in our daily lives, have catapulted the American people and its businesses into the strange new age of "real-time" or instant information; about anything and everything. Computers, interesting toys just three decades ago, now maintain giant data banks capable of securing, storing, sorting, classifying and retrieving instantly all known information about any person or organization. Thousands of newspaper, magazine and TV reporters, virtually all now becoming "investigative" reporters, armed with the instant access of telephones, world-wide data transmission systems and mobile communication equipment (magnetic tapes, disks, cameras, etc.) search into every detail of personal and business activities for interesting information. This national passion for new information ("news"), with media reporters as the public's agents, thrives twenty-four hours a day and fills the newspapers, magazines and TV screens day and night.

The new age of instant communication and information puts both the decisions and operations of today's managers under constant public scrutiny, a condition of business life no previous American managers ever had to cope with daily. As noted above, managers and entrepreneurs of the past in America, including U.S. presidents, operated routinely in private and secrecy, an option modern managers would understandably relish. But the luxury of privacy, secrecy and confidential executive decision making no longer exists in the 1980s. We all, and especially businessmen and public figures, live and move in a fishbowl under ever-watchful public eyes. The public didn't know about the secret Oval office tape recordings of FDR or JFK for several decades (they were discovered and became instant big news around February 1, 1982); President Nixon's tapes, including every minute's recordings, except the famous 18 minutes "lost," were pulled into public view in a matter of weeks -despite Nixon's every effort to keep them secret. The tapes and other evidence revealed unethical behavior in the Oval office and the president resigned. Ethics, and the unethical, do indeed have powerful practical consequences. If "Ethics" conjures up in one's mind images of mere philosophical theorizing or impractical sentimentalizing about vague, unscientific and subjective issues, one might ask Nixon about how catastrophic "Ethics" and its issues can be; in a purely real and practical sense. Or ask other executives and businesses whose unethical practices, soon dragged before the public, led quickly to ruin.

If for no other reason, the practical damage, resulting from misunderstanding or ignoring ethical issues in business decision making, makes "Ethics" a critical element for modern decision makers and managers. Flaws in ethical sensitivity, analysis or judgment in the midst of a well-informed and politically powerful public can destroy careers and entire businesses.

REFERENCES

1 Russell, Avery, The Washington Post, Jan. 25, 1981, page C1
2 An S & L firm in suburban Maryland near Washington, D.C.
3 U.S. News & World Report, Nov. 16, 1981, p. 102 and Dec. 8, 1980, p. 84. See, also, Hill's "Common Sense and Everyday Ethics," Ethics Resource Center, 1730 Rhode Island Ave., Wash. DC, 20036.
4 The authors are Richard Leaky and Roger Lewin.
5 Toynbee, A., Civilization on Trial, Oxford, 1948
6 Keynes, J. M., General Theory of Employment, Interest and Money, 1936
7 From Warren's manuscript of the address on file at The Jewish Theological Seminary. The address was given at the Americana Hotel in New York, Nov. 11, 1962.

For Further Reading

- Friedman, M., Capitalism and Freedom, U. of Chicago, 1962
- Hardin, G., Exploring New Ethics for Survival, Penguin Books, 1973
- Heilbroner, R. L., The Worldly Philosophers, Simon & Schuster, 1961
- Luthans, F., et. al., Social Issues in Business, Macmillan Co., 1980
- Walton, C., The Ethics of Corporate Conduct, Prentice-Hall, 1977
- And see Bibliography at end of book.

QUESTIONS AND PROBLEMS

1. Describe in some detail each of the following concepts or theories:
   (a) Ethics (singular) (b) Ethics (plural) (c) social order
   (d) Social freedom (e) Law (f) Religion
   (g) Evolutionism (h) Business "trusts" (i) Antitrust laws
   (j) Ethics as theory (k) Ethics as "practical"
2. If you had to decide to save just one of two lives with a sole kidney machine, the two lives being a 25-year-old woman the sole support of 3 children and the other the U.S. Secretary of the Department of Defense, which would you choose? Why?
3. Think of an example illustrating every relationship in the diagram on page 18. Does Ethics imply practical consequences? Explain.
4. Explain and illustrate: (a) "Law floats in a sea of ethics;" and (b) "Without ethics a nation is doomed to chaos or dictatorship."
5. Explain and illustrate: "Ideas have consequences." And Toynbee: "Freedom is expendable, stability is indispensable." How does ethics affect (a) social order, (b) social freedom, (c) a free democracy?
6. From newspapers, find examples of unethical (in your view) actions, but legal, and explain why you view these actions as unethical.

2 Business's Moral Quandary

This chapter could be titled "Business's Bad Reputation and How It Got It." Rightly (usually) or wrongly (sometimes), businesses and their managers throughout history have been condemned, even hated, as harsh predatory animals, powerful and cunning, systematically grabbing every last dollar from the work, sweat and meager lifetime savings of farmers, widows and even children in order to amass huge profits – and always in cleverly legal ways. A 1904 newspaper cartoon, for example, pictures the "common people" (on raft at left) with sharks (American "trusts") moving in for the kill.[1] The trusts (commodity monopolies of oil, meat, copper, sugar, steel and other necessities of life) named their price for goods they controlled and people needed; people went broke paying and businessmen profited by the many millions of dollars. The public rage ultimately led to the American antitrust laws and the adversary relationship between business and the American public (it still thrives in the 1980s and is a chief cause of Japan's domination of America in competitive international markets – another practical consequence of ethics and how its issues are understood or misunderstood). The age of the American "robber barons" also led to the current maze of stifling regulatory agencies and powerful trade unions more concerned with member protection than the critical productivity needed for lower consumer prices and effective competition with Japan Inc.

The "Robber Barons"

A number of giant individual entrepreneurs emerged for two generations after the American civil war and in half a century built the giant industries and corporations (many of them "trust") and, of course, became personally multimillionaires. These men embodied in massive scale the spirit of pioneering and Westward-bound America; all had in common a wild, but usually brilliant, trait for courting high risk with raw nerve, unwavering determination and the ruthlessness to destroy competitors (or capture them and swallow them up in their "trusts").* These corporate "gun fighters" became known as the "robber barons" because of their public image as large-scale thieves, protecting their flanks just within the edge of the law by corporation and trust structures while profiting at the public's expense. Among the first of these business tycoons and literally a gun fighter in the dangerous fur trade was John Jacob Astor (left)[2] who, after financial success in the fur trade, became a dominant figure in real estate and one of the few multimillionaires of his time. Astor was ingenious at taking advantage of fine legal points and had a passion for foreclosing mortgages at huge profit based on exact timing.[3]

A sampling of some of the major industrialists of the period following the civil war will illustrate the often less than ethical tone of 19th century business. It must be remembered, however, that the nation was very young and experimental, material survival was each individual's responsibility (with no help from any government) and often reduced survival itself to a Darwinian "survival of the fittest," and ethical niceties were often of low priority in the struggle to live and to prosper. It would seem, too, that, for many, the predatory habit, learned and used successfully to sustain life, continues when the goal is no longer food for survival but great power and money.

In 1833, as a young steamboat operator, Cornelius Vanderbilt (later and for life called "Commodore") was hurt in a railroad accident and for years hated trains. He spent his life making millions of dollars in the steamboat business and ocean shipping.[4] Realizing, however, at about age 70, that railroading was to be the major transportation of the future, he contrived to buy key railroad properties which became the New York Central

* Most business historians agree, however, that American industrial growth would have been much slower without these business titans. And the implication is that this growth was ultimately good.

Railroad. The Commodore never hesitated to use blatant deceit and whatever pressures he could muster in order to secure legal control of any property he set sight upon as a needed part of his growing empire. Stock manipulation was one of his favorite tactics; with the financial power at his command, he would make massive and instant sales or purchases of railroad stocks, depressing quickly the stock prices of property he meant to buy and inflating stocks he planned to use in buying it. In time, he bought or arranged effective control of a huge railroad network throughout the nation. And many millions for himself (he left $100 millions at his death, a sum, adjusted for inflation, equal to many billions today). And he found the time (and energy) to acquire a thirtyish new wife in his mid-seventies. The Commodore was not excessively modest: he planned a monument in New York commemorating the two greatest Americans, Cornelius Vanderbilt and George Washington. Although he or his son, William, is reputed to have made the famous remark "Let the public be damned," old "Corneel," as he was familiarly known, built and maintained (new track, bridges, etc. as needed) the nation's railroads and made efficient nationwide transportation possible for all.[5] *

What Vanderbilt was to railroads John D. Rockefeller was to oil.[2]

In 1860, when Rockefeller was 20, no one had yet gotten the idea that you could dig or drill for oil; oil, called "rock oil" and used to light lamps (Yankee salesmen sold it as a sure cure for every medical problem) was just skimmed from small pools of it in rocky areas of Pennsylvania mainly. When, soon after, companies began drilling for it, Rockefeller foresaw the financial potential of refining oil into kerosene and other uses rather than merely extracting it and using it in its raw state. So, with little to invest but a genius for organizing, he formed a company, lured people to invest in it and, within ten years, was a major refiner in the midwest. He then formed a new firm called the Standard Oil Company of Ohio in which he held a controlling 67% of all

* The historical observations here must necessarily be sketchy. Most readers will want to read one or more of the following detailed business histories: Chamberlain's, short and anecdotal, see notes at end of chapter; T. C. Cochran's Business In American Life, 300 pages but complete, M. Beard's comprehensive (2-vol) History of Business and E. Bursk (ed.) The World of Business (4 volumes) for full details.

stock. At the time, there were many refining companies like his in a chaotic maze of mutual competition with wild swings of pricing. John D came to hate what he called the "idiotic, senseless destruction" and "wasteful conditions" of competition. Thus he systematically "persuaded" independent refiners to combine into Standard of Ohio; as Standard got bigger and stronger, other independents had little choice but to join. The tactics used to absorb all independent competitors were often deceit (25 Eastern independents joined a new combine, Acme Oil, to fight and compete with Standard on equal footing, only to discover later that Acme was itself secretly owned by Standard). The main tactic, however, was the "trust." The trust, an ingenious legal method of combining companies in the same industry thus effectively establishing a monopoly, was invented by a Pennsylvania lawyer named Samuel Dodd who came to Rockefeller's attention and soon became a key Standard Oil lawyer. By the early 1880s, Standard enjoyed effective control of virtually all oil refining in the nation, including all major pipelines and most key railroad tank cars. The oil business belonged to Standard Oil Company and Standard belonged mainly to Rockefeller. Standard was thus able to control prices, production volume and distribution of oil products almost at will (somewhat similar to OPEC's complete control of world crude oil since 1973).* Until public outrage finally created the antitrust laws of the U.S.A. around 1900 (similar state laws had failed: when Ohio in 1892 banned trusts, Standard just moved and became Standard Oil of New Jersey, doing business as usual). One historian characterizes the quiet and secretive Rockefeller as "positively savage" and Standard as a company that "cut to kill," referring to Standard's tactic of price cutting in a region until independents went bankrupt or sold out to, of course, Rockefeller.[6]

Andrew Carnegie (left)[4] built his Carnegie Steel Co. into a huge combine by using many of the "big business" tactics above and especially by buying out companies temporarily near bankruptcy during economic depressions -they asked for help but became part of the growing Carnegie Steel Company. The young Andy Carnegie, a Scotish immigrant whose family was driven to settle and start over in Pennsylvania due to hard times, was working days and nights as a cotton mill laborer at age 13 and saving every cent of his $1.20-a-week pay. In odd hours he studied the business system and became a sharp

* OPEC, the mainly Arabian Organization of Petroleum Exporting Countries, is a cartel, having the same effect as a "trust," setting non-competitive prices, controlling production, etc.

and risky investor. But his risks were carefully calculated and he had the nerve to "wait out" his stocks until they increased a hundredfold. During his twenties, Carnegie worked as a telegrapher (lots of first-hand and profitable information in this line of work) for Tom Scott, head of the Pennsylvania Railroad's Pittsburgh division. Scott was amazed at Andy's cool nerve, mental brilliance and liked the "little white-haired Scotch devil."[7] In 1863 (at age 28), Andy Carnegie recorded annual income of $47,860, only about $2,400 of it from his railroad pay (with no income taxes in his time and adjusting for inflation, he was already a millionaire). Now, with the power of money, and the brilliant mind that had made it, and his incessant diligence, Carnegie, with typical nerve, put all his eggs in one basket (steel). As the years went by, he gained control of the entire steel-making industry and his profits in the late 1990s were $40 million per year. In 1900, aged 65, interested now in philanthropic achievements more than further estate-building (he had said "the man who dies ....rich dies disgraced"), Carnegie sold all his steel interests to a powerful investment banker, J.P.Morgan (inset),[8] for $492 million and Morgan's U.S.Steel Company became one of the most powerful and controlling "trusts" in the nation (see the bigger octopus of the two in the page-23 political cartoon). Carnegie money, like that of Astor, Vanderbilt, Rockefeller, Mellon and the other American robber barons, is still admired today -and sought after by public spirited arts, humanities, university and other organizations-, but Carnegie and the other barons were often a bit unethical in the means used to amass these fortunes. And, despite all the philanthropic good the barons' money represents throughout America today, the means and methods used to amass it, always carefully legal, are the chief cause of American business's current bad reputation as unethical and antisocial -if not, for some inclined to socialism and even Marxism, an outright danger to America. These latter intellectuals, whether university-trained or drug-inspired (but of voting age), want and, in sufficient numbers, could vote for the nationalization of major American industries. A cool analysis of the American system since FDR, who launched the land onto the road to socialism, easily highlights the quite plausible prospect of a fully socialistic America in the decades to come, all industries run by a good and people-oriented government (like the U.S.Post Office!) and the public's movement toward acceptance of this prospect fueled by the memory and practices of America's robber barons. (Again, may we note that the issues of ethics and the unethical do have consequences.)

The Ethical History of Other American Businessmen

The robber barons stand out in American business history because of the gigantic scale of their activities and practices. But the average businessman (retailer, manufacturer, salesman, etc.), on a less historical scale, was not much more, or less, ethical than the barons.

The Yankee traveling salesman (called peddler) is a classic character, welcomed in every small community for his unusual wares and his news from the cities -despite his reputation for blatant cheating. When used as a verb, yankee meant "to cheat." And the peddlers were everywhere; in 1850 there were 10,669 of them licensed and on the road (no one knows how many more unlicensed) and 16,594 of them in 1860.[9] The peddlers guaranteed what they sold (guarantee had a legal basis in their "word of honor" only) such as brooms that fell apart a few days after the peddler's departure, clocks which when wound up operated for a week or two, "solid" metal bowls and plates which rusted quickly to the wood inside, fabrics of far lower quality than presented, and so on. Customers, isolated in western farms, had little knowledge of such products and no way to compare them and their prices (peddlers typically charged at least a several hundred percent markup over costs of goods) so they were easily victimized and usually remained quite ignorant of it.

As sparsely populated western communities (depending on the year "West" was Philadelphia and westward) grew large enough, a central location became a "town," with a saloon, a hotel, a bank and a general store (usually in this sequence and order of importance). The general store replaced the peddlers in such towns because people liked to deal with retailers with roots in the town, men they knew (and could trust?). Local store retailers had the same Yankee streak in many cases as they often engaged in undetected practices such as misrepresentation of goods and quality, short measures and weights of goods, phony or no genuine metal in gold watches or bronze implements, sawdust laced in fertilizers (and perhaps foods like flour) to enhance weights, prices determined by retailers' sales skills along with the customers' ignorance, ability to pay and inability to bargain intelligently with "the only store in town."[10] It would be a long time (about 1900) before the Sears & Roebuck catalog with posted and fair prices for clearly described merchandise came into general usage (Sears prospered on the novel idea that people will remain loyal customers of a store they trust as honest, ethical and reliable). So much so that people often wrote Sears & Roebuck to solve personal problems by means of the honest and cure-all catalog. A schoolteacher wrote

> "I am a lonely school teacher in the dismal hills of Idaho. Be kind enough to assist a poor forlorn teacher in her future happiness by sending the man advertised in your catalog (page 26)."[11]

Even the good Sears catalog, however, was infected with a slight strain of Yankee deceit. Its 1902 edition, for example, suggested miraculous cures for pennies, with bottled solutions for ulcers, female disorders, male impotency, age fatigue and virtually all health problems. Vin Vita

SEARS, ROEBUCK & CO., Cheapest Supply House on Earth, Chicago. CATALOGUE No.112. 389

Wine of Life **VIN VITAE** **Wine of Life**

Retail Price, per bottle, $1.25 **Our Price, 69 Cents.**

A NEW AND PERFECT TONIC STIMULANT FOR THE TIRED, WEAK AND SICK OF ALL CLASSES. A RENEWER OF ENERGY, A STIMULANT FOR THE FATIGUED, A STRENGTHENER FOR THE WEAK, AN EFFECTIVE AND AGREEABLE FOOD FOR THE BLOOD, BRAIN AND NERVES.

NOT A MEDICINE, BECAUSE IT IS DELIGHTFUL TO THE TASTE AND TO THE STOMACH **NOT MERELY A STIMULANT,** BUT A GENUINE TONER AND STRENGTHENER

A Tonic which we find is as yet Unequaled.

was one of its best selling tonics. Ads usually included pictures of a voluptuous young woman and a muscular male youth with a full head of hair, ancient Greek (like the gods) in its massive array and, of course, a direct result of steady consumption of Vin Vitae. And it sold well. Little wonder that we have the FDA (Food and Drug Administration) today to control the manufacture, advertising and distribution of medicine and pseudo-medicines.

Many Western Yankees outdid the Easterners from whom they bought goods for their stores on credit; they just sold the goods in the store for cash, pocketed it, closed the store and went elsewhere undetected and with no forwarding address - they left all bills unpaid, of course, and set up business again in parts unknown (till they did it again). A critic wrote that "after four years of attentive observation and inquiry, my honest conviction is that the standard of moral character is very greatly lower than in Europe." "Business dishonesty (was) a continuing problem, perhaps stemming from high geographical mobility and not curable by large doses of childhood admonition."[12] The merchants' tactic of "cashing out" and ruining a store, and then running off with the cash, was a miniature version of the big tycoons' common practice of buying a profitable company, cashing out its assets to personal accounts -thus ruining it, selling the company before anyone realized it was ruined and walking off quite legally with a huge personal profit. Dan Drew, in mid-nineteenth-century, was an outstanding example (or model) of this kind of corporate gun-fighter: Daniel Drew "bought and sold, built up or ruined properties solely for the purpose of extracting the maximum personal gain."[13] And Dan Drew was always meticulously "legal," but always on the very edge of the law, as he preyed upon and devoured any rising company that appealed to his appetite. (Cash McCaw, in the modern American novel of that title, illustrates more recent methods of acquiring and exploiting companies for personal gain, -and always legally; skilled, but not necessarily ethical, lawyers are essential.)

Peale, an advertising man in the 1917 play, "It Pays to Advertise," sums up the perceived view of businessmen by the public, when he says: "Son, the world is full of bunk. Ninety-seven percent of the people are sheep, and you can get 'em by advertising." Businessmen still do (but much more carefully). Phineas Barnum, the great American showman and publicity genius (the original PR man), exemplified in his "sheer the sheep" attitude toward the public and his Barnum & Bailey circus ads the ethics of businessmen as perceived by the common people -but yet they always thronged to his circus. Philosophers say that people need heavy illusion to shield them from life's harsh realities (illusions such as fairy tales, fantasies, poems, songs, father-figures such as dictators and even the vague otherworld promises of many religions -and, of course, novels and TV "soaps")*; practical businessmen of history find that this illusion-need of the masses precisely matches their own goals of exploiting this human tendency to personal business advantage (by promising much and delivering little but relying correctly on the human need for more such promises as illusions "to live by"). The public is easily "conned" by shrewd politicians, showmen, priests and businessmen who all, naturally, take full advantage of it -and have throughout history.

Leading New England intellectuals about mid-century (Channing, Emerson, Parker, Thoreau, etc.) viewed the new industrial world and its business practices as a menace to human values. Parker was harsh on the "dishonest businessman. The devil of the nineteenth century has gone into trade and advertises in the papers. He makes money; the world is poorer by his wealth.... his patron saint is Judas.... In politics he wants a government that will ensure his dividends; so asks what is good for him but ill for the rest. He knows no right, only power; no man but self, no God but his calf of gold."[14] At about the same time, intellectuals in England were castigating that country's unethical merchants and businessmen. Herbert Spencer, in "The Morals of Trade" in 1859, described in detail a host of tricks used by merchants to deceive the public but noted:"On all sides we have found the result of long personal experience to be the conviction that trade is essentially corrupt ....To live in the commercial world it appears necessary to adopt its ethical code....As, in self-defense, the civilized man becomes savage

---

* The ancient Greek tragedies and comedies (heroes frequently saved by "deus ex machina," a god manipulating ropes that literally drew the hero off stage and out of danger), the poetic sagas of Homer and the religious prophets of the time were the "soaps" of that time.

among savages; so, it seems that in self-defense, the scrupulous trader is obliged to become as little scrupulous as his competitors. It has been said that the law of the animal creation is 'Eat and be eaten'; and of our trading community it may be similarly said that its law is 'Cheat and be cheated.' A system of keen competition, carried on, as it is, without adequate moral restraint, is very much a system of commercial cannibalism. Its alternatives are: use the same weapons as your antagonists, or be conquered and devoured." But Spencer noted, too "the large amount of honest dealing throughout which they (dishonest traders) are dispersed."[15]

So, too, in America at the time, the ethical businessmen probably outnumbered the unethical; but the number of the latter was more than sufficient to earn "business" a generally bad reputation among the public at large. And Spencer's analysis was probably correct: that an ethical businessman was at an unfair disadvantage competing with an unethical rival and the pressure to use similar tactics, in order to survive, was severe.

Business' Ethics and Reputation in Earlier Times

As far back as we can go in recorded human history, people and governments were concerned about ethics in business transactions such as buying and selling goods and services. After all, such is the business of life and even surviving; very fundamental indeed. Although sketchy, records of about 3000 BC reveal that manufacturing and trade were common, accounting (single-entry, of course) for the most minute kinds of transactions was routine,and complex legal contracts were standard media for commercial agreements. Codes of conduct in business,legally enforced, certainly existed prior to that but our best known example is the code of Hammurabi, a great ruler of Babylon about 2000 BC.,whose code consisted of over 300 laws covering every sort of business transaction.[16] "Government regulators" have a long history of controlling businessmen -and suppressing them; although Hammurabi's code supports business in many ways including a crude form of business insurance. For example, merchants had some protection from travelling salesmen or peddlers: "If a merchant gives barley, wool, oil, or any goods of trade to a peddler, the peddler must write down the amount of the money and return it to the merchant; the peddler must take a sealed receipt for the money which he gives to the merchant." And the code of Hammurabi was rough on price fixing and other collusion: "If outlaws hatch (plan) a conspiracy in the house of a wineseller and he does not arrest them and bring them to the palace (for justice), that wineseller shall be put to death."

"Big business" flourished in ancient times too and certainly posed ethical issues in the massive construction projects of Egypt and risky commercial trade along the land and sea areas surrounding the Mediterranean Sea. One pyramid, constructed by the Egyptian ruler Cheops around 3000 BC, was 500 feet high, covered 13 acres, required 2.3 million two-ton stone blocks and 100,000 working men for 20 years. Financing, manning and accounting for the trading ships and overland caravans also involved almost every issue of modern management, including the ethical. Similar big business situations were common in ancient Athens (500 BC), the Roman Empire with its roads and aquaducts and the late medieval period with its cathedrals -and throughout every period the traders and the bankers. All this business has always been necessary as the very basis of life for all except primitive farming tribes -and even they occasionally had to buy metal tools they couldn't make.

Throughout history, societies have tended to be pro- or anti-business in their attitudes, often based on cultural or religious premises about the meaning of human life and the believed prospects of a hereafter. The code of Hammurabi suggests that Babylon was pro-business but wary of it and intent on controlling its unethical excesses. The huge trading cities of Tyre, Carthage and Rhodes owed their very existence to buying and selling goods throughout the Mediterranean area and beyond -and were dedicated advocates of business (until anti-business but hard and militarist Rome destroyed and enslaved these cities with the very swords these traders had sold them).* For different reasons concerning the human value of agricultural, artistic and intellectual life, the leaders and people of ancient Greece were anti-business, too. Most of its great writers castigated business as parasitic and, at best, a necessary evil to be tolerated in as small proportions as possible. Plato, one of the period's two greatest thinkers (the other was his student Aristotle), was especially anti-business in his The Republic and Laws, conceding the human propriety of manufacture (making of shoes, etc.), although noting that such work was the most ignoble man might choose, but condemning trade for money as evil per se ("trade produces nothing," he said). In his Laws, trading and the exchange of money in business, was in most cases outlawed. (His proposed laws were admired -but never adopted.) (Plato, in his The Republic, also and literally banned poets and playwriters as "poison" to the public mind and morals - poisoning minds with illusions instead of building them strong with realities- see p.30 above.) Although Plato's plans for businessmen were never adopted in entirety,

* Interestingly, 2500 years later, U.S. and other Free West nations sell their technology for trading profits to a nation (U.S.S.R.) that might conceivably destroy them with the technology sold to it.

the anti-business spirit inspiring them was generally accepted throughout Greece where businessmen and traders were tolerated but only as a necessary evil.[17]

Beard's History of Business provides the detail about pro- and anti-business societies which is beyond our scope here.[16] Anti-business, like the ancient Greeks and the Roman Empire, were medieval Catholic Europe and Ottoman Turkey; early England (until its industrial revolution about 1800), Byzantium and Russia under the Czars were ambiguous but probably more anti than pro; explicitly pro-business countries were Protestant Europe (especially Scotland, Holland, Switzerland, Germany and Scandinavia and especially in the nineteenth century) and the U.S. after the Civil War until 1929, the year of the great economic crash and depression -and the beginnings of faith in FDR and big government for the means of life and disillusionment with business. America, since the crash of 1929, has been almost violent in its attack on corporate business (except for the 1950s)*, especially in the form of increasingly stringent government regulations affecting business's every decision. Probably the only culture consistently pro-business (for 3000 years) has been Judaism. The Torah (Judaic laws) is explicit in its many laws governing business and, although supporting business, demands a high standard of ethics in selling, buying and advertising as well as manufacturing. The Torah "levels a harsh judgment against the manufacturer or the merchant who deceives by leaving false impressions," let alone by outright lies.[18]

Capitalism Before the Industrial Revolution

A capitalist is anyone who invests his own money or property in order that it earn a profit for him. (Socialist nations, in the economic as well as the political meaning of socialism, have no capitalists since no one is allowed to own property for himself -the State owns all the means of production and distribution as in Soviet Russia today.) In its essential meaning and on a relatively small scale, the history of capitalism goes back to the times of Hammurabi, the Egyptian merchants and the traders of Carthage in Roman Empire days (see above). Traders, for example, invested their own money to build or buy and stock a ship with goods, take these for sale to distant ports at great risk on the sea, hoping that ultimate sales revenue would exceed total costs and thus pay a profit. If not, they took the loss (sometimes their lives at sea).

---

* Interestingly, America's 1950s and early 1960s were its most prosperous years in recent times with only minor government deficits, inflation at about 1% and a high-rising GNP (as contrasted with a trillion dollar debt, annual deficits of 100 billions, near 10% unemployment, 20% interest rates, 10% inflation in 1982).

Historians mark the beginnings of modern capitalism as about 1300, toward the end of the Dark Ages of Europe, with the rise of the petty capitalists. These were the people who invented the "putting out" system: an owner of goods or property or money would put it out for another to use for their later return (as is or the equivalent in value) along with a profit for their use in the form of interest, dividends or other increase in the value of the original investment. Common cases were (a) A loans B money to be returned in six months plus an amount of interest for the use of the money over that period; or (b) A buys goods from local farms for his store and then sells the goods to townsmen at a profit to himself. As the cases suggest, most early capitalists were merchants, traders and money lenders (bankers later) and shopkeepers. In Catholic Europe of the period, an anti-business society as noted above, the business and practices of these early petty capitalists created a furor among the days' theologians and churchmen over the issues of "just price" and "usury." These terms, as used then and now, need clarification: "just price" is now mainly determined by the market, i.e. supply and demand economic realities along with government regulations to maintain fair markets (see antitrust laws related to the robber barons above); around 1300, "just price" was argued and determined (quite disappointingly to capitalists whose businesses were forced "underground" in order to continue) upon purely theoretical and theological grounds (which "proved" that profit was sinful); "usury" today means interest, demanded on the loan of money, which is excessive and beyond the limits of fair interest chargeable by law (100% or 300% per year by a "loan shark," which is illegal, as compared to 21% by a department store, which is legal and probably a net loss to the store in these days of sky-high interest rates); around 1300 and throughout the writings of theologians such as Aquinas, who became soon the "final word" on most issues in Catholic doctrine for centuries, "usury" meant "using" money or its equivalents in any way at all (even a 1% per year interest rate was regarded then as usury) —and the practice of usury for any Catholic was a mortal sin condemning one to hell for all eternity.* Despite eternal punishment in the next life, many Catholics remained petty capitalists (as quietly as possible), but money-lending for interest and profit was, for centuries, mainly the business of Jews (who, as non-Catholic, would not suffer eternal damnation for earning a <u>fair</u> interest rate or "profit" on money or property they let others use).

---

* Aquinas' condemnation of usury was supported by rational grounds developed much earlier by Plato and Aristotle. See page 32 and footnotes on page 35.

Aquinas' condemnation of usury (any form of interest on a loan) was dictated by earlier church doctrine, based on St. Augustine whose views about business were probably inspired by the anti-business Roman Empire in which he lived; but, given the conclusion he was to reach at risk of heresy,* Aquinas reached it and rationalized it upon grounds developed by the Greek philosopher, Aristotle: i.e. that money per se, unlike a living plant or animal, was essentially barren and thus "should not grow upon itself."[16] To conceive of money, a commodity and inanimate, as reproducing itself and procreating as a living being was "against natural law," as well as "divine law," Aquinas argued successfully following the philosophical arguments of the Greek philosopher preceding him by some 2000 years.** The philosophical concept of "natural law" was manipulated increasingly and varyingly for church purposes for centuries (any sort of contraception, for example, was ruled "against natural law" since the act of sexual intercourse was, by nature, intended for procreation -and for no other purpose such as communication or mutually supportive love).

Despite the church in Europe, the petty capitalists thrived upon the use of their money and property for personal profit (often "underground" and always condemned by the church fathers). But the notions and force of capitalism were so viable that gradually the petty capitalists became "mercantile capitalists" (1350 - 1800). The principle of capitalistic operation for the mercantilists was the same as for the petty capitalists, i.e. to sell or loan at a profit, and remains essentially the same in the giant capitalist countries like the U.S.A. Personal gain based on one's individual effort and willingness to take risk, i.e. personal profit, is the driving incentive to produce and do business. The mercantilists differed from the petty capitalists mainly in size of their operations and their international scope; whereas petty capitalists were mainly local businessmen operating locally, the mercantilists roamed across national borders by land and sea selling and buying and doing other business such as loaning money (banking) while usually maintaining their base of international business within the country of their citizenship. In later centuries, national governments came to realize the value of home-based mercantilists, some of whose profits could be drained off to enrichen national treasuries and finance wars of conquest (and discoveries of new

* "Philosophy," the analysis of the real world based upon reason and experience, was then simply a service to theologians whose conclusions were based solely upon faith in the church and its dogma. One's thinking began with a conclusion, based on faith, and then elaborated rational arguments to confirm it. See Bertrand Russell's History of Western Philosophy on Aquinas as a "non-philosopher."

** Aristotle wrote in Greek language, banned in Europe until the time of Aquinas who urged a colleague to translate Aristotle into Latin.

properties and trade opportunities in America); this national encouragement of home-based mercantilists was called "mercantilism" in which a nation grew richer than its neighbors by exporting more goods than it imported –as it grew richer it also grew more powerful in world affairs, including militarily. Thus nations became indirectly capitalistic, living off the profits of their citizen capitalists. The common laborer, struggling to make a sufficient wage to feed his family, was often exploited (as the critics of capitalism charge) in the profit-making energies of mercantilists and their nations; thus raising ethical issues about wage and hours of work, child labor, worker safety and so on, many of which issues persist today in different forms and will be discussed in later chapters.

Mercantilists often became large, if not gigantic, trading and manufacturing companies (corporations, in effect) whose agents travelled the distant international routes, selling and making deals, while company owners remained in their home nation administering the far-flung and complex operations. Ethical issues abounded as the complexity of business and especially its then environment soared: mercantilists took far greater risks than petty (local) capitalists and thus tended to view their business world as a jungle governed by necessity for survival and profit rather than schoolroom or church ethics (business was the real world – ethics merely admirable as abstract mental exercise). Governments, in these late medieval and early modern centuries, had no time and little power to regulate businessmen; nor did they have much inclination to do so (since the governments' treasuries depended increasingly on the very success of businessmen –no matter by what means, ethical or not). In effect businessmen did what they pleased, so long as it produced profits for themselves and their governments; there were few ethical, or even legal, restrictions to complicate or interfere with a capitalist's sole objective: profit, at whatever human costs or by any means one could get away with. During these turbulent centuries, kings and nations (some as small as mere provinces in Europe or today's American counties) were in constant wars, conquering each other, gaining power one day and losing it the next. Businessmen moved among them, often at great risk, from town to town and court to court, unconcerned about the local politics of the moment, concerned about their own function only –selling profitably the goods kings and others needed (clothing, tools, medicines and even food and often arms or the metals to make them). Churchmen, like kings, were also losing power, as popes in Rome and bishops in national regions struggled to merely survive in their positions and make political deals with any current king or prince in power to do so. Churchmen, even if they wanted to –as some did such as Aquinas, had little time or power to control business practices, no matter how unethical; Aquinas and bishops could write tomes or encyclicals against unethical business practices but had little power (moral or legal) to enforce business morality. And, to make matters worse, the church itself had become capitalist, selling indulgences at huge profits,* exploiting tenants and their families living on its properties for huge rent payments in money or goods (else eviction) and generally conspiring with power-hungry princes and greedy businessmen in the interest solely of the personal gain of the church as a whole (popes at Rome) or regional bishops and priests exploiting local business opportunities. The church, no less than political princes or businessmen, was forced by survival instinct to use the general public for its own ends –"the good ends justify (morally) any means necessary," no matter how seemingly unethical, became a common premise (the Jesuits, a religious order of priests dedicated to the service of the pope in Rome, became famous for their skillful practice of "ends justifying means," the then version of today's American CIA). The result of this church corruption, along with some smoldering theoretical reservations about Catholic dogma, was the Protestant Reformation launched by Luther in the 16th century to reform the church and set it on a godly course again. For centuries, European men had another reason for wars, an ancient one, religion: catholics and protestants (of various denominations as the original protest spirit turned back upon the first protestant group) fought and killed each other throughout Europe for hundreds of years(God, it was always claimed, as during the Crusades against Moslem "christians," on each side of such conflicts).

Given the church and state environments of religious and political chaos over these centuries, churches and states could afford little real interest in regulating business. In most cases, it would have been a case of the expected regulator needing regulation of itself most of all. Petty capitalists, early in the period, and mercantilists, later, thus operated completely free of any regulation or codes of conduct –except their own as they did business with each other. Business ethics did not, and could not, exist in the turmoil of these times. A kind of "jungle ethics" (survival of the fittest) ruled the practical lives of businessmen as well as princes and churchmen, whether catholic or protestant.

---

* An "indulgence," in the Catholic system, was a guarantee by the church, often in writing and often by the pope himself, of avoiding eternal punishment in the fires of hell after death and/or of reducing punishment time in "purgatory" before entering "heaven." Indulgences were "retailed," especially to the dying, at all prices & estates.

The Industrial Revolution and "Big" Capitalism

By the mid-eighteenth century, the industrial revolution was well launched in Europe, especially in England, and even in America. The industrial revolution consisted essentially of the invention and use of more efficient tools, usually machines, for manufacturing products. Two of its key features were mass production on assembly lines and the use of interchangeable parts as in the making of guns. This revolution was indeed that: it changed drastically the way men worked and the nature of production (and later marketing too). The spinning jenny and frame, the steam engine, machining interchangeable parts for assembly line production of guns, the power loom and so on led rapidly to the building of factories and very detailed specialization of labor (whereas, in the past, most products were tailor-made by craftsmen, one at a time, usually in a workshop in their homes, hence the so-called "cottage" industries, the industrial revolution forced workers into large factories and to work stations on an assembly line where they performed a tiny and tedious job as just one simple part of hundreds of similar tasks resulting in a product emerging from the line). Small children could do these tasks because of the new simplicity of most jobs and child labor (at very low wages) became an integral part of the factory system. A child was virtually born in a factory, worked there all day except for a night's sleep at home, and by mid-life usually died there. Many regarded this as gravely unethical but its efficiency could not be denied; child labor and subsistence wages increased the profitability of business, the treasury of governments and the national success of export-over-import mercantilism - thus all interested parties talked much about child labor but did nothing about it. The novels of Charles Dickens dramatized the drudgery of life in the factories.

The industrial revolution made petty capitalists obsolete (but not, of course, mercantilism, which was enhanced, especially in England with its wool and clothing trade). The industrial revolution was mainly a manufacturing revolution; petty capitalists were mainly merchants and shopkeepers (marketing) and knew nothing of the new economics created by factory production of goods. As factories and systems of machines grew larger, "big" capitalism quickly replaced the earlier "petty" version. The role of merchants was determined by the big factories and the new corporate managements which designed the factory systems as well as the routine and controlled distribution systems of which merchants became a part.

Two factors in human development were chiefly responsible for the new age called the industrial revolution: (1) one was the idea and spirit of capitalism (again "ideas have consequences") driven by the essential idea and incentive of personal profit; efficient manufacturing methods cut costs which directly increases profits, and thus the more efficient factory system and machine inventions to cut costs were inherent goals within the concept of capitalism (if and when such could be accomplished by the mind of man); (2) the other was the idea and spirit of a new, and unused, method of human thinking, the "scientific method," which logicians call "induction,"* which began in earnest when Galileo about 1600 AD decided to look through a telescope to discover the facts about our universe by observing it scientifically rather than merely believing what centuries of churchmen and philosophers had deduced about it from theoretical scriptures and theological dogma (Galileo was, of course, imprisoned by the church for heresy but we know today that the church's geocentric notion, i.e. Earth as the center of the universe, was wrong and Galileo's scientific observations were correct). Galileo's scientific method of thinking was probably the greatest human revolution of them all and every major technological advance of man since stems from it. Since Galileo, scientists have patiently gathered facts and objective conclusions about all the knowledges we today call physics, chemistry, biology, astronomy, anthropology, nuclear medicine and so on; inventor and engineering minds, using scientific knowledge as it developed, led man to new machines and technologies, i.e. the industrial revolution as well as the many technological revolutions since (computers, TV, miracle-type surgery to save lives, an amazing quantity of effective medicines, etc.).

The industrial revolution followed Galileo's thought revolution by about two centuries and both revolutions continue to change the world in which people live and work. Specifically, the industrial revolution began the age of big corporations and industries, many run by "robber barons" as explained above, and occasioned an even increasingly "bad" reputation for business and businessmen, who, many believed, were as unethical -or more so- as before but now on a giant scale.

The Reputation of American Business Today

As noted above, business practices in general and giant "trusts" in particular led to a massive public outcry and its political repercussions

---

* The concept of "induction," as a method of reasoning pre-dates Galileo by at least two thousand years (but Galileo's revolution was to use it seriously). Aristotle (400 BC), in his books on Logic and human thinking processes, distinguished in great detail mental "deduction" (arguing from general statements to a conclusion, the standard method in theology such as in Aquinas' writings) from the "inductive" process of observing specific facts and arguing upon it.

about 1900 (the process in a democratic society is diagrammed on p.18). This took the form of new laws and government regulations controlling every aspect of business practices and every American industry, beginning with antitrust laws in 1890. The political process in America is torturously slow (an uneasy trade-off of the rights of "due process" for all against the evaporation of rights by "justice's delay," as Shakespeare noted in his Merchant of Venice). So it was decades before the public rage about trusts and other business practices worked its way through Congress, court tests for constitutionality and finally became effective as enforceable laws. And, also, the political mood of the American public is notoriously vacillating and inconsistent, including rage against business trusts comfortably combined with a generally pro-business feeling: millions of average wage workers in the booming 1920s believed the then American credo that "the business of America *is* business" and had their life savings invested confidently in "their" companies on the stock market -which was bound to keep rising and multiplying everyone's profits forever. Until October 29, 1929 when the stock market crashed, banks went bankrupt, life savings and large fortunes disappeared, homes were foreclosed, the Great Depression set in and a third of the nation had no jobs or source of income for food and other necessities. The real causes of the 1929 crash and the depression (which lasted a full decade)* are still debated, but the public blamed big business and its unethical nature; "hate business" articles and cartoons (like the one on p. 23) were again popular in the public press and sold newspapers; people began to seek salvation elsewhere, many in the religious movements of the time and most in the promises of FDR's "New Deal" government to divert the wealth of rich businessmen to the common people -by means of government regulations and programs.[19]

Most of FDR's social programs ultimately proved unrealistic but, in the desparate 1930s and the idealistic 1960s, the majority of people, each with at least the power of political vote (however uninformed and illusion-seeking), supported ever-increasing central government, its social spending for rising benefits for all (except taxpayers) and America

* Despite FDR's big government programs in the 1930s, which relieved some human distress temporarily and certainly (with FDIC) put banks back on a sound foundation, the depression persisted through that decade essentially unchanged in its catastrophic misery; World War Two (1939), not government economic programs, ended the depression (all Americans rallied into the war effort, bought war bonds, worked overtime, saved money; new attitudes led to victory and the strong American economy of the 1950s); soon bigger social spending began. See Galbraith, Mitchell, etc. (References) on the depression.

systematically became pro-government and anti-business. Whether rational and based on accurate facts or not, American voters chose to support the growing paternalistic government and to restrain business.* Government regulation of business began in 1890 (antitrust laws), grew slowly and interruptedly into the 1930s but then soared into today's maze of government agencies regulating, restraining and often stifling every action of business. Given the history of American business and general economic conditions for the common people (voters), the public today places its trust in government (including Social Security!) and distrusts business. Even a sampling of today's government agencies, each costing $ millions to operate and dedicated to the regulation of business, strains the alphabet for merely naming them: FTC (trade), FDA (food and drugs), SEC (stocks and securities), ICC (commerce), FAA (aviation), DOE (oil and gas), and literally hundreds of others governing every detail of American industries and practices such as pricing, safety, hiring, communications, radio, lawnmowers, interest rates for banks versus S & L savings institutions, advertising in general or to kids or not at all (cigaret and liquor ads banned), and too many others to name, much less describe, in a short book. A sizeable portion of the federal budget each year, in the many billions of dollars, is earmarked for p o l i c i n g the businesses of the nation and keeping them honest. Many will maintain that the bureaucratic maze of business regulation, draining efficiency from national efforts in competition with other nations such as Japan, is business's fault: even a child or individual criminal, unable or unwilling to control himself, must be controlled by persons or systems despite the cost (the average annual cost for each prison inmate in America, during 1981, was $25,000, twice what most could earn if employed) - thus, if business is inherently unethical, external controls, no matter how costly, must be maintained. Other observers (I among them) say that, despite its past infractions of ethics, common alike among princes and churchmen of the past as well as businessmen, American business and its leaders have matured to a point of ethical sensitivity where they can exert <u>self</u>-control in lieu of government control.

The question today becomes, then: "can businessmen be ethical?" Frank Abrams, Chairman of Standard Oil in 1960, sensed the issue: "The job of professional management is to conduct the affairs of the enterprise in such a way as to maintain an equitable (ethical) and workable balance <u>among the claims of interested groups - stockholders, public etc.</u>"[20]

* Implied in this statement is the critical issue of "universal suffrage" (laws permitting <u>all</u> to vote quite apart from ability to read or comprehend issues of national significance). America's founding fathers explicitly excluded it, confining the voting privilege to citizens of proven education, understanding and personal responsibility.

Surveying American Opinion

Just as Sears & Roebuck's listed prices for merchandise represented a quantum leap upward in ethical level (p.28), so today's average consumer enjoys a level of fair and ethical treatment from businesses far superior to American (or other) consumers of a century or more ago. At least, this is the opinion of many observers of the business world. In the great majority of cases today, when a consumer does business with a big department store or bank or food supermarket or well-known automobile dealer or drug store or long-established home builder or most specialty merchants (tires, watches, clothes, etc.), he can buy quickly and calmly with relatively high assurance that he is being treated fairly. This is even true with the many kinds of repair and service businesses (plumbers, electricians, A/C & heating, auto service shops, fast food chains, etc.), especially if one deals regularly with the same businessmen who then are anxious to retain your business by treating you ethically. Big businesses (GM, IBM, Exxon and other Fortune 500 or 1000 firms) are especially careful about their ethical status, as well as their legality, given the shadows of the robber barons constantly present and the electronic media always scrutinizing and searching them in the public interest (and often just parochial or political interests which can be furthered by attacking big businesses or utilities as "on the other side"). As noted above (p.20), our age of "instant information" has become a powerful sanction against unethical, let alone illegal, behavior. American business seems to be today far more ethical than business at any earlier time or place.

And yet, the newspapers and TV News are often filled with recent exposures of business (and government) corruption. And the media and public seem to relish every saga of misconduct (and the retribution for it), much the same as Elizabethans enjoyed the unfolding of Shakespeare's tragic plays or later English villagers a public hanging or today's TV watchers a juicy scandal. Those of us with an anti-business bias or with an anti-government bias -or both- can comfortably enjoy the media exposés of our choice to confirm our original biases. Those of anti-business stripes will concede some of the flattering interpretations of modern business in the preceding paragraph but hasten to add that business is per se unethical (driven to profit by any means) and would be no better than the robber barons and petty business cheats of yore except for the new laws and penalties and government-enforced regulations put into effect over the past century. It is strong laws that fine and jail excutives who fix prices or make unsafe products that improve business ethics. To be sure, the government regulation itself is costly and often inefficient (accounting partly for America's low productivity) but it is necessary. Pro-business people hate regulation but find the above argument strong.

Is Business Morality Watergate Morality?

In the 1960s the nation was rocked by the disclosures of massive price-fixing conspiracies by the major manufacturers of electrical generators and other equipment (Westinghouse, GE, etc). This business corruption was dimmed by Government's own corruption in the 1970s which caused the first resignation (in disgrace) of an American president (Richard Nixon). This scandal is called "Watergate" after the name of the Washington D.C. building in which the Democratic Party's headquarters were broken into by operatives of Nixon's Re-election committee whose crime, when discovered, was covered up by an elaborate system of payoffs and lies reaching to the White House itself and Nixon. "Watergate morality," however, does not refer to the break-and-entry crime; that was simply a bungled burglary ordered by over-zealous managers of Nixon's re-election committee without Nixon's knowledge until it failed, the burglars were caught and charged with that crime. Then, when top White House aides and finally Nixon himself learned of the details of the crime, all of them, including Nixon, conspired by lies and payoffs to cover up the incident. It is the lying, bribery and conspiring to obstruct justice that "Watergate morality" refers to -and will for the remaining history of America.

Soon after Watergate, Archie Carroll, a management professor at the University of Georgia, conducted a survey of business managers to get their views on business ethics as related to the (political) Watergate experience.[21] Two-thirds of these managers agreed that they feel under pressure to compromise personal standards of ethics to achieve company goals (90% of the survey respondents were top or middle-level managers, not just first-line supervisors). Over two-thirds agreed that, despite a general ethical credo at the top-management level, pressure for results from the top leads down-line managers to consider compromising or to actually do so.* About half of the respondents agreed that 'big business' is somehow mixed up in the whole constellation of events labeled today "Watergate" and that business will suffer from Watergate because it will lower public confidence in business as well as in the political system. More than half (60%) agreed that the junior members of the President's Re-election committee went along with their bosses to show loyalty and "this is just what young managers would have done in business." This is the frank view of managers themselves, many the future leaders of banks and other major American industries.

The view of the public at large, including legislators, labor groups, university students (and professors) etc., rates the ethics of business as

* In the big electrical company cases of the 1960s, the "guilty" executives said they felt extreme pressure for "bottom-line" results.

even lower. Rightly or wrongly, deserved or undeserved, business still has a "bad reputation. As businessmen realistically assess their world (and their image), this is just a fact of life -either to be lived with, or changed.

REFERENCES

1 "The Castaway,"by Fred Opper, New York Public Library (Hearst)
2 Picture: Courtesy Brown Brothers
3 Chamberlain, John, The Enterprising Americans, Harper, 1963, p.84
4 Picture: Courtesy Library of Congress
5,6,7 Chamberlain, op.cit., 144-159, esp.p.144, 153, 155, 156
8 Courtesy: N.Y. Geneological & Biographical Society
9 Bursk, E.C., et.al. (ed), The World of Business (4 vol), Simon, 1962, 280
10,11 Bursk, op.cit., p.305 and 332
12 Cochran, T.C., Business in American Life, McGraw-Hill, 1972, p.91
13,14 Cochran, op.cit., p.79 and 100
15 The Westminster Review, Apr., 1859 and see Bursk, op.cit., p.585-9
16 See M.Beard's scholarly 2-vol. History of Business, U.of Mich., 1962
17 Bursk, op.cit., p.9 and 567-569
18 Rabbi D.H.Panitz, Address on file at Temple Emanuel, Patterson, N.J.
19 See Cochran, op.cit., relevant chapters and index
20 Fortune, August, 1960, p.108
21 Archie Carroll's "Survey of Managerial Ethics," Bus.&Soc.Review

For Further Reading

- Business Week, Jan.10, 1977, on U.S.corporations' overseas "bribes"
- Carr, A.Z., "Can An executive Afford a Conscience?," HBR, 7/'70
- Galbraith, J.K., The Great Depression (Causes of, etc.)
- Jay, A., Management and Machiavelli, Holt, Rinehart, 1967
- Fuller, J.G., The Gentlemen Conspirators, Grove Press, 1962
- Mitchell, B., Depression Decade, 1947
- Russell, Bertrand, History of Western Philosophy, 1945
- And see Beard, Bursk, Chamberlain, Cochran (above) and bibliography.

QUESTIONS AND PROBLEMS

1. Explain the following terms (including historical context if useful):

(a) trusts	(b) robber barons	(c) Darwinianism
(d) Standard Oil Co.	(e) OPEC	(f) Yankee peddler
(g) legal but unethical	(h) price-fixing	(i) capitalist
(j) usury	(k) mercantilists	(l) scientific method
(m) Industrial Revolution	(n) socialism	(o) universal suffrage

2. Give reasons why business has a bad reputation, in the past and today
3. Rank the following occupations in order of "most ethical" to "least ethical" (and explain it): bankers, car dealers, dept.stores, food stores, husbands, lawyers, politicians, professors, repairmen, salesmen, wives.

3 Ethical Theories and Concepts

The two chapters so far have demonstrated that, in today's world of instant electronic information, a good reputation for ethical behavior is essential for long-range business success (simply a practical necessity) but that business and businessmen in the past and still today suffer from a distinctly bad reputation (as generally unethical). Both of these key themes will be pursued further in later chapters, but first we must be very clear on the central concepts for any serious discussion of these issues. Ethical and moral issues (abortion, capital punishment, sex, interest rates, etc.) typically touch people deeply and tend to be discussed emotionally rather than analytically; in most cases, even in college classrooms, such discussions are emotion-laden interchanges of conclusions without proof (the stronger one feels about a proposition the more self-evident it is to him, with or without rational proof); in most cases, the participants in such arguments are unable or uninterested in even defining the critical terms used, although rational clarification of terms is the most elementary condition and foundation for any rational examination of the merits of any proposition. This chapter and the next, therefore, are devoted to the rational necessities of defining and analyzing the essential concepts of ethics. Although cold logic and tedious detail to many who would prefer to charge directly into the "hot" and exciting ethical issues themselves (i.e. application of ethics in the absence of clear concepts to apply), these two chapters on the fundamentals of the discipline of ethics are necessary.

ETHICS DEFINED

Few words suffer such semantic butchery or vagueness as "ethics" or "ethical." When I beat my competitor, it is the superiority of business acumen and my hard, but ethical, fighting; when he beats me, I easily detect his "dirty tricks" and unethical practices that beat me unfairly.

Some regard themselves as highly ethical if they operate just within the law but on the edge of it. Others feel ethical as they rationalize their sharp practices by emotional appeal to abstract ideals or standards which can be selected carefully, while ignoring other moral criteria that might clearly condemn such actions as unethical. For example, even the universally admired "golden rule" ("do unto others as you would wish them to do unto you") can be applied cleverly to rationalize cheating a child in a store purchase ("it will teach him a good lesson") or working a subordinate into a near-breakdown of his health ("it will train him to hard work the way I was"). Other ethical standards easily used to justify actions, or abused to excuse them, are patriotism (for terrorist actions), love of family (for hurting neighbors -including feuds and wars), "love thy neighbor" (for passing poor students into the next school grade or for occasional adultery) and so on. Such superficial interpretations of "ethics" are limited only by the imagination and emotionality of the wielder of the word. Obviously, we need clear definitions.

What is "Ethics?"

"Ethics," as traditionally defined, is a set of standards, or code, by which human actions are determined as humanly right or wrong, good or evil.*

Ethics, therefore, is in its strict sense normative, a set of criteria to judge actions as right or wrong. Ethics are standards of conduct. Ethical theory is the philosophical theories or religious systems of belief which underlie ethics, lead to it and provide its foundation or rationale.** For example, Aristotle (ancient Greek philosopher who had no religion at all) and St.Augustine (fifth-century theologian of the Catholic religion) developed thought systems or theories differing greatly but their ultimate ethical standards (ethics) emerged as similar in many respects, except, of course, respecting religious rituals (the philosopher had none). The expression "ethical standards" is itself redundant or tautological but occasionally useful in communicating one's meaning; the field of "descriptive ethics," despite its significant contribution to the human understanding of human beings, is not ethics in the strict sense but rather a history of ethics, as actually practiced, at different times and places, often a subset of anthropology. These terms will be used reasonably strictly throughout this book.

---

* "Ethics" is used as both a singular and a plural noun, depending on context. See footnote on page 11 above.

** Philosophy (reasoning based on experience) and Religion or Theology (based on prior faith and beliefs) are very distinct terms. See p. 35.

The definition of "ethics," however, depends, for its clarity, upon two other terms used within it: "good" and "humanly good or right."

The Concept of "the Good"

Many words, like "democracy," "love," "fear," "pain" and "good," are so common and used so often that no one ever stops to define them; they suggest sufficient meaning in daily life for most purposes of practical living, despite little or no exact definition. When, however, such words are essential terms in a philosophical analysis ("democracy" in a technical book on international political systems or "love" in a professional text on marriage and the family), the key terms must be elevated from vague suggestion to strict and clear definition. Since the term "good" is a critical part of the definition of ethics, it too needs clear definition. (Surprisingly to many, who have "taken for granted" such words for a lifetime, their much-used words are difficult to define and often can be defined only imperfectly - such as the word "good".)

Based on the patient analysis of "the good" by philosophers since Plato and Aristotle,* "good" is defined as that which is desirable or sought after as an end or goal.** Many kinds and degrees of good can be identified, arranged in hierarchies of means-and-ends relationships, lower goods or ends contributing as means to higher goods or ends. As a hammer is called good because its particular form, skillfully used (this human skill a good too), places nails to hold planks of wood together in a securely built house, a higher good itself contributing to the still higher good of warmth and shelter for its occupants (who make nails for a living). Thus "goods" can be classified as practical goods (a good tool or good skill), athletic goods (a good tennis racket or player), aesthetic goods (a good painting or painter or a good pianist), gourmet goods (a good meal or cook), sexual goods, professional goods (a good doctor or dentist or engineer or computer programmer), and so on throughout every aspect of nature. And the "good" is relative at most intermediate levels (a good meal relative to taste might be bad or fatal to a fat man with a bad heart just as a large inheritance of money is good for security but might destroy a young man's incentive to become worthwhile for himself). Sorting out all these goods and their interrelationships in hierarchies of accomplishment, skills, knowledge, pleasure and so many others, what is -or should be- man's ultimate good? That good to which all other goods lead. That good which is proper to a human being -and final.

* Plato's Republic, VII, Symposium, Phaedrus; Aristotle's Ethics.

** Philosophers learned early that concepts such as the good (and the true, the beautiful and even "being" itself) are so-called transcendental notions that cannot be defined in the required form of a species within a genus (eg:man as a rational animal). They can only be defined by pointing at them in the real world.

The Humanly Good as Man's Ultimate Good

What this ultimate and final, most proper and important, good is for a man (as a human distinct from all other animals and living things) is the most important question that thinking men have asked of themselves throughout human history. Religions and philosophies have proposed theories about man's ultimate good or goal ranging from happiness in a next world (heaven, nirvana, etc.) to patriotism, intellectual development or sensual pleasure in this life. However, whatever values man accepts as his ultimate good, whether from religious belief or his own philosophical thinking, these become the ethical principles or theories from which a particular set of standards (ethics) derives. Just as the purpose of a tool, such as a screwdriver or automobile, determines the standards (specifications) for building or using the tool, so a man's conception of his ultimate purpose as a human being (his "value system") determines his most basic standards of human conduct (his ethics).

Although exactitude or uniformity about human value systems is not attainable,* there is sufficient consensus about certain values in most modern civilized nations to generate a general and workable ethics and to establish some body of laws for orderly, rather than chaotic, relations among men (in their families, business, work and other social interactions).** Also, there is sufficient clarity about such values and ethics to distinguish among the vast variety of goods in the human hierarchy. The context of a discussion makes it sufficiently clear that we mean different kinds of goods in statements such as: "This batter has good eyes;" or "she has good looks;" or "he's a good runner" or "she's a good lawyer" or "he's a good man" or "he's a good person, a good human being." Only the last statement refers to the good as ultimate for a human being rather than intermediate and a means to a further human end in life.

The Good Doctor as a Bad Man

At the conclusion of World War II, records seized from Nazi prison camps revealed that several doctors had performed experimental surgery on unwilling prisoners, many of whom died (they were to be killed anyway in the gas chambers) but the surgery attempted and the skills manifested in the surgery were technically superlative, not just good but the best. By the ethical standards of most civilized people, the surgery,

---

* Aristotle, even 2500 years ago, although a stickler for precision in his Logic (Organon) and Metaphysics, insisted that exactitude cannot be hoped for in ethics (see his Ethics) because of inherent subjectivity about intangible values, semantic difficulties, etc.

** The similarities and variations of value systems and ethics will be discussed fully in later chapters.

forced upon victims as experiments and needless for their health —and often killing them, was viewed as a moral (ethical) atrocity. The doctors who performed these acts were good surgeons but evil men. Despite the inexactitude of ethics (and many other human studies), where the precision of mathematics and chemistry are impossible, ethical standards are clear enough to distinguish in most cases good men from the bad, however good they may be as engineers, athletes, movie stars, lawyers, teachers or preachers or in any other intermediate life skill.

Imperatives

An imperative (grammatically a verb form) is a "do" or "don't" statement, a command. As contrasted with categorical verb forms ("you are standing") or interrogatory ("are you standing?") or hypothetical ("if you want the job, you will stand"), the imperative is an order or command ("stand!").

Ethical standards are directly imperatives ("do not steal") or always implicitly imperative ("stealing is wrong"), implying what ought to be done or not done. The laws of nations are also imperatives as are the rules and rituals of religions, the normal procedures and policies of organizations, the norms of courtesy in social and business behavior, etc.

Sanctions That Enforce Imperatives

The effectiveness of (obedience to) any imperative depends upon the *sanctions* imposed for obeying or violating such a command. A sanction is a reward for obeying an imperative (positive sanction) or a punishment for ignoring or violating an imperative (negative sanction). For example, positive sanctions are public praise for donating money to an admired charitable organization such as the Salvation Army, or even self-satisfaction for achieving a difficult personal goal, or a military medal for courage in action; negative sanctions are imprisonment for stealing, or excommunication from one's religious community for violating its rules or rituals, or rejection by a peer group, or a loss of self-esteem and sense of inner integrity because of a violation of one's own personal code of conduct.

The notion of sanctions will be critical in many later chapters concerning the effective application of ethics in business (especially its ethical codes of conduct); negative sanctions, although not so called in our first chapter on the practical importance of ethics, were a dominant theme throughout that chapter (unethical businessmen ruined by public disclosure, on TV and in other media, of unfair business practices, public perceptions of business as unethical and thus requiring strict and growing government regulation, and the forced resignation of a U.S. president).

Moral Philosophy and Moral Theology

There are two main sources from which ethical values and standards evolve: philosophy and religion (theology, which is the study of God). Philosophy is a body of knowledge, much of it about metaphysical things such as the human soul and the ultimate meaning of human life, based upon human thinking and analysis of actual human experience. That part of philosophy which deals with ethical values and standards is called moral philosophy. Religion (often called Theology when systematized) is a body of beliefs based upon faith in the authority of some person (like Christ or Buddha) or some holy writings (Hindu or Judaic scriptures). That part of religion which deals with ethical values and standards is called religious ethics or often moral theology.

Throughout this book, the terms "moral" and "ethical" will be equivalent. "Morality" or "morals" will be defined exactly the same as "ethics" (above).

As sources or principles of ethical standards, philosophical thinking and religious faith (often operating together*) are very distinct operations of the mind and function very differently. One's mind may be mainly, even entirely, either philosophical or religious -or partly both but still dominated by the one or the other mental tendency. In its pure form, the religious mind is the "true believer," seeking and finding security in someone or something perceived as a final authority about the meaning of life and proper behavior during it. Ambiguity or gaps in what can be known about man and his meaning (if any) are intolerable and must be resolved into certainty and mental security by submission of the mind to some authority (person or institution) which guarantees the needed certainty. Such persons literally cannot function at all without the security provided by complete faith in their particular religions, prophets or holy men (for some, a psychiatrist or priest or guru or other counselor serves sufficiently in the latter capacity). The purely philosophic mind is the thinker. He shuns authorities and religions, thinks for himself and discovers whatever truth can be found by thoughtful analysis of reality and human experience as he and other humans know it. This inevitably entails living with high degrees of doubt, uncertainty and scepticism, but he is up to, or actually enjoys as many philosophers have, tolerating such ambiguity and uncertainty.

These two mind-sets, the religious and the philosophical, create the value systems from which ethical standards are derived.

* Thomas Aquinas, 13th century, the giant mind dominating Catholic thought into modern times, was always a man of faith in his religion first, but showed in his writings exquisite skills in philosophic methods of reasoning and analysis, drawing especially on Aristotle.

LAW

Law refers to the laws of states and nations and, like ethics, is a set of imperatives,actions to do or not to do. Unlike ethics, however, laws are enforced by the power of the state after being established and promulgated by the state as law. The sanctions for unethical action are a guilty conscience, excommunication from one's religion, personal disrespect or contempt from friends, family or the community at large. The sanctions for violating laws range from fines and loss of property to jail and being put to death by firing squad, burning or hanging.

Laws and Ethical Standards That Coincide

Typically, throughout history, societies (tribes,nations,etc.) have been monolithic, i.e. strictly structured and homogeneous in their value systems. Virtually everyone in such monolithic communities held identical beliefs, learned from birth, reinforced in the society till death, and rarely challenged by serious questioning or alternate beliefs (the rare challenger was, by definition, abnormal and either exiled or executed as, for example, the heretics of the European medieval centuries). In such societies, the value system of beliefs (ethics) rapidly became formalized as laws subject to enforcement by state authorities quite apart from existing intangible sanctions of the society's religious leaders. In many cases, leaders were "two-hatted," simultaneously the head of both church (religion) and state (excommunicating a violator and condemning him to hell by his authority as religious leader while also sentencing him to death by his authority as head of state). In the Christian empire of the medieval period in Europe, for example, kings (the state) usually enforced as law the church rulings of the pope and bishops; a heretic was declared such by the church and excommunicated but his execution was ordered by state authorities as a violation of law. Church and State were essentially the same in the content of their imperatives, different only in the manner of establishing and sanctioning them (the Church by divine revelation through holy men sanctioned by blessings or curses, the State by order of rulers in power sanctioned by physical force). In such cases and societies, ethics and laws coincide in their imperatives; but, conceptually, ethics and law are still very different and, in many societies, lead to quite different results and imperatives -often in direct conflict.

Conflict Between Laws and Ethics

In the early 1940s, the Nazi government in Germany (Hitler and his ministers as a dictatorship) established laws requiring citizens to report the identity and location of Jews and, later, requiring military officers and soldiers to murder them. Although these actions violated the ethics of many who participated in the atrocities, failure to comply with the Nazi laws carried the sanction of swift imprisonment or death. This is a case in which laws are in conflict with the ethics of many, if not the majority of a nation's people. In such cases, the decision to comply with one's conscience (ethics) or the law is a personal decision -often an agonizing one; in the Nazi period, one would have to believe in his ethical principles enough to literally die for them as early Christian martyrs died in the Roman coliseum rather than obey the laws prohibiting worship of the Christian God.

Cases of conflict between law and peoples' ethics in American history include: Federal laws prohibiting polygamy among the Mormons, laws of taxation and mandatory public schooling among the Amish, conscientious objectors to military draft laws, abortionists and their clients until recently (and maybe again, if antiabortion laws pass), sale of contraceptives until recently, civil rights protestors against racist laws in the 1950s and so on. These conflict situations are so common, especially in pluralistic societies (such as the U.S. where people are free to follow different religious faiths with minimal legal constraints), that we have an expression to convey the notion: civil disobedience. Coined by Emerson and Thoreau (19th century New England transcendentalist philosophers), "civil disobedience" is the violation of laws, deemed unethical, including the awareness and willingness to suffer the legal penalties for violation of such laws. Thus civil rights protestors violated the law knowing they would go to jail -and so they did. So did conscientious objectors earlier in the century. In a pluralistic society, like America, civil disobedience often performs the useful function of highlighting "bad" laws and eventually changing or repealing them. Thus today conscientious objectors are given other and acceptable options of service, other than military, by which they can both preserve their ethical posture and act within the law; the prohibition laws of the 1920s, which made millions of law-abiding citizens violators of the law in their "speakeasies," have been repealed as ill-conceived laws (the powerful organized crime these laws spawned, however, to service the millions of civilly disobedient, still plagues us); recreational users of marijuana and other illegal drugs still today engage in civil disobedience by the millions; homosexuality, once illegal, is now quite lawful; but some Mormons practice polygamy illegally and "underground" and some, who refuse to pay IRS taxes on well-founded ethical grounds, are nevertheless in jail.

Thus laws and ethics are not necessarily the same things at all. In most cases, they coincide; but often they are in conflict. Often, also, what is legal is quite unethical and what is illegal is quite ethical.

Ethical Knowledge vs Ethical Action

Knowledge and action must, obviously, be distinguished. One may know what is ethically right and still, under pressure or temptation, act otherwise. Most men who embezzle funds from an employer, cheat on IRS tax reports (or their wives) know their actions are unethical or illegal -but do the actions anyway. A professor of ethics might be an adulterer, thief or liar: he knows clearly what is unethical, but acts otherwise.

Ethical ignorance or insensitivity is even a more unfortunate case: the man who acts unethically, or even illegally, because he does not know or is unable to analyze correctly what is right vs wrong, especially in complex business situations or in the midst of heavy emotional pressures.

This book is concerned about both ethical knowledge and ethical action, but primarily the former: improved human skills in the ethical analysis of managerial decisions and heightened ethical sensitivity for any and all ethical issues latent within such decisions.

BUSINESS ETHICS

Business ethics is the application of an individual's or community's ethical standards to specifically business-type decisions; just as medical or legal ethics is their application to medical or legal practices. By virtue of similar distinctions among the various applications of ethics, we could distinguish among ethics for dentists, priests, salesmen, wholesalers, engineers and so on. "General ethics" would mean ethics as it applies to the general lives of all, apart from the particular occupations or professions of each.[1]

Business ethics, therefore, deals with those issues of ethics which relate to the specific functions of business, i.e. the production and distribution of goods and services, usually for a profit or, at least, with profit as the intent. Thus, if one business owner murders another, this is a matter of general ethics (and law too), murder being an issue generally applicable to all members of a society if any commits that act, not at all specific to the human functions of conducting business; misrepresenting a product for sale, however, or charging an unfair price for it is specific to business and, therefore, an issue of business ethics.

In reality, the categories of application cross among specific lines as well as general life. A medical doctor is also a citizen and a businessman as, at different times, he performs surgery (ethically or not), makes demands upon his wife and children (ethically or not) and charges patients different fees for similar services (ethically or not).

It would be merely academic and boring to note these distinctions as they occur in later chapters; having established the distinctions among specific and general lines, the reader will easily note them as they occur in the text.

POSITIVE ETHICS

The tendency in any discussion of ethics is to emphasize avoidance of evil, i.e. the unethical. This kind of emphasis is usually called "negative" ethics, and it must necessarily be the dominant theme of ethics as normative (as distinct from descriptive ethics, p.46).

But there is such a thing as "positive" ethics: stressing actions that are ethical or even beyond merely being ethical; such as helping others beyond any conceivable obligation to do so, selfless charity, heroism, and so on.

OBJECTIVE ETHICS AND SEMANTICS

Are the ethics of individuals and peoples merely subjective, relative to the value preferences of particular humans at different times, places and situations? In this view (often called "relativism" or situation ethics), there is no absolute or objective ethics by which certain actions are *per se* wrong, *always* unethical no matter the time, place or situation; rather, the ethical nature of any action depends upon either the value preferences of people (their conception of ultimate good,p.48) or the unique situation to which ethical standards are being applied, or both.

Or is there some objective foundation for ethics, a source rooted in reality and human nature itself by which certain human actions can be absolutely and universally known as always ethical or always unethical? If so, this would be called "objective" ethics or absolute ethics.

Subjective vs Objective Ethics

The philosophical debate between subjective and objective ethics theorists has burned through the centuries since the early Greek philosophers 2500 years ago -and still continues.* The problem of objective ethics is no nearer solution now than it was then. Nevertheless, we must consider here the nature of the problem and how it affects the

---

* Tending toward the side of objective ethics were Plato, Aristotle, Augustine and Aquinas (theologians), Descartes, Spinoza, Locke, Kant (a paradox, whose "categorical imperative" is absolute but whose metaphysics demanded subjectivism in everything), and many others. Tending toward or explicitly advocating subjective ethics were Protagoras, some Protestants, Hume, Mill, James, Dewey, etc.

development of a workable and practical ethics here and now in America.* First let's consider briefly the case for and critics against the two views.

The human desire for an objective ethics is deep and enduring since, if it could be found or established under the belief that it had been found, men would enjoy the satisfaction of clear knowledge about the most profound issues which concern them, good and evil, right and wrong. Man, among all living things, is unique in possessing a moral sense, a sense of guilt or moral self-satisfaction (and the sought-after esteem of peers and others) surrounding his every action. His sense of moral rectitude, for good actions, is exhilarating and his guilt can be agonizing as he broods daily about evil actions (murder, betrayal, lies) committed in his past. Often worst of all is gnawing doubt about good and evil, what is really right and wrong, and the obsession with it that generates an unsureness of mind, ambiguity about moral concepts and situations, weakness of will, collapse of determination and inability to make decisions. As Shakespeare put it: "thus conscience (which meant awareness and thinking in his times) doth make cowards of us all."

Given the powerful yearning for objective ethics, man found or created them in many of the great philosophical systems (Aristotle and Confucius) and world religions (Catholicism and Aquinas). Throughout the Catholic centuries of medieval Europe, for example, the church, gifted with the gem of absolute infallibility at its head (the pope), provided everyone with clear directions and certainty about what was right and wrong in virtually every human activity (eating, working, sleeping, sex, money and its uses, etc.). The Catholic church still claims the gem of infallibility on moral matters and this offer of relief from agonizing doubt and mental insecurity about the "right thing to do" attracts and retains church members by the millions. Men yearn for certitude and objective ethics provides it.

Critics of objective ethics (and even its possibility) admire it as a goal but find the prospect of objective ethics an illusion and merely "wishful thinking." They abandon the effort and search for any absolute

---

* Philosophy and theology (religion) are not like modern "science" which is based upon observation of empirical facts (see p.39) and gradually settles problems once and for all, such as cures for diseases. Philosophy and theology deal with metaphysical issues that are unobservable and cannot be proven (or disproven) factually, such as the soul, a next life, God, freedom of will, and ethical values. Thus, debate about these issues can, and does, go on forever and few such debates are ever settled with any finality.

ethics and, often reluctantly but realistically in their view, accept the necessity of subjective ethics (relativism or situation ethics). Subjective ethics forfeits certitude, abandons the hope for any final set of moral guides and acknowledges, even promotes, scepticism about all ethics. Often its critics are harsh, as, for example, Samuel Clarke (1705):

> "Moral truths are so notoriously plain and self-evident that nothing but the extremest stupidity of mind, corruption of manners or perverseness of spirit can possibly make any man entertain the least doubt concerning them."[2]

John Locke, thirty years earlier, was equally explicit:

> "Those only doubt of a supreme ruler (God) and universal law who would willingly be under no law, accountable to no judge; those only question another life hereafter who intend to lead such a one here as they fear to have examined and would be loath to answer for when it is over."[2]

But the advocates of subjective ethics do not perceive right ethical (or moral) standards as self-evident, absolute or universal. They note that, throughout human history, different religions have taught different and contradictory "absolutes" of morality, and, surely, all could not be "true" simultaneously; nor could the Gods appealed to as their moral sources of knowledge since they "reveal" through different churches different and contradictory ethics as absolute and universal. By the definition of the word, neither the moral absolutes nor the Gods are universal. Nor, say the relativists, are ethics or its principles and standards. Objective ethics is a supreme yearning of man but, being beyond the realm of the observable (metaphysical like God, soul and moral values), it is theoretically impossible; and the history of cultures, civilizations, religions and philosophy (actual human experience) shows little that is absolute or universal about ethics - quite to the contrary, ethics among peoples have always been varied, contradictory and subjective.

So the debate about objective ethics continues. The current star among contemporary American philosophers, Robert Nozick, just completed a book, a large portion of which is devoted to the new search for objective ethics but conceding (vaguely and sadly) that it poses severe difficulties.* Nozick's latest is a brilliant work but it merely continues the debate over objective ethics and certainly will not end it.

---

* Nozick, R, Philosophical Explanations, Harvard U. Press, 1981. Since Charles Peirce, mathematician and later a philosopher, probably America's greatest, objectivist in intent but subjectivist at the end of his enquiries, and Wm. James and J. Dewey, America has had no stars. Nozick will be worth watching.

A Massive Problem of Semantics: Aggravating the severe problem of objective vs subjective ethics at the very foundation of ethical inquiry, the very meaning and definition of words (semantics) create ever-present difficulties. Unless one is scrupulously precise and careful in the definitions of ethics-related words, ambiguity and confusion always contaminate such words as "moral,""virtue,""rights,""obligations," "unethical,""evil,""fair or just,""scandalous,""obscene,""ungodly," "brutal,""love," "integrity,""character" and so on. Unlike modern science, which defines terms in reference to observable facts and realities (objective things, see p.55 footnote), the essential subject matter of ethics is metaphysical with no reference to empirical realities. Ethics is the analysis, not of what is (facts), but of what ought to be (value judgments which are normative, not merely descriptive as in science). Moreover, an additional cloud marring the clearness of ethical sight is human emotion, often at white-heat intensity, that dominates most discussions of ethical issues: all the words in quotes above are usually laden with emotion as used in human communication.*

Workable Ethics Amid Incomplete Theory

The purpose and scope of this book explicitly exclude any attempt to review or critique any of the theoretical foundations of ethics such as objective vs subjective ethics, Plato's vs Aristotle's metaphysics, Christian vs any other religious foundations of ethics. The "Philosophy" and "Religion" sections of libraries are full of such books which the reader can consult for full-length book explorations of such theoretical foundations.

Despite the controversies over ethical theory and the semantics of it, our purpose here is a practical one: to identify, in our present American society, a set of ethical standards sufficiently clear (pp.48-9) and in fact accepted by the American public such that they can and do serve adequately as a workable ethics. As we shall see, this can and will be done in this and the following chapters -despite the theoretical problems of ethical inquiry.

It follows from our purpose that sections and chapters relating to ethical theory and the history of philosophy or religion are intended to provide clear understanding of ethical concepts, not at all to validate or critically analyze them. But some sense of the history of human experience about ethical inquiry is necessary for both the definitions and

---

* Mutually meaningful communication among people about ethical issues is difficult and laden with problems of conflicting meanings, perceptions, values and attitudes. These are explained at length in Ch.9 of the author's Theory and Practice of Managing (1982).

clear understanding of current ethical issues.

ETHICAL STANDARDS THROUGH HISTORY

Although we cannot here either prove or disprove the validity of various ethical standards developed by past human societies, it is necessary that we know and understand what they were. In this section, we will list and consider many of the most prominent ethical standards used by millions through human history (brief references to the origins of each are amplified in more detail in the next chapter concerning the history of ethical theory).*

1. Might Makes Right.

This standard of human conduct is the most ancient of all and is also referred to as "jungle ethics," "the law of survival of the fittest," "the ethics of necessity," or, some would say, "business is business." Although best formulated by writers such as Hobbes, Machiavelli and Nietzsche (see Ch.4 for detail on these and other origins of ethics),* the law of might and survival of the fittest dominated man's early history and his constant wars among tribes, families and nations. Even in very recent times, the European courts of Louis XIV and Peter the Great were dominated by those who could command the army and its lethal weapons; English kings lived by the sword (many of their sons were killed young, by aspirants to the throne, to prevent them from ever claiming kingship); the average "World History" text is almost entirely a chronicle of wars, conspiracies to seize power or land or money, the weak fading from most of human history and the strong surviving and <u>writing</u> it (their way).

Darwin, in his monumental work on the natural evolution of animals and other living species, discovered the natural law that only the fittest animals survive long enough in life to <u>reproduce</u> their kind; the weaker are killed off early by the strong and, unable to reproduce, become extinct. Spencer, in human and social studies, found the same dominant tendency among humans through history, accepted freely as the *only* realistic ethical standard, only the strong and fittest survive or "might makes right." In the economic world of men (business), Adam Smith, a professor of moral philosophy, wrote his <u>Wealth of Nations</u> (1776) which made "pure competition", or survival of the fittest in business, the main

---

* The listing of major ethical standards is a chronological one, as far as this is possible; certainly not a listing in order of importance. The reader will probably accept some of them, as valid in his own personal value system, and reject others. But all of them need to be understood.

determinant of healthy personal and national economies; driven by this ethics of "enlightened self-interest" and free-market capitalism, smart and strong businessmen became increasingly efficient (and wealthy), the inefficient were weeded out and failed to survive as unproductive, and Americans, somewhat ruthlessly (see "robber barons,"p.24), built the most prosperous nation in human history. Despite the semantically harsh and offensive tone of the words, the ethics of "might makes right" and "survival of the fittest" underlies much of the American success experience.* This is not necessarily admirable from a moralistic viewpoint, only a fact.

Semantics again becomes important. "Might makes right" and "jungle ethics" are offensive words. So are the words "death" and "taxes." Thus, often, humans, with the gift of words, shield themselves from realities by using euphemisms such as "passed away" or "in his final sleep" (for the reality, death) or "revenue enhancement" (for the reality, taxes). Hobbes and Machiavelli, in their classic works, cut through the semantics and the euphemisms, observed the hard realities within human societies (including the issue of survival within them): if you were strong, smart and productive, you survive; otherwise not. So, as an historical reality, it has always been among men. Adam Smith and his followers would, of course, have to say the same about all men struggling in the real world of business now and throughout the past.

A harsh ethics, indeed. But Hobbes and others would say it is the only realistic one.

2. Justice (Fairness to all)

This standard also goes back to man's early history, codified by Hammurabi as early as 2000 BC, established in the Judaic scriptures as the law of "an eye for an eye," developed as a central human virtue in the philosophy of Aristotle and the foundation stone of Roman law.

Justice (or fairness) is defined by Aristotle and others as "the act of giving oneself or another what is due him." This statement implies the notions of "rights" and "obligations" (with which we will deal more fully later) but, put simply, means equity in the transactions among

---

* In the past several decades, Americans have retreated from a norm of productiveness ("work ethic") as the rule for all and moved to a "welfare" ethics: today, in America, millions of adults live on the work of others (taxpayers) by means of government welfare payments and food stamps and other gifts from government; such Americans survive not as "fittest" but by government edict. And, since they are technically an "overhead" cost of otherwise productive national business, Japanese companies overwhelm Americans in the markets.

people. Thus, if I save your life, you owe me yours when I ask it; if you destroy my home or my horse, you owe me the same either by restoring or replacing mine or permitting my destruction of your home or horse as compensation; if I loan you my horse, car, money or wife (a common practice in the past), you are obligated to repay in kind or other mutually accepted substitute (such as repaying me in money for losing or killing my horse). In short, an "eye for an eye,""a life for a life" and all other forms of mutual equity and compensation among men. Virtually all law since the times of Hammurabi is based on justice.*

3. The Golden Rule

Like the test of justice, the test of the Golden Rule is virtually universal among civilized cultures as a measure of ethical good and evil. The Golden Rule, in its simplest form, states: Do unto others as you would have them do unto you. This is the Christian version (book of Matthew) but the sense of it is found among religions and philosophies alike. Confucius, a philosopher rather than a theologian, states it in the negative around 500BC (in Analects): Do not unto others what you would have them not do unto you. Buddhism, Islam, Judaism and all world religions have some form of the Golden Rule buried deep among their roots.

As generally interpreted, the Judeo-Christian norm of brotherly love (see "Love Thy Neighbor" below) and the Golden Rule are quite different. The Golden Rule is closer to the law of justice in governing the actions of men toward each other; the element of equity among men (not equality necessarily) suffuses the Golden Rule.

The major flaw in the Golden Rule seems not inherent but a possible ambiguity in its interpretation or application; since all people do not want the same things and "one man's meat is another's poison," a literal -if not perverse- application of the Golden Rule can justify (?) a person treating another harshly or in unwanted ways based on the agent's wants only (for example, I like a cool room and keep the thermostat down even when you occupy it despite your need for a very warm room). Thus many, including the playwright Bernard Shaw, interpret the genuine meaning

---

* Mercy is the noble and unrequired act of forgiving an injustice and declining to demand any sort of repayment for it in kind or otherwise. Shakespeare covered the distinction well in Merchant of Venice as the lawyer, Portia, pleaded with plaintiff for mercy for the defendant instead of the "pound of flesh" required by justice. In similar manner, the loser in fair combat often asks for mercy from one he sought to destroy but who now has bested him and holds the power of life or death over him. Mercy is positive ethics(p.54).

of the Golden Rule as more like: Do unto others as you would have them do unto you if you were they. Application of the Golden Rule, in its real meaning, thus requires empathy, understanding the wants and needs of others by their perceptions and conditions of life before applying the Golden Rule to them. A professional NFL football player, running a Senior Citizen Exercise group, would kill most of his class by over-exertion if he applied the Golden Rule based on his physical needs and wants rather than his students'; so might an unmarried, workaholic and achievement-oriented boss drive competent subordinates to mental breakdowns or divorces as he applies the Golden Rule by his needs and life goals rather than theirs.

Human Life as Transactions or Exchanges: As noted by Chief Justice Warren (p. 15 above), primitive man became civilized and "human" because his developing brain and societies discovered the practical use of an inner ethics in governing the transactions among men toward an effective mutual survival (Golden Rule) rather than mutual destruction (Jungle ethics, as above). Even today, modern nations of people use most of their energies destroying each other by military spending and conflict (Poland and Russia for 500 years or more, now Russia and the USA) rather than cooperating toward prosperous economies and security for both nations in their mutual transactions. But, in international as well as business exchanges among people, the Golden Rule becomes often "intelligent self-interest," "do unto others before they do unto you," "we will stop arming or shooting only after you do it first" and, especially in American business, "you pat my back and I'll pat yours but you pat me first."

The Golden Rule is one of modern man's soundest and a powerful advantage for his species. But, to be effective, it must be applied correctly and carefully.

4. Love Thy Neighbor

This norm of brotherly love, making oneself responsible voluntarily for another's welfare while owing him nothing, goes far beyond justice and the Golden Rule. When such love exists and is expressed consciously,* it is positive ethics as common among the early Christians and by parents for their children. As unconscious and instinctive behavior, such "love" by parents for their offspring is essential for the survival of

---

* "Love," in the English language, is a most ambiguous and often abused term, representing such diverse states of emotion and will as sentimental affection, friendship, pity, sexual passion or very temporary infatuation. In its purist sense (agapae in ancient Greek) love is an act of will, willing and wishing the good of another.

most animal species (for example, parenting birds and mammals feeding their helpless young for weeks or months or, for bears, many years). In the animal world, in quite practical terms, as practical as Darwinian survival of the fittest, "love," operating instinctively by genetic code, is the norm for survival. It is the same for humans except that acts of love are done consciously or withheld or otherwise perverted by human consciousness about what they are doing and human freedom of will to do it, continue to do it, cease doing it or make no efforts at all to do acts of "love."

Interestingly, "love," in the strict sense used above and operating instinctively without consciousness of it, is not a noble "sentiment" or luxury in the animal world; it is a main practical means of survival itself -and, for man, also an animal species, is the ethics of "love" any less necessary for his survival?

Love and Reciprocity: The practical (survival) value of the ethics of love, and of justice and of the Golden Rule, lies within the concept of reciprocity: humans, and animals too, tend to treat, help or hurt others as they have been treated, helped or hurt. A mad dog (unless it is diseased with rabies) attacks humans because it was maltreated by them as a puppy; treated kindly as a puppy, the dog will reciprocate in kind, friendly and loving to all humans encountered; a (human) child, beaten or verbally abused by its parents or early teachers, will typically hate, fight and hurt others until he ends up in prison (unless he finds a way to channel his hostility constructively, joining his nation's army or building a business from scratch).

Pure "love" does not always require reciprocity (the abused wife who remains loyal to husband and children is the classic case of this); but the law of justice and the norm of the Golden Rule operate strictly upon reciprocity and the full expectation of it in all transactions. In effect, the ethical norms of justice and the Golden Rule are the ethics of ultimate reciprocity. Instinctively (for animals) and very consciously (for most humans), mutual transactions are governed by this law of reciprocity.

5. The Golden Mean

Formulation of the Golden Mean, as the ethical criterion of virtue as distinguished from vice (evil habits), was first developed by a pagan philosopher, Aristotle, around 400 BC (see his Nicomachean Ethics). Aristotle explicitly rejected the religions of his times (as had Socrates before him) and, recognizing no "afterlife" such as the Christian heaven, determined man's ultimate good and goal as well-being or happiness (physical, mental and emotional) in the one life he has on earth.

For Aristotle, man's ultimate good was the proper use and development of his natural functions as a series of goods beginning with physical and culminating with that good specific to man alone, the use and enjoyment of his intellect. Man shares many physical and even mental goods with other animals; development of his intellect is the unique, special and specifically human good of man. Thus, at every level of human life (physical, emotional, mental, sensual and intellectual), being and living "good" (ethical) consists of voluntary and self-determined habits that promote proper -and enjoyable- use of man's functions (virtue) and avoid their abuse (vice). With few exceptions, Aristotle's analysis of all man's living functions found that "good" use of them consisted in a mean between the extremes of excess and deficiency. For example, excessive eating shortens life and often causes discomfort while insufficient food weakens or kills; only a right amount and kinds of food are best for overall well-being and physical health (despite the urge often to overeat). Similarly, for most categories of human behavior (drinking, exercise, work, play, risk-taking, expression of emotion, etc.), the "good" or "best" emerges from experience as the "golden mean" somewhere between the extremes of possible behavior.

This analysis of human experience thus led Aristotle to his theory of "virtue," the habit of good conduct, and to his typology of human virtues. Illustrations of virtues are courage (the mean between recklessness and cowardice), temperance (the mean between licentiousness and insensibility), magnanimity (the mean between vanity and meekness) and so on. Aristotle recognized, of course, certain obvious limits in applying the Golden Mean: some human actions are per se evil in any degree such as lying, stealing, murder, rape, treason and so on. His argument for the concept of intrinsic evil (actions per se or "by nature" wrong) is based entirely on reason, analysis of actual human experience and his concept of the human good (as above). Thus, too, he was the originator of "natural law" ethics which profoundly influenced Roman philosophers such as Seneca and Cicero, medieval theologians such as Aquinas and the Thomists, and many modern philosophers, especially John Locke whose version of it influenced and became a part of the new American Constitution.

6. Natural Law

The concept of natural law itself, as originated by Aristotle and interpreted into modern times, must be listed as an ethical standard; although, more so than any other, it has been interpreted by different users in different -and even contradictory- ways. In essence, however, "natural law" or the intrinsic laws of nature are the built-in functions and purposes of any living being, including man, by virtue of its inner nature as known by its "natural" behavior.* An analysis of specific functions, especially their ends, is explicitly included in natural law ethics; for example, the purpose of human speaking is to communicate facts, information and truth -and therefore lying is a violation of a law of nature, i.e. unethical; by similar reasoning obesity, drunkeness, vandalism, sloath and all the vices chronicled by Aristotle, as "extremes" deviating from the golden mean, are all perversions of nature, violations of natural law and unethical.**

Historically, "natural law," as an ethical criterion, has led to a great deal of controversy in its interpretations and when applied to very specific functions of human life. Generally applied, as Aristotle used it in his Golden Mean applications, "natural law" emerges as a useful guide to ethical conduct. But, philosophers and theologians have often used (or abused) the spirit of the concept either to engage in sophistries about minute details or to rationalize pre-conceived beliefs already implanted in the mind by reason of religious, political or other prior conditioning. (The modern philosopher, Bertrand Russell, was particularly suspicious of this mental process which profoundly confuses the purely reasoning processes of philosophy, and of science, with the belief processes of religion, politics and other cultural conditioning; see footnote on page 35.) Thus, for centuries, Thomists and other Catholic theologians used "natural law" as the church's major argument for condemning birth control (except by sexual abstinence), abortion, usury (any interest taken for money loaned) as violations of the natural ends of sexual organs (to procreate) or money (as merely a means of exchange of goods by buying and selling). Planned parenthood groups today, following Malthus' 1798 Essay on Population and alarmed at the self-destructive multiplications of humans in poverty-ridden lands such as India, China and Mexico, use the "natural law" argument to encourage birth control by any effective means (human breeding to the point of starvation for an entire society is a violation of natural law); the Japanese, who condone abortion, interpret natural law as requiring by any means strict

---

* Technically and unfortunately, there is a bit of question-begging (a logical fallacy first and ironically identified by Aristotle) in the use of the "natural law" criterion: as one observes human behavior, how does one distinguish between "natural" and "unnatural" to infer conclusions about the "inner" and true "nature" of anything? The inner criterion of nature is needed to judge its actions as natural.

** Although obvious, let's note explicitly that "law" as used in the expression "natural law" is an analogy only to the strict meaning of the term (p.51 above). Strictly, laws are statutory, not discovered.

population control for a race of people living on a group of small islands with no possible expansion of food and other resources; merchants (petty capitalists) appeal to natural law to justify the earning of interest on money loaned as the only reasonable reciprocity among realistic men for the one borrowing it to use it or the other delaying and risking the use of his property.

"Natural law" seems, on balance, a strong and rationally accessible guide to ethical behavior when used generally and with cool reason; otherwise, it often leads to contradictory interpretations and conclusions about what is ethical or unethical.

7. The "No Harm" Standard as a Test of Ethical Action

Many test the ethical integrity of their actions by asking "will it hurt anyone?" If not, they are ethical. This approach is a practical version of the Golden Rule, put into the form of an operational test. Many modern people use this test to justify "alternative life styles," especially in sexual behavior, such as homosexuality, premarital sex, group "marriages", and other formerly "sinful" behavior provided it is "among consenting adults;" others appeal to the "no harm" test to justify (or rationalize?) cheating huge impersonal bureaucracies such as banks, insurance companies, IRS and government welfare agencies by means of embezzling, falsifying reports, forgery, false testimony as a witness, "skimming" cash, checks or goods, and so on. In these latter cases, the "no harm" rule is being applied ignorantly -or perversely- insofar as, at least indirectly, all these actions do indeed hurt individual people in the form of higher prices, costs of control and policing, rising insurance premiums and tax rates, and so on.

8. "If Everybody's Doing It, It's Ethical!"

This ethical test is a paradox: the bold statement of it seems crass, ignoble and expedient, seldom acknowledged as a standard in words or public print -only by peoples' actual behavior; and yet, the spirit of this test is one of the principles underlying political democracy (laws established by majority vote). Until recently, human slavery was justified by this test of general (and actual) practice, even in democracies like America where the majority deemed it morally acceptable.

Even more than a paradox, an as yet unresolved philosophical dilemma is involved: is truth absolute or a result of the subjective opinions of the majority of mankind?* Common sense seems to favor the former

---

* This dilemma about "truth" (and what it really is) is essentially the same as the dilemma about objective vs subjective "good" (ethics) as already discussed on page 54 above.

view of an objective reality and therefore objective truth about it; the Earth is not flat nor the center of the universe just because virtually all medieval scholars and churchmen ruled that it was as a matter of dogma. Based upon different methods of ascertaining "truth" (mainly scientific method), the large majority of intelligent people today "know" that the Earth is a round planet, among many others much larger, orbiting a star. But, then, common sense itself seems often deceived and, indeed, fully supports the medieval view (the Earth appears flat and centered to anyone upon casual glance at the horizon or the stars in the night). Will the (new) common sense of today yield to "truths" just as different in the future development of human knowledge as today's "knowledge" differs from that of ancient or medieval humans? Modern physicists, for example, are discovering increasing evidence suggesting that "matter," as we perceive it through our senses, does not even exist but, like the atom, is merely a system of positive, negative and other electrical energies. This kind of speculation leads one closer to the second view: that, given man's historical experience of error accepted as truth, the best criterion of truth is the majority opinion of the most intelligent men of a particular period.*

Apart from speculation and as a matter of practical necessity, some method must be used to establish an essential body of political, legal and cultural "truths" by means of which people can organize and pursue their lives whether they live in ancient Rome, medieval Europe, an African tribe of primitives or colonial New England. Three methods for achieving such a "working" body of knowledge and enforcing it within most human societies are:

(1) by custom: what people believe and how they are expected to behave are fully familiar bodies of knowledge handed down from ancestors beyond any present memory; often the origins of such knowledge are explained by later legends which also become part of the unquestioned current knowledge. (In the cases of societies which developed written forms of language, such as scriptures, historians are familiar with the common cultural tool of "redaction" by which manuscripts and

---

* The field of philosophy which deals with this inquiry into "truth" and "knowledge" (and human capability of achieving it) is called "Epistemology" and has been a central concern of virtually every serious philosopher from Plato and Aristotle to America's Peirce, James and Dewey. It led the latter to the philosophy of pragmatism. James and Dewey finally conceded that absolute truth is not possible and established pragmatic methods of thinking as substitutes; Peirce, who preceded them, staunchly held to the possibility of objective truth, discovered by slow advances in pragmatic method

sacred scriptures are later revised to fit current political or doctrinal ends and thus slip new doctrine into ancient scriptures, all of which will then continue to be unquestioned truth - as an example, redactions of the Christian Bible, especially the Four Gospels and the Epistles of Paul, have been so redacted that many scholars abandon hope of every knowing the genuine "originals" except within controversial degrees of probability.)*

(2) by fiat: what people believe and do is dictated by leaders with authority and the power (usually physical or military but often psychological and religious) to enforce the dictated beliefs and actions. This method of establishing truth (i.e. truth for all practical purposes as it affects an individual's life) has been often and easily combined with the method of custom, usually after two or three generations after the old have died off and what were originally dictates by force have become accepted custom, enforced mainly by peer pressure and habit.

(3) by majority vote: the opinions of the majority prevail as, at least, the practical rules of conduct for all. In a certain practical sense, if everybody believes it is so, it is. Which is not far from "if everybody's doing it, it's ethical."

Fortunately, the "majority rule" test, as used through American history, seems guided by other ethical standards (Golden Rule, justice, etc.) which are more fundamental. Thus, gradually, through open debate of issues, what the majority believes to be so increasingly approximates the ethical judgments determined by the more fundamental standards (for example, slavery and other practices, once a majority view, are now deemed unethical -and illegal- based on changing majority opinions). This gradual refinement of truth by continuing use of the pragmatic method and open discussion was the basis of Charles Peirce's belief that objective truth, although not yet attained, was attainable (see footnote on previous page).

The standard under discussion in this section would probably offend less and enjoy a truer sound if expressed differently: "if, gradually and after long discussions in open debates, everybody arrives at a similar opinion, the truth and morality of that opinion have increasingly higher probability of being right - at least in practice, if not in theory." This formulation of the standard has the strength of the democratic American experience in support of it.

---

* Epistemologists (see footnote on previous page) find it interesting or, sometimes, frustrating to their theories that such redactions, by which original and "absolute" "truths" change quite regularly to fit new realities and purposes, usually serve effectively the practical needs of human living in particular times and places. Mormons, Baptists, Catholics, etc. have varying truths; but they're viable.

9. Intuitive Conscience

Many believe in the existence of an inner awareness (conscience) within man that tells him intuitively what is right and wrong. In varying ways, this concept of intuitive conscience appears in ancient religions (especially oriental), Plato's philosophy, tribal priesthoods as the enlightened class among primitive societies, philosophers of "feeling" such as Rousseau for whom the "heart" rather than the "head" is the intuitive guide for action, and, in our day, the many versions of new existentialism (Kierkegaard, Heidegger, Sartre and even Freud).

A recent American candidate for the presidency (Goldwater) built his campaign slogan on this theme: "In your heart, you know he is right."

Intuition, by definition, is immediate awareness, without the slow and systematic steps involved in reasoning; like the senses of sight or hearing, by which one has immediate awareness of shapes, colors, tones and sounds or no awareness at all, one either "sees" or does not (hence the word "seer" for wise men). Thus intuitive conscience, as a concept or functioning entity, is inaccessible to reason or critical evaluation; those who accept and live by it can no more prove it valid than those who reject it can prove it invalid. It remains a matter of faith on the part of individuals and, like religion, cannot be argued rationally. One either believes or does not -and reasoning has nothing to do with it, except, possibly, to rationalize prior belief (see footnotes, pp. 35 & 50).

However, history would seem to show that intuitive and emotional beliefs create human fanaticism (Islamic executions for adultery, suicide squads in religious wars, religions barring life-saving blood transfusions, and self-destructive cults like that of Jim Jones in Guiana involving the mass suicide of a thousand people). All of which is disturbing to a rational mind. Moreover, it seems obvious that there is no universal conscience common to all men since the "conscience" of various cultures and religions has led historically to a multitude of contradictory beliefs (human sacrifice vs abolition of capital punishment, ritual murder vs loving thy neighbor, etc.).

Certainly, in our dealings here with business ethics, the criterion of intuitive conscience is too vague, variable and inaccessible to reasonable debate to be of practical use.

10. The General Law Standard (Kant's "Categorical Imperative")

Immanuel Kant (d. 1804), one of the few giant minds of modern philosophy, gained his major influence through his *Critique of Pure Reason* and *Critique of Practical Reason*. He spent a lifetime teaching and thinking out these two books, along with a few minor ones, but published nothing of significance until he was almost 60 years old. Then he finally published the Critiques, essentially epistemological works (see p.66), which profoundly influenced virtually every philosopher since his time as well as many Protestant theologians and even physicists such as Einstein. What concerns our subject here, however, is a short work of Kant's called Metaphysics of Morals in which he developed his central moral principle for all moral reasoning (which, incidentally, he was unable to derive, as he had wished to, from the system of concepts in his Critiques).

Kant's moral principle (or standard) is his "categorical imperative," an imperative that is absolute rather than hypothetical or subject to any contingencies of time or place. His elaborate method of deriving it is beyond our scope here but, in essence, Kant's categorical imperative states that "everyone should always act in such a way that his action and the principle underlying it could be made a universal law promoting the general welfare of all men." Many moralists now refer to Kant's categorical imperative as the "General Law Standard."

Examples of the use of Kant's General Law Standard as a clear test of any action (if it fails the test, the action must be deemed unethical): Jones, under severe financial pressure from creditors, desparate, trapped in debts he incurred to help his family and friends when they were in extreme need, is a bank officer and knows an easy and safe way to embezzle the money he needs to get out from under the debt that is about to cause him a nervous breakdown, loss of his job and ruin his life; strong (emotional) reasons to make the decision and take money from his bank, justifying his action by virtue of desparate need and pressure; despite his stress, testing the action against the General Law Standard confronts him with the easily derived and generalized "law" of his action that "anyone with a financial problem is permitted to embezzle or otherwise steal," a general law no one could accept rationally as a universal rule of human conduct. Jones might, indeed, crumble and perform the act anyway; but, having tested his action against the General Law Standard, he will at least have no illusions about the act being essentially wrong and unethical. Other actions, emotionally tempting but usually failing the General Law test, are: lying on the witness stand in court (just this one time); cheating on IRS and other tax reports; falsifying a resume or other application form to qualify for a desired job; seducing another's wife into bed (just this one time); falsifying test data on a Defense contract in order not to lose the contract; cheating on college exams; etc.

Although not a major aspect of Kant's powerful thinking, which was a revolution in epistemology rather than in ethics, his General Law Standard or "categorical imperative" is one of the clearest and most unarguable ethical criteria developed by man's pure reasoning power. It is compatible with and clarifies most other ethical standards as well.

11. The Pragmatic Test ("Long-Range Utility Standard")

The philosophy of pragmatism, as we call it today, was named and popularized in America by William James and John Dewey but formulated in its essentials by the ancient Greek philosophers, particularly Protagoras and Epicurus. It was developed to a fine point, under the name "Utilitarianism," by Jeremy Bentham and J.S.Mill (the latter's major work of 1861 was entitled Utilitarianism). The formulations of pragmatism vary greatly and range from the (seemingly) crass selfishness of Protagoras and James to the sophisticated versions of Mill and Dewey (the most sophisticated -and rigorous- pragmatist of them all was Charles Peirce whose erratic personality and refusal to publish in "stuffy" journals still denies him the status he deserves in American philosophy).

In simplest form, the rule of pragmatism is that "what works is good." Stated thusly, pragmatism (and James) can be faulted as mere here-and-now expediency; if it serves my needs now to steal, then do it.* But, as insisted upon by Mill and certainly by Peirce and Dewey, the pragmatic rule is valid only if applied in long-range terms, i.e. over the entire lifetime of an individual or over many centuries for societies.

Thus, the version of the pragmatic test we will use is stated as: "So act that your act will produce, over the long range, maximum personal happiness and well-being in terms of its ultimate consequences."

So stated, the pragmatic test, although limited in its applications, covers many moral situations quite well. And a chief merit of pragmatism is its inherent or built-in sanctions: anyone who violates the pragmatic rule, as stated above, ultimately suffers the consequences of earlier acts -intelligent people, therefore, operating solely on practical and very realistic "enlightened self interest," can project ultimate consequences of current actions and, by means of the pragmatic test, avoid "bad" actions and pursue only the "good." Thus, even a purely self-oriented attitude, if guided by intelligent self-interest and pragmatically for the long range of life and the ultimate consequences of every personal act, will lead one to pursue generally ethical actions and avoid the unethical (as simply and ultimately practical). No abstract moralizing or religious sentiment here; only practical realities urging ethical behavior.

For example, in our world of instant information and data banks, a bank considering foreclosing a home on technical grounds but ruthlessly and unfairly could quickly determine the action unethical based on

---

* In fairness to William James, it must be noted that his later work makes it abundantly clear that pragmatism is valid sometimes for short-term situations (too much drink tonight works poorly for one tomorrow) but essentially applies to individuals and societies viewed in very long-range terms (how an action now will ultimately work for goods desired decades or centuries later).

the pragmatic long-range utility standard (see case on page 12 above). An embezzler, in most cases, will ultimately be discovered and thus the act is ultimately impractical -and unethical as well as illegal. If one stops to consider the pragmatic test before acting, he can usually identify a tempting action as unethical -and, in practical terms, just stupid.

The long-range utility test is at once simple to apply, realistically concerned with one's own self-interest, and goal-oriented in terms of ultimate practical consequences.

11. The Pleasure Principle (Hedonism)

Hedonism ("eat, drink and be merry" and the devil with the consequences), often also called Epicureanism, is wrongly attributed to the ancient Greek philosopher, Epicurus, who in fact led a very ascetic life along lines dictated by Aristotle's golden mean or the later long-range utility standard. (Epicurus had a bad stomach all his life and ate only bits of bread and cheese!) Unfortunately, mainly because of the misinterpretations of the Roman Stoic philosophers as they read translations and redactions of Epicurus, he was wrongly ridiculed as a crass hedonist and still is today.

From earliest childhood, our common sense ideas of the good mainly concern pleasure: seeking food, cool water, rest, friends, security, later sex, relaxing drugs, interesting work, love relationships and, for some (as Aristotle said), intellectual activity. Hedonism usually refers to a life of seeking only sensual pleasures and these to excess (food, alcohol, drugs, sex, excitement, etc.). Often hedonism is justified by intuitive conscience, the "no harm" test and/or atheism; although most atheists will live lives as or more moral than religious believers based simply upon such considerations as long-range utility, the golden mean or enlightened self-interest. Most Roman stoics were atheists and lived ethical, if not noble, lives such as Cicero's and even gave their lives heroically or died with historic dignity. They, and most other people, discard hedonism as a serious ethical standard simply because it is ultimately irrational.

Unfortunately, many philosophers whose views are totally opposed to hedonism (Aristotle, Epicurus, J.S. Mill, Bentham, and William James) used the word "pleasure," meaning not solely sensual pleasure but the deeper and lasting human satisfactions (pleasures) of work, achievement and intellectual activity. Thus, wrongly, they are associated with rude hedonism and discarded simplistically by those who have not bothered to read or understand them precisely.

Pragmatism, in its real meaning, is worlds apart from hedonism.

12. The Work Ethic

After Luther and the Protestant Reformation, many different forms of original (Catholic) Christianity developed such as the Lutheran, the Mormons, the Anglican church, the Baptists and the Calvinists. One particular dogma of Calvinism (John Calvin, d. 1564, in his Institutes) was the concept of predestination according to which every man, at his very birth, has been predetermined by God as destined for saving (i.e. heaven) or a lost soul (hell, or, with luck, limbo). The theological rationale for this doctrine, at the time, was partly practical: to render invalid and useless a major money source for Catholic churchmen, indulgences which popes, bishops and priests sold at high prices in exchange for their guarantee of eternal salvation for the purchaser (price bargaining favored vendors as prospective purchasers were near death and final judgment by God and the church). (See p. 37 footnote.) In a world of Calvinist predestination, indulgences became a useless expense. Importantly, however, in Calvinism was another doctrine which, after several interpretations, drove Calvinists toward the life-goal ends of hard work, thrift, personal diligence, individual initiative to succeed in business, and demonstrable achievement in clear capitalist terms (money earned and in the bank). The doctrine was that, although at birth every man is predestined to heaven or hell, his demonstrable success in life is a sure sign of his predetermined destiny in the next life. Thus, for all practical purposes, every Calvinist made it his life ambition to use every minute in hard work, striving for success (money), ascetically cutting every personal cost possible in the interests of thrift, and ultimately amassing the savings and wealth which constituted a sure sign of his earlier predestination to heaven rather than hell. In strictest Calvinist terms, the rich (capitalists) went to heaven, the poor to hell, and the mediocrities of the middle class would never know their destiny -until after death (even for them, however, it was best now to try harder for the sign).

These are the historical beginnings of what we today call the "work ethic." The Calvinist spirit ran deep in the heroic work efforts of all who first ventured by ship to America and carved out a survival here and then prosperity. They knew and lived for nothing else than hard, constant and intelligent work, for every waking moment of every day. Not that all pilgrims to the new America were Calvinists, of course; they represented virtually every Christian sect, including Catholic and Lutheran and, especially, Anglican - but, in the developing theological texture of each sect, there was the essential mandate of the "work ethic." All lived by it, respected individual work and initiative, held high the value of personal pride and individual responsibility, and cursed the lazy.

Over the last several decades in America, the "work ethic" has been generally discarded, especially by labor unions favoring less work for more pay, government workers coasting through the average day but with unchallengeable job security (often based on current concepts of civil rights and EEO statutory requirements) and, most blatantly, by the many millions who live on government welfare and do virtually no work at all. The work ethic survives, however, elsewhere such as in Japan where, for reasons of family-oriented cultural values, the incentive to work hard and with pride for quality work is almost the primary value of life as it was for early Americans (Japanese domination of international markets, especially the American market, by means of quality products at lowest prices, is a painfully obvious result of the Japanese work ethic alive and well).

The "work ethic" is clearly related to other ethical standards above such as long-range utility, the pragmatic test, Kant's General Law and even (economic) "might makes right."

The "work ethic," as an ethical value, may return to America, in time, for the simple and practical reasons of long-range utility and pragmatic consequences for individuals and the society at large when the inherent relationship between work and personal prosperity is again fully understood. Given America's current socialistic leanings, such basic understanding of the ethical value of work may take a while. One can only hope it happens soon enough to avert America's decline to a second-rate nation.

13. The Lesser-Evil Standard

It is not uncommon, especially for business decision makers, to be faced with decisions in which all options available, including doing nothing, are clearly evil in some respect. The classic case, based on a true story, is that of Captain Holmes, summarized as follows:

> After an ocean vessel sank, two lifeboats were left, each having a capacity for twelve persons. In a large wave, one of the boats tipped over and floated away. The people were soon hauled from the water into the single remaining boat which now had twenty-four persons aboard. It soon became apparent that the boat, overloaded as it was, could not stay afloat in the stormy seas. The senior officer, a Captain Holmes, made the decision to eject all from the boat except twelve strong men to row, a nurse and himself. The situation facing Captain Holmes was a *forced option*. Even if he did *nothing*, a decision would have been made. Incidentally, all reached port and survived.

A manager, faced with the choice of firing or retaining an alcoholic worker, knows he chooses some evil in whatever option he decides upon. In situations such as these, often called cases for "lifeboat ethics," the common norm is the Lesser-evil standard: "So act, in circumstances where action is unavoidable and all available options appear unethical, that your act, judged by the usual ethical standards (above), is the lesser evil."

The Lesser-evil standard is found in many philosophies and in moral theology (beginning with St.Augustine) because, in a real and complex world, the circumstances cited in the rule are quite common. Managers, particularly in military and industrial environments, often face decisions in which every available option contains a large measure of evil; but, still, somebody has to make a decision -often the hardest part of the managerial job. And, as discussed above, in our current world of information availability and public sensitivity about ethics, a manager's "tough" decision must be defensible on strong ethical grounds; if it is thoughtless or overlooks critical aspects of ethical analysis, it can be a disaster for him and his organization (for example, price-fixing decisions made by America's largest electric companies -see p.43 above).

In the case of Captain Holmes (above), his choice seemed to be to do nothing and let everybody die or to take the harsh action he did and save a dozen people. The British Admiralty court, which tried him, naturally had to find him guilty (or else condone officers "playing God" with people's lives), but, implicitly considering lesser-evil aspects of the case, he was given a remarkably mild sentence.

ETHICAL CODES

A code of ethical conduct has essentially the same definition as "Ethics" or ethical standards (p.46 above) but tends to be very specific. The Golden Rule, as a standard, is quite general and broad; the ten commandments of Christian tradition are very specific and constitute a code. Both standards and codes are essentially ethical imperatives; the distinction between them as being more general or more specific is merely a convenience, not critical. What is critical is their content and real application. Also, specific codes are usually derived from the more general standards, the latter as principles forcing the mind to codes as conclusions. If, for example, one accepts the Golden Rule as a guiding principle of action, one can hardly escape as conclusions in the form of specific codes such propositions as "every bank customer paying on a home mortgage but late in payments will be given a five day's notice of time to pay before the execution of foreclosure on his home" or "every customer will be fully informed of any defects in a used car before the car dealer completes the sales transaction" and so on.

The ancient code of Hammurabi (p.31) is a classic example of the distinction between standards and codes: virtually all 300 of the statements in that code are minutely specific. Statutory law, such as federal and state laws in America, is always specific or attempts to be (as in the attempts to write antitrust laws which are not too general). The broad standards which are the principles underlying such codes and laws are rarely stated explicitly but can usually be inferred. Often the principle underlying a law is an ethical standard generally accepted by the public.

Codes As Interpretations of Standards

Ethical standards, like the Golden Rule or the General Law standard, are broadly-stated human values, most of which have endured virtually unchanged for hundreds and thousands of years. Codes, however, spell out in minute detail what a standard means, specifically what a person can or cannot do, as interpreted in a particular time, place, situation or culture. Thus codes, especially viewed over long periods, are highly changeable. Business codes -or implicit norms- of today vary sharply from those of just a hundred years ago in such specific areas as child labor, safety requirements, worker compensation, consumer protection, packaging, labeling, product liability, wages, work hours, and so on into the hundreds. Such changes are even more dramatic when viewed over spans of a thousand years or from one culture as compared to another. Yet, in most cases, the enormous variation in codes can be found to be interpretations of similar general standards.

The Practical Importance and Functions of Ethical Codes

A society, organization or even an individual without pre-set codes (often called "policies") is vulnerable to ethical error, if not chaos, as broad standards must be applied to specific here-and-now situations with little time for reflection and often in the midst of highly-charged emotional states. Decisions, without coolly considered and pre-set codes which apply standards intelligently, will often be arbitrary and inconsistent. Moreover, pre-set codes permit rational discussion and the benefit of many views in a calm atmosphere before a code is set; and, often, most or all agree on the code's appropriateness before the force of it in application affects them in an actual and pressure-laden situation. A code is, therefore, the practical intermediary step between broad standards and actual decisions in particular cases; a code facilitates ethically correct decisions as firmly based in generally accepted ethical standards. In today's complex and changing world of business, ethical codes are essential for consistently ethical decisions.

For example, many companies without codes have gotten into deep ethical trouble on the issue of vendor gifts to a company's purchasing agents. If each purchasing agent is left without specific guidance, each inevitably applies broad ethical standards differently, some willing to accept gifts from vendors at Christmas only or gifts with a set dollar limit while others accept gifts in any "reasonable" amount as a token of appreciation, all "certain" that such gift-taking will not influence buying decisions unfairly (to the competing vendors as well as the company). Even with generally ethical purchasing agents, this kind of ambiguity invites ethical abuses, some of them very possibly quite subconscious in favor of one vendor over another for reasons other than the only right one: best product for the company at the fairest price. To avoid such ethical disorder -and even protect managers from unfamiliar situations and superskilled salesmen who might influence unfairly-, the average sophisticated corporation today has a written code (policy) explicitly prohibiting purchasing agents from accepting any gift of any kind for any reason; this code being the rational interpretation of the "fairness,""General Law" and other broad ethical standards.

Typical Ethical Codes in Industry and the Professions

The need for ethical codes can be traced back thousands of years for vital professions such as medical practice. The Hippocratic Oath, an ethical code for medical practitioners, was an explicit and specific code developed in ancient Greece. Today, a major function of every national professional association, such as the AMA, is to refine, update and enforce ethical codes upon which the essential integrity and reputation of the profession depend. The sanctions can be powerful, even apart from any penalties of the law: a doctor can lose his very license to practice medicine. State bar associations disbar lawyers for proved unethical practices. In the aftermath of Watergate (see p.43), over 100 lawyers were called before their state bar associations and cited for disciplinary action.

Increasingly, business corporations are following the lead of the professions and developing codes of ethics for their officers, managers and other employees. IBM, for example, has its code of ethics in writing in the form of an 84-page booklet, Business Conduct Guidelines, which all managers are required to read annually and then certify in writing that they understand it. Violators are subject to instant dismissal. Certified Public Accountants (CPAs) have, for years, been subject to their association's code of ethics. Although these codes are far from perfect, their continuing development and refinement are essential to any serious pursuit of improved ethical sensitivity and action.

Ethical Codes and Government Regulation

Many pro-business writers, including myself, are appalled at the strangling maze of government regulation that has multiplied like a living thing over the past several decades in America. But we are forced to note (as on pages 19 and 41, above) that business has brought much of this upon itself, beginning with the practices of the robber barons and other unethical practices which the public will not tolerate. If business will not regulate itself ethically, then, in America's political system (p.18), the public -through government- will do the regulating even if unwisely and excessively. A chief function, therefore, of industrial and other associations is to develop sophisticated and fully effective codes of ethics in order to forestall or reduce counter-productive external regulation.

Arch Booth, former president of the U.S. Chamber of Commerce, stated this theme strongly in 1976:

> "Is it possible to prevent business and the professions from sinking further and faster into the quicksand of government regulation? Is it possible to make a deliberate choice between further loss of freedom or of using voluntary action to raise the standard of ethics and morality in the commercial community?
>
> The answer is that ....it is now being done by numerous enlightened associations...The commentaries and the codes that follow are some of the brightest examples of what can be accomplished by taking the initiative through excellent professional leadership...Today most association leadership and members are filled with concern and good intentions. But... positive emotions about right and wrong are of little help. They are a poor answer to the crying need for action. Trade associations are in an ideal position to provide the essentials:
>
> - a code of conduct or set of guidelines for those within the association;
> - a process, a method, an arrangement of steps to be taken by the organization to encourage compliance and to discourage or penalize noncompliance;
> - professional leadership to provide the planning, the procedures and, most important of all, the sustained action so vitally necessary."[3]

(The "codes that follow" refer to some 100 pages of examples of ethical codes of associations in the fields of public relations, direct selling, TV and broadcasting, news media, real estate, etc. The final article in the series, by William Simon, former Secretary of the Treasury, is a rationally and persuasively argued paper on the same idea.)

Ethical Codes and Laws

The critical distinction between ethics and law must be noted again (p.51,above). Thus ethical codes and Federal or state laws are not the same at all although both are necessary for an orderly and ethical society.

As Chief Justice Warren emphasized (p.16), laws are cumbersome to enforce and, in a free society, must be kept to the minimum essential for societal order; laws cannot cover every minute transaction between people except in political dictatorships or police states. Exchanges between people, not covered by law, must be covered and regulated voluntarily by the ethical codes of the people, at least most of them -otherwise laws must multiply to take the place of ethical codes with resulting sacrifice of people's freedom. The relationship between laws and freedom in a society is at once profound and subtle: profound in that, as Toynbee noted (p.13), order in any society (as opposed to chaos and anarchy) must always take precedence over people's desire for freedom and even comfort, order being absolutely essential to the very survival of a society; the relationship is subtle in that order can be achieved and maintained only by increasing numbers of laws (to handle every possible threat to order) which, in the same proportion as increasing legal restrictions, decreases or virtually eliminates the desired freedom of the people -unless the people are willing and able to regulate themselves voluntarily in most of their actions by voluntary codes of ethical conduct.

Thus, the prize of human freedom and living in a free society is technically a privilege, not a right*; a privilege possible only among people with sufficient self-discipline and intelligence to maintain proper order in their society by generally voluntary ethical codes which, therefore, require only a minimum number of state-enforced laws. In the long history of mankind, most peoples have been unable or unwilling to sustain the consistent self- regulation and ethical codes voluntarily which are essential for a free society, without anarchy, civil disorder and restrictive laws. Most Oriental (China), East European (Poland, Russia),African and South American nations which have occasionally "experimented" with a free political system, usually American-style democracy, have quickly failed to reconcile freedom with essential societal order; the resulting anarchy and social disorder, utterly fatal and intolerable in any society, always lead to a "coup," usually a firm

* This term "right," as in "human rights," has a strict technical meaning to be explained shortly, as do other central ethical terms such as "duty,""responsibility,""accountability" and "obligation."

and sometimes bloody military one, which restores order and maintains it by means of oppressive laws, brutal enforcement of these and a strict dictatorship.* Throughout human history, societal order has required (seemingly) cruel oppression of people by the state and the church, with minutely detailed laws covering all human behavior (as with children), including the desparate measures of burning some to death publicly (for stealing or heretical statements that might arouse seditious emotions) in the ultimate interest of maintaining essential societal order for all.**

America is one of the rare peoples able to sustain social order with minimum legal restriction and consequent general freedom for most of its citizens in most of their personal endeavors. Even the classic city state of Athens, whose freedom was earned by Pericles and defended by the orator Demosthenes but questioned by Aristotle,*** could not endure long as a free democracy. The free Athenian political pattern quickly yielded to the dictatorships (harsh but insuring order) of Alexander the Great, the Roman Ceasars, European monarchs with the "divine right of kings," unchallengeable popes and other churchmen and other dictators of people's every action and thought into modern times -most notably the contemporary absolute control of people by Communist governments. Toynbee merely recorded historical facts of human societies; and they universally demonstrate the reality that, as he often said, "freedom is expendable, stability and order ore indispensable."

But, obviously, America, still young and an experiment in the long-range viability of a free and democratic society, must improve in its understanding of ethics and effective use of ethical codes, as opposed to completely restrictive laws, as the consistent means of insuring order in business and other human transactions. American freedom depends on it. If, ultimately, American citizens, businessmen and government officials are unable to develop and enforce voluntary self-regulation, then government-imposed regulations and laws will continue to restrict American freedom to a point where it hardly exists as a reality. How close has America actually come to this already? Ivan Hill, who has

* Often such military takeovers are prompted by mere personal lust for power - but sometimes by agonizing application of the "Lesser-evil" ethical standard (p.73), social disorder deemed worse than deprivation of freedom for the people at large. Depending on one's interpretations of history, cases in point are the medieval popes and kings who pursued the bloody Crusades into the Moslem world.

** Critical views of the medieval church (including mine) must be tempered by the historical context of the times, in which kings and churchmen alike were desparate for social order (Lesser-evil ?).

*** Aristotle (Politics) and Plato (Laws) advocated intelligent monarchy and rejected democracy. Universal suffrage would be unthinkable.

studied the issue for a decade (p.13,above), seems convinced that we are almost there, soon to yield to the necessity of virtual government dictatorship (probably in a socialistic form) to insure social order, control crime, contain business abuses of ethics and the general irresponsibility of many citizens who are incapable of using freedom properly. Hopefully, a more serious appreciation of the role of ethics in a free society and a determined concern by all Americans for effective ethical codes, both business and personal, will prove Hill wrong.

The next several decades in America will probably determine the ultimate direction of the nation. History will probably show that the success or failure of the Reagan administration and the congresses of the early 1980s in their efforts to reduce irresponsible government spending, especially for politically popular social benefits, was America's turning point, either toward the use and preservation of freedom or the abuse and loss of it. Personal ethics, including probably some form of the old American "work ethic," as well as effective business ethics codes will be critical in America's efforts to make its short experiment in freedom a lasting one.

Ethical Codes, Congressmen and Government Officials

Considerable emphasis has been placed thusfar on codes of ethics for businessmen, associations, the professions and even the average citizen. The need for codes of ethics is probably most urgent in the government sector, especially among congressmen, state legislators and top government executives. Political corruption, or even today questionable actions "just within the edge of the law" performed -or condoned- by government officials, weakens the ethical posture of America in the most radical way, right at the roots of the American system and its basic Constitution. If America's highest-placed citizens and leaders find it necessary or expedient to compromise on <u>their</u> ethics, in their public actions, average Americans, including businessmen, inevitably remain cynical about ethical behavior at their level. Thus, where effective ethical codes are needed most is in Congress, state legislatures and all executive levels of the government. To be sure, Congress has its "ethics committees" and the Senate forced a member to resign after his conviction for blatant felonies;* but currently these committees concern themselves mainly with blatant violations of law, not with the blatant violations of generally accepted ethical standards. Congress, for example, has no code of ethics covering unnecessary junkets abroad at tax-

* Senator Williams (New Jersey), in March 1982, would have been the first senator expelled from the Senate since the Civil War but he was given the option of resigning instead, which he did.

payers' expense or conflict-of-interest deals made among them to pass spending bills. Until they do, it must be assumed they have no serious interest in ethics, as distinct from basic law, and would be hypocritical (or comical) in urging others, such as businessmen, to adopt effective ethical codes for business practices. If cynicism about ethics exists and is generally publicized (as in the example below) in the actual behavior of congressmen, only wishful thinkers and the naive could expect that average Americans will ever take ethics seriously.*

One example is the way in which congressmen typically deal with each other on the development and spending of the national defense budget. Gary Reich, a Wall Street financial analyst who specializes in defense contractors as investments and has followed the industry closely for twenty years, explained recently in Barron's the inner workings of the industry and the role of congressmen in it.[4] It makes somewhat frightening reading which is confirmed by many other similar full-length articles in The Atlantic Monthly (by James Fallows, a top analyst of the defense establishment), Reason (by Dina Rasor), Wall Street Journal, New York Review and Across the Board.[5] His essential point, as related to our theme here, is that congressmen handle the multi-billion dollar annual defense budget more for their local political ends than for national security. Reich reports, for example, quite casually and a bit surprised that it is news to anyone that:

> "(This is) where what I call the 'Pegasus Law of Inertia' sets in. It states that a program in production tends to remain in production. ...I'm not aware of any major program (over the past 20 years) that has ever been canceled once it's gone into production.... Once the Defense Department gets a program going, it is Congress that's reluctant to kill it. In each Congressional district, there is some piece of defense spending, and there is an unwritten rule that says (to all congressmen) that 'you leave my programs alone and I'll leave your programs alone.' As a result, they go on building things long after there's really a need for them. For example, the LTV A-7 airplane. For years, we've built 12 of them annually and for years the Navy's never asked for any."[4]

In like manner, Reich, Fallows and other analysts of the military-industrial-congressional complex (which Eisenhower warned of in the

* Actually (and fortunately) business and professional associations are taking ethics seriously (see p.77 above) and developing codes of ethics far exceeding the minimum requirements of existing laws. These businessmen and professionals are quantum-leaps beyond the lip-service motions of Congress in their pursuit of genuine ethical codes. Why don't the citizens demand ethical codes of Congress? Because Congress should lead the way and citizens will do likewise

1950s) question the integrity of major military-spending decisions such as the B-1 bomber, MX missiles and the two aircraft carriers now budgeted at $7 billion into the mid-1980s (actually the carriers will cost more like $20 billion or more when necessary equipment, aircraft and payroll etc. are added). An added irony is that most public analysts (Reich, Fallows, top military officers writing in Harpers etc.) report that many of these multi-billion weapon systems are utterly impractical and, assumedly, continued for reasons of local congressional interests. For example, as Reich put it, "the whole concept of an aircraft carrier is really antique. Royster recently said it beautifully recently in the Wall Street Journal. He called aircraft carriers today's dinosaurs. They are the most vulnerable weapon system ever built."

Considering the gigantic sums of money the decisions of congressmen control, even a minimum level of ethical commitment would require that congressmen insist on programs that most efficiently pursue the purpose of the military budget (national security), not their personal political ends. This would take courage.* But, as dramatically shown in J.F.Kennedy's Profiles of Courage, each a profile of a highly ethical American government official, courage and ethical commitment are possible - and urgently needed.

The Ethical Test of Disclosure

In the recent effort to develop effective ethical codes for business and the professions (p.77), many executives are relying strongly on a "test of disclosure." This test operates more like a sanction than a standard and is fully implied in the major ethical standards above (Fairness, Golden Rule and especially Kant's General Law standard). The "disclosure test," however, certainly helps put actions being contemplated into a clearer perspective. The Quaker Oats Company (Code of Ethics) expresses the test thusly:[6]

> "A reasonable and practical standard of ethical behavior in business decisions and actions is that which would not be embarrassing to you, your family, or your company if it were revealed publicly."

Such a test obviously presumes that ethics is far broader than law and that business ethics is much more than mere conformity to law. As stated

---

* "Universal suffrage" (p.41 above) is again the underlying issue. Especially congressmen, who must face a popular vote every two years (many voters incapable of responsible judgment), are clearly vulnerable to the cries of the (voting) crowd more than they are guided by sound judgment about long-range national interests -or abstract considerations of ethics. The chief goal is to get elected.

in the Caterpillar Tractor Company's code, Worldwide Business Conduct,

> "The law is a floor. Ethical business conduct should normally exist at a level well above the minimum required by law."[6]

Kopper's company chairman, Fletcher Byrom, phrased the disclosure test as follows in a speech to his co-workers in June 1976:

> "Possibly the best test (of whether an action is ethical or not) might be to think whether you would be happy to tell your spouse and children the details of an action you are contemplating or whether you would be willing to appear on television and to explain your action in full detail."[6]

Such executives are realists -and practical- in their pursuit of strong ethical codes.* They base their determined campaign for improved business ethics on such practical standards as long-range utility and the realistic implications of the "disclosure test," not merely on vague moral sentimentality or religious platitudes.

RIGHTS, DUTIES AND RESPONSIBILITIES

Except for the word "ethics" itself, it would be hard to find words of daily usage in the press that are as little- or ill-defined as the key words "rights,""duties" and "responsibilities." Most people now use these terms, as propagandists would, for emotional clout (these words carry the sound and connotations of basic truth, not even to be questioned much less challenged). Thus lobbyists in Washington for vested interests, workers discharged for blatant nonperformance, many of the unemployed waiting -but not seriously looking- for jobs, people living on welfare and food stamps, and others claim categorical "rights" to whatever it is they are seeking; correspondingly, it is the "duty" and "responsibility" of others to provide it for them. When particularly hard-pressed ("rights" being implemented too slowly or not at all), the public appeal is usually to "constitutional rights," claimants having learned that this adjective escalates the emotional clout of their claims and the probability of a federal court actually converting them into constitutional law (a daily occurrence in the courts on issues such as bussing children, rights of homosexuals, proper living accommodations

---

* One executive, not only a realist but also quite philosophical, is Fred Collins of Sperry and Hutchinson Company, who said that, despite quantum leaps in education (including science and technology), "there has been no appreciable moral and emotional growth among men. The mind is a fearfully fine instrument for analysis but the mind is totally amoral."[6] (Emphasis added.)

for convicted felons in prisons, apartment rents, etc.). One must read the newspapers daily to keep up with "new" constitutional "rights,"discovered or created by American courts, especially its federal judges.*

For serious analysis of ethical issues, we obviously need precise definitions of these three central terms as well as the rational use of them.

Definitions of "Rights,""Duties" and "Responsibilities"

Consider the statement of a man saying "I have a right to food, protection from predators who might kill me on the street, housing and clothing to shelter me in the winter." What does this mean in real and cool rational terms? (Amazingly, no book I know of in recent years, whether on business or philosophical ethics, attempts a full and precise definition of this key term, "rights;" going as far back as Sharp & Fox, the 1937 classic Business Ethics, the concept is mentioned, on p.201, merely as "correlative with duties" but neither "rights" or "duties" is defined as an operational term; even Garrett's excellent 1966 text on Business Ethics ignores analytical definition of these terms, his page 16 on the subject merely referring to but not defining them.[7]) But, drawing mainly from fundamental thinkers such as Aristotle and Aquinas, whose mental discipline could not tolerate even a single undefined term, let's define these key terms.

A "right" is a claim upon another person or thing insofar as the claim is substantiated by the real power to enforce it ("might makes right," as on p.58) and/or by genuine considerations of the human norm of justice. This is a brief, but essentially correct, definition of "right" as drawn from the analytical treatment of the subject, many pages in length, by Aristotle and Aquinas.[8] Key terms in the definition are, obviously, "claim,""substantiated,""enforce" and "justice." So let's examine them.

A claim, per se, is simply a person's demand for something (food, money, land). As such, the claim can range from a child screaming for a candy bar to a desparate man begging for his life from a kidnapper or national court of law. Most people, intuitively, would discard the candy bar claim as mere childish whim, merely a "desire" rather than a "right," but take more seriously the claim of the man for his life. But, still, in strict analytical terms, what is the real basis for the man's emotional (and understanable) "claim" for his life? Per se, nothing.

* In the American system, the judiciary branch of government only enforces laws or interprets them (putatively); it is not supposed to create them (that is the task of the legislative branch!). But, for decades, Congress has avoided voting (for the record) on controversial issues (could affect elections); so courts create many laws.

Any such "claims" (for the candy bar or one's life) become "rights" only to the extent that they are -or can be- substantiated.

Claims are substantiated (thus becoming "rights") mainly* by force** ("might") or by effective appeal to justice. To be effective (a key word), an appeal to justice must have the following characteristics:

- the appeal must be recognized as legitimate in a society;
- the justice appealed to must have real sanctions (such as penalties of law or of ethical codes for violators); and,
- the appeal must be specific (I demand my TV back from the named man who stole it), not general (I want justice).

For example, in our American society, I thus have a "right" to pay by an employer for work done by contractual agreement because my claim to it will be enforced by law. I also have a right to attend meetings of my University's Senate, not by Federal or state laws, but by virtue of the recognized policies (organizational "laws") long established by custom, peer pressure favoring and enforcing the right, i.e. by voluntary ethical code and its human sanctions.

Thus it becomes clear (conceptually) that all "rights," except those enforced by sheer physical strength, such as military, are statutory, either explicitly or implicitly. Rights are enforced by explicit statutes of law or implicit precedent (custom as binding, as in "equity law" of England); or by similar statutes, explicit or implicit, sanctioned by peer pressure in the form of codes of ethics. Considered technically, using the concepts analytically, there is no such thing as inherent*** "rights" residing per se within any man by virtue of the mere fact of his birth or needs or emotional claims. Per se, mere claims, without the substantiation of force or appeal to justice, no matter how emotionally expressed, are claims, not rights. A man alone and starving in a jungle has only a desire for food, not a right to it (unless he is strong enough to find, collect or catch it). On a larger and pathetic scale, many thousands of people die annually of starvation in lands where population keeps expanding beyond the capacity of the land to feed it (Garrett Hardin's classic article, "The Tragedy of the Commons," in

---

* We must qualify with "mainly" because, strictly considered although rarely a reality, other substantiations of rights are possible: such as appeals by the needy for charity (not justice) or for mercy (see p.60)

** Physical (or other) force is the basic "right," overwhelming all other claimed rights throughout the human history of wars, coups, etc. If I put a gun to your head for your money or the USSR proves that it can destroy America without retaliation, only I or the USSR has rights.

*** Philosophers can quibble with the word; the reality has been clearly explained in the above paragraphs. Semantics (p.57) are critical.

Science, December 13, 1968, analyzes the realities of population increases ; he finds few rights to life, mainly unrealistic desires for it).*

Thus, except for raw force, no one has a right to anything unless others owe it to him by virtue of justice. So, finally, we come to the concepts of duty and responsibility.

Duty is my obligation by justice (law, ethics, etc.) to do something for another. For example, by justice and law, I have a duty to repay money borrowed from a bank; and the duty to help another in kind or its equivalent for help given. Or to be given (American pioneers all accepted as binding the duty to help a neighbor in need with the firm mutual expectation of equal reciprocity when they were in need - see p.62 above). Duty, then, is a derivative of justice -and that only. If I give money to help the poor in India, I do it for reasons of pity, love, guilt, hope for God's blessing or just the joy of it; the act has nothing to do with duty.

Responsibility (or accountability) derives from duty but focuses on the person(s) to whom I owe the duty and/or the person(s) who will enforce the obligation by sanctions for performance and nonperformance. For example, in the American system of justice, having borrowed $100 from a bank, I have the duty to repay it (plus interest) and will be held responsible to and before a court of law which will punish me if I fail to perform my duty. Similarly, in managerial delegation, my boss gives me the duty of sending a monthly check to a supplier but I am ultimately responsible for performance to my boss (who can fire me) as he is to his boss (who can fire him).

These terms are being defined carefully here because of the human tendency to use them meaninglessly, as merely emotional expressions or rhetorical tools. We will need to use these terms very accurately in later sections of the book dealing with such issues as "rights" of people to jobs, living wages, retirement security, protection from discrimination, and other popular "claims," some of which are rights and some not. (Interestingly, some American businessmen are plugging into the popular theme and planting into the public consciousness -or conscience the notion of a corporation's "rights to a fair profit.")

---

* Hardin's full-length book on population increase and its consequences, Exploring New Ethics for Survival (Viking Press, 1972), contains the original Science article in an Appendix. Anyone with a serious interest in the subject has studied it -or should. Hardin is at once a scientist (biology), a fact-oriented realist, but also most sensitive to the central issues of philosophy and ethics -and his prose is refreshingly clear with an abundance of realistic examples.

As an example of the complexity in use of these terms (and the need for rigor), consider the not uncommon situation of a corporation facing severe losses in sales, revenues and profits (GM, Ford, Chrysler and others in the early 1980s). And some of the ethical questions. Who are responsible for the layoffs, unemployment, bankruptcy of supplier firms, investor losses and declines in cities' revenues causing collapse of many social services? And, if responsible, then to whom? And why? Are the unions and high wages responsible? Government regulations on pollution control, safety factors such as seat belts that few drivers use, consumer protection? Who is responsible for creation of these regulations? Do workers, laid off or put on part time, have rights to a secure job and a fair wage? If so, whose duty is it to provide it? Do investors have a right to a fair return on their stock in auto companies?* Who is responsible in large organizations where personal responsibility gets lost in decision making committees, recommendations of staff groups and external consultants, automated data systems which virtually determine decisions and civic pressure groups insisting on rights while taking no responsibility for consequences of decisions demanded? Don't people have rights?**

We will return to these questions in later chapters and hold to the strict and accurate use of the key terms. In this way only lies clarity.

REFERENCES

1 Camenish, P.F., "Business Ethics," Bus.&Professional Ethics Journal, Fall, 1981
2 See American Spectator, Jan. 1982, p. 12 (Emphasis mine)
3 The Ethical Basis of Economic Freedom, ed., I. Hill, 1976, p.257, 502
4 Barron's, Mar.22, 1982 (Barron's is a major financial newspaper.)
5 Atlantic Monthly, May'81; Reason, Apr.'82; Washington Post, 8/23/81, p.C1; Wall Street Journal, 3/13/81, p.25; New York Review, 4/2/81; Across the Board, Mar., 81, p.3; and many others.
6 Walton, C., ed., The Ethics of Corporate Conduct, Prentice, 1977, p.5
7 Garrett, T., Business Ethics, Appleton-Croft, 1966
8 See Index of Aristotle's and Aquinas' standard works (in Engl. trans.)
9 See Paul Taylor's Problems of Moral Philosophy, Dickenson, 1972, 277.

---

* This particular question is academic. Investors, especially the big institutional ones including pension managers, simply sell GM and other "loser" stocks and reinvest in winners just as American autoworkers buy foreign cars. (Ironically, less than 1% of GM's giant pension fund, $13 billion, is now invested in GM!)

** Basic Rights, by a philosopher, Henry Shue (Princeton, 1980), is a recent example of sheer confusion in the use of the key term "rights".

For Further Reading

- Bartels, R. (ed.), Ethics in Business, Ohio State Univ., 1963
- Baumhart, R., Ethics in Business, Rinehart & Winston, 1968
- Carr, J.L., Life in France under Louis XIV, Putnams Co., 1966
- Clark, J.W., Religion and the Moral Standards of American Businessmen, South-Western Pub.Co., 1966
- Corson, J.J., Business in the Humane Society, McGraw-Hill, 1971
- Gould, J.A., ed., Classic Philosophical Questions, Merrill Pub., 1975 & 1971 (one of the best anthologies of key excerpts in the lit.)
- Hancock, R.N., Twentieth Century Ethics, Columbia Univ., 1974
- Massie, Robert, Peter the Great: His Life and World, Ballantine, 1980
- And see References above and Bibliography at end of book.

QUESTIONS AND PROBLEMS

1. Define and give a modern example involving the following concepts:

(a) ethics	(b) philosophy	(c) religion
(d) theology	(e) the "good"	(f) "ultimate good"
(g) imperatives	(h) sanctions	(i) moral philosophy
(j) Law	(k) Business ethics	(l) positive ethics
(m) objective ethics	(n) subjective ethics	(o) semantics
(p) scientific method	(q) "rights" & "duties"	(r) Golden Rule
(s) Justice (fairness)	(t) Golden Mean	(u) Love
(v) "Natural law"	(w) Democracy	(x) universal suffrage
(y) intuitive conscience	(z) Kant's "categorical imperative"	
(aa) pragmatism	(bb) long-range utility standard	
(cc) Lesser-evil standard	(dd) ethical codes	(ee) the work ethic
(ff) a church (religious)	(gg) a "cult"	(hh) Disclosure test
(i i) ethical knowledge vs ethical action		(j j) responsibilities

2. What are the main arguments for and against "objective ethics?"
3. Name, explain and illustrate 10 major ethical standards (for example the Golden Rule). Which three do you find most valid and live by?
4. What is the practical usefulness of ethical codes for business, the professions and even government (if any)? Should your school or company have such a code? Why? Can codes help families? Why?

Practical Exercise

1. Interview a parent, uncle or other relative or friend who is now engaged fulltime as a manager or employee in a small business or a large corporation. First brief him and explain the key concepts of this chapter as the framework for your interview. Then find out from him his real views about the practicality of ethics and codes & why.
2. Library Research: Choose any key concept (eg: rights, love) used in this chapter, search out and read material on it in your library and prepare a short report on your research -possibly to be read in class.

4 Historical Development of Ethical Theories and Practices

The previous chapter presented and explained the essential concepts of ethics and ethical theory. This chapter will sketch a brief history of their sources: the men and cultures that invented, developed and institutionalized the ethical systems which separate civilized man from his earlier primitive species.*

The Sources of Ethical Theory

As early as 2000 BC, Hammurabi promulgated and enforced a detailed code of law and ethics (p.31,59 and 74 above). The 4000-year-old Hammurabi code is evidence of civilized man thousands of years before the Christian era. It is also evidence of human thinkers who invented ethical ideas and theories long before they were refined in the code of Hammurabi. By the time of Christ, many traditions of ethical thought existed among the Greeks, Chinese, Jews and other cultures. Many of these were absorbed into and refined by Christianity as well as later philosophical systems.

The number of books describing and analyzing the hundreds of religions, philosophies and cultures comprising ethical sources literally fills entire libraries. (Many of the books are cited at the end of this chapter and in the book's bibliography.) The purpose of this chapter, therefore, is very limited in scope: merely to sample some of the major traditions, theologians and philosophers responsible for the ethical ideas of Western man and to provide a brief historical sketch of these. This is exciting intellectual fare, even in the brief format of a single chapter

---

* This chapter is not essential for readers who wish merely to know the major ethical standards (but not their sources) and how to apply them after ethical analysis.

as required here, because of the practical consequences of the ideas of the great philosophers and religious leaders for literally billions of human lives throughout history. (Reread Keynes' version of the "ideas have consequences" theme on p. 15 above.)

So, in this chapter, we will attempt to bring to life some of the highlights of this rich history of ideas and some of the men who created them - a profile of giant minds and their thought. Such a voyage, even brief, through history offers the advantage of enhanced understanding of the real meaning of thinkers' ideas by viewing them at birth in their historical context. Thus this chapter will clarify and elaborate upon the key concepts of the previous chapter and, also, prepare the mind better for the modern applications of ethics in the following chapters.

THE HEBREW TRADITION

Of all the ethical systems discussed in this book, the typical American reader will be most familiar with the ethics of the Judaic and Christian systems. Most Americans are taught one or the other as children and the memory (and habits) of it linger throughout adulthood even for those who later reject religious beliefs. Fortunately, as we shall see, many of the key ethical standards taught by Judaism and Christianity are fully confirmed by the purely rational ethical systems of the great philosophers -and thus accessible and binding for religious unbelievers as well as active believers in Judaism or Christianity.

Justice

The cardinal ethics of early Hebrew thinking is justice (see. p. 59), an eye for an eye, a life for a life. In the harsh deserts stretching from Egypt to the Dead Sea, life had to be governed by the hard laws of justice and these were confirmed, as needed, by God himself through the Hebrew leader, Moses, and the commandments he received from God. These, condensed somewhat here and drawn from Exodus 20,3-17, are the Hebrew Decalogue (ten commandments):

1. Thou shalt have no other gods before me.
2. I am a jealous God and punish, for generations, those who disobey.
3. Thou shalt not take the name of the Lord thy God in vain.
4. Keep holy the sabbath. The seventh day is the Lord's.
5. Honor thy father and mother, that your children honor you.
6. Thou shalt not kill (meaning murder, not self-defence).
7. Thou shalt not commit adultery.
8. Thou shalt not steal.

9. Thou shalt not lie or bear false witness against others.
10. Thou shalt not covet thy neighbor's house, ox, ass or wife.

The ethical values developed by the Hebrews, and sanctioned by harsh and clearly known penalties (often death), were justice, loyalty, truthfulness, absolute respect for and obedience to authority (mainly the authorities of God, his church, his prophets and priests, and parents) and a sacred right to one's property (especially livestock and wives as stressed repeatedly in Commandments #7, 8 & 10). God, and his priests who implemented his Will,* demanded severe and swift punishment for anyone who dared to violate His commandments, including thousands of derived rules and rituals (about food, travel, sex, church worship, etc.). Commandment #2 legitimized any and all sanctions needed by God's priests to enforce His Will (as interpreted by God's prophets and priests). Only a harsh God could govern human lives effectively in the harsh climate and desparate conditions of that time and place. But, probably because of those laws of God and his priests, that race of men (Hebrews) survived, unlike many others which became extinct.

Justice Tempered by Mercy and Love

About 740 BC, Hosea tried (only partly successfully) to modify the stern law of justice among the Hebrews by introducing ideas about that part of God that was merciful, loving and forgiving. But, still, many centuries later, Christ's cruel death was accepted as a necessary sacrifice for man's sins, as a requirement of justice. In God's view and his priests', even then, the human law of reciprocity (p.62) was absolute, no exceptions made even for a son of God. So God's own son, Jesus, was tortured and crucified as a massive act of justice: the life of God's son as recompense for the trillions of sins of men (all offenses to God the Father). This is how highly valued was the ethics of justice as a critical ethical norm for the orderly control of human behavior.

THE CHRISTIAN TRADITION

Christianity, of course, has been by far the most dominant religion in Europe, the Americas and the near-East. The many and complex threads of Christianity defy any adequate summarization as it evolved into its major forms of medieval Catholicism, Eastern Orthodox versions,

---

* The concept of the "Will of God" is central in Judaism and Christianity (and other religions). It functions psychologically as both a decision mechanism in societies as well as a sanction to enforce decisions. The habit of obeying the "Will of God" renders a people sufficiently malleable as to accept hard decisions about their lives with minimum resistance, thus aiding government and social order.

Thomism (based on Aquinas), Protestantism (beginning with Luther about 1500) and literally thousands of Christian sects as offshoots of Christianity and the Bible (the Old Testament representing the Jewish tradition and the New Testament mainly the Christian tradition).

Christianity and Judaism

The relationship between Christianity and its Hebrew origins is equally complex, somewhat but only superficially similar to the Protestant break from Catholicism in the sixteenth century. Suffice it to say here that the latter was a series of religious revolutions (including wars) while Christianity arose quietly and evolved into a major religion. But more about the sixteenth-century upheavals later.

As noted above, the essential ethics of the Hebrews was the law of justice embedded throughout the Decalogue, the ten great commandments. But, Judaism had its progressive elements (Hosea for example), especially from about 100 BC until the completion of the sacred books called the Talmud about 500 AD. Progressive Jewish thinkers slowly expanded the metaphysics of the Hebrew religious tradition to include such new concepts as personal immortality of the human soul, ultimate resurrection of the body, heaven and hell as sanctions for obeying or violating the laws of God, etc. From the time of Christ himself and over the next five centuries, Judaism and Christianity obviously had a great mutual influence upon each other in the development of religious ritual, organizational administration of the churches and clerical hierarchy, systems of orderly succession of leadership at all levels, moral theology (ethics and specific codes) and emerging metaphysical concepts (nature of God, afterlife, sin, redemption, soul, etc.) as the theory underlying ethics.*

Brotherly Love and the Golden Rule

Although the Golden Rule preexisted Christianity in Hebrew tradition, as essentially an enlightened form of justice and reciprocity (pp.60-62 above), the Rule rapidly expanded beyond justice as the

---

* The terms "metaphysics" and "metaphysical" will occur often and should be accurately understood. They refer to things "beyond" ("meta" meaning "under" or "beyond") the physical realities we can see, hear, touch and know through our senses. They are in stark contrast to "scientific method," including "physics," as on p.55 above. Metaphysics is the realm of theology (religion based on faith without observable evidence) and philosophy (inferences based on pure human reasoning). (See pp.35 and 46 above.)

minimum ethical requirement of man to the rule of Brotherly Love and mutual Love between God and man. The two ethical standards which dominated early Christianity were:

- The Golden Rule ("do unto others etc." as on p. 60 above);and
- Love Thy Neighbor (as on p.61). (As noted, "love," in this context, is an act of will, doing what is good for another, not merely an emotional state or deep "feeling" often more an exercise in self-satisfaction than genuine interest in or concern for the real welfare of "the object of one's affections.") Special and specific terms existed then for (brotherly) love, "agapae" in Greek and "caritas" in Latin. As in the New Testament, it meant the will to give one's very life for a friend or for love of God (as Christian martyrs did in the Roman coliseum).

As history shows, often shockingly, the purity and innocence of the early Christians, although always present in some isolated individuals who were often canonized as saints, eroded ultimately into the gross church practices (such as selling of indulgences -see p.37 and 72) that caused the final break from the church in the form of Protestantism. In a single century, huge proportions of Christians abandoned the corrupt original church (as the Eastern Orthodox had done centuries ago) and became fervent Lutherans, Calvinists, Anglicans and so on. Once the original break was made from the original church, that had dominated Europe for a thousand years, Christianity splintered into thousands of Christian sects, each reformers of earlier errors or corruption and/or reinterpretations of the basic Bible and its continuing redactions.

For realists, the history of Christianity is neither surprising nor scandalous; it is simply human and political. In practical terms, considering especially the desparate conditions of human life in the middle ages (see p.36), popes, bishops and kings alike could survive and maintain their political control only by difficult and practical decisions. For kings and princes, practicality meant frequent exercise of force, wars, murders and assassinations of other kings (often very young ones before they could grow to adulthood and handle power); for popes, bishops and lesser churchmen, survival for themselves personally and for their mother organization also meant practical decisions such as converting holy concepts (intangible assets but powerful in their potential influence on serfs) into cash flow, as was done with the marketing of indulgences, burning heretics as external threats (equivalent to today's concept of "treason"), compromising expendable principles in mutually-advantageous deals with kings and princes with current political power, canonizing saints for urgent political ends and generally surviving by whatever means needed.

By word, the church preached Love and the Golden Rule; in action, its ethics was the long-range utility standard (but not wisely interpreted in the century before the Protestant Reformation!) and often probably the lesser-evil standard (pp. 70-73).

But, still, Christianity, despite its ambiguities in official actions and its departures from ideal principles when required practically, has survived as a human institution for 2000 years and, in its own way, promoted -and even institutionalized as ideal behavior- the ethics of Love, the Golden Rule, Justice, Reciprocity and many virtues such as those codified in the Hebrew Decalogue.

PLATO AND PLATONISM

We move now to an age and place in history, the land of Homeric legends and the birth of philosophy as a serious intellectual activity, in which small corner of history -and only for about a century- the pure reasoning of the mind (philosophy) was the supreme ideal. Not religion. The time and place were about 600 BC in Greece, mainly Athens. The men were Parmenides, Heraclitus, Zeno, Epicurus, Democritus, Socrates, Plato, Aristotle and others who, in an amazing few years of original intellectual inquiry, developed virtually all of the basic philosophical, political and other ideas that have ruled the lives of Western men ever since.

Three Giant Minds

Three men, influencing each other during overlapping lifespans, are chiefly responsible for the "golden age" of classic Greek philosophy: they were Socrates, Plato and Aristotle. The 100-year period from about 422 BC (when Socrates was at his prime) until 322 BC (when Aristotle died) laid the intellectual foundations for virtually all of Western thought up to the present time (in the fields of logic, epistemology, metaphysics, mathematics, science, law, politics, etc.). Every modern man's education owes much of it to these three giant minds whether he has encountered them by name or works or not.* Even Christianity, except for its religious origins based in faith, depended mainly on these Greek philosophers for its logical elaboration of concepts, its systematization into the science of theology and its deduced

---

* Time was (prior to the 1970s in America) when college students were required to take at least one course in philosophy, much of it built around readings and discussion of the key works of Plato (which included Socrates' ideas) and Aristotle. Unfortunately, the liberal '70s wiped out tough requirements for easy electives.

applications to the (practical) moral and political life of men such as, for example, in the ponderous tomes of canon and ecclesiastical law of Catholicism as it grew into gigantic proportions over the centuries. The concepts of Plato -and his way of thinking- dominated medieval Christian thought until the 13th century (especially Augustine, the first great Christian theologian) when the greatest Christian theologian in history, Thomas Aquinas, virtually obliterated Platonism in favor of Aristotle. Aquinas prevailed upon a friend, William of Moerbeke, to translate Aristotle's works from the original Greek into current Latin, and then made Aristotelian thought the basis of his theology.

Although Plato was Aristotle's teacher, as Socrates was Plato's, Aristotle's thinking gradually grew into directions radically different from Plato's. Since their time, "Platonism" and "Aristotelianism" have represented the two basic intellectual options every man sorts out and chooses between: searching for truth and genuine reality by looking inward into one's self, one's soul and innermost thoughts (Platonism) or looking outward at the sensible world for truth and reality. These two intellectual "temperaments" -and complex mergings of the two- are the basic foundations underlying virtually all of the systems of Western thought from medieval Augustianianism and Thomism to modern Kant and Existentialism.

Let's look first at Plato's world and his teacher, Socrates.

Socrates, the Teacher

Athens, about 400 BC, when Plato was a student in his twenties and Socrates (in his sixties) was his principal teacher, was already an exciting intellectual world. Thinkers from all parts of Greece gathered in the "schools" (usually outside) of Athens and the discussions were alive with virtually every human question and theory now known to modern man. Thales (the "father of philosophy") had raised questions about the basic nature of things. Parmenides' subtle reasoning (and Zeno's too) raised questions about the very reality of our observable world of constant change. Heraclitus retorted that change (birth, death, motion, etc.) was the only reality. Democritus resigned himself to a common-sense materialism based on his theory of "atoms" as the basic building blocks of all things while Parmenides became the first pure idealist, asserting that the world of the senses was an illusion and true reality was an immaterial and unchanging "oneness" somewhat like pure concepts in the mind. Pythagoras, the "universal genius," excelled in his insight into mathematics, philosophy and everything. This was the teeming intellectual world in which Socrates taught.

And world events, as usual, had their influence upon philosophical thinking. The twenty-seven year (Peloponnesian) war with Sparta had just ended in a stalemate but permanently weakened all the Greek city-states which, within a century, would succumb to the militarist power of Macedon to the north and become part of the empire of Alexander the Great. Such times of threat and uncertainty were echoed in the philosophical scepticism of the "sophists" and "cynics." Protagoras even questioned the existence of the gods and was exiled (freedom of speech in Greece was not that free). Socrates himself, although never a sceptic or sophist, was later misinterpreted and executed for impiety. Many, including the young Plato, rose in defense of Socrates before the Athenian judges. But the judges wanted to be rid of Socrates and gave him the choice of exile or death, never dreaming that Socrates would, on principle, refuse exile and accept death instead (it was 399 BC and Socrates was 70 years old). Socrates refused to admit any evil in his teaching and, to the contrary, used the courtroom as his final "classroom" to teach high personal integrity and virtue as the only good life and peaceful intellectual inquiry and questioning all things in the search for truth as the essence of a truly human life. This was the ethics Socrates taught which can be summed up as the standard of "honesty." Socrates' final words to the court, much shortened here, are typical:*

> "Let us consider also how good reason there is to hope that death is a good thing. For either it is nothingness, so that the dead have no consciousness of anything or, as many say, it is a migration of the soul to another place. If the former, then it is merely dreamless sleep; if the latter, what wouldn't any of us give to meet with Orpheus, Hesiod and Homer? In either case, death is not to be feared.

> Thus you also, judges, must regard death hopefully and bear in mind this one truth: that no evil can come to a good man either in life or after death. I am not angry with those who have accused me and condemned me. However, I make this request: when my sons grow up, trouble them as I have troubled you; if they seem to care for money

---

* Socrates (inset above) did not leave any written works. The early dialogues of Plato, including The Apology from which Socrates' final courtroom statement is excerpted, are our main source of knowledge about the philosophy of Socrates. Scholars on Plato (Shorey, Ross, etc.-see bibliography) find no reason to doubt Plato's account of Socrates' philosophic views.

or anything else more than for virtue, rebuke them because they do not care for what they ought.

But now the time has come to go away. I go to die, and you to live; but, which of us goes to the better lot is known only by God."

The ethical principles of Socrates can be summarized in three propositions: (1) virtue is knowledge (i.e. the reason for wrongdoing is simply ignorance of the personal damage one does to oneself by vice - an interesting version of "long-range utility" as on p.70 above); (2) thus all wrongdoing can be avoided by correct knowledge and constant search for truth (a philosopher would say later that "truth sets you free" for a truly human life, which centers on knowledge, truth and virtue) and (3) it is better to suffer injustice than to inflict it (again for reasons of ultimate maximum self-satisfaction).[1] Socrates is often misunderstood as a sentimental do-gooder or idealistic truth-seeker, like Diogenes with lantern. He was all of these but, most importantly, he was convinced of the simple realism, cosmic justice if you will, that immoral and "inhuman" acts gradually erode away a man's greatest personal possession, his humanity and joy in living it to the fullest as human rather than merely another species of animal life. An example of Socrates' ethical stance is useful: if you inflict an injustice upon a neighbor, such as cheating him of money due him, you gain the means of increasing animal-like enjoyments but suffer a scar in the integrity of your unique humanity and lose, to that extent, the personal joy and pride of it (it is better to be cheated -than to cheat- since the money lost can be regained but one's integrity can't - that much of it is lost forever).

Interestingly, Socrates' courtroom speech illustrates the new (deductive and dialectical) forms of human thinking being perfected in the Athenian schools. Thales, Pythagoras and Parmenides discovered deductive reasoning (although it would remain for Aristotle to codify and conceptualize it later in his logical works) but it was Socrates - and then Plato in his many Dialogues - who perfected dialectical thought processes including, especially, hypothetical examination of alternative ideas, their meanings, consequences and possible validity.* This is illustrated in Socrates' courtroom discussion of what death is or might be, each hypothetical alternative examined as to meaning, consequences and validity. In Socrates' reasoning at that time, death and all of its possible meanings were concluded as either good or harmless. So he chose death over abandonment of principle and his life work.

* Aristotle later grasped this basic thought form and established the rules of hypothetical syllogisms, the basis of computer science now.

Plato, the Teacher

Plato was thirty when Socrates died. Socrates was only one of his teachers. The richness of Athenian culture constituted many others. Plato, as an educated man, certainly had witnessed the great plays of Sophocles and Euripides (Oedipus Rex, Medea, etc.) and the great body of poetry from Homer to the Greek lyricists (he later condemned poetry of all forms as a distraction from "reality"). His written works make it clear that he had read carefully all the literature in every field of thought, possibly even some oriental and Judaic fragments. In his years with Socrates, he had often visited other schools, crossed verbal swords with such as Gorgias, Protagoras and many of the sophists and cynics. No school of philosophy was unknown to him. He was also involved in civic and political affairs (which is evident in his later works called the Laws and The Republic). At the time of Socrates' death, he was already more qualified than any of his peers to begin teaching. But, first, Plato began a series of travels to the coastal cities of Italy, Asia Minor, Sicily, Egypt and most of the Greek city states. During these travels, he talked with all the great men of his age and drafted many of his dialogues.* In these, the main lines of his thought are already apparent. Although he returned often to Athens, it was ten years of constant traveling over the then-known world before he settled in a permanent home and "school" in Athens (at age 40). He purchased a large home and a nearby grove where he established his school, called the Academy. The Academy soon became a world center for scholars and ambitious students (like Aristotle). The Academy was a life of pure thinking and Plato was at the center of it for forty years until his death in 347 BC. During those years of traveling, thinking, writing and conducting the Academy discussions, Plato's thinking became "Platonism" and dominated the Christian world (later) completely until the 13th century and significantly even into modern times (Platonism is a deep part of Kant, for example, and even William James and certainly the modern Existentialism of Kierkegaard, Heidegger, Sartre and the great Protestant theologian, Paul Tillich).

Apart from his particular doctrines and philosophy which came to be known as "Platonism," Plato in his Academy perfected what Socrates

* Except for a few of his written works (Laws, The Republic), most of Plato's writings are in the form of dialogues, "conversations" and discussions of key issues, usually titled after a real or imaginary discussant. Throughout such dialogues it is obvious what Plato's opinion is -and those of Socrates when he appears in them. This literary form was his invention, is long (sometimes tiring), possibly used to avoid attribution for controversial ideas. It was used often in the middle ages to express new ideas without dying for heresy.

had initiated: the search for truth as absolute and rigorous "critical thinking" as the only acceptable method for acquiring it. Socrates, Plato and the other early Greek thinkers were the first to pursue truth objectively, by critical reasoning alone and into whatever ultimate conclusions that honest search might lead (this intellectual spirit was wiped out under the Roman emperors and Christian popes until the 16th century when it was reborn in Protestantism and the beginnings of modern science which, by empirical methods unknown to Plato, adopted his same firm determination for truth, began finding it by patient research and thus created our modern world of chemistry, physics, medicine, computers, and genuine knowledge).* Galileo could be characterized as Plato, 2000 years later, but with a telescope in his hand.

Plato's Theory of "Ideas"

The centerpiece of Platonism is Plato's elaborate theory of pure "Ideas" as the essence of the real world. Ideas, as Plato uses the term, are not what most of us think of when we use the word to mean mental thoughts or ideas in the mind. Plato acknowledged ideas in the mind, of course (let's use ideas with lower-case "i" for these) but reasoned to the existence also, and more importantly, of real entities, independent of the mind's thinking, and corresponding to mental ideas. These he called (real) Ideas, immaterial or spiritual realities, somewhat similar to what Christian theologians would later call "soul," "God," and pure being as "divinity," more real than any material body in this life (we will use a capital "I" for these). No wonder Christian thinkers were enthralled with Platonism and the Ideas: Plato, by pure and pagan reasoning, had discovered the reality of the spiritual world a thousand years before Augustine, the great early Christian theologian, who then would detail it (minute descriptions of God, angels, heaven, hell, etc.) in ways never imagined by the philosopher, Plato. The average man in the middle ages "knew" far more about the Ideal world of God, souls, the paradoxical divine trinity, heaven, hell and purgatory (and the spiritual effect of prayer and indulgences) than he knew about farming, food, tools, sex, business or the chemistry and physics of the material world.

* There is no reason why "modern science" could not have been established in the several centuries following Plato and Aristotle. During that one bright intellectual century, the objective attitude to use the mind to search for truth was there. But seeking truth - and especially finding it- threaten old customs, ideas, religions, states and powerful people currently in charge of them. So truth-seeking was effectively abolished and punished for 2000 years.

Like Parmenides and others before him, Plato's reasoning led him to question the reality of things known through human senses, physical and moving objects. Indeed, these seemed so real as well as the intense emotional reactions to them -such as running in fear from a charging bear or army. But how much of this intense (internal) mental and emotional activity was merely illusion, although powerful in its effects? The same effects will occur, including the sense of dread and sweating, as one awakes from a d r e a m about such dangers.* Are the objects in a dream real? They seem to be. Are the objects we sense in daily life real? They seem to be. But, based mainly on the rational arguments of Parmenides proving that true being and reality cannot admit of change or physical dimensions, Plato drew the necessary, but unpopular, conclusion that true reality is indeed pure and immaterial Ideas, not the generally accepted world perceived by the senses of human and animal bodies.** Few Christians of the next 2000 years ever examined the long and tortuous rational argumentations of Parmenides and Plato (in his Dialogues), but, strange as it may seem to our common sense of the physical world around us, most intuitively rejected this physical world as mainly illusion and strove by all means for salvation and happiness in the next (purely spiritual and Ideal) world of genuine reality.

Plato's Epistemology and Ethics

Platonic epistemology (see p. 66-67 above) and ethics derive directly from Plato's metaphysics (theory of Ideas). Regarding the first, where is truth to be found -and how? Regarding ethics, how is the good to be defined? For both, truth and the good (ethical), it is fruitless to examine and analyze observations of the physical world (seemingly) all around us -since it is all essentially an illusion. Thus, knowledge about true Ideas, the genuine reality, must be found in this life by looking inward into the mind (not outward at illusions). Patient attention to and analysis of the ideas within the mind will provide an essential glimpse of the true nature of their corresponding realities, i.e. Ideas such as Beauty, Truth, Good, God, Oneness, Love and so on.

* This analogy and analysis of human dreams to make the point of the probable illusion of the physical (sensed) world is essentially true to the Platonic spirit, but it is not to be found in Plato's works. It is in the Discourses of Rene Descartes (d. 1650), the founder of modern philosophy and one of the founders of modern mathematics (recall your cartesian geometry and coordinates).

** Plato's "analogy of the Cave," where people mistake the familiar shadows on the cave walls for the real animals outside projecting them, is well known. The best short description is Bertrand Russell's.[2]

Platonic ethics is, therefore, not a particular set of standards - although all of Plato's later works advocate key concepts such as justice and love. And, of course, the ideals of honesty, virtue and peaceful search of truth as taught by the teacher he loved, Socrates. Platonic ethics is rather a mental orientation, an attitude, a way of searching for the good and the ethical - by looking honestly within one's own mind and, by a kind of immediate intuition, knowing the true and the right when it rises as such there, one's own and to be believed absolutely despite the sensed illusions of the physical world surging all about. The truth and the (ethical) good are to be found only within oneself. And no one else can dispute it since it is not subject to common sense or laws (Plato, nevertheless, wrote in later life his Republic and Laws).

ARISTOTELIANISM

Plato's brilliant student, Aristotle, learned and understood well all his master could teach. But, as his own mind developed, Aristotle came to question and then reject the basic Platonic philosophy. He also soon discarded the literary form of dialogues, used by Plato, and all of his now known works are highly organized essays, articles or texts very similar to these literary forms today.

Aristotle was born in 384 BC at Stagira in Thrace near Byzantium, gateway to the Black Sea and the mid-East. He had the advantage of an excellent education from his earliest years, longed someday to study at the intellectual centers in Athens, far away at the opposite edge of the Aegean Sea, and, at age 17, went to Athens. Except for occasional travels, Athens became his home until his death in 322 BC. He spent the last year of his life in Thrace where he had been exiled on charges similar to those against Socrates (impiety, dangerous ideas, etc.).

When, at 17, after a long voyage, Aristotle arrived at the city of his early dreams, he chose and was accepted for study at the already-famous Academy of Plato. Plato had just left for three years of travel and Aristotle, anticipating with excitement the return of Plato, worked at a furious pace for three years reading and absorbing every book, play and philosophical school known to Athenian intellectuals. (Aristotle's parents had died when he was in his teens and he inherited considerable wealth from his father, an eminent physician of Thrace; he was able, therefore, to purchase in Athens the incredibly costly luxuries called "books" today but then laboriously-hand-written manuscripts.)

When Plato returned to Athens, he was at the height of his physical and intellectual development (at age 60) and Aristotle was a very mature and superbly educated 20-year-old. With intermittent interruptions for reasons of military service, business, government assignments, Aristotle studied with Plato at the Academy for about 20 years until Plato died (a natural death) in 347 BC at age 82. After Plato's death, Aristotle travelled in Asia Minor for several years until he was persuaded to live at the court of Philip of Macedon (343), as tutor to Philip's son, Alexander (then 13).* Soon after, Philip was murdered, Alexander became king of Macedon and Aristotle returned to Athens to establish a school.

Aristotle and the Lyceum

Plato's Academy continued to prosper after his death and, as noted, the influence of Platonism was dominant till the 13th century and firm even into modern times. But, as much as Aristotle admired and loved the man Plato, his own thinking had diverged radically from his master's. So he founded his own school, the Lyceum, when he returned from Macedon to Athens (at age 48 then) where he thought, taught and wrote until his death at 62 in 322 BC (the same year Alexander died).

Aristotle's Lyceum rapidly grew to eclipse all other schools in Athens in numbers of teachers and students, world-wide influence and fame. The excitement and power of Aristotle's ideas and writings created an almost daily frenzy for the latest news from the Lyceum. His physical and mental energy was such that he lectured while walking in long strides in the paths and gardens of the Lyceum, students following and listening as best they could, until he and his students became affectionately known as the "peripatetics" (the walking philosophers). And, at all hours of day and night, when not lecturing, he was writing prodigiously (the Organon, his works in Logic, Physics, De Coelo, Generatione, De Motu, Meteorologica, Historia Animalium, De Anima, the Metaphysics, Constitution of Athens, Politics, Nicomachean Ethics, Eudemian Ethics etc.) and constantly revising, editing and updating these and other works. Like Plato, Aristotle produced two kinds of writings: detailed lecture notes which were drafts and re-drafts of tentative material which was

---

* By this time, most of the city states of Greece, including Athens, had come under the military and political control of Philip of Macedon, the great military power to the North. Philip's son, to become Alexander the Great, went on to conquer most of the then known civilized world, in just about fifteen years, till he died in his mid-thirties far away from home. Despite what some dramatic historians like to suggest, Aristotle had little influence on young Alexander, who was interested only in the art of war and conquest, not philosophy.

still being thought through -"work-in-process"- and final, fully edited and finished, published books. Unlike Plato, whose finished books survived, only the notes and drafts of Aristotle's survive today. The fully finished and final books of Aristotle, so much praised and imitated in their style by the Roman Cicero, were lost or destroyed over the years. We have, today, Aristotle's thinking, but not his style. This is not unimportant: centuries after Plato and Aristotle, the beauty and almost poetic power of Plato's finished Dialogues probably created devotion to Platonism as much as the theory within the words; while the rough notes, drafts and paraphrases of his students were all that became left to posterity of Aristotle and his thinking. But, despite the awful style of Aristotle's extant works, the essence of his thinking remains and has had, even into modern times, an influence probably greater even than Platonism. Much to the point of this book, Aristotle's final books on Ethics are lost. What we have today are the literal notes from his lectures preserved by his son (Nicomachus) and a dedicated student (Eudemus, one of Athens' prominent mathematicians). (A recent discovery, in the sands of Egypt, of Aristotle's Constitution of Athens is the only finished work of Aristotle's extant -and it exhibits the smooth and graceful style Cicero admired.)

The Philosophy of Aristotle

Aristotle's epistemology (uses of the mind to find truth) and his metaphysics (theories about the ultimate nature of reality) were utterly opposed to Plato's. Whereas Plato had concluded that man's senses absorbed only a world of illusion or dreams, Aristotle established the "empiricist temperament," as William James would later call it (in his Pragmatism), and held firmly that all human knowledge begins from and through his senses, what he sees, hears, feels, smells and touches. For Aristotle, the human mind at birth is a "tabula rasa" (blank tablet) with no inborn knowledge (of the Platonic or other sorts); all knowledge the mind acquires comes from what is sensed and then analyzed by reasoning. Any other so-called knowledge, by religious or other beliefs, by the saying of seers or priests, by mere personal "intuition" or by deep need for something to be true (such as the gods, a next life of heavenly joy, etc.) was fraudulent or ignorant assumptions unless and until it could be proved empirically and by logical analysis. Aristotle was mankind's first great empirical scientist (facts only and always), although his spirit was suppressed until after the Protestant Reformation when Galileo and a new host of scientists began implementing Aristotle's ancient spirit and thereby created our modern world. For Aristotle, only facts as we sense them, and then logically analyze them, are the valid source of truth and systematic knowledge. Using the concepts of Parmenides and

Plato about "illusions," Aristotle held that mental abstractions and even Plato's Ideas were pure illusion (he would, of course, have said the same for later Christian "Ideas" about God, divine trinities, heavenly bliss and other assumed joys of the "next world," none of which being empirically verifiable); in Aristotelianism, human senses and logic are far from "illusion;" they are the only path to truth and knowledge.

Given Aristotle's epistemology, his way of searching out truth, his metaphysics differ radically from Plato's. The real world is the physical world we sense and inhabit - there is no other, except by assumptions inspired by hope or questionable traditions (which any rational mind must indeed question).*

Aristotle's Ethics

Aristotelian ethics derives from its epistemology and metaphysics. Unlike Plato who would look within the mind for the knowledge of good, Aristotle examines external human experience and the workings of the physical world. This does not mean that Aristotelian ethics is merely a description of what men do or have done ("descriptive ethics," as on p. 46) but only that the ultimate basis for (normative) ethics is real, i.e. observable and sensed, human experience. Given this basis, Aristotle's ethics is developed by careful rational analysis of human experience in terms of acceptable human life goals and the optimum means for achieving them.

Aristotle's ethics is entirely teleological, i.e. fixed to the human seeking of human goals (or goods in a hierarchy from least to most proper for the unique species called man). This analysis of human good leads Aristotle to the doctrine of the "golden mean." This need not be repeated here. It is fully explained earlier (pages 62-63 above).

ROMAN STOICISM

In the decade before Alexander the Great died, he conquered all of Greece, Persia, Babylonia and all lands as far east as Afghanistan and as far west as Egypt and southern Italy. Alexander's armies and the traders who soon followed spread the culture and philosophies of Greece, especially of Athens, throughout this new empire. Also,

---

* Only the broadest kind of sketch of the philosophy, epistemology and metaphysics of Western thinkers is possible in this book, just enough to suggest the philosophical or religious framework forming the basis for their ethical theories. For the reader desiring more detail, carefully selected histories of philosophy and religion can be found at chapter's end and the bibliography. One of the most readable is Bertrand Russell's History of Western Philosophy.

Greek philosophies began to be influenced by the Eastern philosophies of Zoroaster (an Indian-Iranian religion affirming life as God), Buddhism and Hinduism, especially their concepts of life-after-death, contempt for this present world of pain and the knowledge of the senses, and the notion of re-incarnation.* These Eastern ideas reinforced the already entrenched Platonism of the West. Aristotle's common-sense kind of empiricism provided little human comfort or hope for common people of that day, struggling daily and painfully against famine, sicknesses, harsh climates and generally miserable (and short) lives. The Eastern and (later) Christian religions, reinforced by the Platonic system of Ideas as real, promised relief in death and the sought-after joys of life in a next life. No wonder, considered in terms of human psychology, most people preferred the promises of religion and Platonism to the disheartening limitations of Aristotelian empiricism and rationality. No wonder, too, that Platonism dominated the West for almost 2000 years and Aristotelianism receded rapidly in influence, including the finished copies of Aristotle's books.**

But all men did not adopt the promises of religion or the idealism of Platonism. A relatively few, but influential in military and political positions, opted for the here-and-now practical but hard doctrines of Stoicism or the sensual goods advocated by Epicureanism (or hedonism). As Alexander's hard-won empire crumbled (he had never made effective arrangements for his <u>own</u> <u>succession</u> or permanent organization of his new empire, once won), the practical and militaristic people of Italy became supreme and, over several centuries, established the Roman empire. The Romans had never developed philosophies or ideologies on their own (only Vergil's <u>Aeneid</u>, circa 100 BC, a literary masterpiece but, like the early Greek Homer's <u>Iliad</u> and <u>Odyssey</u>, an inspirational national "history," not a systematic philosophy). Thus they reached back into the Greek culture they had conquered and, avoiding of course the idealistic and "impractical" Platonism there, fixed ironically upon two contemporaries of Aristotle (rather than Aristotle himself) as the new basis for Roman philosophy. These two men were Zeno and Epicurus.***

Zeno

Among the many new schools of philosophy developing in Athens at

---

* Kung Fu Tse (500 BC, Chinese philosopher known as Confucius to Westerners) must be excepted from this characterization of Eastern religions. He was an atheist but practical philosopher of ethics.

** Even the draft copies of Aristotle's works became unknown in Europe until the 13th century. The Arabian philosophers had preserved and used them in their own systems, especially Avicenna and Averroes.

*** Epicureanism was wrongly named (see p.71) but is not standard.

about the time of Aristotle's death, two survived to become influential throughout the empire of Alexander and later the Roman empire. They were Stoicism and Epicureanism.

The founder of Stoic philosophy was Zeno, originally a native of Cyprus but, like Aristotle, an Athenian for life. Unlike Aristotle, Zeno had no patience for the subtleties of either Platonic or Aristotelian reasoning. He saw life as hard, simple, uncompromising and not to be "sugar-coated" with the idealism of Plato or even the elaborate logic and syllogisms of his colleague, Aristotle. Zeno simply rejected all of "metaphysics," i.e. the possibility or relevance of anything beyond the physical world as experienced. Even Aristotle's "teleology" (p. 104) is too abstract and removed from the "real" world for Zeno. Needless to say, Zeno rejected the Greek gods of his day (a view somewhat more safely and fashionably pursued than at the time of Socrates' death) as well as the mystery religions, prophets and "saviours" common in his times and more so in later centuries. Zeno was a "materialist," who believed only in the observable natural order about him in which any man, like any other animal or plant, became a small part of life for a short time until he died and was replaced by the next generation of his kind. Human life was that, no more or less. Thus, the wise man just accepted the reality of his existence, including its joy, pleasures, intellectual excitements and its pain, frustrations and ultimate end. The wise man, the philosopher, wasted no time on the illusions and luxury of imagining that he was some kind of eternal being -which he isn't- or is destined for some kind of afterlife of cosmic significance -which he doesn't have at all- or that there are gods to protect him -which there aren't. Better to live the zestfull and courageous life of a realistic man, accepting with inner strength and dignity the fate of his life when it is painful as well as when it is pleasant. The only real reward for a man is his inner satisfaction for a life well lived, filled with as much accomplishment and admired deeds as possible and the joy of knowing always that later generations will remember him, even honor him, as one of the best of his kind.

Stoicism began in Athens but grew into a national passion among the Romans. Roman homes were full of their "house gods," not gods at all but small statues of ancestors remembered for great deeds, noble character, feats of self-control (especially under conditions of pain, torture or death) and a virtuous life often exceeding that of religious zealots such as the Christians (who, of course, did it for different reasons). Many great Roman Stoics earned, by their lifetime efforts and deeds -and were mainly motivated by the prospects of- huge marble statues of national, not merely family, significance insuring the memory of them for posterity. Ceasar, Cicero and other great Romans spoke of such aspirations often in their writings and speeches in public forums and the Roman Senate.

Thus Stoicism became an ethics of "virtue for its own sake," duty perceived and done no matter the personal cost or pain. A man was truly great only insofar as he excelled in virtue, sense of duty, self-discipline and deeds to be honorably remembered after his death. The true Stoic pitied, or despised, weak or fearful men and would routinely suffer any pain or death rather than sacrifice his personal honor or virtue (his mind and motives were always centered upon posterity and its final memory of him as a man).

For completely different rationales, the ethics of Stoicism arrives at about the same catalog of "virtues" developed by Socrates in his way, Aristotle in his and many religions in theirs. Already a pattern begins to emerge which is of critical importance for the practical purposes of this book: despite a perplexing diversity in the philosophies and religions developed by man, these many roads lead to similar conclusions about ethical standards, "virtues" and good human conduct. The significance of this is profound in a pluralistic society like America where people are free to practice a huge variety of religions and philosophical convictions which, fortunately, agree greatly on at least one practical issue, a basic body of generally acceptable ethical standards.

Epicureanism

Epicureanism (often called hedonism) is incorrectly named after Epicurus (d. 270 BC). Epicurus is probably the most misunderstood philosopher in history. His ethical views were closest to Aristotle's (a hierarchy of goods, only the highest and most human to be sought by man, the golden mean of virtue, etc.) and he lived the ascetic life of a Stoic or medieval monk. But he used a wrong and much misinterpreted word: he taught that the goal of man's life was pleasure. He meant by this word the highest human goods (p. 47 above) which ought to please man most, essentially the same as Aristotle's concept of ultimate human good or happiness (p. 63 above). But the word is easily interpreted into the crude meaning of merely sensual pleasure, "eat, drink and be merry" and sex of course. And so it was. A life of mere sensual pleasure, usually in life-shortening excess, came to be called "Epicureanism." The influential Roman Stoic philosopher, Epictetus (Discourses, II, 20), firmed the title "Epicureanism" when he characterized Epicurus' life as one of "unworthy eating, drinking, copulation, snoring, etc." (Like so many absurd "facts" of history, this is still believed into modern times.) An "epicure" today is someone dedicated to exquisite food. The historical Epicurus lived mainly on bread, water and bits of cheese. Despite poor health from his earliest years, he founded a school of philosophy in Athens about ten years after Aristotle's death, administered it and taught there regularly for forty years.* His chief pleasure in life was his friends, intellectual discussions and writing the long, very selfless and helpful letters to his friends and members of his family when, as often was the case, they were in trouble or depressed.

But hedonism, my preferred term for "Epicureanism," is indeed a common human tendency: the animal desire to sleep late, overeat, escape responsibilities with alcohol and other drugs, hide behind father- or mother-figures for protection and survival needs (or a benign government), seek tactile comforts in irresponsible sex and sensual experience, and so on. The tendency toward hedonism is sufficiently strong and common to create the need, from man's origins, for law, cruel control of peoples by realistic authorities, punishment as a universal reinforcement (motivator) and a host of similar social systems (especially family and formal education) to curb animal appetite in men and channel it constructively. Hedonism cannot seriously be considered an ethics, even if many choose it as a life-style; quite the reverse, ethics -and law- were necessarily developed by man to prevent hedonism from destroying him as a species (see the Chief Justice's views, pp.15-17 above).

AQUINAS AND THOMISM

We must move ahead a full 1500 years for the next truly great and original thinker, Thomas Aquinas, the 13th-century Catholic theologian. This is a huge historical leap, of course, but appropriate and necessary for the purposes of this book. By 200 BC the fundamental options of human thinking had been established by the Greek philosophers (Thales, Pythagoras, Parmenides, Heraclitus, Anaximander, Democritus, Zeno, Epicurus, Sophocles, Euripedes, Socrates, Plato, Aristotle, and others), by the great religions (Judaism, Hinduism, Buddhism, Zoroasterism, Taoism, etc.) and all had spread throughout the civilized world. The Roman empire invented no new religions or philosophies but excelled in its practical arts of farming, building, public entertainment, war and political organization of the empire's many power hierarchies. Romans

* Epicurus and his school became known, in <u>his</u> time, for a subtle version of the "pleasure principle," more compatible with Zeno's Stoic philosophy than Aristotle's very positive ethics and concept of the good. Epicurus taught that pleasure is the <u>absence of pain</u>, a negative thing, and a chief goal of man is to avoid pain and to help others do the same. Hence he himself ate little and shunned all excess. Gautama Buddha (Buddhism) promoted the same way of life (India, 500 BC), passivity, meditation. We use tranquilizers.

used, even perfected, the ideas of others and organized them to maintain the most enduring empire in history. The sole metaphysical (ideal) invention within the Roman empire was the all-powerful one of a new religion, Christianity. But Christianity was not born of or in Rome; its origins were in the Judaism that was developing new directions at about 200 BC. The concept of a messiah, a savior born of God but in human form, to save man from his sin and misery, had intensified within later Judaism until, for some, it became a self-fulfilling prophesy - the coming of the Christ was so deeply believed that it finally actually happened.* Roman authorities, however, rejected and even persecuted the new religion; but, over several centuries, it was Christianity that literally absorbed and re-structured the Roman empire into a Christian world. Christianity grew slowly at first and became a systematic religion by gradual additions of ideas and doctrines. No one giant mind (except possibly Augustine) shaped it as a thought system until Aquinas appeared in the 13th century.**

Augustine

Once launched by its founders and established as a growing sect with a huge following throughout the Roman empire, Christianity in its third century was seething with a variety of beliefs, doctrines, rituals, practices, rules and traditions but none of it was systematized and all of it increasingly vulnerable to sectarian dissolution into sub-sects or minor religions (in fact, this happened in the 16th century but the Protestant "sub-sects" were sufficiently large to become major religions on their own). Internal conflict within Christianity, regarding doctrines and growth strategies, had existed from the beginnings (for example, Peter and Paul and the early bishops) and now, three centuries later, threatened to accomplish what savage Roman persecutions had failed to do: splinter and destroy Christianity as an influential religion. That this did not happen and Christianity survived to become a dominant world religion is probably due to Aurelius Augustinus, known later as Saint Augustine or, simply, Augustine.

---

* Many, including some Jewish believers, still doubt the divine origin of the Christ of Christianity and regard him as a myth. If so, a very successful myth indeed with millions of adherents today. (Christ and Jesus are not given names but generic terms: "Christ" is the Greek translation for the Hebrew "Messiah" and "Jesus" is Greek for the Hebrew "Joshua," meaning "savior." From about 200 BC, in Asia Minor, many claimed to be "Christ" or "Jesus.")

** Thus we pass over many interesting thinkers in this book because they added little (not already covered so far) to ethical theory.

Augustine was a native of Africa and a "pagan" before he converted to Christianity, an agonizing and soul-searching conversion of mind and passions revealed in his Confessions (still regarded as a major work of literature). His passions (and hedonism) in early life were as strong as his subtle intelligence and need for a philosophy to "explain and settle" life in his mind. His discovery of Christianity provided him a personal control over his passions and a mentally satisfying outlet for his need for certitude about the meaning of his life and its destiny. All of this is caught dramatically in his story of a man's mind, Confessions. After conversion to Christianity and resolving his doubts of mind, he finally had a focus upon which his brilliant mind could concentrate. In a few years, Augustine rose rapidly through the ecclesiastical ranks and became bishop of Hippo (near Carthage) about 400 AD where he worked and wrote until his death 30 years later.

But Augustine was not a Plato or Aristotle, capable of generating a major thought system out of thin air. He needed a system already in place and established which he could use as a foundation and also adjust and modify toward his purposes of a Christian theology, a clear and systematic exposition of the religion. For reasons stated earlier (p.99), Platonism was the ideal choice (not Aristotelianism).* Throughout his mature works (On Free Choice, Confessions, Commentary on Genesis, On the Trinity, City of God, etc.), Augustine clearly finds Platonism as a pure philosophy and Christianity as a religion ideally made for each other. His Christian faith set his goals and ultimate beliefs about God, the trinity, immortality, the nature of Christ and so on; but his Platonism provided the systematic logic to organize and relate religious beliefs to each other, develop the huge collection of Christian beliefs into a coherent theology, and importantly extend its scope (by further deductions from the base system) to increasingly wider areas covering both this and the next life. Augustine became thus the "father of all Christian theology" and his Platonic Christianity (or Christian Platonism) dominated the thought and lives of the Christian world for over 1000 years.

Augustinian ethics is based theoretically upon the "innatism" and "intuitionism" ("looking inward" for truth) of Platonism. However, its ethical conclusions about standards and specific ethical codes are a full and systematic confirmation of the earlier Christian norms and virtues of justice, charity, love, temperance, the "golden rule," and so on. As noted, even non-Christians such as Aristotle and the Stoics concur.

---

* Three brilliant, but non-christian, platonist philosophers around Augustine's time were Plotinus, Origen and Boethius (whose classic De Consolatione Philosophiae was written while awaiting death).

Aquinas and the 13th Century

Almost a thousand years elapsed from the time of Augustine to that of Aquinas, most of it recorded by historians as the "dark ages" in Europe dominated by abject misery in the conditions of life (about 2 children in 10 born lived to adulthood and their average life expectancy was age 30), by totalitarian suppression and continual wars of actual and would-be kings, by absolute obedience to religious orthodoxy and by a virtual absence of any original intellectual activity.* Galileo and scientific inquiry, the printing press and other human developments (especially of man's mind and mental methods), the keys to unleashing man's potential, had to wait till the 16th century. But Thomas Aquinas (ironically, since he would never have intended it as the fully obedient priest he was) began the rational (rather than merely religious) tradition of Western man -or at least renewed it- by restoring Aristotelian methods of thinking and spirit of inquiry into the main stream of 13th-century thinking and establishing Aristotelianism as the foundation block of his massive new construction of Christian theology. Aquinas questioned everything, although his ultimate conclusions were guided by religious orthodoxy,** and two centuries later such questioning led to Luther and Protestantism as well as Galileo and science. Critically, along with accepted truths of his religion, Aquinas was guided intellectually by Aristotle, not by Plato.

Thomas Aquinas, son of the Italian Count of Aquino, was born in 1225 and died just before his 50th birthday. In that short lifespan, Aquinas and Thomism (as his thought system is called) became the turning point of medieval thinking. Because of Aquinas' thought and writings, intellectual history must divide the medieval period into two parts: the thousand years from Augustine to Aquinas (when Platonism was dominant) and the two centuries following Aquinas (during which Aristotelianism grew dominant and the rational spirit of it led to the beginnings of the modern period).[3] As noted earlier (p.95), it was

---

* During this thousand-year intellectual trough, when man's "mind stood still," many interesting writers made minor contributions such as Bede, John of Damascus, Erigena, Gerbert, Avicenna, Lanfranc, Avicebron, Anselm, Roscelin, Champeaux, Abelard, John of Salisbury, Averroes, Maimonides, Albert (the Great), R. Bacon, etc.

** Bertrand Russell (History of Western Philosophy, p.463) thus concludes that "there is little of the true philosophic spirit in Aquinas. He does not, like Socrates, set out to follow wherever the argument may lead. Before he begins to philosophize, he already knows the 'truth' ... and the conclusions in advance...This is not philosophy."

Aquinas who had the works of Aristotle translated into Latin and introduced Aristotelianism into medieval thought. Aquinas himself wrote an enormous quantity of works, each of which has exerted almost absolute influence on Catholic theologians and philosophers. Thomism is still the orthodox doctrine taught in most Catholic colleges in the U.S.A. Most influential are his Summa Contra Gentiles and his huge multi-volume Summa Theologica which contain his final word on virtually every theological, philosophical and ethical issue of importance. But his other works, lengthy Commentaries on all of Aristotle's works, etc., have been also greatly influential and almost too numerous to mention. Aquinas (left), although as a person a man of quiet temperament and humble habits, was a revolutionary in his times; his thinking and writings were so comprehensive, thorough, incisive and powerful that they became virtual dynamite that wiped out ten centuries of thought systems preceding him. In his own times, he changed the world of thought as radically as Freud, Einstein and Darwin revolutionalized their worlds.

Thomistic Ethics

As one would expect, Aquinas' philosophical ethics and moral theology are quite distinct in the mental methods of developing them, although they generally coincide in content and ultimate conclusions. His moral theology is based upon his Catholic faith and begins with the conclusions appropriate to it and already declared "true" as revealed by God through His Church (see footnote on previous page and page 92). His philosophical ethics follows the purely rational approach of Aristotle and arrives at essentially the same conclusions (the "golden mean" etc. as on pages 62 and 104 above). If there were only this natural world of men and no God or supernatural next life (a dialectical assumption used often by Thomas in his Contra Gentiles –and dangerously*), then he concluded that a life of virtue still emerged, even without the guidance of Catholic faith, as the only good and ethical life for a human being as dictated by pure reason and its analysis of actual human experience. If one abstracts from Thomas the Christian and theologian, as he often did, and reads Aquinas when he is writing as (hypothetically*) pure philosopher, Thomas and Aristotle (separated by 2000 years) are 'brothers' in

---

* Thomas' books increasingly threatened old and established ways of thinking as well as powerful princes and priests with vital vested interests in crushing the ideas of this new 13th-century rebel – or, if necessary, the man himself. Thomas was often charged with the act of heresy –and its consequences. His books were burned in Paris.

mind, thinking, spirit and world-view. They exhibit in all their works similar zest for the adventures of intellectual activity and speculation, mental problem-solving and precise organization of solution-options and their ultimate conclusions, and almost a single mind on ethics.

Aquinas and "Natural Law"

Aristotle, and Aquinas after him, were the supreme metaphysicians (p.92), ever searching for the inner, but intangible, nature of all things, that inner essence and inherent "form" (as Aristotle termed it) determining the entire activity and functions of a being as well as its appearance.* Thus both, Thomas mainly following Aristotle, built their ethics upon the inner "nature" of men (and their functions, such as seeing and hearing). This tendency to search out the "natural law," controlling the lives and every function of human beings, was implicit within Aristotle's ethics but became explicit and dominant in Thomism's doctrine and details of natural law ethics. Remaining implicit in Aristotle's ethics and governed by common sense, the law of nature became a very sensible "golden mean" of human conduct. Unfortunately, after Thomas' death, Thomism and subsequent Catholic theologians (not Aquinas himself) came to interpret "natural law" for and toward preconceived and church-dictated purposes such as bans against interest on money loaned and all forms of birth control (church policy favoring large families, despite the misery of most of them struggling to feed even a few with scarce resources, and approximately geometric increases in numbers of the faithful and the consequent power of the church). The medieval church was notorious for its sole concern for the quantity of human lives and its derived and growing power based on their continuing increase; it had little or no interest in the quality of life. (Review p.64 above for more details of such abuses of the concept of natural law.) The pure and rational mind of Aquinas would not have liked many church doctrines deduced pragmatically from Thomism. Several centuries later, John Locke, the brilliant English philosopher, again, like Aristotle, combined common sense with the basic natural-law concept and developed from it the ideas of rights and human freedom later embodied in the American Constitution and Bill of Rights. Frustratingly for ethicians, the natural-law concept, depending upon interpretations of it, has been equally useful in supporting thought-control and totalitarian religions as well as philosphers who launched the American system of freedom (Paine, Locke, etc.).

---

* In the same spirit but by modern scientific methods, today's biochemists have found DNA molecules (genes) as the innermost factors determining virtually every aspect of any individual's life.

THE PROTESTANT REVOLUTION

The Protestant Reformation (more accurately a virtual revolution) is usually associated with Martin Luther, an Augustinian priest and professor of theology at Wittenberg, who publicly attacked the sale of indulgences by Tetzel, the ever-traveling ambassador of the Roman pope (see p.37 about indulgences). For Luther, however, who died in 1546, Tetzel's visit, to improve sales revenues needed by Rome, was the occasion for the public break with the Catholic church, not the underlying cause. The real cause was both doctrinal and very personal. Luther, like Augustine (Confessions), lived in mental torture about his ultimate salvation. Unlike Augustine, who finally found peace of mind in the early church and its doctrine of divine forgiveness for sin, Luther, inspired by the spirit of his role model whose writings he knew by heart, suffered from increasing doubts that the same church, a thousand years later, was still the same and valid church of the early Christians. In contrast to the words of Christ and the early Christian spirit of love and forgiveness, the Catholic bureaucracy of Luther's times, as he perceived it, was corrupt, laden with rules that made salvation impossible (feeding the need of all for selling all they owned to purchase indulgences), hypocritical in the daily practices of its pope and bishops, and concerned only with money and political power. Obsessed with the need for his own personal salvation, having at an early age given his life as a monk and servant of the church till death, Luther's studies and experience drove him to the conclusion that only a return to the original church of Christ and the Bible could guarantee salvation. The Roman Catholic church, over the centuries, according to Luther, had gradually claimed infallibility in its interpretations of the Bible and merely exploited it for the churchmen's real goals of money and power over people. Thus, till his death, Luther rejected Rome's interpretations of Christ in the Bible, advocated a renewed and honest interpretation and, in effect, founded the new Lutheran Christian religion based on salvation by pure faith only in the mercy of God, not in "good works" as defined by Roman popes.

Luther

The response of fellow Germans was phenomenal: over several generations, virtually all of Germany and northern Europe became Lutherans. (It should be noted that the Catholic church -too late- began an internal reformation at this time, to eliminate and control abuses such as the sale of indulgences, an effort often called the "counter-reformation," but the spirit and momentum of Protestantism were already unleashed.) Luther was not even the first of the "protestants" (John Wycliffe, d. 1384, had opposed the established religion in England, and died for his efforts) and a host of protestant Christian religions followed soon after Luther.

John Calvin and Other Christian Protestant Religions

The essence of Protestantism was twofold: escape and freedom from papal (Roman Catholic) central control of every detail of religious life and rules, especially papal interpretation of the Bible as the infallible will of God; and, as the positive side of it, private (personal and purely individual) interpretation of the Bible as the final basis of every man's conscience and religion, this personal faith in Christ and interpretation of his Word the ultimate keys to salvation. This latter is what finally provided the peace of mind Luther had sought over his early years of mental agony about his own salvation. Ironically, Luther had found the germ of the concept of "private interpretation of the Bible " and the primacy of each man's individual conscience in the writings of his role model, Augustine, the founder of the Catholic Church's theological system. A thousand years later, however, intuitive faith -and Platonism- had been replaced by Thomistic logic -and Aristotelianism; and, in the view of Luther and other early Protestants, these new thought systems were merely exploited by current Catholic popes and bishops for their own worldly and ungodly purposes. Needless to say, Luther and other Protestants returned to Augustine, rather than Aquinas, as their prime theologian and to Plato, rather than Aristotle, as their prime philosopher -these allegiances are still paramount in today's huge array of Protestant sects. Once the concept of private interpretation of the Bible became established, soon after Luther, the natural result was the rapid founding of a vast multitude of Christian religions, all Protestant and each based on its own interpretations of the Bible.* 4

Calvinism, founded by John Calvin (left), requires a special attention because one of its theological doctrines led to the powerful religious support of an economic system condemned earlier by all previous Christianity, capitalism and the "work ethic" (p.72 above). Calvin, in his Institutes (c.1550), set forth a strict and harsh form of Protestantism in France that, for centuries, punished wrongdoers and burned heretics alive as fervently as had its mother church, Catholicism (which it was "reforming"). The God of Calvinism was as vengeful and

* The Anglican church, established by England's Henry VIII (for mere marital and political reasons, certainly not religious), was an early and most influential example which, despite its founder and his low personal character (executing wives and friends like Thomas More), grew into one of the most respected religions in modern times - and a dominant one in modern America. Calvinism was another early version. Today, there are literally thousands of Protestant religions based on the Bible such as Adventists, Baptists, Methodists, Unitarianists, Presbyterians, Mormons, Shakers, Evangelists, etc.

demanding as today's God of Christian Evangelists and born-again converts is friendly, loving and forgiving. A unique doctrine of Calvinism was "predestination:" no mortal man could determine his ultimate salvation by "good works" or anything else;* only God could do this and, in fact, God predestined most miserable men to hell at the very moment of their birth but a chosen few to salvation and heaven. How could any man, agonizing over his eternal fate, know whether he was among the many to be condemned or the few predestined by God for heaven? There was nothing any man could do to cause his salvation; but there were two signs, manifested throughout the history of a man's mortal life, which proved to himself and all others that God had indeed chosen him for salvation. These signs were: abandonment of false religions (Catholicism and, later, other Protestant religions) as exhibited in active membership in the Calvinist religion; and, visible (public) evidence of success in this life as demonstrated by prestigious positions in the Calvinist church, high public office, professorships in universities and by the clearest sign of all, insofar as it is quantitative and easily compared among men, wealth and personal income. Thus, for most Christians for several centuries,** the "work ethic" dominated their lives: the sure way to salvation was hard work every waking moment (for many, especially Puritans, any sort of recreation such as dancing or music was condemned as sinful); only work, accomplishment, success, income and wealth (capitalism) were proper in a truly Christian life. Thus Protestantism created the "work ethic" which, powered later by the philosophical and political concepts of America's founding fathers in their Constitution and Bill of Rights, launched the "American Experiment" and the marvels it has achieved in its first and young two centuries. (Whether America can sustain and continue its past success remains a critical question; see p.40, 79 & 13.)

Protestantism and Ethics: Although the specific ethical codes and rules of the various Protestant religions vary greatly and range from strictly enforced (Calvinists, Mormons, etc.) to broad and lenient groups of Baptists and born-again Christians, the central ethical standards are still those of justice, the Golden Rule and the standard virtues (p.93).

---

* Luther's rejection of "good works" as the cause of salvation (p.114) actually carried the astounding implication of divine predestination but he never dared draw the obvious conclusion (if he realized it was indeed buried there in his theology); Calvin made it explicit.

** In (theologically) complicated ways, most Protestant religions, especially Anglicans, Puritans, Methodists and others adopted this notion of success as essential to Christianity while rejecting specific Calvinist docrines about divine predestination.

MODERN EMPIRICISM

Ironically, and as the exact opposite of his personal intentions as a fervent Catholic, Aquinas' Thomism laid the seeds which, within two centuries, unleashed the human tendencies toward Protestantism, empirical science and many aspects of the Renaissance (which began in Thomas' homeland, Italy, and spread rapidly throughout Europe -not many years separate Galileo, the Italian, Thomas More, the Englishman, and Erasmus, the "internationalist" thinker of that time). The conceptual "genes," sown into the European thought-system by Aquinas who got all of them from Aristotle, can be summed up as a revolutionary and new method of human thinking, not necessarily new conclusions (although the latter followed rapidly upon the new methods of thinking). In a word, the new method, the new "genes," amounted to the unimpeded use of human reasoning and the full potential of its development. Thomas (especially in his Summa Contra Gentiles) vivified Aristotle's methods of pure and powerful reasoning to convince non-Christians (of Arabia and North Africa) to accept the conclusions of his Christian religion as conclusions demanded by rational analysis of universally-known and basic human experience rather than by religious authorities they rejected. In general, non-Christian readers of Aquinas admired and learned from his methods of logic and rational analysis - but used these very methods to reject his conclusions (determined at the start, of course, by Thomas' Catholic religion -see footnote p. 111). As brilliant a mind as his was, Thomas never realized he was opening the Pandora's box of free and unfettered use of human reason (as opposed to prior religious faith); the use of it soon led to the modern world of science, Protestantism and rapid material progress (health, quality of life, longevity, etc.) in the daily-life conditions of mankind radically exceeding the life-norms of all prior human generations. This latter development of human life and its conditions has become supreme in the lives of modern Americans.

The Renaissance

The beginnings of the Renaissance, a complex mingling of great evil with brilliant intellectual innovation, are usually associated with 15th-century Italy, especially the city-state of Florence and the powerful Medici family. The essence of the Renaissance was free-thinking, much of it nonsensical grasping at old myths and ancient legends, all of it secular and anti-church; but some small part of the new and free thinking of the Renaissance became the works of Petrarch (poetry), Da Vinci and Michaelangelo (art), Dante's epic, Erasmus, Montaigne and Thomas More (criticism), Pico, F. Bacon and others (philosophy).

And, especially, Galileo. Galileo, an Italian, was born in 1564 and was educated in the classical languages, logic and the science of his time. He gradually rejected the latter as based on and deduced from the conventional wisdom of the past as well as theological premises instead of being discovered from empirical observations and the analysis of these (called "induction," p.39 above). For example, the church had always declared as dogma that Earth was the center of the universe (this early Greek Ptolemaic theory appropriately placed Earth, the single part of the universe visited by God in the form of Christ, in the center of God's creations); just before the birth of Galileo, Copernicus had proposed as a possibility (not a doctrine -that would be heresy) a theory of the Sun at the center and Earth a planet revolving about it along with other even larger planets. A generation later, after formulating the Law of Isochronism of a Pendulum from patient observation of a huge lamp swinging in the cathedral at Pisa, Galileo (left) heard reports about the telescope and he constructed one himself and kept improving upon it until his fine instrument was in great demand throughout Europe. And, with his own telescopes, he spent years observing the stars, moon and planets, and concluded, from actual observations rather than mere theory (Copernican) or theological deductions (dogma) that, in fact, Earth was a planet circling the Sun along with many other such planets, the Moon was a minor-planet or satellite circling Earth, other similar satellites circled the huge Jupiter which was itself a planet of the Earth's Sun, and that the Sun itself was just one of many (the Milky Way). The key word above is fact: Galileo's specific discoveries, as startling as they were, are today insignificant compared to his revolution in man's methods of thinking, induction and scientific observation rather than merely deduction from the conventional wisdom and premises of the past, and absolute dedication to the search for truth (facts). In spirit, Galileo was an objective philosopher with truth his sole goal, no matter where the truth led (review p.99 and footnote on p. 111); in his actions, he was the beginning of modern empirical science and all of its wonders (medicine, horseless carriage, aircraft, telephone, computers). The same spirit of rational inquiry was also invading philosophy, displacing blind faith in religions, challenging age-old traditional myths and launching the free and new thinking through which the Renaissance led man into the modern world.

Rene Descartes

In indirect ways, the Renaissance produced the phenomenal mind of Descartes (Cartesius in Latin as he was known for centuries). Although many thinkers, including Galileo, have changed their worlds by their ideas, only five emerge as the gigantic minds of Western thought: Plato, Aristotle, Aquinas, Descartes and Kant.

Descartes, born in France in 1596, became not only one of history's greatest mathematicians (we have all studied cartesian coordinates and analytic geometry in college math) but also the great systematic philosopher who framed virtually all of the questions and philosophical alternatives dominating modern philosophy since his time and into ours.* Like his mathematics, Descartes' philosophy is rigorous logic and deduction. His aim was to begin with a self-evident axiom and, like a Euclid in his geometry, continue to deduce conclusions to become premises for further conclusions -until the entire mystery of the universe was laid open to man's understanding.** His starting axiom was his famous statement "Cogito ergo sum" ("I think, therefore I am")*** from which he ultimately deduced two existing worlds: the spiritual world of God, whose existence Descartes proved deductively in the manner of rigorous mathematics, and then the physical world governed by mechanical laws established by his already deduced God.**** His philosophical system was flawed in its exact details but the profound questions it raised led to the two main paths travelled by modern philosophy: (a) idealism, rejecting the existence of the physical and "apparent" world (Hegel, Kant) and (b) empiricism -or materialism-, accepting only the physical world as discovered and known by the human senses (Aristotelianism again and soon Locke, Hobbes, Malabranche, J.S. Mill, Spencer, James, Dewey).

Descartes (left), like Thomas Aquinas, was a faithful and fervent Catholic but, like Aquinas, sowed the seeds of intellectual inquiry that led ultimately to the rejection of Catholicism by the large majority of modern Europeans and Americans.

Cartesian Ethics: Descartes was a mathematician and metaphysician (philosopher) and gave little explicit attention to ethics as such. His practical ethics were those of Christianity

* Leibniz (d. 1716), like Descartes, was a supreme mathematician as well as an influential philosopher (Monadology being his classic in philosophy). He, independently, in Germany, invented Calculus at the same time Newton did the same in England.

** Descartes suffered severe and continuing illness most of his life (he managed, however, to live till age 54) and was convinced that his philosophical system would reveal the cures of all disease -and his.

*** The cartesian "Cogito" is usually, and wrongly, interpreted as an inference. It was, however, self-evident: I am (esse) thinking.

**** In his personal life, Descartes was a fervent Catholic and faithful.

but the profound influence of his overall philosophic system of thought generated later the specific ethical systems of idealists and empiricists alike. All of them, idealists such as Hegel and Kant, and empiricists such as Locke and Mill, used Descartes' works as their starting points.*

John Locke

John Locke (1632-1704) was an English physician of modest income and slight physical appearance. But his major life interest was philosophy, especially political philosophy, and over his lifetime he wrote two major works (Essay Concerning Human Understanding and Letters on Toleration) which, respectively, founded modern Empiricism and provided the conceptual foundation for the American Constitution about a century after his death. Locke's Letters on Toleration and the companion volume, published a year later, Two Treatises on Government were read avidly by influential Americans and shaped the American mind over the century more than any other intellectual influence. Locke's passion and cool arguments for man's individual "natural rights," freedoms of speech and religious belief, toleration and respect for all by all, pervade America's Declaration of Independence and the Bill of Rights of its Constitution. Although not physically a founding father of America (like Washington, Franklin, Jefferson, etc.), the most influential mind among the founding fathers was Locke's. But Locke's political philosophy and values, incorporating an obvious ethics, were derived from the more basic level within his thinking: his emphasis upon the facts of human experience and his resulting Empiricism.

Locke's Empiricism

Locke's Essay, published about ten years before his death, examined and rejected the innate ideas proposed by Descartes as the basis of knowledge and certitude,** and concluded with Aristotle that all true knowledge comes into the mind through the senses (rather than from within the mind itself) and that any certitude about the real world is far more elusive than Descartes (and Plato earlier) had thought. He distinguished always in the Essay between sense knowledge of the real world (which reaches reality, i.e. the external world, but not with any

---

* Descartes' major works were his Discourse on Method (1637), and Meditations (1641) and Principles of Philosophy (1644).

** Mathematics is one of the few fields that yields certitude (given certain assumptions about a numerical system, 2+3=5 for sure). Descartes ambitioned similar certitude about the whole of reality.

certitude) as distinguished from mental constructs (concepts in the mind -like mathematics or other abstractions- which yield certitude but are quite independent in both their existence and their representation of the external world of reality). Useful, although not certain, knowledge of reality is attainable, according to Locke, only by sensation and then human reflection upon it. Only thus, not by deductions from innate "first principles" (Descartes) or by any sort of intuitions of the mind examining its own "innate" contents (Platonism and most of Christian theology), is valid although imperfect human understanding possible. Locke exhibits always a clear and understandable style of writing (a relative rarity among philosophers, theologians -and economists, too) as well as a refreshing "common sense" (equally rare among many of the learned). These qualities ultimately earned him an international reputation, near the end of his life, as the apostle of common sense, human freedom and pure honesty of thought. But, expectedly, his thinking -and its conclusions- (although not yet published) marked him as heretical and dangerous to both church and state in England and most of Europe. A man of common sense, and with no ambitions for prison or martyrdom for his "cause," Locke prudently exiled himself to Holland in 1683 where he finally wrote and published his major works.*

Locke and Ethics

The key to Locke's overall value system and ethics is in his chapter entitled "Of Degrees of Assent" where he insists that man's passion for certitude drives him to give assent to religious and other propositions that have little or no basis in fact or reality. In Locke's view, this quest for absolute certitude was the mark of the hoping child, not the thinking and realistic adult. The degree of assent we give to any proposition must be confined to the degree of factual evidence, reasonableness and probability supporting the proposition. Human understanding is thus a slow, patient, sceptical and (for Locke) friendly discussion and sifting of conflicting opinions in the ever-growing light of facts, objective analysis, experience, reasoning and probability. Never certitude. Locke came to despise "certitude," the quest for it and the human insistence on it as the single major cause of intolerance and its consequent tyrannies by churches and states over the minds and lives of men -and the monumental suffering imposed upon men by other men in the

* Locke spent six years in Holland, at that time a major sea power and center of international trade as well as the only European nation which tolerated religious and political differences and freedom of speech. In Holland, Locke was free to write his *Essay*, *Letters on Toleration* and *Government Treatises*. The "Glorious Revolution" in England (1688) was inspired by Locke writing in Holland.

name of religious "truth" and the cruelties (including major religious wars) used throughout history to force men to accept it. Locke preferred tolerant reasoning and discussion of evidence as far better than religious "truths" (all contradicting each other) intolerantly implemented by physical or other force. This is his ethics: friendship, mutual respect among people and nations, sympathetic tolerance for all views and lifestyles within the bounds of reasonable laws, recognition of all human rights and freedoms that constitute the dignity of a human being; and, most importantly as the source of all of these, intellectual honesty, the tentativeness and scepticism about even one's own ideas that permits careful listening and respect for the ideas of others. As befits a genius, there is much in Locke of both Socrates' spirit (p.96) and Galileo's factual methods (p.118) as well as their rare common sense.

The Age of British Empiricism

Locke was able to return to England for the last few years of his life and, for two centuries, British philosophy was dominated by one generation after another of Lockians who created the powerful tradition of British empiricists. To name just a few: Toland (d.1722), Norris (d.1711), Berkeley (d.1753),* Butler (d.1752), Hume (d.1776), Hartley (d.1757), Smith (Adam)(d.1790), Reid (1796), Bentham (d.1832), Stewart (d.1828), Paley (1805), James Mill (d.1836), J.S.Mill (d.1873), and, in America, Charles Peirce, William James and John Dewey. The British empiricists varied greatly among themselves ranging from the very religious Berkeley to Spencer, the champion of "ungodly" evolutionism, and from the sceptic Hume to the positive ethical thinking of James and J.S.Mill. Adam Smith began his career as a moral philosopher and ended it as the first systematic economist (Wealth of Nations, 1776, the same year Locke's political philosophy became action across the Atlantic). But, despite their many differences, the basic empiricist theme (the senses as the source of human knowledge), established by Aristotle and championed by Locke, pervades them all.

The scope of this book allows consideration of only those thinkers directly bearing upon ethical theory. In the above list, these are Smith, Bentham, J.S.Mill, Peirce, James and Dewey, to be dealt with later.

Materialism

"Materialism," as used in our philosophical context, is one of the

---

* George Berkeley, deeply religious and a bishop, drew ambiguously from both Descartes and Locke, concluding ultimately that human senses provided knowledge but distorted knowledge. How distorted is sense knowledge raises the "epistemological question" of using the doubtful senses as the very measure to evaluate their accuracy.

legitimate deductions from empiricist premises (unfortunately, so are absolute scepticism and nihilism).* Technically, materialism accepts as true only what we can sense and as real only these same sensed data. Since the senses reach and know only physical (extended) things such as shapes, color, sounds, motion, smells, tastes, tactile objects creating physical pressures or resistances, etc., and since many philosophers, including Aristotle and Locke, found cause to distrust "innate" mental constructs (Platonic Ideas and Cartesian "first principle" concepts as the major cause of human enslavement by visionaries and their religions), it is one obvious deduction from empiricism that the only true "reality" is that which can be sensed. All else, "invented" by the creative "mind," must simply be illusion and convincing, but deceptive, mental and conceptual manipulations -similar to the fascinating manipulations of mathematics and no more "real" than these are (albeit useful as models often to "simulate" and manipulate things in the real world). Thus, materialism accepts as actually existing only sensed (material) things as reality; all else is of the mind, there only, and no part of the actual (real) world (thus it follows that no such "things" as God, souls, angels or other putative spiritual entities possess any reality -except in the mind of man). Needless to say, religious leaders and all churches (whose major asset was a spiritual God and His Will) fought all manifestations of this new heresy (materialism) and, especially, any of its inventors or advocates. Historically, materialists have not fared well against the ingrained and aggressively religious opposition of Western Christian tradition (even today, only 20% of the world's people are atheists or otherwise non-religious while the other 80% are believers of one or another of the thousands of Christian and other religions still extant[4]).

Insofar as the "materialist" conclusion from empiricist premises is so easy, obvious and a natural deduction, the intellectual historian has to wonder why the "materialist" philosopher is still so rudely shunned, condemned and excluded from serious membership in the scholarly world. Possibly it is a function of emotional ties to traditional beliefs rather than the cool rational thinking (and friendly discussion) Locke liked.

Thomas Hobbes, Materialism and the Ethics of Physical Power

Like Machiavelli's Prince (c.1500), which taught Renaissance rulers in Italy the intricacies of political power and physical survival in a jungle-like world of intrigue and assassinations for power, Hobbes'

* Strangely, but logically, modern Existentialism (its nihilistic versions as with Kierkegarrd and Sartre) as well as standard absolute Scepticism (the Cynic School of ancient Greece and the modern Hobbes) derive easily from Empiricism (but also from Idealism!).

Leviathan, published in England in 1650, did the same for English kings and, also, justified any use of royal power to suppress the king's subjects in order to achieve the ends of the nation, order, stability and resources (taxes) for wars. Expediency, for both Machiavelli and Hobbes (left inset), takes priority over all other ethical considerations - the end always justifies any means, no matter how brutal or "unethical" the means seem in them selves. In short, "might makes right" (p.58 above). Thomas Hobbes (d.1679) was technically an empiricist like his contemporary Locke but, unlike Locke, drew a purely materialist conclusion and, further, views of men and human government totally opposed to Locke's ideas of human freedom, rights and intrinsic dignity. Hobbes had a horror of anarchy and the ever-potential bloody and chaotic rebellions of the common people. He viewed the average man as naturally barbaric, a savage animal, controllable and made useful only by the absolute power and "might" of the state -this, preferably in the unambiguous hands of a single man (monarch, tyrant or ruler). Ethics, for Hobbes, is the simple and harsh practical judgment to do anything that is *necessary* to control men, use them properly and maintain civil order among them. Human life is a warlike struggle among men, tribes, nations and classes (poor vs. rich, etc.) for the scarce resources needed for survival; what ethics, except expediency and "might," works for survival under conditions of perpetual war?

Nietzsche (d.1900)

Although Friedrich Nietzsche's Zarathustra and Geneology of Morals were written about two centuries after Hobbes, Nietzsche must be mentioned here as Hobbes' logical descendent. Nietzsche's concepts of physical power, "superman" and "super-race" were the ideas Hitler embraced to cause the greatest upheaval in human history (World War II and its consequences both in lives and political turmoil since).* Despite the horrors caused by Nietzsche's philosophy, he and his ideas are still admired, even in modern America.** One must wonder, or sweat, amid the speculation of Hobbes' and Nietzsche's ideas taken seriously as a national policy (any nation's) in today's nuclear age. These ideas were taken seriously in the Germany of the 1930s; could it happen again (say in Russia) in the 1980s or the 1990s? (History has a tendency to repeat itself; those who don't read it, tend to repeat it.)

* Ideas do have consequences. Review p. 14-15.

** W.J. Dannhauser, "The Trivialization of Nietzsche," American Spectator, May, 1982

Despite much controversy among philosophers about what Nietzsche really meant, any interpretation of Zarathustra (who speaks for Nietzsche without risky attribution to him) makes it plain that he preferred war over peace and fully deserves the description of a "Fascist" in all of its forms. Zarathustra "abounds with stated preferences for war... and equates the preferences of the ancients for peace with their preference for being over becoming, rest over motion, contemplation over the life of action -all of which he considers part of a sleepy doctrine inimical to the glorious vitality preached by Zarathustra " (Dannhauser, footnote p.124). Nietzsche relished the action and vitality of disorder and revolutions leading to new orders, these in their turn to be dismantled and restructured by change, mass revolutions and war. This is how animal species war among themselves toward the "survival of the best" and how human history has created great civilizations upon the bones of the meek and peaceful.* Peace is for sheep wanting rest away from predators; the lions among men yearn for glorious and exhilarating achievements through fighting, might and war. And the history of both animals and man demonstrates that the Earth belongs to lions, not sheep. Thus spoke Zarathustra. Many, even today, seem still to be listening!

Darwin, Spencer and Evolutionism

Charles Darwin (left) was, like Galileo, the patient, fact-finding and truth-seeking scientist and, like Galileo, changed his world radically and for all time. Galileo shocked the church by pulling Earth from the center of the universe and placing it where it belonged as a minor planet, using his telescope to prove it scientifically; his true revolution in thought, however, was his new "scientific" method of human thinking and discovery of truth, opposed at its very roots to the traditional methods of generating "truth"(p.118). Darwin shocked the church and most Christians of his time by crediting the slow processes of the material world and Nature with the creation of animal species and of man himself (rather than the God of Genesis and the "historical" voyage of Noah's ark). Darwin's own voyages and

---

* Nietzsche reveals always the influence of the historical dialectic theories of his countryman, Hegel (whose influence upon Marx became "dialectical materialism" dominating Communist lands today), and of Darwin's evolutionism (Origin of Species and Descent of Man were published and well known when Nietzsche was a young man).

research on the islands of the world, and the animal species inhabiting them, consumed twenty-five years of his life. He reported his thousands of observations finally in his Origin of Species (1859) and Descent of Man (1871). Scientists (mainly biologists) and Christians have fought over these books ever since.* Darwin himself was a quiet man, dedicated only to his fact-finding, avoided publicity and the public, and detested the controversy rising over his work; he could not affirm a God but he upheld Christian ethics.

The essence of Darwin's theory of evolution is that higher species evolved into existence as a result of slow and accidental changes in earlier species as these adapt to their changing environments. It is not a matter of conscious design but chance development of characteristics that make some species more fit to survive and others less so (the latter become extinct). For example, a rabbit might, by genetic accident, be born with the characteristic of longer hind legs, transmit this by normal breeding to its descendents until gradually a species of faster rabbits is able more successfully to outrun predators and survive while its slower cousins (without the characteristic) are caught by predators, eaten before they can reproduce and thus gradually become extinct. Every kind of plant, animal and man existing today is the result of this kind of slow development of "successful" characteristics making it most fit and able to survive against all other forces constantly changing -and adapting- in the balance of nature. Rabbits still exist by having developed faster legs and reflexes to detect and escape danger; lions developed huge claws, teeth and strength; birds wings to fly from danger; man a brain to think and outsmart his way through danger and to survival -and ethics.** In Darwinian evolutionism, existing species of today (cats, dogs, horses, roses, lilac, pines and man as known over our 5000 years of recorded history -"today" meaning thousands of years as anthropologists measure time) evolved over millions of years of "natural selection" and "survival of the fittest;" they were not created by a God in an instant nor did they emerge as such from a Noah's ark. No wonder Darwin's books hit the nerves of Christians of his time and created the controversy he disliked.

---

* For example, as recently as the 1925 Scopes trial in Tennessee in which the state, represented by the famous presidential candidate William Jennings Bryan (the "golden orator"), successfully stopped a teacher (Scopes) in his efforts to teach Darwinian evolutionism in a state school (Scopes was defended by the dramatic Clarence Darrow; Darrow lost the case, but Bryan, from strain, died 5 days later).

** Since Darwin (and Spencer, the philosopher of evolutionism), many philosophers regard ethics itself as subject to the natural process of evolution and the survival of the fittest ethical standards.

In fascinating ways, Darwin's contemporary countryman, Herbert Spencer (left), both preceded and followed Darwin's ideas about evolution. Spencer, in his times, was one of the great English philosophers and, early in his career, fixed his thinking upon change and development as the "first principles" for explaining all realities in man's life, societies, political government and ethics. Spencer wrote and re-wrote one master work, editing and re-publishing it often, from 1861 to 1892, entitled First Principles of Biology, Psychology, Sociology and Ethics. When it first appeared, it vaguely suggested the kinds of evolutionary phenomena which Darwin had discovered in fact and was then in the process of publishing. After the publication of Darwin's Origin of Species and Descent of Man, Spencer became an ardent and aggressive follower of Darwin's ideas, now fact and not just theory. Unlike Darwin, Spencer thrived upon controversy and public combat of ideas (an essential part of his philosophy as he practiced what he taught) and became the public advocate of Darwinian evolutionism as well as his own applications of evolutionism to societies and human life. The superb prose of the English scientist, later great literary master, Thomas Huxley, soon and often appeared in the defence of evolutionism. Huxley's brilliantly phrased and rigorously argued essays advanced the growing popularity of evolutionism as much as Spencer's academic backing and far more than the quiet creator of evolutionism, Charles Darwin.

The Ethics of Evolutionists: Although by no means confined to evolutionists, the ethics of the latter tend toward relativism or modern "situation ethics" (p.54 above). Relativists honor, in general, most or all of the ethical standards (Golden Rule, Justice, etc.) dealt with so far but insist that, in any given actual situation, the ethical action is never necessarily any single prescribed one but varies with the unique circumstances of that situation. Killing, for example, or stealing or lying might be ethically wrong in some situations while ethical in others. American law recognizes "relativism," as another example, in the much used -or abused- "insanity" plea for vicious murderers of entire families or even Senators, Robert Kennedy's assassin, Sirhan, and President Reagan's would-be assassin, Hinkley. And, more in line with common sense, the courts impose different punishments today for an old woman stealing cat tuna from a supermarket to supplement her own diet as compared to a financial tycoon stealing the savings of senior citizens by means of deceptive, convincing but worthless investment proposals.

Despite the fame and views of "might-makes-right" materialists such as Hobbes and Nietzsche, most materialist and evolutionist philosophers hew close to traditional ethical standards (as did the Stoics).

Auguste Comte and Positivism

Comte (1798-1857) lived through one of the most unstable periods of French history in terms of political changes and social upheaval. He was a child of the bloody French Revolution (1789), grew up in its aftermath of passion and emotional "causes," and displayed throughout his main work, Course of Positive Philosophy, a firm preference for facts and reason instead of emotional faith in religious or metaphysical abstractions. He rose up (somewhat dangerously, to him) against his many predecessors who spun doctrines, beliefs and passionate faith in them from mere abstractions, intuitions of visionaries and human hope of the masses for relief and salvation in these imagined abstractions (God, heaven, etc.). He was, expectedly and by understatement, not popular in his times with the clergy (whether Protestant or Catholic) or the reigning metaphysicians in the universities (a few unimportant and obscure scientists of the time appreciated his ideas). He died generally rejected by his academic colleagues and a popular target for contempt by the ignorant masses easily propagandized against his name and his stereotyped ideas (few of his contemporaries ever actually read Comte).

Comte's revolt was directed against metaphysics (both religious and philosophical) and its endlessly argued abstractions, none of which can be substantiated or empirically verified in any way -the arguments, wars, over them continue to destroy people meaninglessly. Comte was determined to develop and promote a method of human thinking aimed at eliminating human conflict over abstractions and replacing it with constructive solutions based on facts, reason and common sense. He coined the term "positivism" (as in emphasis on positive facts as sole legitimate basis for reasoning and conclusions) for his new approach.

According to Comte, human history developed in three stages in generally chronological order but greatly overlapping (many minds still operating in the first stage even in modern times): the first stage was the theological stage of human life guided and dominated by superstitions, priests' knowledge based on intuitive examination of stars or entrails or earlier sages' visions later legendary and "divinized" into firm religious belief - faith in such perpetuated by routine training of the young to orthodox ideas, monolithic reinforcement and peer pressure; the second stage was the metaphysical stage (mainly philosophers, not theologians), a radical advance over life by faith into life by reason as men attempted to understand the universe and their own nature but still with little systematic attention to empirical facts; the third, and final, stage, developing in modern times, is the stage of positive (factual) knowledge in which dogmatic assumptions and faith begin to become replaced by systematic examination of facts (science) and reasoning upon this solely factual base. Thus Comte's intellectual standards made him a pure form of materialist and placed him directly within the track of modern empiricism.* Comte is today known as the first sociologist.

Comte, as might be expected of any historical respecter of the facts of human relationships and societies and essentially in the tradition set by Aristotle, advocated an ethics similar to Aristotle's "golden mean" (p.63) and based, also, upon traditional standards (Golden Rule, Justice, etc.) insofar as these were deducible by reason (as they are) and the positive experience of human history.

Materialism and evolutionism were two major forms of the empiricist tradition invented by Aristotle and popularized by Locke. The most powerful form of empiricism, however, especially in its effects on ethics and moral philosophy, was Utilitarianism -later called Pragmatism. This stream of empiricism was developed by Bentham and J.S. Mill in England and Peirce, James and Dewey in America. We will deal with it later but, before that, a brief discussion of Idealism, especially Kant, is necessary.

MODERN IDEALISM

"Idealism," in the history of philosophy, is a technical term meaning the very opposite of empiricism.** Although appearing in many forms, idealism questions or denies the very possibility of the senses to produce valid knowledge of reality and therefore relies upon innate ideas in the mind for man's only valid knowledge. Ideas, not the senses, are the source of human knowledge; hence the term "idealism." Platonism is an early and major form of idealist philosophy and, to a great extent, the model for all forms of idealism since (please review pp.99-100 for an explanation of Plato's "theory of Ideas").

Immanuel Kant

Kant is one of the five gigantic minds of Western philosophy mentioned above (p.119). He was born and died in Konigsberg (1724-1804), travelled never any further than thirty miles from that German town in his lifetime, taught at its university and wrote nothing of importance

---

* Ludwig Feuerbach (1804-1872), born in Germany about the same time as Comte's birthdate and ultimately of the same materialist temperament, must be mentioned here. Unlike Hegel and Marx, Feuerbach is not well known but Marx, fascinated with him linked his materialism with Hegelian dialectic to form Marxist dialectical materialism ("Communism") which dominates half the world today.

** The term is used here solely as defined; with no connotations of necessary nobility, personal dedication to causes, etc.

until almost age sixty. But, when he finally set pen to paper, his major works were published rapidly (Critique of Pure Reason, Critique of Practical Reason and Metaphysics of Morals, published about 1787)and became a profound influence on virtually every Western thinker since. To understand Kant and Kantianism, we must consider the two men who most directly influenced his thinking, Descartes and Rousseau.

As noted earlier (p.119), Rene Descartes, determined to establish human knowledge on a rock of certitude instead of the often-deceived senses and the mere probabilities they provided, began his philosophical system as an idealist; searching for bottom rock ideas in the mind about which there could be no doubt as to their certitude and validity. His "Cogito, ergo sum" ("I am sure I am thinking and my existence at least as a thinking being is, therefore, certain") was the foundation idea, absolutely certain, upon which he could with mathematical certitude deduce other ideas in logical series until systematically all that was to be known about reality would indeed be known (by essentially the same mental methods he used to develop Cartesian geometry and others used to discover calculus*). Thus, soon, his deductions proved the existence of God and, since God placed our sense images of an extended, physical world in our minds, therefore bodies and matter do actually exist, our own bodies physical mechanisms independent of our minds but somehow linked to them.** This "link" became the fatal flaw in Cartesian philosophy, establishing a "dualism" of mind and body that was never solved in his own work or his immediate followers' (Malebranche, Spinoza, etc.). Mind, as known by ideas, and body, as known by the senses, could not be reconciled into a unity; thus, man could be only mind (body an illusion) or only a mechanical body and brain, not both. Descartes himself resisted this conclusion and strove hard and always to maintain the being of man as a mind/body unity. But the generations of philosophers following him felt forced, for reasons of logic and consistency, to view man as essentially either mind only (idealism) or body and matter only (empiricism and materialism).***All of Kant's thinking struggled with this basic dilemma posed by Descartes.

Jean Jacques Rousseau (1712-1778), most strangely, was the other powerful influence upon Kant. Strangely, because Rousseau, emotional

---

* Newton and Leibniz, a generation after Descartes, independently deduced the mathematical principles and methods of calculus.

** Descartes' subtle but rigorous reasoning is lengthy (see his works on p.120,footnote) and beyond our scope here. But, essential in his approach is that the physical world, including man's body, is not known through sensation but by ideas of it in the mind (idealism).

*** Thus, from Descartes' dualism, arose modern empiricism (Locke,etc. see p.120) stressing sensation as basic and idealism (Kant, Hegel).

French writer and passionate believer in what he sensed and experienced, was so different in temperament from the cool, logical idealist we find in Kant's writings. Unlike Kant, Rousseau wrote early and much (Emile, his book on education, Social Contract, on the ideal government, Causes of Inequality Among Men, etc.). Clearly a deist, and technically a citizen of Geneva (for protection from heretic-hunters), Rousseau was the French intellectual of his day along with Voltaire.* His strong feelings permeated Rousseau's writings. He was incensed at how common men have been oppressed by both states and churches, all human freedom obliterated by arbitrary laws and church persecutions. He demanded a radical reform and restitution of the natural order where all could pursue happiness by their own work, desires, reason and feelings. This, he said, is a matter of human right -and will prevail, despite all states, churches and governments. (The underscored expressions appear often in America's Declaration of Independence and Constitution, and, later, in the French literature just preceding the French Revolution.) Rousseau's books, Social Contract and New Heloise, written in the colorful and vivid style Rousseau became known for, greatly influenced the American and French revolutions, and Kant.

In Kant's mind, a strange, but most productive, relationship grew among three opposites: Descartes, Rousseau and Kant himself. Descartes provided the intellectual framework, Rousseau the spirit of freedom and human rights, Kant the system of thought combining rigor and intellectual freedom in philosophy (not only for idealists but especially, as it happened, for empiricists and pragmatists**). Kant was especially enticed by Rousseau's style of writing. His biographers note that Kant abandoned his precise clock-like routine for three days to read and reread Emile "first to enjoy its style and beauty, then to comprehend its concepts." Little of Rousseau's easy and moving style of writing is in Kant's books (unfortunately; those who read Kant suffer his style in the quest for his powerful ideas); but Rousseau's spirit of human freedom and rights permeates them.

Kant's Critiques

The term "Critiques," as used in the titles of Kant's works, is very technical, not merely descriptive. In the philosophical world of Kant's time, a "critique" was a powerful, sometimes fatal, usually final, pub-

---

* Francois Voltaire, the famous French dramatist and historian, who shared the French intellectual stage with Rousseau all his life (both died in the same year, 1778), originated the perceptive expression: "If there is indeed no God, man must invent one" (for his psychological needs for security and peace of mind). Voltaire loved freedom.

** Wm. James, great American pragmatist (below), is a prime example.

lished position taken on an important issue, widely publicized as one's final view of it and argued with the most rigorous, logical and precise thinking the writer was capable of. Kant's critiques, thought out over a lifetime and finally published near the end of it, so exceeded the usual norms of rigor and rational argument that they astounded his world and changed its directions (America's scientists, especially Einstein, acknowledged credit to Kant for new and fundamental directions in their thinking).

In his Critiques of pure and practical reason, Kant (left) concluded that pure reason can produce certitude about its ideas and their relationships but cannot know the real (external) world which he called "things-in-themselves" or "noumena" as distinct from "phenomena" (things as they appear or are perceived). There is (probably) a real external world but man's mind, in the very act of forming knowledge about it, changes it as it exists in his mind from the way it actually exists prior to being known. It is something like what scientists encounter in using powerful microscopes to examine a tiny organism: the strong light energy of the scope alters the organism on the slide before and as it is examined; it is not exactly the same as known as it was before being known. This is a very rough analogy to the marvelously sophisticated process reasoned out in Kant's Critiques (and beyond the scope of this book). Theoretical physicists, like Einstein (who knew Kant's work intimately and often drew from it), routinely build "mental models" of molecules, pictured as circles of atoms, electrons, and other named particles, knowing well that the mental models, though useful, are in no way a literal representation of the "thing-in-itself."

In Kant's view, our knowledge of the real world consists partly of "something" really out there and external to the mind (noumena) but mainly of qualities and attributes imposed upon it as and in the very act of knowing it: attributes such as quantity, substance, space, time, etc. In sum, Kant maintained that the human mind cannot know reality as it really is; only as organized into logical groups of attributes mainly products of mind. Reality, at least as we can know it, is solely of the mind. Thus Kant earns the name of a classic idealist, along with Plato. He totally rejected the "naive" realism of those who assume the external world is literally the same as it is perceived through the senses.

Despite the inability of pure reason to produce genuine knowledge of reality, Kant conceded that our practical life, as we sense and experience it, goes on and must be explained. This is the role of man's practical reason which postulates (assumes) the existence of the real, external world since in no other way can the appearances of sensation (phenomena) be rationally explained. But still it would be grossly naive to assume that our perceptions and "mental organizing" of things-in-themselves are literal representations of them as they actually are; this latter simply cannot be known.* Thus, from a practical viewpoint (which includes ethics, as we shall see), man's mind must interpret its perceptions and concepts of "reality" as best it can and often "act as if" these were valid representations of the external universe (in somewhat the same way we speak and act as if the "sun rises in the East" when modern evidence shows it is the Earth rising about and over the sun, just the opposite of our naive perceptions; or we "see" a grain of sand as a solid mass when, under a microscope, it is mainly empty space as is most of the material world according to theoretical physicists).** Thus Kant's theoretical mind was in profound conflict with his practical mind: "things are not what they seem;" but the practical mind must review, critique, sort out and interpret the "appearances" about him for the practical purposes of life as experienced.

Analogies, starting with Plato's classic of the "cave" (p. 100 above and Descartes' "dreams" (p. 100), lend plausibility to the idealists' deep scepticism about man's naive tendency to accept uncritically things as they seem. The often-used analogy among recent philosophers is the man born with blue-tinted glasses who is, of course, convinced that all trees, animals, men and other realities are really blue; so convinced that he would stake his life -and others' lives- upon it as "true" (if they disagree). Critically considered, blue-tinted eyes will never see the world as it really is any more than green-tinted or other-tinted eyes. If, as Kant reasoned, the entire mind of man is "tinted" by its own filters and "organizing categories" of thinking, then it likewise knows nothing of the world as it really is. But history is full of differently-tinted human views, especially religious and political perceptions, in defense of which men have been killing each other with fervent belief and determination since their beginnings. Men have fought wars, died and killed by the millions, persecuted and excommunicated the enemies of orthodox truth over such theories ("tinted" views and beliefs) as a

---

* Kant's reasoning is infinitely more complex than its oversimplification here. His analyses of a priori propositions (contributing certitude) and synthetic propositions (based on experience), of the categories of the mind's operations (substance, causality, space, etc.) and of conceptual systems uniting these into meaningfulness are the sophisticated ideas forming the thought of all great thinkers since his time. Here we can only suggest the general direction.

** Physics now views bodies (mass) as illusion and mainly pure energy.

geocentric universe (p.118), infallibility of the pope (p.114), divine rights and power of kings (p.121), indulgences (p.72) and hundreds of other views of man and the universe. Rousseau deplored man's cruel inhumanity and intolerance (as, of course, did Locke), wrote movingly against it and for freedom of mind, and became a major influence upon Kant.

The Categorical Imperative (Kant's "General Law" Standard)

Kant's ethical theories were developed in his Metaphysics of Morals and derived from his analysis of practical reason (as above). Briefly, and in essence, Kant accepts on practical grounds (despite his theories of pure reason) the necessity of traditional Christian and Aristotelian rational ethics (virtues and standards as above) as essential to man's daily life for civilized order and relationships rather than chaos and anarchy. The centerpiece of his ethics, however, is his concept of the "categorical imperative," an ethical command wholly unconditional, inherently known by reasoning about human experience, commonly referred to now as his "General Law Standard." Which has been explained earlier (pp.68-69).

Idealism After Kant

After Kant's death, thinkers of every variety, from idealist to empiricist, religious to atheist, absolutist to pragmatist, found some fundamental insight in his writings to expand upon and interpret anew. As noted above, theoretical scientists, like Einstein and Heisenberg, found in Kant's notions of mind as "organizer" of reality the conceptual basis for their own "theoretical models;" Protestant theologians, like Niebuhr and Karl Barth, found in Kant's "leap of faith" from the impotence of pure reason to the necessity of practical assumptions (belief) a new and sophisticated justification for religious faith over reason; American pragmatist philosophers, especially William James, found their sound conceptual foundation in Kant's "act-as-if" of the practical reason.*
And, most of all, the absolute forms of idealism (Fichte, Schelling and Hegel) were easily and enthusiastically deduced from Kant's devastating critique of pure reason as a source of knowledge of the real world.

---

* Einstein's theory of relativity contradicted men's "common sense" views of space, time, matter (mass) and energy; Werner Heisenberg (German physicist, b. 1901) received the Nobel Prize for his theory of quantum mechanics (published at age 24) and soon after proposed his "principle of uncertainty" relating to the conflict between matter as it is and as it is observed; Reinhold Niebuhr and Karl Barth founded liberal Protestantism; James is discussed below.

Johann Fichte, who died ten years after Kant, was quick to deduce absolute idealism from Kant's Critiques. If man's pure reason is flawed and cannot know reality (noumena), then why just postulate or assume such a noumenal external world? Obviously the latter cannot be proved to be; and thus must be rejected as non-existent and merely an illusion of the senses -which merely create and "imagine" an external world. As much as we think it to be and want it to be, no such external world really exists at all, except in our imaginations and mental concepts. A practical conclusion, however, emerged from Fichte's analysis of the mind and its workings: that men operate on faith (usually blind) rather than by knowledge and reason; thus Will, not Mind, is the critical factor in the world of men. Reason is useless and academic; those with the strongest Will control the world of men. The last years of his life were devoted to the theme that the German race was -or should be- the most powerful Will for action and dominance over men. Nietzsche (p. 124) dramatically improved upon this theme and Hitler tried to implement it.

Friedrich Schelling, Friedrich Schleirmacher, Friedrich Schlegel and Georg Hegel followed Fichte (and, of course, Kant) elaborating various forms of idealism with, usually and ironically, powerful practical consequences. Except for Kant, Hegel became most influential. And deservedly, in the sense of his integrity as a pure philosopher. G. W.F. Hegel (Georg Wilhelm Friedrich), preferring initials to full names as is customary among military officers today, returned to the pure origins of idealism, Plato and Kant. Kant's Critique of Pure Reason was his bible, to be thrust and deviated from, not followed literally (a common mind-set of new founders of new Christian religions, based on the Bible but expanding and interpreting it liberally by their own lights) and Hegel rejected Kant's other works on Practical Reason and Morals as unworthy of the master's masterpiece (on Pure Reason). In his first major work, Logic (1817), Hegel concluded that thought and reality are one, the external world is purely a product of mind, and the minds of all are simply parts of a universal mind, God.* Hegel's most influential concept was his "historical dialectic" in which opposites (thesis and antithesis) collide, destroy each other, and form a synthesis of a new order which itself becomes a new thesis generating its opposite, and so on. As noted (p. 129), Marx combined Hegel's idealist "dialectic" with Feuerbach's materialism to develop "dialectical materialism." Hegel's influence on ethics was indirect insofar as it contributed to ethical (or unethical) systems such as Marxism (and Nietzsche).

---

* A view often called Pantheism, the idea that all things are really an actual part and manifestation of a supreme being, God. For different reasons, Pantheism is common in Eastern thought.

MODERN PRAGMATISM

One of the most common forms of empiricism (see Aristotle, p. 103, and Locke, p. 120) has been the philosophy of pragmatism. (Other forms of empiricism are materialism, evolutionism,* Stoicism, etc. as above.) The most influential pragmatists, often entitling their philosophies differently although substantially similar in their basic pragmatic thrust, are Protagoras, Bentham, J.S. Mill (utilitarianism), Peirce (pragmaticism), James (pragmatism) and Dewey (experimentalism).

Protagoras, the First Pragmatist

Although the pragmatic temperament ("seek that which works") is universal throughout human history, pragmatism as a systematic ethics and philosophy begins with the Greek philosopher, Protagoras (410 BC). Protagoras spent his life traveling the cities of Greece, teaching and lecturing for fees (for a living!). Plato faulted him (see dialogues Protagoras and Theaetetus) for accepting money for sharing knowledge, a "trading" in knowledge (Plato was independently wealthy whereas Protagoras was not -nor are most modern university professors). Protagoras was not a pure or doctrinaire sceptic (like the Greek "cynics" and "sophists" of his time) nor an atheist; he was a moderate sceptic and an agnostic (the difference is critical: atheists "know" there is no God; agnostics simply doubt whether this can be known one way or the other).

Protagoras was a moderate sceptic whose views seem best described in Locke's "Degrees of Assent" (p. 121). Certitude is rare; only degrees of it can exist in a critical mind, depending on the degree of evidence available -or possible. The philosophic mind must resist the naive urge for certitude as well as the cynical surrender to total doubt (nihilism). Protagoras lived in the difficult middle-road between these extremes. For example, he begins his work, On the Gods, as follows:

> "With regard to the gods, I cannot feel sure either that they are or that they are not, nor what they are like; for there are many things that hinder such knowledge, both the obscurity of the subject and the shortness of human life."

---

* The classic economists, at least in their discipline, are social evolutionists (like Spencer, p. 127). Adam Smith (Wealth of Nations, 1776), a professor of moral philosophy before becoming the world's first systematic economist, based economics on pure competition, the "survival of the fittest" producers for their own profit (the incentive) and the best products at lowest prices (for the economy as a whole); Smith's economics, still the theoretical foundation of pure capitalism, often called "laissez faire" and raw individualism, called for survival by individual effort -and no government help. Th. Malthus, Population, said the same for survival.

Within the context of his moderate scepticism, the central statement of Protagoras' pragmatism is:

"Man is the measure of all things, of things that are that they are, and of things that are not that they are not."

Historians of philosophy have generally interpreted this statement as a rejection of absolute or objective truth for truth based on the subjective perceptions or judgments of each individual human (relativism, see p.54). Each man is the final measure of truth, determining it as he sees it. This led Protagoras in practice to support the democratic political systems of the Greeks city states: despite different views, men cannot exist in any sort of civilized order, without chaos, unless, as a practical matter, all abide by the ethical standards, codes and laws of the majority. Truth, in practice, at any given time and place, is relative and depnds on the subjective views of the majority -or, if this fails, the single view of a dictator (strong man) after he restores order out of chaos. (See p. 16.)*

Bentham and Utilitarianism

Less known than other famous modern pragmatists (except Peirce, below), Jeremy Bentham (1748-1832) followed Locke in his empiricist temperament and preceded Spencer as a social philosopher; and he was the founder of modern pragmatism (which he came to call utilitarianism). His major work, Principles of Morals and Legislation, published in 1789 (the year of the French Revolution), approached ethics as a macro-system, advocating norms for government and legislation. He was greatly influenced by the nature and dynamics of the American Revolution and the new American constitutions. He concluded that the purpose of any government and its legislation is to promote the "greatest happiness of the greatest number of its people," a continuing optimizing balance between public and private interests toward the best good of the most people. He was enthusiastic about and admired the new American government as 'the only good government' because it clearly sought these ends.

Three principles came to govern Bentham's system of ethics: happiness (equivalent to "pleasure"), the "association principle" (long before modern psychologists), and his "greatest-good-for-the-greatest-number" norm.

Men naturally seek, he said, their maximum (or optimum) good

* Except in the ancient Greek city states, modern England and Japan and several European nations, and in America, democracy has rarely been successful for more than a very short time. Even Aristotle (Politics) was very sceptical about its survivability; Plato (in his Republic and elsewhere) rejected it outright as absurd and favored a strong, enlightened and benevolent monarch as the only way to maintain order among unruly humans. Most of human history seems to prove it - as in South American and African nations today.

as personal pleasure or happiness, which Bentham called a "utility." A man's accumulation of such utilities over a lifetime (his pleasures and times of happiness), minus his pains and times of unhappiness, sum up the net value of his life. Bentham later abandoned the term 'utility' as stressing excessively the quantity of pleasures rather than their more important quality - but the term stuck and his version of pragmatism is still called utilitarianism. Bentham defined a "utility" as "any source of pleasure, happiness, benefit, good, or advantage, or any means of avoidance of pain, evil, disadvantage, loss of benefit or unhappiness." (Inclusion of 'avoidance of pain' in his definition covered both sides of the controversy over whether happiness is something positive or merely the absence of pain - a mainly, and typically, argument over the words and semantics of an issue rather than its substance.)

Bentham began his analysis of human ethics on the macro level of societal relationships; and concluded with the norm of the "greatest good for the greatest number." Implied in this idea and conclusion is the notion of "marginal utility," developed by the economists, such as Adam Smith. And an eternal issue with politicians as they balance the various utilities for their diverse constituencies (especially their numbers and voting power). But "marginal utility" applies to individuals too. An act of a man often causes both pleasure and pain, the latter usually consequent upon the former (as a morning-after hangover following the joy of the night-before party or the lifetime responsibility for a child following a few minutes' impulsive sexual pleasure - the party and the new child often linked as respectively cause and effect). Thus, the core of Bentham's ethics (for individuals) is the evaluation of long-range consequences against the pleasure of any immediate act (the essence of the "Long-range Utility standard," p. 70 above, as expressed by American pragmatists such as James and Dewey). Bentham developed methods for calculating the utility vs the dis-utility of any human action (often called his "calculus of pleasure") by evaluating the pleasure and pain effects of any action based on seven criteria: intensity of pleasure, its duration, the certainty or ranges of probability of it, propinquity, its fecundity (probability of causing consequent pleasures), its purity (not contaminated by unpleasurable effects) and extent (potential for sharing it with others).

By the "association principle" Bentham sought societal order and proper control of a society's members. For example, a man might wish to steal; but, if laws and their enforcement make it certain that theft will end in pain (jail or worse), he will associate theft with pain, and thus avoid it. (Bentham would smile knowingly at the failure of the criminal justice system currently freeing and rewarding criminals in America.)

Thus Bentham's ethics evaluates the goodness of an action by its long range consequences for the happiness of individuals and society as a whole. This is the essence of pragmatism, meaning, literally, the judging of an act -or anything- by the criterion of whether it works or not.

John Stuart Mill (1806-1873)

James Mill was 25 years younger than Bentham and his ardent disciple; and friend, too (Bentham gave James Mill a fine home, formerly owned by the poet Milton, and helped in the education of his son, John Stuart). John, a genius by any standards, was educated from birth with an intensity that drove him to a nervous breakdown. He learned Greek by age 3, studied Plato's dialogues at 7, taught his sister Latin at 8, and so on. At this young age, he shocked a conservative conversational group around his father's dinner table, who were discussing the long-standing thomistic argument for the existence of God as first cause of everything, by asking innocently "Who caused God?" With sour glance at John, his father quickly changed the subject.

Mill (left, and always now referring to John Stuart) was first a master logician. His Logic, including his conceptualization of scientific method for the first time and still standard today, was published in 1843. "Mill's methods" of agreement, difference, etc. still underlie modern science and statistics.

But it is Mill's major work in ethics (Utilitarianism, 1861) that concerns us here. In it, he faulted Bentham for stressing the quanity of pleasures or happiness over their more important element, their quality. Actually, as noted above, Bentham had tried to correct this impression -especially with his seven criteria of happiness. But not to Mill's, or other critics' satisfaction. Mill admired Bentham's general pragmatic direction but contested his "calculus of pleasure" and his seeming stress upon quantifying "utilities." For Mill, it was the human quality of happiness that must be emphasized over Bentham's seeming quantitative approach. Else, Mill said, it would not matter whether the animal enjoying itself were a man or a pig. "It is better," he said, "to be an only partially fulfilled human being (in terms of sensual satisfaction) than a fully satisfied pig; better to be Socrates dissatisfied than a dull and insensitive fool fully satisfied." Thus, Mill modified Bentham's pragmatism and "calculus" to stress, as utilities, the specifically human joys and happiness proper to a human life (a full circle back to Aristotle's concept of human happiness, p. 63 and 104 above). Mill's version of pragmatism, which he ironically kept calling "utilitarianism" despite the quantitative tone implied and rejected in his own Utilitarianism book, emerges as fully compatible with and greatly identical to the "golden mean" of Aristotle (p.63). In the very broad spirit of the term, Aristotle could be called a pragmatist -along with Bentham, Mill, James and Dewey (and with Charles Peirce's conclusions -but not his methods).

Charles Peirce, the First American Pragmatist

While his friend, William James, was first a psychologist and later the acknowledged leader of pragmatic philosophy in America -and also Europe, Charles Peirce was first, even in his early twenties, and always, the master of logic (including especially mathematics) and a profound philosopher in the classic tradition. Peirce is pictured at left at the age of twenty. His version of pragmatism is only a small part of his intellectual work but, still, the most fundamental development of the essentials of pragmatism before or since his writings. Of the three famed and great American pragmatist philosophers (Peirce, James and Dewey) Peirce excelled as the profound thinker; James and Dewey, albeit gifted with powerful minds as well as the will and writing style to apply and popularize American pragmatism, were great but not genius minds as was Peirce. Despite, or possibly because of, his rare power of mind, Peirce is generally unknown today as a philosopher, mathematician or pragmatist. Ironically, he was notoriously inept in the way he lived his own practical life: he was so solely dedicated to the development of his ideas, in the privacy of his study, that he found practical projects like securing a professorship at Harvard University not worth filling out the forms or dealing seriously with the pedantic professors governing the intellectual but (Peirce felt) superficial thinking and research there. (William James secured such a professorship at Harvard and used it as his base for establishing himself and pragmatism throughout America.) Instead, Peirce earned his living as a mathematician with the U.S.Coast and Geodetic Survey for thirty years but devoted every moment before and after his job hours to his really important hours of developing and thinking out his philosophy and his version of pragmatism.

Peirce began with Kant and his powerful concept of *a priori* propositions (p. 133 above). *A priori* propositions, always products of the mind relating its ideas to each other with absolute certitude (such as 2+3=5), are useful -and essential- in the mind's manipulations of ideas; but, like Kant, Peirce called that mind naive which assumed such ideas or certitude possible about the world of reality. He insisted that it is foolish to talk of "true" or "false" statements when dealing with the real, and external, world in which men live. Like Kant, Peirce viewed all statements about the real world as merely *provisional* as to their truth; unlike Kant, he was convinced that truth about the real world was obtainable -and at increasing degrees of *probability**- by testing any statement against the cumulative bank of actual human experience, especially human acts and their historical *consequences*. Consequences were critical as a continuing experimental *test* of what statements and ideas proved valid vs. invalid along the span of probability about each one's real worth. Only time and testing would prove out the worth of any human idea. (John Dewey later converted this method into his new "experimentalism" which virtually controlled American philosophy and educational methods in schools and universities for decades.) This slow, methodical and patient approach to the discovery of truth -and the probabilities rising or declining based upon experiential testing of all such "potential" truths- was called "fallibilism" by Peirce.

Of the three great American pragmatists, Peirce exhibits by far the greatest intellectual power and the most profound philosophic inquiry; James and Dewey arrived at pragmatism by mainly practical individual and social necessity, not by the purely philosophic analysis developed by Peirce (who disassociated himself from James' methods, even insisted on calling his approach "pragmaticism" instead of pragmatism and, in turn, was rejected by the main stream of philosophy in his time**).

Like Descartes, Peirce examined the problem of "how to make ideas clear" (the title of his first major article on pragmatism) and concluded (totally opposed to Descartes -and Kant) that the sole meaning

* Peirce was profoundly influenced by Blaise Pascal (left) who invented theories of probability (c. 1650), excelled as a great French philosopher of his time and influenced the field of statistics profoundly -despite his early death (at age 39). Peirce built his notion of truth on the degrees of probability about any statement's truth, not the naive belief that a statement is either purely true or false (except for *a priori* propositions such as those of mathematics).

** A collection of *Peirce's writings* was published after his death in 1914, the publication appearing not until 1940.

of any idea is the sum total of its effects or consequences (often today called the operational definition of an idea). An idea is made clear only by examining the total effects of the idea. For example, "hard" is a meaningless idea until described in terms of an object's resistance against being scratched, broken or otherwise penetrated. Over many years, Peirce's effort to subject ideas and their real meanings to his operational test of clearness led him to reject many common ideas (especially metaphysical and religious terms) as literally meaningless, i.e. having no real or operational meaning at all.* (Peirce thought it useless human tragedy that so much war and misery has been caused by violent conflicts over unclear and meaningless ideas.)

Peirce's major interest, as a philosopher, was epistemology (p.66) and the human search for truth wherever that led. His ethics derive from his philosophy as pragmatic, similar to James' but arrived at by more intellectualistic (analytical) methods. Like all ideas, moral ideas have meaning only in terms of their consequences in the real world. Thus an action can be called ethical if its effects ultimately, over the long range of experience, actually contribute to man's highest ends, human happiness. Accepting the specifically human concept of happiness, as developed by Aristotle (p.63), Peirce's ethics becomes essentially the long-range utility standard (p.70).

William James (1842-1910)

Although Peirce established the foundations of pragmatic thought in America, his eccentric personality and life style barred him from universities and publishers. He seemed to have little interest in applying his pragmatism to the issues of human life, especially psychology and ethics. Application and popularization of pragmatism became the life work of William James, generally (and correctly) regarded as the most influential of all American pragmatists.

James' publications of many books and articles, his many lectures and his professorship at Harvard established him as the intellectual leader of two fields at the turn of the century: psychology and philosophy. He enjoyed the benefit of being raised in highly cultured surroundings. His father (Henry, Sr., a theologian) and his brother (Henry, Jr., who

---

* The best recent introduction to Peirce's quite complicated philosophy is James Feibleman's An Introduction to the Philosophy of Charles S. Peirce (M.I.T., 1969). Peirce's operational approach to determining the meaning of ideas influenced A.J. Ayer and the Logical Positivists (the "Vienna Circle") who concluded that most metaphysical and religious terms were, upon analysis, "non-sense" terms, i.e. terms spoken but lacking any real meaning or sense.

became one of the great American novelists) enriched William's life and kept him stimulated by the historical and most recent intellectual trends in world literature. This included, especially, the most recent

intellectual developments in Europe. Henry, the novelist and writer, was a constant traveler and was more at home in France and England than America, his birthplace. William James (left) visited Europe often and became personally acquainted with its top thinkers (Bain, Spencer, Wundt, von Helmholtz, etc.) and its traditions, especially Kantianism. He was always a man of vibrant energy, variety of interests, painstaking effort to do best whatever he attempted and, at the same time, a man of intense sensitivity - living close and often to nervous breakdowns. In his youth, he devoted much of his time and energies to painting (his later writings in psychology and philosophy, famous for their clear and sharp prose style, manifest always his visual manner of conceiving and expressing the most abstract ideas of psychology and philosophy).* Then, for years, he studied medicine and science, fixing finally upon psychology as his central focus. His Principles of Psychology (1890), still sound and recently reprinted, stands as the classic work in that new field.

Ultimately, however, James turned his lifetime energies to philosophy and, then, to the development of American pragmatism. His writing was prolific: The Will to Believe (1897), Varieties of Religious Experience (1902), Pragmatism (1907), A Pluralistic Universe (1909), Problems of Philosophy (1911), Essays in Radical Empiricism (1912) and many others. In many ways, James was not the intellectual genius that Peirce was; but few philosophers excel James in his efficient and professional approach to the production of ideas and their distribution in the media available to thinkers and writers.

The Pragmatism of William James

All of James' mature writing exhibits the struggle between what he himself termed the two mental "temperaments" of man: facts vs feeling. James himself was a man of deep religious feeling within the Protestant tradition (his father, indeed, a theologian); but, he was also trained

* Reading James reminds one of Kant's joy and enthusiasm in just reading the style and prose of Rousseau (p.131). Whether one agrees or disagrees with his ideas, James' style of writing about them must be admired as superb English prose. His abstractions are always converted into concrete images and examples, refreshingly clear and interesting (unlike most philosophers, especially the idealists Kant and Hegel, who are often unintelligible). In the tradition of James, this book uses examples often to clarify ideas.

in medicine and as a scientist where facts, not feelings, generate conclusions about life and death. The tension, often intense, between the two temperaments pervades most of James' books –and even their titles. For example, in Pragmatism the fact-oriented temperament dominates whereas in Will To Believe it is the religion- and Kantian-inspired man of feeling "overcoming" logic and facts in a leap of faith to certitude about himself, his fate and the fate of mankind. (By strange combination of ideas –but psychologically sound, willing to believe and to act accordingly often becomes the practical and most pragmatic thing to do.)* James coined the terms "tough-minded" and "tender-minded" as descriptive of these two basic human temperaments.

James' formulation of pragmatism is essentially the same as Peirce's: the true meaning of an idea consists of its total effects if it were considered as if it were true and used. Kant's influence (p.133), acting as if an idea is true when reason cannot prove it, is clear and acknowledged by James often. Unlike Kant, James relies upon the pragmatic test of an idea's consequences as the criterion of truth. As James himself summarized his views in Pragmatism (quotes are from the chapter "Pragmatism's Conception of Truth"): "The pragmatic method tries to interpret each idea by tracing its respective practical consequences... If no differences can be traced between the consequences of two ideas, then they are practically the same and it makes no practical difference which one I believe." James shunned the metaphysical controversies of philosophers (and theologians) over such ideas as God's nature, sin, natural law, etc. as usually meaningless; although, in his Will to Believe, strongly influenced by Kant, James advocates belief in God's existence, not because it can be proved rationally, but because it has the practical effect of making life happier, more successful and psychologically secure (one is reminded of Voltaire's apt remark, p.131). James also advocated a high ethical code for the same practical reasons: good ethics in the long run manifest good practical consequences.

James, of course, rejects any ethics as objective or absolute (p.54) (Peirce accepted the possibility of such). Instead, James was a relativist as, for example, in these key statements:

> "The 'true' briefly is only the expedient in the way of our thinking, just as the 'right' and 'good' are only the expedient in the way of our behaving. Expedient in almost any fashion; and ex-

---

* Chapter 14 of this author's The Theory and Practice of Managing, concerning personal methods of career and personal development, draw explicitly from key concepts in James' Principles of Psychology and Will to Believe. James' ideas about self-development by acts of will, cultivating of positive habits, etc. can change a man's life.

pedient in the long run and on the whole." (Emphasis James')

Thus James subscribes to the Long-Range Utility Standard (p.70 above). Despite the seeming reservations implied in the word "almost," here is James' next statement:

> "The 'absolutely' true, meaning what no farther experience of man will ever alter, is that ideal vanishing point towards which we imagine that all of our contemporary truths will some day converge.... Meanwhile we have to live today by what truth we can get today, and be ready tomorrow to call it falsehood. Ptolemaic astronomy, euclidean space, etc. were expedient (i.e.'worked well') for centuries, but human experience has boiled over those limits, and we now call these things only relatively true, or true within those borders of experience. 'Absolutely,' they are false; for we know that those limits were casual, and might have been transcended by past theorists just as they are by present thinkers."

The obvious implication is that the "truths" and "ethical absolutes" of the 20th century are no less relative than those of the 5th or 15th centuries and will be "transcended" in later centuries as human nature, its experience and its ethics, continue to develop and expand. James again

> "True ideas are those that we can assimilate, validate, corroborate and verify. False ideas are those that we can not. This is the practical difference... The truth of an idea is not a stagnant property inherent in it. Truth happens to an idea. It becomes true, is made true by events. Its verity is in fact an event, a process: the process namely of its verifying itself, its very verification and validation." (Emphasis James')

James' pragmatism was (and is) often criticized as crass selfishness, egoism and the justification of means by ends, quite apart from adherence to absolute principles. James would prefer the term "intelligent self-interest" (Adam Smith's economics is based on it -p.136) and human progress over stagnation. A later American pragmatist (Dewey) made pragmatism more respectable by changing its name (to Experimentalism) and stressing its positive benefit at a social, rather than merely individual, level.

John Dewey (1859-1952)

Dewey, like James, was a New Englander, pure American pragmatist and prolific writer. Just a few of his books are: Logical Theory (1903), Ethics (1908), How We Think (1910), Influence of Darwin on Philosophy (1910), Experimental Logic (1916), Democracy and Education (1916), Experience and Nature (1925), and Quest for Certainty (1929). In Common Faith, Dewey espouses a purely naturalistic and humanistic faith which he terms natural "religion."

In his early years, Dewey was intrigued by the dynamic dialectic that powered Hegel's philosophical system (p.135), although he rejected Hegel's idealist framework that contained it. Dewey, like all pragmatists, was at root an empiricist in the tradition of Aristotle and Locke -and, of course, Peirce and James. But the Hegelian dialectic led the young and the mature Dewey to think always in terms of large, dynamic social systems (rather than the issues of individuals stressed by James). Karl Marx, equally intrigued by Hegel, did the same but in a communist and socialistic context rather than the clearly democratic and free one always espoused by Dewey. And Dewey made the pragmatic test of continuous experimenting with social ideas his basic method, searching always for the real and practical consequences of every idea. Darwin, Spencer and the evolutionary thrust of man, still evolving, run deep in Dewey's books; social ideas and ethics itself survive or die by evolving appropriately to the dynamic development of the human mind, its changing environment and the new worlds it is constantly creating. As with James (quoted above), for Dewey truth is not stagnant but alters its nature, "happens" as an event in itself and becomes true as 'fit' to 'survive' in changing human times and environments. Ideas (social, philosophical, political, scientific or religious) that don't "work" for ultimate human welfare must -and will- be discarded. That is the key pragmatic -and evolution's- test of all men and ideas. An often quoted statement of Dewey's catches his spirit of thinking:

> "Every thinker puts some portion of an apparently stable world in peril and no one can wholly predict what will emerge in its place. If we once start thinking, no one can guarantee where we shall come out, except that many objects, ends and institutions are doomed."

EXISTENTIALISM

Of all philosophies, "Existentialism" is the most difficult to define because of both its vague conceptual roots and the wildly diverse forms it has taken. Its common roots are found in the age-old controversy over "existence" and "essence," reaching back to the early Greek philosophers Parmenides (who first posed the dilemma), Plato and Aristotle. But most philosophers have struggled with the controversy, especially Thomas Aquinas, and been forced to develop their own solution to this basic issue of essence vs existence and being vs becoming as central to the subsequent directions of their philosophies. (The field of philosophy dealing with this issue is called "Ontology" or, more broadly, "Metaphysics".) The amazingly diverse forms of existentialism run a range from the deeply religious Kierkegaard to the atheist Sartre, the theologian Karl Barth to the psychiatrist Freud and the Catholic existentialists (mainly in Europe) to philosophers of Will and raw power such as Nietzsche and Martin Heidegger (who justified and fueled the reign of Hitler). No general philosophy (or theology) contains such starkly opposite thinkers as are routinely found calling themselves modern "existentialists" (the only thing that comes close is Christian roots in the Bible and the radically diverse forms of that religion today).

Essence vs Existence, Being vs Becoming

Classic writings, books, debates and controversy over the ideas of essence, existence, being and becoming would fill a large library –and are beyond the scope of this book. It must suffice here to merely highlight the main points as they relate to modern existentialism. The first problem is that these key terms cannot be defined –they are too basic. Generally, however, every thing can be said to "exist" (if it does) and in a particular way (its nature or "essence," as existing as a horse or man with the natural properties of that "kind" of thing). "Being" means to exist and by a particular nature or essence. "Becoming" (change) is especially a shocking phenomenon to the intellect (filled with well-defined and stable ideas, i.e. descriptions of essences) since to become signifies birth of new "being" and death of old.

Existentialists have this in common: they charge that most historical philosophies and theologies stress essences over existence and becoming, firm and stable "being" (and ideas of it) over new, exciting and revolutionary "existence" coming to be –and challenging old ways of being. Although the term "existentialist" is only a century old, the first existentialist was the early Greek Heraclitus who, opposed to the eternal and unchanging "being" of Parmenides resting in the mind, declared that only becoming and change "exist" in reality; essences do not. Existentialism thus stands for movement of ideas and events over staid and stable "being" and *status quo*.

Kierkegaard

Soren Kierkegaard died young in 1855 at age 42 and, like Peirce, was generally unknown until many years after his death. His writings, *Philosophical Fragments* and *Post-scientific Philosophy*, finally became regarded as the serious beginnings of modern existentialism. He was deeply and emotionally religious in his own way but rejected orthodox (institutional) Christian religions as inhibiting man's inner feeling and personal experience or "existing" with God. The existing, living person and his experience are paramount, not stifling systems of abstract ideas (essences).

Sartre

Irrationalism (rejection of human reason as a guide for men) is implicit within existentialism, including Kierkegaard's version. Life and its meaning cannot be reasoned out; it must be felt and experienced - with no reference to abstract ideas or essences. One exists anew each day, growing in the life of inner feeling and experience, becoming a new existence. Jean Paul Sartre, 20th-century French philosopher, unlike Kierkegaard, became an atheist and glorified the life of inner feeling as well as sensation, testing the full range of experience in his novels and other writings. Existentialism, based entirely on inner subjective feeling, could thus take any direction -which it has in the wide diversity of existentialists today in literature, movies, cults and so on. Existentialism has little, if any, applicability to the scope of this book.

REFERENCES

1 Shorey, Paul, What Plato Said, 1958, p.21
2 Russell, Bertrand, History of Western Philosophy, 1945, p. 125
3 See the classic The Thirteenth, Greatest of Centuries.
4 See the new World Christian Encyclopedia, Oxford Univ. Press.

For Further Reading

- Brinton, Crane, History of Western Morals, 1959
- Ferm, V., History of Philosophical Systems, 1950
- Jaeger, Werner, Paideia: Ideals of Greek Culture; and his Aristotle
- Larson, Martin, Religions of the Occident, 1959
- Ross, W. D., Aristotle, 1949
- Taylor, A. E., Plato, 1957
- Weber, Alfred, The History of Philosophy, one volume
- And Russell and Shorey, as above, and see Bibliography.

QUESTIONS AND PROBLEMS

1. What are the major similarities and differences (if any) between the philosophies and ethics of the following pairs of thinkers?
   (a) Aristotle & Plato; (b) Plato & Christian thinkers; (c) Plato & Sartre; (d) Stoics & Hebrews; (e) Plato & Kant; (f) Kant & W. James (g) Descartes & Locke; (h) Bentham & Dewey; (i) Rousseau & Kant; (j) Marx & Dewey; (k) Galileo & Comte; (l) Peirce & J. S. Mill; (m) Augustine & Plato; (n) Aquinas & Galileo; (o) Spencer & Smith; (p) Calvin & W. James; (q) Epicurus & the Christian thinkers.
2. Project: Select and read your favorite book title of your favorite thinker in this chapter -and get a taste of the "real thing."
3. Define: categorical imperative; empiricism; idealism; law; ethics.

5 Applying Ethical Theories

The two previous and necessarily lengthy chapters establish our framework of ethical theories (conceptually in Chapter 3 and historically in Chapter 4). Now we move to the major purpose of this book which is to apply ethical theories to the business and organizational world of reality in America of the 1980s. As we shall see, application of theories is far more difficult than developing them in the abstract.

Knowledge vs Skill

Skill in a field of human activity, whether physical or mental, is far different -and usually more difficult- than mere knowledge of it. And skill does not always depend upon prior knowledge -although usually the understanding of an activity helps in doing it well. Many famous performers, for example, in athletics and dancing (baseball, ballet, etc.) have been poor coaches; they could hit homeruns or execute exquisite ballet turns by learned experience and instinct, but they didn't understand -and couldn't teach- the principles and knowledge underlying their skill. Reversely, many outstanding teachers, coaches and professors, with comprehensive knowledge of an art, are poor performers of the skills they teach. The top baseball hitter, Ted Williams, was a poor coach; a top professional football coach, Vince Lombardi, was a poor player. Knowledge of an art is not the same thing as the skill to do it. It is the same with ethics: expert knowledge of ethical theory is quite different from the solid skills (and will) to judge surely what is ethical in a here-and-now set of concrete circumstances and to will to do it. In the case of skills of ethical behavior, however, knowledge of theory -at least the essentials as summarized in this book's last two chapters- is usually necessary for consistent and deliberate judgment in the sure application of ethics. (No book without the essential theory, therefore, is adequate in the new field of business ethics and its applications.) You have the essential knowledge and theory (in the last two chapters); now we must examine the problems and skills of applying ethical theory.

Why Theories Work or Fail

Man could well be defined as a theory-inventing animal. A theory is a broad model or explanation of some reality (even including some purely mental things such as geometry to explain space). Most of man's early theories were religious models of the universe with a god(s) and specified relationships with him as explanations for observable events such as rain, death, fertility, thunder, sickness and so on. Man's unique capability is that he can communicate verbally, think and ask the question "why?" about everything within his experience. Even early man needed answers so intensely, to avoid the mental agony of "not understanding why" people got sick, died, etc., that he had to invent the answers (theories) as the satisfaction of that deep human need (see p. 121 and Voltaire's statement on p. 131). Thus rain came and crops grew because of minutely ritualized actions of men to please god (including human sacrifice). Then came the more modern religions (Hebrew, Christian, etc.) with more sophisticated, but still God-oriented, theories to explain man's life and its meaning.* Then the philosophers, using pure reasoning from human experience, developed such theories as Aristotle's, Plato's and Kant's (the entire previous chapter is mainly a profile of these). Finally, science and scientific method (Galileo, experimental physicists, chemists, etc.) developed theories based upon observable facts. Thus, atomic theory, genetic theory, Newton's laws of mechanics, Einstein's theory of relativity, Boyle's gas laws, etc, use models (mental, verbal or graphic) to explain the facts of the world as we actually experience it.

Today, all three basic approaches to theorizing (religion, philosophy and science) coexist, not always amicably but at least in a fair competition for the minds of men (i.e. in free, pluralistic lands like America).

Theories are often regarded as true or false, right or wrong, working or failing. The reasons lie within a number of factors which will pervade this chapter: the theory is simply in error (Ptolemaic, geocentric astronomy and creationsim based on literal interpretation of Bible); or the theory is merely tentative and subject to further refinement (the atomic theory as modified constantly over the past century); or theory is basically sound but <u>applied</u> with poor judgment, either wrongly or to the wrong situation. The latter is usually the reason for ethical misjudgments among business and other managers who genuinely wish to conform to high ethical standards but are unskilled in the analysis and application of them. Improved skills in ethical <u>analysis</u> and <u>applying</u>

---

* Anthropologists generally classify modern religions as those espousing <u>one</u> God as opposed to the polytheism of early Greece, etc.

ethical theory are the purpose of this chapter (and others that follow).

A Word on Good Will and Good Intention

In the following sections (and chapters) on improving one's skills in ethical analysis and application, the distinction made earlier (p.53) between knowing what is ethical and willing to do it is critical. We must assume throughout the book that managers and others reading it already have the good will and intention to wish and try to do the right thing, the ethical action, and that our aim here is to sharpen the skills of discovering, by sound ethical analysis, and thus knowing consistently, just what is the right and ethical action to pursue. This sense and will for personal integrity is not gained from a book, but brought to it, and lies in the most basic traits of every human being.* Robert Bartels, in his Ethics in Business (1963, p.3), expressed this theme well:

> "If a person tries to discover what is right and what is wrong, what is better or worse in a specific situation, and tries to act accordingly, then he has already made a very basic commitment. If one is commited to try to do right and avoid evil, he has already made the most necessary commitment to ethics. He may make mistakes, he may be misinformed, he may seek goals which differ from yours and mine, but by this very commitment -that for ethical reasons some things should be done and others avoided- he is taking a very big step." (Emphasis added)

A GENERAL SYSTEM OF ETHICAL THEORIES

Before applying ethical theories, we must deal with the issue of their huge and rich variety. Our previous chapter's profile shows thinkers and their ethics ranging all the way from religion to science, from Platonic Ideas to James' expediency, from Augustine's pure faith to Sartre's cynicism and life of sensation, and from Protagoras' form of pragmatism to Kant's idealism. How can one apply such diversity of theories to anything? Fortunately, for the purposes of this book, the confusing diversity lies mainly in the metaphysical systems of these diverse thinkers, these systems being that part of their ethical theories

---

* The trait theory of leadership, basing managerial effectiveness on a man's inner personal characteristics, always found 'integrity' as a necessary trait in any man's ultimate and long-range success as a practical manager. See Chapter 7 of this author's The Theory and Practice of Managing (1982) for full explanation and documentation as well as his article "A Reappraisal of Leadership Theory and Training," (Personnel Administrator, November, 1981).

providing the principles from which their ethical standards were finally derived; the ethical standards themselves reveal essential similarities. (This emerging pattern of similarity of ethical standards, despite huge diversity of fundamental philosophies and principles, was noted earlier in our discussion of Stoicism as related to Aristotle's "golden mean" standard -page 107 above.) The similarities of ethical standards are so specific and consistent as to permit the attempt at a "general system"* of ethical theories, based on the ethical standards arrived at rather than the philosophies, religions and principles from which they were derived.

A Common Thread of Ethical Standards

The key, then, to a practical use and application of ethical theory by managers (or anyone else) must be found by (1) systematizing the many and radically different theories by schemes of classification, and (2) discovering, through these systems of classifications, those central thrusts or common threads constituting a workable consensus of ethical values. It is the latter, then, that can be applied to business decisions by managers. Our focus, as usual, is mainly on American managers in the 1980s.

Given the multitude of ethical theories through history, many hundreds of classifications of them are possible (for example, by time, by religion, by geographical region, by number of adherents, etc. and by any combination of such bases). Most such classifications into systems are mainly of academic and research interest. Two, however, are useful for our practical purposes of application to the real business world: (1) the classification of ethical theories according to their ultimate sources (the systems of religion, philosophy or metaphysics as first principles), in order to clarify and acknowledge their great diversity; and (2) the classification of ethical standards (i.e. the final results as norms of human action). It is the latter that reveals useful common threads and sufficient consensus about ethics for our purposes of practical application.

---

* We are drawing here explicitly from "General Systems Theory," a new field originated by Ludwig von Bertalanffy ("General System Theory," General Systems Journal, Vol. 1, 1956). See, also, Norbert Wiener (Cybernetics, M.I.T., 1961) who pioneered systems concepts as holistic information systems (which run our electronic world of communications today). Conceptualization of a system of ethical standards (a theory organizing lower-level theories) seems appropriate in the case of diverse ethical theories.

For example, as different as are Aristotle (empiricist, philosopher and probably atheist) and Christian theology (platonic, God-oriented and based on religious belief), they arrive by different theoretical paths at remarkably similar standards of ethics (golden rule, virtues, justice, etc.). (It must be noted immediately, however, that their similar standards were often translated into far different specific codes of conduct. See pp.74-77 above on the nature of codes.)

The Classification of Ethical Theories (by Sources and First Principles)*

I Outward-looking (tending toward Empiricism):
- A. Ethics based on Happiness as Human Goal (known and experienced by reasoning upon sense information):
  1. Aristotle (virtue as "golden mean")
  2. Epicurus (virtue as avoidance of painful effects)
  3. Pragmatists ("good" = that which "works" well)
     - Protagoras • Bentham • Utilitarians
     - J.S.Mill • Peirce • James • Dewey
     - Aristotle, Epicurus and Spencer fit here too.
- B. Ethics based on Realism (whether aiming at happiness -or not)
  1. Scientism ("scientific method" as key source of truth)
     - Galileo • Comte • Darwin
     - Naturalists (Spencer, Darwin, evolutionists)
  2. Materialists (Stoics, Hobbes, Nietzsche, Marx, Sartre)
  3. Social Evolutionists (Spencer, A. Smith, economists)
  4. "Natural Law" empiricists (Stoics, Locke, Aquinas)

  (Note: Human success, as a form of happiness, is implicit as human goal in the above four categories.)

II Inward-looking (tending toward Idealism):
- A. Ethics based on (eternal) Happiness defined by God/religions (Hebrews, Christianity, Islam, virtually all religions)
- B. Ethics based on Idealist Philosophies (other than religions)
  1. Intellectual Intuition (Innate Ideas)
     - Platonism • Descartes • Kant • Hegel
  2. Emotional Intuition (feeling and "heart" as guide)
     - Poets • Rousseau • Sartre & Existentialists
     - Most emotional religions would fit here too.
  3. Will and Duty (Voluntarism) as ethical norm
     - Stoics • Kant • Nietzsche • Wm. James

---

* Review p. 95 above on the basic distinction used here between Inward- and Outward-looking thought systems. Also, see Index to review key terms and thinkers as named above. Naturally, this chart is oversimplified, classifying all systems by dominant position

When the giant thought-systems and thinkers of the Western world are reduced to their essentials "in one sentence or less" and compressed into a hard, logical classification (necessarily stereotypical, of course), as on the previous page, their fundamental theories are obviously so diverse as to be irreconciliable with each other. Such opposites have few things in common (Platonism vs Aristotelianism, empiricism vs idealism, religion vs atheism, Augustine vs Aquinas, Descartes vs Peirce,etc) except the ethical standards most of them ultimately arrived at. In a free and pluralistic modern America, we enjoy the right to accept and live by any of these diverse religions or philosophies (so long as this infringes not on rights of others to do the same); fortunately, the ethical standards of most of them exhibit essential similarities, as outlined in the following classification.

The Classification of Ethical Standards

I Standards defining ethical action as based on Virtue*
- A. Christian virtues (as in Catholicism, Protestantism, Judaism)
- B. Aristotle's "Golden Mean" of virtue (vs vice)
- C. The "Golden Rule," almost universal in world ethical ideas
- D. Justice (as in early Hebrews, Christians and Aristotle)
- E. Charity and "Love Thy Neighbor" (as in Christianity)
- F. Honesty with self and others (Socrates and Plato)
- G. Virtue as dictated by "natural law" (Locke, Aquinas, Stoics)
- H. Virtue as "work ethic" (Calvin, Protestantism, A.Smith)
- I. Kant's "General Law" standard of virtue as "duty"
- J. Virtue as deduced from idealist systems (Descartes, Kant)
- K. Virtue, the good thing, as by intuitive feeling (Rousseau)
- L. Pragmatists: virtue as that which "works" for happiness (Some evolutionists fit here - virtue as survival;see H)

II Standards based on norms other than Virtue
- A. "Might Makes Right" (Hobbes, Machiavelli, Nietzsche)
- B. Some Materialists and Evolutionists (survival as in A above)
- C. Intuitive Conscience ("inner feeling" as norm of action") -Some poets, novelists and Existentialists (Sartre, etc.)

---

* Like the term "idealism" (defined on p.129), the term "virtue" is used throughout this book in its technical philosophical meaning (as defined by Aristotle, p.63) without any connotations of "stiff," "stuffy," "righteous," "inflexible," "virtuous" etc. unfortunately associated today with the term. "Virtue" is defined as "a firm habit of good human action" (as opposed to vice, the habit of doing evil). Key word in the definition, of course, is "good" (discussed on p.47)

Note carefully, in the classification of ethical standards, that most -almost all of them-, throughout the human history of religions and philosophical thought, despite its wide differences in origins or sources, end up with "virtue" as the only recommended and honored (and ethical) manner for man to live his human life. Pragmatist philosophers would remark, of course (probably correctly), that this is to be expected simply because good habits (ethics) "work" toward ultimate long-range happiness -and this is obvious from a study of human experience.

Note, too, that the few standards not related to virtue (Part II on previous page) are no longer of much relevance in American business today as some of them were a century ago. The American Robber Barons of the 19th century used "jungle" ethics (Hobbes' "might makes right") with dramatic success and personal profit; today they would be in jail or, at the minimum, a public embarrassment and liability to themselves and their organizations. (The reasons why "jungle" ethics is no longer practical and simply fails to work in modern America were examined fully in Chapter I above, especially pages 19-21.) As for "intuitive conscience," pure feeling and existentialism, these are far too subjective and unanalyzable as ethical standards for managers who must today justify decisions in public forums either within or outside their organizations. Always in the public eye and subject to scrutiny, managers must be able to justify decisions on common ethical grounds with their critics, i.e. by ethical standards generally accepted. And these are the ones listed in Part I of the classification (previous page).

Ethical "Tests"

But the Part I list is still too general and abstract for effective managerial application. The general consensus running through it must be expressed (deduced) in more operational or usable terms -as reasonably understandable "tests" against which any action can be evaluated as ethical or not. Such ethical tests have already been listed in Chapter III as concepts, prior to discussion of their rationales and sources in Chapter IV. The full list of ethical standards, relevant to modern America (i.e. based on Part I on the previous page), is summarized below as operational ethical tests (numbers in parentheses refer the reader to pages above for full explanation of standards and tests).

Ten Tests of Ethical Action

- Justice and Fairness (59)
- The Golden Mean (62)
- Natural Law (63)
- Kant's General Law (68)
- Long-range Utility (70)
- The Golden Rule (60)
- Love Thy Neighbor-Charity(61)
- "No harm to others" (65)
- "Work Ethic" (72)
- Lesser Evil Standard (73)

Virtue: A Hard Operational Term

As noted (footnote, p. 154), the term "virtue" (or "Virtuous") has accumulated today the unfortunate connotations associated with words and expressions such as "stiff," "stuffy," "ritualistic," "inflexible," "religious fanaticism" or, even worse, "religious sentimentality," "prim and virginal," "Mary Poppins," "Donald Do-Good," and other words suggesting weakness, meekness, passivity and inability to make decisions or take strong actions. Because of this, a writer's temptation is to just abandon the word as lost -in terms of its original, strong and precise meaning.* Choosing to do otherwise in this book, we will salvage and use the word "virtue" often, in its historical meaning of strong, goal-centered, self-controlled and active habits of pursuing and doing the right and good action (rather than sinking, by weak or passive personal character, into habits of evil, i.e. vice). In this, the original and historical, sense of the term, virtue was the proud personal goal of all great ancient Greeks (called "Paideia" or Pride[1]) and of the strongest and noblest of the Romans (called "virtus"). From these Greek and Roman times, and throughout Western history (until recently), the word "virtue," attributed to any man, constituted the highest of compliments; most men, overwhelmed by and yielding to their animal instincts, lived vicious lives (dominated by evil habits -or vice) while the few who rose above vice to hard-earned virtue in their lives are remembered and admired for the self-control and achievements of their time on earth.

Thus, here, we will not wink at -or apologize for- the use of the term. As defined here -and used for several thousand years, virtue is the final measure of any man's true character, traits, worth and life achievements.** For example, specific manifestations of lives of virtue among men (all passing the "Ten Tests" as on the previous page) include such hard, life-long actions and habits as:

- keeping every promise
- paying all debts on time
- being fair, and kind, to all
- risking life itself, if necessary
- honestly telling the truth
- never over-eating (drinking)
- helping, never hurting, others
- meeting every responsibility
- working hard and always to be able to do the above obligations etc.

---

* The ancient Roman (Latin) term, "virtus," means, depending upon context, honesty, excellence, strength, character, goodness of soul, chastity and fidelity, loyalty, courage in battle, brilliance of mind, risking one's life for others, and a human life like God's.

** Traits, such as firm, personal integrity, are the fundamental ingredients of virtus (see footnote above). (See, also, footnote on p. 151.)

PITFALLS IN THE INTERPRETATION OF STANDARDS

The delineation of the Ten Tests of ethical action (p. 155), derived from their diverse sources and systematized in the classifications above, is the essential step in translating broad ethical theories into usable (practical) form for application by managers. But, still, there are huge cautions and conditions of individual judgment to be carefully considered as one moves into the next step of actually applying the ethical standards (the Ten Tests). The following are the major ones.

Subjective and Varying Interpretations of Common Standards

One perennial problem of practical ethical analysis is the subjective variations in interpreting common standards, especially over long periods. Several centuries ago, slavery was regarded as ethically acceptable while today it is unethical and illegal in most civilized lands. The ethical standards (the Ten Tests) had not changed; but this specific interpretation of "Justice," "General Law" etc. had changed greatly. As noted on p.67, fortunately many errors in interpretation seem, in a free and pluralistic democracy, to be self-correcting. This was the key to Peirce's optimism about "testing" ideas by their effects until "truth" was increasingly refined and found (p.141).

Another example: in any labor-management negotiation, all parties accept "fairness" (Justice) as their common test of proposed actions but disagree usually on its specific interpretations; labor focuses mainly on what is fair to workers, management on what is fair to stockholders, and so on. Similarly, a hard- and self-driven executive might use the Golden Rule to drive his subordinates into his own workaholic style, damaging their health or marriages. Again, good will (p.151) can take one a long way in avoiding blind, one-sided and facetious interpretations of the ten tests, especially those obviously self-serving.

A common fault in ethical analysis is the interpretation of standards perversely to rationalize an action one desires out of sheer determination to do it, whatever its real ethical value as good or evil. Open discussion, even debate, of such issues and actions in meetings and public forums aids greatly in sorting out honest interpretations that honestly disagree from transparent rationalizations. This, as Peirce and Locke forever emphasized, is a supreme value of an open society (America and freedom of speech and religion) as opposed to closed societies (Roman empire, the Holy Christian empire, modern Russia, and, unfortunately, most historical and modern nations). In an open system, constant critical discussion can refine specific interpretations toward a reasonable consensus on issues such as capital punishment, abortion, discrimination, fair profits, conflicts of interest, wages, etc.

Knowing the Facts of the Situation

A most common pitfall in ethical analysis is applying sound standards to concrete real situations which have been poorly or wrongly understood as to the actual facts of the situation. Ethical standards in their abstraction are universal propositions; but individuals and event in the real world are very specific, often unique. Every situation can be said to be unique if one examines into every minute, factual detail of it. Since it is obvious that the "facts" of any actual situation are virtually infinite in number, depending on how much detail one can or does seek, we can rarely wait or delay decisions until literally "all" the facts are known. Realistically, this theoretically ideal goal is impossible (despite decision-making textbooks with steps requiring that "first one gets all the facts"). Thus, realistically, our knowledge of the facts of any situation ranges from utterly insufficient to reasonably and acceptably adequate, in the context of constraints such as time, money, human energy and genuine interest.

For example, any of the following situations look the same upon superficial glance but even major details of fact vary greatly and substantially affect one's application of ethical standards in each case: two homocides (one by a hired assassin, the other by a robbery victim who panicked when attacked); two rapes (one by a midnight intruder breaking into a woman's apartment, the other by a youth "teased" into it throughout a long party); two lies (one under oath profoundly affecting the lives of men on trial, the other diverting a salesman by telling him, as secretaries must often do, that her boss is "in conference" or "out of town at the moment"); two thieves (one cleverly stealing funds of old clients by means of his powerful lawyer's letterhead and orders on it which manipulate such funds to his personal profit, the other concealing several cans of cat tuna for her own meal as she is checked out of a supermarket); and so on. The above examples exhibit extremes of varying circumstances, just to illustrate the point; but even subtle or unknown details of any situation can radically change the application of ethical standards and rational conclusions of the mind as to what is ethical or unethical, truly, in each case -as it is carefully analyzed in terms of the true facts of the situation. Too often, we apply sound standards to situations without a proper attention to the realities, the facts, of the situation. Such attention to detail, to facts, in ethical analysis is essential (as we shall see in later chapters on current issues).

Ethical analysis, therefore, operates at two levels: establishing general standards and systematizing them into usable form (this now already accomplished in the development of the Ten Tests, p. 155 above); then searching for the true and adequate facts of the real situations to which the ethical standards must be applied (with careful judgment).*

The White and Black of any Situation – and then the Gray Areas

Upon analysis of adequate facts, many actions will, fortunately, be "clearly right" or "clearly wrong" and provide sound guidance for final ethical decisions. Unfortunately, many situations lie ultimately in the gray area between clearly right and wrong. For managers, dealing with marginal workers, some slightly or greatly alcoholic, some tending to low or merely tolerable productivity –or even attendance and time records, some slightly or greatly of poor or destructive attitudes, etc., managerial life and decisions typically face daily the gray areas, not the easy black and white situations. Today's managers, at every level, must be skilled in handling properly (and ethically) –and with learned judgment– the gray areas as well as the easy black and white ones.

The irony is that a manager's right decisions go unnoticed and are taken for granted; his occasional wrong ones –often just one– ruin him and sometimes his organization (review, again, the practical effects of managerial decisions, as on pages 19-21). Most such wrong decisions, as judged in retrospect, could be avoided by even the simplest kinds of ethical analysis –but they aren't (and weren't in the case of President Nixon and his cohorts) due mainly to lack of these skills of ethical awareness and analysis.

Semantics and Emotional States as Conditions of Ethical Analysis

Semantic confusion (about the true meanings of words) is a constant source of misunderstanding and conflict in ethical analysis (as already noted, pp.57 and 59). Unlike the terms of science which refer to observable physical things (weight, speed, toxic, fatal, etc.) and can be accurately defined, the terms of ethics refer to metaphysical things (fairness, evil, inhuman, ethical, good and other normative values) and have no direct referent in the physical world. Words used on the previous page are examples: "murder," "rape" and "lying" are difficult to define because these words refer not only to observable acts but to a normative judgment about them as ethical, unethical or somewhere in between. (Charles Peirce, as we have seen on p.141, tried to clarify

---

* Often the toughest part of an ethical analysis is the factual part of it. No one disputes the ethical standards (the Ten Tests); but all perceive the actual situation very differently and with different facts. A classic case: a picture in an urban newspaper showed two white policemen roughly dragging a small black girl toward a police car. Her face was contorted, she was clearly in great pain and held hard. Police brutality? No. They had rescued her from a fire.

such metaphysical ideas by examining the real effects of these ideas as used.) Except for pragmatists (Peirce, etc.) and positivists (Comte, Ayer, etc.), however, words used in ethical analysis are often defined carelessly and usually by reference to other metaphysical ideas just as unclear and ambiguous.

The problem of semantics in ethical analysis is not insuperable, but strict caution is always necessary to remain alert for the semantic effect on ethical analysis and careful definitions where needed. For example, the word "murder" might be used loosely for the more neutral "homicide" and confuse a discussion of capital punishment; or "rape" in a case of a semi-willing woman where "seduction" might be more accurate;* is it a "lie" (unethical) for my secretary to tell a salesman on the phone that I am in a meeting when I'm right at my desk but busy on a budget with deadline just hours away? Such words, including a pre-judgment as to ethical vs unethical as applied to an act ("murder" presumes an act to be unjustified homicide), are "loaded" terms; loaded with pre-judgment and usually, also, with strong emotions.**

Emotionality is probably the most deadly of all mental blocks stopping or contaminating clear and factual application of ethical tests (standards) to real-life situations. Other than desparate need for food, sex, water or shelter, few human issues fan the fires of passion to hotter heat than those involving ethics: a quiet, living-room discussion fires up into a blaze of emotion as soon as someone broaches the good or evil in issues such as abortion, capital punishment, birth control, bussing of children for racial integration, sexual affairs, use of drugs, etc.; as much, or more, heat is generated when these issues are argued in staid boardrooms at corporate headquarters, PTA (Parent-Teachers Association) meetings, city/county meetings of mayors and commissioners, and -at highest emotional heat level- in the conference rooms of Congress and the White House. Heat-levels are a measure of energy output, not cool, rational, fact-oriented analysis. For reasons of political survival

---

* Current anti-discrimination policies of the U.S. government reveal bizarre instances of semantic confusion over key words. Even the expression "affirmative action" is one of them. Government executives must hire and promote on "merit" while simultaneously meeting "quotas" of many racial and ethnic categories. The key terms are left carefully undefined; executives live in anxiety about "ad hoc" criticisms charged against them by hindsight. "Sexual harassment" policies are unintelligible in application (many women like some attention from men, some degree of "harassment").

** In the footnote, p.160, "brutality" was "loaded" despite the facts.

(getting elected every two years), congressmen are forced to humor the masses (the deep constitutional flaw of universal suffrage, again, p.82) and excel at emotional rhetoric rather than cool and sound analysis of issues. Public officials, probably intelligent, but forced for survival into positions of irrational government spending for "goodies" for "all" (however irresponsible the childish demands for more), resort typically to vote-getting emotional rhetoric, rarely to statesman-like analysis of facts and realities. As many proverbs testify, nothing deprives the human mind of its inherent and powerful tool of reason as surely as do strong passion and emotionality. Irrational wars, killing millions, are historical and continuing evidence of this.

Human emotionality cannot be eradicated and is a threat to sound (cool, rational and analytical) decision-making; alert to this common condition affecting a man's judgment, one must consciously attempt to compensate for it, adjust the mind against distortions caused by it, force an objective and rational mode upon oneself (quite easily done, if one really tries), and be sure that one's emotional state and feelings are in control by the powers of one's reason (rather than momentary passion!).

Human Subjectivity

Every person lives in his own world of opinions, attitudes and values implanted (conditioned) in him from his own particular early life experience. This personal subjectivity, slowly molded by the authority figures in one's life, his religious or cultural training, the fixed ideas and prejudices of his time and place, operates consciously -and subconsciously- in all of one's thinking and communicating. It makes one very vulnerable, unless clear and critical thinking become an explicit personal habit, to a host of mental errors such as confusing perceptions with facts, stereotyping, jumping to conclusions (wrong assumptions or inferences), failure to listen carefully (especially for facts rather than reinforcement of preconceptions), and so on.*

Degrees of Ethical Good and Unethical Evil

Obviously to be considered always is that ethical actions vary in their degrees of good and unethical actions in their degrees of evil. All other things being equal, donating 20% of my income is better than

---

* Human proneness to error in thinking, analysis and communication is a huge subject in itself requiring full-length books and courses (Logic, Fallacies of the Mind, Communication, etc.). A good recent one is J. & A. Kaminsky's Logic: A Philosophical Introduction (1974); a shorter treatment of the essentials is in Chapter 9 of my own The Theory and Practice of Managing (1982).

10% as charitable contributions; mass murder worse than simple assault. The method of ethical analysis called "Force-field analysis" (next section below) incorporates this key factor (of degrees) along with others.

Degrees of evil among many unethical options become critical in the analysis of situations often called "forced options." A forced option is a situation in which all available actions, including doing nothing, contain some degree of evil (judged by any or all of the usual ethical standards, the ten tests above). In such cases, and they are much more common than realized in the lives of managers who must make decisions, the test of the Lesser-Evil standard (p.73) must be used. In such anxiety-ridden forced options, the decision-maker must opt for an act containing the least degree of evil. Let's note immediately that, in the inexact field of ethics (p.48, footnote), the concept of "degrees" can be used analogously only: i.e. to suggest in a meaningful, but not literal, sense the "more" and "less" significant variations in actions (considered ethically) based on their kind, quality, circumstances and the "degrees" of each factor. The classic case of Captain Holmes (p.73) illustrates his judgment that allowing 24 people to die by inaction was a higher degree of moral evil than taking action to forfeit 12 lives in order to save 12 others. Not usually in this sort of utter life-and-death situation, it is quite typical for managers to face similar forced options such as closing an inefficient plant (jobs lost) to protect stockholders' equity, or firing an alcoholic father of small children who is endangering fellow workers, or cooperating in a payoff to a foreign nation's contracting minister to secure a huge order saving the life of a near-bankrupt company and its workers' jobs, and so on. Life-and-death decisions, too, are not uncommon on managers' desks: to cut costs and improve profits by eliminating from product designs safety features clearly understood by engineers as needed but only vaguely noticed by price-conscious customers (until they need it -and sue the manufacturer for lack of it); to reduce tests of a new pharmaceutical agent or medicine (or distort or manipulate them) to meet marketing and profit objectives; and so on.*

We will return to some of these examples in the next section on force-field analysis, where forced options and degrees of moral evil are necessary considerations in many, if not all, ethical analyses required by modern managers.

---

* This (safety) issue, now termed by lawyers the product-liability issue, was central in many recent cases affecting automobile (and other) manufacturers. The proneness of the Pinto automobile's gas tank to explode in rear-end collisions cost the manufacturer many millions of dollars. Such liability is growing as an ethical issue.

THE FORCE-FIELD OF ETHICAL PRIORITIES

Assuming the good will and intent to act at high levels of ethics and integrity, the "easy" ethical decisions are those that pit a clear good against a clear evil. Like honesty vs blatant cheating of customers, financial clients or children (of any age) in a candy store or investment management firm controlling the total savings of retired workers. Neither laborious nor sophisticated ethical analysis is needed to know that cheating an old couple out of their life savings is unethical as is, also, raping a woman with a gun at her head. Cases like this are clear to the mind; there is no ethical ambiguity or difficulty in knowing what is right or wrong.

The Gray Areas of Ethical Analysis

Unfortunately, as noted on p. 159, the "right" or "wrong" of many managerial decisions and other human actions is not clearly black or white, but lies rather in the ambiguous or gray areas for reasons already mentioned:

- the true facts of a situation are unclear or unavailable;
- semantic problems cloud or load the meanings of words;
- human subjectivity and personal (one-sided) perceptions build barriers against clear sight of issues and honest efforts toward objective analysis; and,
- emotionality, typical of discussion -or fights- about most ethical issues, blocks out reason and cool rational analysis.

The above, and other, factors, described earlier in this chapter, create ethical issues more usually gray than merely black or white. Force-field analysis, developed by the author over the last decade, can aid greatly in coping with and understanding the "gray" ethical conditions.*

The Premises and Mechanics of Force-field Analysis

Force-field analysis combines analytical power with simplicity of use. It consists essentially, in its application to ethical analysis, of the objective listing of factual realities, their probable consequences and the ethical forces of ethical standards (the Ten Tests, p. 155) to depict, in a diagram form, all the incentives for or against any -or many-

---

* The general concept and method of force-field analysis were developed by Kurt Lewin in the 1950s (Field Theory in Social Sciences and many ground-breaking articles in major journals). The Force-field of Ethical Priorities is a new, hopefully useful, application of field (and systems) theory to practical ethical issues.

human actions. It is best explained by a simple example.

Suppose the case of a supervisor with a subordinate, named John, who has a serious drinking problem. John typically sneaks a drink at various times before coming to work, at lunch, at coffee breaks and his productivity is less than half the average output of the other workers in his department. He has been counseled often and even formally warned of dismissal if he continues drinking on the job; but nothing seems to change John's bad habit. He has even been suspended for two weeks but, upon returning to work, began his same pattern of drinking on the very first day back. The only remaining alternatives are to fire John or to ignore his drinking and "live with" the problem. Although this case has been greatly oversimplified, for our purposes of a clear illustration, the ethical analysis of such a case is aided by simply listing the factors to be considered in the decision(s) as forces or arguments for and against each decision alternative available, as diagrammed below. The length or thickness is a convenient way to suggest the strength (or significance) of each factor. In complex cases,

FORCE-FIELD ANALYSIS OF DECISION TO FIRE OR NOT FIRE EMPLOYEE

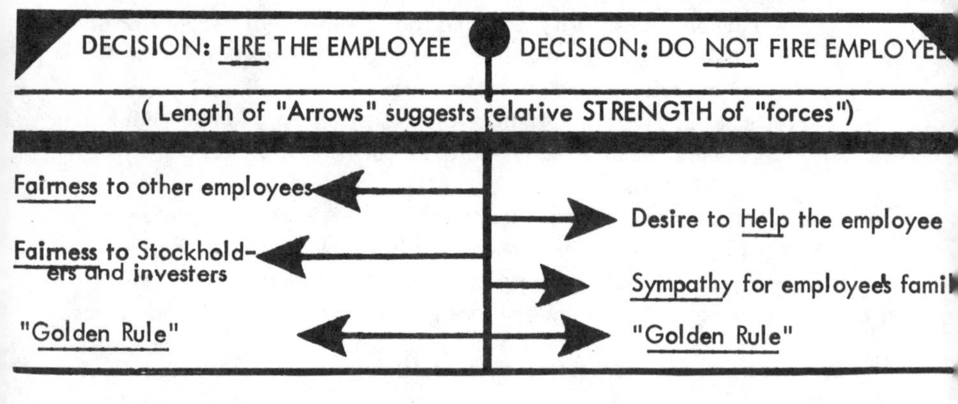

particularly, a force-field diagram requires a decision maker to identify explicitly and evaluate all important factors for and against each available decision option.

Force-field analysis (including diagramming) is thus a method of decision making.* In John's case above, the decision maker evaluated the left-side option (to fire) as the more ethical based on the tests

---

* The mental steps in formal decision making usually include the following: identify the problem, describe the facts of it, determine its causes, list and evaluate alternative solutions. See Chapter 4 (and 5) of my Theory and Practice of Managing (1982).

of justice (fairness) and the Golden Rule. The tests of charity and desire not to harm John's family show some merit (short arrows) but are overwhelmed by the factor of justice to others (workers and stockholders) wrongly harmed by John's own actions. The Golden Rule cuts in both directions: one might want to be treated with pity and charity if failing to carry one's responsibilities but, even more so, one expects to receive one's rights in justice, as a hard worker and owner in a firm, to protection from wrongful threats against the fruits of work and ownership (i.e. against John's willful poor performance in the firm). Other ethical tests (p.155) could have been used in the force-field diagram, such as the General Law standard (p.68) which would probably add a long arrow on the left and a short one -or none- on the right side. It would be difficult to justify a general law based on John's behavior. Emotionally, the supervisor making this decision (to fire John) will probably feel depressed, even "guilty," after his action and, indeed, might not have arrived at his decision or the will to do it without the objective, rational analysis of force-field diagramming. (American combat commanders, fighting off the world threat of Nazism in WW II, had to order thousands of men into combat deaths; if they had acted on emotions such as pity instead of objective, rational analysis, the supreme good of human freedom now enjoyed by Europeans- some of them - would not exist.)

Force-field analysis is, therefore, a simple but powerful method of (1) identifying and organizing relevant factors, (2) explicitly forcing one's mind to consider each, (3) evaluating all factors by rational decision making steps, and (4) forcing one's judgment to operate on objective reason rather than emotion and blind impulse. For these reasons, force-field analysis will be the central method used in our later chapters on current ethical issues. It should also be central in the reader's analysis of the cases at the end of this book.

A Force-field Analysis of the Classic Case of Captain Holmes

Many, or most, force-field diagrams reveal unfortunately the need of the Lesser-evil standard as in the Captain Holmes case (p.73, above) where the Captain had the forced-option situation in an overcrowded lifeboat of doing nothing (and letting all 24 in the boat die when it capsized) or ejecting 12 people into the ocean and letting them die in order to save the remaining 12 in a boat that could safely carry that number and provide a realistic probability of rescue (in fact, the 12 were rescued and, of course, Holmes was tried on criminal charges in Admiralty Court). A simplified force-field diagram of Holmes' decision options, as 24 people sat in the hopelessly overcrowded lifeboat, is as follows, based on Holmes' court testimony:

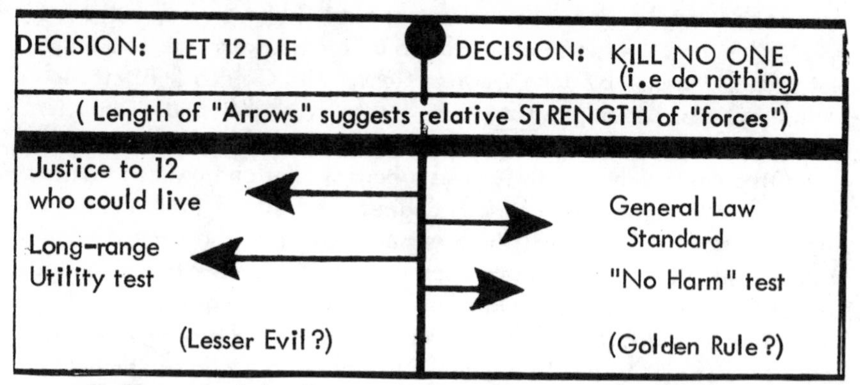

In the analysis by Captain Holmes (diagram above), the key tests, favoring his decision to eject 12 people from the lifeboat and let them die, were justice to the half of that lifeboat population with a good chance to live -if he made the difficult decision and enforced the act-and long-range utility (i.e. the greatest good for the greatest number in long-range terms). Clearly an excruciating Lesser-evil decision situation. Favoring the "do nothing" option, in Holmes' view at the time, were weak (short arrows) considerations of the "No Harm" test (but, given the certain-death circumstances, death itself was certain for at least some or all of the lifeboat population). And what about the arrow representing the General Law test? The Admiralty Court, in its evaluation of Holmes' action as a general law ("playing God," as it were, and deciding who lives or dies by the autocratic single-man decision of someone in power at a particular moment), extended that General Law arrow in the diagram so far as to become determining: Holmes was found guilty of unjustified homicide by the court's decision (but the court, appreciating the lesser-evil constraints of Holmes' decision situation and judging these to be valid, ethical and extenuating circumstances, imposed a very light sentence; protecting the necessities of law and precedents as easily abused in the future but, at the same time, admitting the purely ethical validity of Holmes' decision when he had to face it).

The obvious question for our readers is: if you had faced the Captain's decision to make in the lifeboat, what would have been your decision -and why (diagram your own force-field analysis)? Diagramming the issue, as you must in a force-field analysis, the results of reasoning and rational analysis (as opposed to emoting with deep "feeling") might surprise you. As simple as it is, force-field analysis and diagramming is a powerful mental method for converting confused and emotional feelings about ethical issues into rational and objective decisions.

Force-field Diagrams of Three or More Dimensions

The illustrations of force-field analysis thusfar (the cases of John and Captain Holmes) were simple two-dimensional diagrams depicting two decision options. The same force-field principle, however, can be used when three or more decision options are involved (tri-dimensional or multi-dimensional diagrams respectively). Three decision options create a tri-dimensional (three-sided) diagram, i.e. a triangle; four options create a square diagram; eight an octagon, etc. Let's illustrate just one of these varieties, a tri-dimensional force-field diagram, based on a case developed by Garrett.[2] Apex Corporation, before the stringent era of FDA (Federal Drug Administration), is rushing to market a new sleeping pill even though tests show harmful effects on unborn children of female users. Apex plans to attach a package label warning, "Not to be used by pregnant women," but is aware from market research that few users read such caution labels.* Further research and testing (too costly for Apex) can easily remove the dangerous side-effect. Only if Apex merged with a larger firm could the resources become available for the needed research and testing. Moreover, Apex is near bankruptcy and must market the pill soon in order to survive.

Apex employes 500 people. Its major options are (1) sell the drug immediately, (2) close down the company and liquidate assets, and (3) merge with a larger firm. The three-sided diagram (below) shows

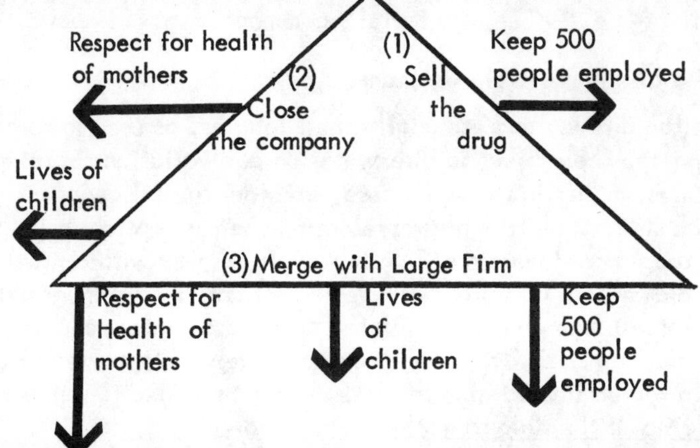

the major factors in the force-field analysis. If one agrees with the approximate weights (strengths and significance) suggested by the

---

* The current (1982) Surgeon General's warning about smoking cigarets as "dangerous to health," fixed by law to be labeled on all cigaret packages and ads, is widely known to be useless -but satisfies certain constituencies of congressmen who need votes.

arrows representing the ethical forces for each option, the third option (merging) prevails as the most ethical (containing the least evil effects and the maximum good). The worst of the options is to sell the drug.

A Note on Methodology and Interpretation of Force-field Diagrams

It must be noted explicitly (again) that the appearance of neat categories of factors and exactitude in force-field diagrams is an aid in analysis, not to be taken literally. It is an illusion to expect any kind of quantitative precision or exactitude in ethical analysis.* On the other hand, the opposite extreme is to make no efforts at organizing, systematizing and rationally analyzing issues that are unquantifiable. Force-field diagramming is used here as a sensible middle-ground between these extremes -provided that allowances and interpretations are made for the inevitable factors of subjectivity, semantics, unclear facts and emotionality, as noted on p. 163.

> Garrett's comment on the Apex case recognizes this problem:[2] "In a case of this type, there is often room for disagreement as to the weights to be given to various factors. However, if the method (of ethical analysis) is carefully followed, the businessman can at least be sure that he has made an honest attempt to act ethically. One can demand little more in human affairs where risk and uncertainty are a part of the fabric of life." (See also Bartel's comment on p. 151 above.)

The Arrows in a Force-field Diagram

Even the arrows, and especially their lengths, as used in force-field diagrams, are subject to interpretation and variations in using them. For example, in the Apex case, consider the following:

- The side of the triangle representing the first option (sell the drug) could have a different graphic display with arrows drawn both outward (positive forces) and inward (negative forces) from the line (only the outward arrow appears in the diagram as drawn on the previous page). "Negative" arrows, directed inward from the line, could be added to represent risks of the drug to mothers and children.

* The same must be said for many fields within the social sciences (psychology, sociology, economics, politics and general management itself). The word "science" itself, borrowed from exact physical sciences, such as chemistry, implies quantitative exactitude with full use of numbers, statistics, percentages and computers. There exists today a field called Management Science that often traps itself into rash quantifying of subjective realities.

- A fourth option might be added for consideration (therefore a square diagram) such as a temporary layoff of some of Apex workers and shifting the cost savings into immediate testing of the pill (if that's feasible); or a fifth option (a pentagon).
- Different people might, in honest disagreement about values or facts available, differ over the proper arrows to add, delete or change as to their length and significance. (If you value human freedom far higher than social order and I value them oppositely, although we agree both are of high value, then we will evaluate differently –and our arrows will vary in length– such ethical issues as capital punishment, probation terms for criminals, bail rules, prison living conditions, etc. Review Bentham's "association principle" on p. 138.)
- Different people, again in honest disagreement, will rate the value of the applicable ethical standards (the Ten Tests, p. 155) differently, while agreeing that all ten are of high value. You might rank Charity (Love thy neighbor) and the Golden Rule as #1 and #2 on your list of the Ten Tests while I, indeed, rank them #5 and #6 (after Long-range Utility, Justice or "fairness," the General Law standard and Aristotle's Golden Mean, respectively, as #1 to #4). What does this say about me and my highest-priority values in any human life? (Or about you?) At least this much: we both honestly intend to seek a high level of ethical action, but differ in our interpretations and applications of that intent (in its details).

Non-graphic Force-field Diagrams

It would be cumbersome to fill the following pages with fully-drawn (graphic) force-field diagrams of the many issues to be analyzed. Thus, usually, we will retain the principle of force-field diagramming, but more succinctly, by simply outlining the options, forces and degree of force of each in linear outline form, the number of 'pluses' (length) suggesting the strength and significance of forces as listed.* For example the Apex case would now be represented as follows:

Option 1 Sell the Drug
++++++++++++ Keep 500 people employed ('plus'=Positive)
-------------------- Health risk ('minus' signs = Negative)

Option 2 Close the Company (Liquidate)
++++++++++++++++++++ Avoid health risk ('No harm' test)

Option 3 Merge with Large Firm
++++++++++++++++++++ Avoid health risk
+++++++++++++ Keep 500 people employed

* + = positive force; – = negative force; length of them = strength.

REFERENCES

1 See Werner Jaeger's Paideia:Ideals of Greek Culture (2 vols.)
2 Garrett, Th., Business Ethics, Appleton-Century, 1966, pp. 19 & 23

For Further Reading

- Kuhn, J. & I. Berg, Values in a Business Society, Harvard University
- and Garrett, as above.
- Donaldson, T., Ethical Issues in Business (1979)

QUESTIONS AND PROBLEMS

1. Define and illustrate the following concepts:
   (a) "knowledge" vs "skill" (b) theory (its nature and purpose)
   (c) social sciences (specifically, psychology, sociology etc.)
   (d) trait theory of leadership (e) the "Ten Ethical Tests"
   (f) "Outward-looking" vs "inward-looking" ethical theories
   (g) pragmatism (Bentham, etc.) (h) natural law ethics
   (i) empiricism vs idealism (j) religion vs philosophy
   (k) philosophy vs science (l) "scientific method"
   (m) evolutionism (Darwin, etc.) (n) virtue vs vice (as habits)
   (o) General Law Standard (Kant's Categorical Imperative)
   (p) Golden Rule (q) Golden Mean (Aristotle)
   (r) Long-range utility standard (s) Lesser-evil standard
   (t) Human Subjectivity ("perception," "semantics", "emotionality")
   (u) Force-field diagram (v) "Degrees" of good and evil
2. Prepare a non-graphic force-field diagram on the issue of a student cheating on and passing an exam (in college, medical school, etc.) (Hint: Try the General Law standard on a brain surgeon who cheats)
3. Prepare a defense pro (and con) Hobbes' "might-makes-right" ethics (refer to pp.58 & 155 as a help). What situations might justify -or rule out- this kind of "jungle ethics?" Are you an evolutionist?
4. Making reasonable assumptions to fill in possible facts in the following short case, (1) prepare a non-graphic force-field diagram and (2) reason to, and defend, your decision -if you had to make it: Wall Street Journal (7/2/79): In "Bribes and Business," the president of a heavy construction firm is angry that his firm has lost several huge contracts (one a $40 million brick plant in Iraq) in foreign countries where a private payment of money to a high official (a "payoff" or "bribe") is considered routine and expected in order to finalize a contract. Such payments are illegal for American companies while legal and routine for German and French firms which got the contracts which the American firm lost. Things to consider: is "bribery" a "loaded" term (see p.160)? Is the American law cited above fair or ethical? Should it be repealed? Why? Be sure to cite ethical "tests" in your analysis.

6 The Purposes of Business

The previous three chapters constitute the framework of theory and analytical methods for the application of ethics to business decisions. The remainder of the book will examine specific current issues of business and organizational life and their ethical implications. We will begin, in this chapter, with the purposes of business.

Business is More Than Just Economics

As we shall see shortly, the first theoretical formulations of what business is came from the economists, especially Adam Smith's Wealth of Nations (p. 136 above). But in modern America, business is far more than merely a matter of pure economics or economic models. The last paragraph of Robert Heilbroner's recent book, Economics Explained, puts it well:

> "The real challenges of our time do not lie in its economic problems, but in the political and moral values that *always* enter into our economic determinations. Economics is the language we use to talk about the workings and options of our system, but it is not the language in which we appraise the value of the system or decide what elements in it to preserve or change. *Politics* and *morality* -our collective wills and our private value systems- remain the bedrock of society. The outcome of the crisis of our times will reflect the strength of that will and *quality of those values*." (Emphasis added)[1]

Edgar Fiedler, an economist reviewing this very book and others in Across the Board (June, 1982, p. 50), put it even better:

"A number of otherwise well-informed people have the notion that economics can provide all the answers....Economists with this notion often search for the answers in econometric models. But the models can't provide answers because they rarely contain all the appropriate economic relationships and,more important, because the equations never contain the appropriate social, ethical and political relationships. This last point is almost always the fatal flaw. Some economists may object to my saying so, but the best economic forecasters and, especially, the best analysts of government macroeconomic policy are not necessarily economists. They are, rather, what we might refer to as "social philosophers." They must fully understand how the economy works, of course, but they must understand the prevailing moral values of society and how these values are changing." (Emphasis added)

A business decision, therefore, based solely upon economic considerations, rather than moral considerations as well, will often be a bad decision. This has been a major theme throughout this book, of course, as for example on page 21 above.

"Business" Defined

Business is the production and distribution of goods and services. Economics is the theoretical study of this process. In a strict sense, business refers to the private (nongovernment) activities defined but, in many countries, government organizations are so deeply involved in controlling and regulating business (as in America) or actually engaged in production and distribution (Russia and Sweden) that, depending upon context, business can refer to either private or government activities affecting the production and distribution of goods and services.

Note that the definition of business purposely excludes the idea of "profit." Thus the definition includes not only business conducted for profit (capitalism) but also nonprofit business such as by governments, voluntary organizations and entire state-run systems (communism). (A definition confining business to profit-oriented capitalism only would be quite parochial; although our focus in this book will be mainly upon business in the American capitalistic system.)

Business and Its Complex Relationships

Centuries ago, the average business (a farm, manor,trader,etc.) was relatively small and simple, interacting with a few employees, a few customers, possibly a few investors, and subject to norms clearly dictated by the state and religion in power at the time. Today, in

America, the average business is relatively large and many gigantic, with complex relationships with banks, stockholders, labor unions, government employment rules, regulatory agencies such as EEO, FDA, FTC, etc., business associations, Better Business groups, lobbyists, politicians, vendors, tax laws, social security and other benefits programs, consumer groups, community concerns and issues, etc. as depicted at left.[2] The ultimate and lasting success of a business depends not only on its skills and efficiency in producing or distributing particular goods or services but also its understanding and cultivation of the many complex relationships constituting its environment.

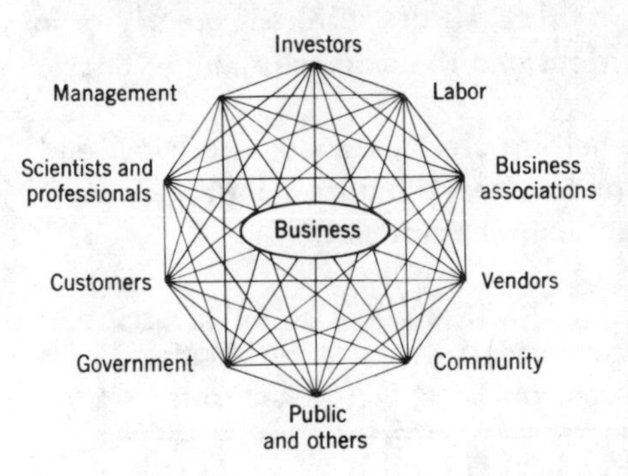

BUSINESS AND ECONOMIC SYSTEMS

As emphasized in the quotations above, business and political (moral) systems cannot be separated in the real world. In the 1980s, as one scans the political-economic systems of the world, ranging from 5-year central government planning in communist (totalitarian) nations (Russia, China) to democratic but socialist Sweden (or Britain) to strong-man dictatorships (Cuba, most of South America) to free enterprise, profit-oriented and democratic systems (America), it is no wonder one is confused by the many and contradictory systems by which people are governed (the political part) and produce and use goods and services (the economic or business part). Let's try to clarify these first.

Political systems are essentially either <u>dictatorships</u> (a nation's decisions and laws made by one or a few top rulers with no voice or vote permitted to citizens) or <u>democracies</u> (sovereignty of all citizens, votes on decisions and laws and majority opinion prevails) or somewhere in the range between the two pure systems of dictatorship and democracy.

Economic (business) systems range between the pure forms of free-market and profit-oriented <u>capitalism</u> versus <u>socialism</u> (complete control, including usually ownership, of all businesses, production and distribution -the state, not a free market, decides what is produced and to whom it is distributed for use, and in what quantities). Insofar as any particular nation might represent a political system anywhere in the range between dictatorship and democracy <u>combined</u> with an economic system ranging anywhere between capitalism and socialism, the variations of political-economic national systems today are just as many as there are nations of the world. All are different greatly or in some degree along both the political and the economic ranges of systems.*

The following diagram will help to clarify the pure political and economic systems combinations and suggest the almost infinite variations between the four (combined) extreme systems:

		ECONOMIC SYSTEMS	
		Government Controls	Free Market Controls
POLITICAL SYSTEMS	Dictator	Dictatorship or totalitarian Communism (Russia, Iran)	Dictatorial but with limited Capitalism (Chile, Argentina)
	Free Elections and Vote of the People (Democracy)	Democratic Socialism (Sweden, Britain)	Laissez Faire Capitalism (U.S.A., Japan, W. Germany)

The term "socialism" is often (and wrongly) applied to Russia's or China's political system whereas "socialism" describes an economic arrangement as defined above. Strictly speaking, the term "communism" also describes an economic, not a political, system and, as such, is essentially the same as "socialism." Russia's economic system is, indeed, socialist (communist) but politically it is a dictatorship with no free elections. (Today's tendency is to use the term "communism" loosely to refer to both the political and economic aspects of the Russian, Chinese or other "communist" country systems.) Thus a nation can be a genuine democracy (politically) with people voting for a socialist economic system (Britain, Sweden, and to some extent, most noncommunist European nations today as well as America

---

* Semantic ambiguity and confusion (some probably by design for public relations purposes of national leaders -review this concept on pp. 159-160 above) are common with the words used here, especially "socialism" and "communism." One must be very clear about these terms. "Communism" means common and fair use of all resources produced by all for all, apart from who individually produces most (or least) or needs most (or least), as in a family. "Socialism" is simply government control -or even ownership- of business whether by dictatorships or by democratic vote of people.

since the 1930s.)

It is rare, of course, that any nation would exactly fit into any of the "pure" systems charted above. Even China and Russia are using some limited capitalist methods (and there's a lot of profit-oriented capitalism in their thriving "black markets" where people trade on the basis of supply and demand, not central government rules and prices). Many South American countries are essentially "strong-man" dictatorships which, however, encourage a substantial degree of carefully monitored capitalism. America in the last century was close to the pure form of capitalism, with virtually no government intervention or control; today America is a combination of capitalism and socialism -probably still closer to the former than the latter, a modified capitalism.

Let's examine briefly the values, real or perceived, to be found in these political and economic systems.

John Locke, Adam Smith, and Capitalism

Although petty capitalism (p.34) is almost a thousand years old, national systems of capitalism grew from the political foundations for it, developed by Locke (p.120), and the conceptualization of it by Adam Smith (p.136).

Locke, as we have seen, based all his ethical and political ideas on the concept of "natural law" or "rights." Five of these (called the Lockean Five) were brought to America by the 18th century colonists and formed the essential foundations and beginnings of the new nation. The five ideas are:

(a) Individualism and Individual Freedom. The individual is primary (not the state, church or any group which is secondary and the mere sum of its parts -individuals, with each his own rights and freedoms). Implied also was equality (meaning equality of opportunity).

(b) Property Rights. The best guarantee of individual rights is the right to free and private use of one's property (against predatory tendencies of state, church and others to deprive individuals of it). The ideal state, unlike oppressive states and churches of the past, will set forth and enforce such individual and property rights as basic in its very constitution (a century after Locke's death, the American Constitution did exactly that in its Bill of Rights - a very strange and heretical document in its time and even today in most parts of the world).

(c) Free Competition among Individuals. Individuals must be free to use their property, talents and diligence in their own interests, each profiting by his own personal effort in fair competition with others for the goods that can be gained or produced from the natural world. A century after Locke, Adam Smith built economics on this basic idea.

(d) Limited Government. Locke lived in an age when the state (the king) and the church (pope and bishops), each in its own way, were absolute in power and there was no such thing as an individual having any rights -except those granted occasionally and arbitrarily by the king, prince, pope or bishop reflecting a particular mood or purpose, not any sort of inherent individual right to life, property or anything else. Locke himself, as noted above, had to exile himself from his native England to gain the freedom to write his major works. Locke, as well as every founding father of America, deeply distrusted central government power (as always abused to exploit the individual). Their motto: "the least government is the best government."

(e) Specialization of Knowledge and Work. Progress requires that more and more people become increasingly educated, specialized or "expert" in narrow and specific fields of knowledge and skill (like medicine, law, war, manufactures, trade, teaching, science, etc.).

Laissez Faire and Adam Smith's "Invisible Hand"

Locke's new and heretical ideas simmered in the minds of many Englishmen (on both sides of the Atlantic) for a century, gained more and more acceptance in the colonies, grew into specific and workable form in the minds of Americans like Benjamin Franklin, Tom Paine, Thomas Jefferson and James Madison, and, finally, 1776 became the "Lockean year," when his thinking and his ideas burst forth, full-grown, ready to found the world's first free and democratic nation as well as the specific economic system of capitalism permitted within it and fueling its power: in 1776 the American colonies issued their historic Declaration of Independence and began drafting a national Constitution based on Locke's five ideas; in the same year, Adam Smith's Wealth of Nations, the "bible" of capitalists, was published.

By profession, Smith was a professor of moral philosophy with an English university but gradually developed a series of concepts (called "economics" today) to explain and advocate the optimum system for producing and distributing goods and services by and throughout a nation. He said that, if every individual worked his best at pursuing his own interests (profit), without external (government) interference, the best interests and strength of the nation as a whole would also be perfectly served "as if by an invisible hand." Given a free market and pure competition among individuals, each will have the incentive to produce goods more efficiently and at a lower prices than competitors so that consumers will buy his goods and he will profit by it. Thus, by an invisible hand, the very act of seeking personal profit forces one to contribute to society the benefits of the highest quality goods at the lowest prices to all consumers -and everyone gains. Like Locke,

Smith assumed a completely free market with no government interference ("laissez faire," as it came to be called, meaning "let it go"), a thorough hands-off policy by state, church and every institution - except the free market of producers working as efficiently as possible and consumers buying the best products at the lowest prices. This is the essence of capitalism and it thrives by the natural forces of the marketplace.

Locke's five ideas (above) are clearly embedded in Smithian capitalism, especially individualism, human freedom and property rights; without the Lockean five, essentially political democracy, a free market -and hence capitalism- are impossible (as is obvious in Russia today and even Sweden -see Case # 11 below).

Capitalism, working freely (laissez faire) throughout the first century of the American nation, tapped enormous human energies and resourcefulness, built it into the most prosperous and powerful nation on earth and the highest average standard of living ever known in history. But, by definition (best and most efficient competitors gain customers and profits), capitalism involves a kind of "survival of the fittest" value system, "Darwinianism" a century before Darwin's work on evolutionism (see p. 125). "Rugged individualism," do-or-die incentive which was the early traditional American spirit, proved to be the most powerful economic force in history; but it also meant misery for the weak or unlucky who failed to survive the rugged competition.

Inherent, too, within Lockean, Smithian and American capitalism was the "work ethic" and capitalist spirit initiated in the early protestant religions.* Ben Franklin summed it up succinctly:

> "The way to wealth, if you desire it, is as plain as the way to the market. It depends chiefly on two words, industry and frugality; that is, waste neither time nor money, but make the best use of both. Without industry and frugality, nothing will do, and with them, everything. He that gets all he can honestly and saves all he gets will certainly become rich...."[3]

Plato, Marx, and Socialism

Two human tendencies, always in political conflict, dominate history; the one that prevails in a society and its government sets the fundamental philosophy and style of the society, usually for centuries or millennia: they are the desire for freedom vs the desire for order, stability and safety. The latter is so powerful and basic that virtually

* The "work ethic" is a key concept in this and later chapters. It can be reviewed above on pages 72-73, 80, 115-116. It is a value system favoring hard work and saving as opposed to leisure and spending (i.e. consumption, except for essentials necessary for life).

all societies and their thought leaders have sacrificed, even utterly suppressed, freedom (anarchy and its terrors) in order to insure the absolute essential of a civilized society, societal order and stability (see Toynbee's profound analysis of this human dichotomy, p. 13 above). The few exceptions, historical societies which achieved democratic freedom (for example, the ancient Greek city states), soon abused their freedom, became soft and lazy, spent their money on luxuries instead of defense from aggressors, quickly went bankrupt in money and national spirit, and survived as free democracies for only short periods of time.* (Modern America, of course, is another exception, but so far only a 200-year-old "experiment" and, many say, already deteriorating as a survivable society, diseased by the usual abuses of freedom.)

Instinctively, all human societies throughout recorded history have opted (by necessity, despite deep desire for freedom) for a firm, dictatorial central government control, preferring order and safety to the dangers and chaos of freedom. Plato was the first to conceptualize this preference in his *Republic* and other writings. The historian, Plutarch, tells how Plato was invited as a "consultant" to aid the new dictator of Sicily (Dionysius II) in forming his government - and Plato advised strongly against any kinds of democratic methods. Plato had no interest in progress, freedom or human adventurism; he was deeply dedicated to preserving societal order, stability and safety. It should be added that Aristotle, who differed so radically with Plato on most issues, also (in his *Politics*) favored dictatorship or monarchy over democracy (which, he said, usually is or becomes chaos and dangerous anarchy).

Since the conquest of democratic Athens by Philip of Macedon 2300 years ago there have been no democratic societies; only societies ruled and held stable by strong (often necessarily ruthless) state and church dictators. The entire history of Europe's states, kings, emperors, churches and popes demonstrates the ultimate preference for order and stability rather than human freedom.

Marx and Modern Communism

Karl Marx (1818-1883), a German social philosopher, is clearly

---

* Ancient Athens, under the brilliant leadership of a general, the famous Pericles, defeated its foes and soon became the greatest of the Greek city state democracies. The citizens increasingly voted for more building programs, grain subsidies for all, fewer troops in the field and ships at sea, and less taxes. In less than a century, the world's greatest orator, Demosthenes, delivered his three great speeches (called the "Philippics," about 345 BC.) to try to inspire the Athenians to realistic action. He failed. (See p. 102)

the chief theorist of modern socialism (called communism in Russia and many other countries). Fascinated by the Hegelian dialectic, but not Hegel's idealist setting for it (see p. 125 and 129), he adopted a philosophy of dialectical materialism and founded, upon that basis, the economics of socialism. (His philosophy and economics are not *necessarily* related as they happen to be in the Russian and Chinese systems today, combining materialism, atheism and socialism; many modern nations are socialist, following Marxist economics, while at the same time theistic or democratic or both.) We are here concerned with Marx's *economic* theories (socialism) as published in his early *Communist Manifesto* (1848 when he was only 30) and his later, mature and monumental classic, *Das Kapital*.

Marx was incensed at the cruelty of capitalism and its "survival of the fittest" acceptance of misery for the weak, the uncompetitive, the average worker in mines and factories who barely eked out a living in food for his family while owners and managers drew high profits from the labors of the worker. Marx became determined to destroy the world's capitalist systems and replace them with his own socialism. (Essentially, Marx's socialism eliminates private property, places all resources and means of production in the hands of the state -which therefore owns all property, lets the state by central planning for all employ all workers to produce what is needed for all and then to be distributed to all, "each contributing according to his *ability* and receiving benefits according to his *needs*," like a communal family - hence the convenient term "communism" - all working their best for the family as a whole regardless of differences in each man's production as compared to his needs and uses of communal production.)

In Marx's view, capitalism and its individualistic striving for personal profit through economic competition made the strong stronger, the weak weaker, the worker a slave and capitalists rich. These riches must be distributed to all who need them, not held by a lone capitalist. But socialism could replace capitalism only by revolutions (political) destroying existing governments and replacing them with new leaders dedicated to establishing the socialist system. The Russian revolution of 1919, establishing a new socialist order, was Marxism's first major conquest for its ideology. The strategy has never changed and is going on daily today: foment revolution in a capitalist nation, replace old leaders with socialist-oriented ones, establish and administer socialist systems and laws. Even if by dictatorship, if necessary (as it always is).

Socialism now prevails, in absolute or some degree, in virtually every modern nation, including America since the 1930s. In America, the current tension between the two major human tendencies (freedom and free market capitalism vs social order and stability through central government socialistic control of production and distribution of goods) is the ongoing and intense political -and ethical or human value- issue. Insofar as America is a democracy, the people will decide on the extent to which they prefer capitalism vs socialism. This is the most fundamental value issue boiling, and often near explosion point, in America.

Two Views of the Purposes of Business

The two basic human tendencies identified above can be polarized as dictatorship vs democracy (political arrangements) and socialism vs capitalism (economic arrangements). (See chart on p. 174.) As noted already, any nation and any reader's value preference will probably lie somewhere between the extremes on either the political or the economic continuum. One hundred years ago, America was almost an absolute democracy with the people dominant and government weak as well as purely capitalist with almost no government control of business. It was a nation of individualists, self-reliant and suspicious of government, near-chaotic and disorderly democracy, passionate pride in each individual's freedom and personal opportunity to compete for position, profits and wealth. Today, America has shifted sharply from the earlier pure or extreme positions (pure democracy and capitalism) into a midway position on both continuums: still a democracy but this limited by a powerful central (federal) government, often enforcing virtual dictatorial control; and still a capitalist nation but with clear and growing elements of socialism (best exemplified by distribution of income and profits from successful societal members to the unsuccessful by means of federal taxation and welfare spending). On the p.174 chart, today's America is somewhere near the center of the chart.*

Along the economic continuum, capitalism and socialism view the purposes of business quite differently. In both systems, the objective (or inherent) purpose of business is to produce and distribute goods and services. In both systems, every man is both a producer and a consumer producing goods as a working employee (in a factory, farm etc.) and consuming goods produced by the economic system. The radical difference between capitalism and socialism is in the human mechanisms by which (a) producers (workers) are motivated to produce, (b) what products and how much of each are produced, (c) which consumers and in

* Although this author, being human, has his own strong value preferences along both the political and the economic continua, the purpose of this book is to clarify and improve ethical analysis of such value judgments, not here to advocate his own. Thus, all sides of all issues will be presented as objectively as possible.

what proportion each benefit from the society's production, and (d) the regulation of all these complex producer-consumer relationships. Under capitalism, the mechanism for accomplishing these four economic objectives is free market forces and the "profit motive;" under socialism, the four objectives are accomplished by central government ownership of all property and capital, central planning of all production (what and how much), government distribution of all goods produced by government-determined wages and prices (all workers are employed by the government) and complete central control of the entire economy (there is no such thing as a free market or profit motive).

Thus, in short, the purposes of business under capitalism are two-fold: not only the production and distribution of goods and services, but also personal profits for producers in the use of their property (i.e. capital) and their varying degrees of industry and skill. Personal ownership of property and capital along with the "profit motive" are the key elements of capitalism as distinct from socialism's state ownership and eradication of the "profit" system. Therein, in essence, stand the eternal differences between the philosophers Locke and Marx and the economists Smith and Marx.

THE SOCIAL RESPONSIBILITY ISSUE IN AMERICA

According to classical capitalist theory, the purpose of a business is solely to maximize its profits by its optimum efficiency in producing and selling highest quality goods at lowest prices. Maximum personal profit is the fuel driving individuals and businesses to maximum effort and innovation to please consumers, gain their purchases and keep good paying customers. Apart from anyone's natural desire for profits, the function of the profit motive is to handle efficiently the four key problems of any economy (as above): (a) hope for personal profit provides intense motivation to work hard and gain rewards in proportion to one's efforts and skills; (b) what is produced, and how much of it, is constantly determined by millions of individual buying decisions in the free market (profit-oriented producers produce more of what is selling and stop producing what is not selling); (c) profits and wages earned by successful personal efforts in satisfying consumer needs (sales) and employer needs (degrees of effort and skill of workers to be hired) determine greatly varying degrees of personal income and purchasing power, i.e. the amount of money each individual has to make and pay for a buying decision (capitalist economists call this "demand" which controls supply of goods); and (d) kinds and amounts of production and consumption become, therefore, automatically regulated by each hard-working individual seeking always his own best interest (profit) in each of millions of economic transactions constantly going on in the economy.

For example: (a) a small businessman or young engineer in his first job is willing to work his hardest day and night and invest his savings (capital) in a reasonable expectation of a high return (profit) later (in socialist Russia, such efforts merely produce more for the state treasury, not oneself personally, and, therefore, such individual effort is uncommon; without personal profit in working hard, few do); (b) if a merchant finds his sales of fish down and that people are demanding more beef, he immediately stops his orders for more fish and increases orders for beef from his suppliers -who, in turn, produce less fish and more beef; in this way, throughout all industries, to avoid losses and make profits, everyone produces or stocks in stores only that which is selling (in Russia, central state planners set annual quotas for what is to be produced -and how much of it; usually the plan fails and people are lined up at stores for fish they don't want and beef "out of stock" as state planners guessed wrong on their quotas, not to mention the lack of incentive for anyone to please and attract consumers); (c) one man works hard and patiently for years and finally succeeds in buying a small home of his own; his brother works little and never receives the benefits of one's own home (in Russia, apartments and homes are doled out by one's position on a waiting list, not by past efforts or present purchasing power); and (d) a man wants a luxury car and, from his life earnings, that being his free choice, pays the price for it and gets it (in Russia, a luxury car -or even average cars- seldom appear in the national state production plan and are simply not available except on the "black market").

These are examples of capitalism and the "profit motive" at work as compared to socialist state central planning. More comprehensive details about the free market capitalist system are tempting but beyond the scope of this book. The interested reader should read the modern classic on, and advocating, free market capitalism, Milton Friedman's Capitalism and Freedom (University of Chicago, 1962) and later works by Friedman.

Maximizing vs "Satificing" Profits

Pure capitalism, i.e. individual "raw" competition for profits with no government or legal regulation of it, lasted about a century in America (see Robber Barons, p.24-29 above) - and then failed as a pure system. Marx had prophesied that "pure capitalism had within it the seeds of its own destruction," and he proved correct on that key point. In briefly tracing the history of American businessmen in the last century, especially the "Robber Barons," it is obvious that their lawless and unethical competition inevitably led to a single victor in each major industry (a monopoly) who then controlled production and set prices sky-high as he pleased, gouged the public unmercifully and pocketed a personal fortune in "maximized" profits. Ironically, as Marx had predicted in Das Kapital, pure competition led inevitably to its opposite, monopoly controlled by profit-hungry capitalists. In both theory and practice, Marx's solution was, of course, to abolish capitalism and let the fair and impartial state monopolize all production and distribution (socialism) to avoid the evils and human misery caused by the individual profit-seeking of capitalism.

The American solution (in the early 1900s beginning with anti-trust laws, p.18 above) was to retain the powerful productive energies of capitalism but to regulate them by laws against monopoly and other unfair effects of pure capitalism. Thus, about 1900, America began to be a system of "modified capitalism," operating in a free political democracy where the people by voting decided on what laws were needed to modify and control capitalism. In America, the political system of democracy is more fundamental than the economic and, indeed, modifies it as it sees fit at the ballot box. As explained in the diagram on p.18, the American voters, if they come to wish it, can "modify" the nation's capitalistic system all the way to the opposite extreme of democratic socialism. In fact, over the past 50 years, that is the distinct direction being set by the majority of American voters - in order to impose "social responsibility" upon profit-oriented business.

Thus, today, few American businesses attempt any longer literally to maximize profits. This was the pure philosophy of the "Robber Barons" and is obsolete today. Any major business even appearing as maximizing profits, at the expense inevitably of perceived responsibility to the society as a whole, causes a public outcry and possibly great damage to the business by new and restrictive laws voted in by critics.

Economists today describe American business's profit-seeking more accurately as "satisficing" profits, i.e. trying to make a satisfactory profit, enough to provide dividends to shareholders, reinvest profits into the business to sustain it and at the same time discharge its proper responsibilities to consumers and society at large -as perceived by the public (each with vote in hand as he watches what business does).

The Beginnings of the "Social Responsibility" Movement

Pure capitalist theory, of course, held that business has no responsibility at all to society - except to seek maximum profits which, by the "invisible hand," would result in a benefit to society in the form of good products at low prices. Poverty, sickness, unemployment, inadequate education of citizens, etc. are, in pure capitalism, not business problems, but social problems for people to handle themselves or, if they can't, for government to handle, if it can.

Gradually, toward the end of the last century, the American public concluded that business should be responsible to society rather than the mere maximizing of profits. America's antitrust laws and other early 20th-century laws regulating business practices were the beginnings of the so-called "social responsibility" (of business) movement.

The formal beginnings of the social responsibility concept in the management literature can be found mainly in Oliver Sheldon's The Philosophy of Management (London, Pitman & Sons, 1923). Here, within a decade of Taylor's "scientific management" movement in America (methods of maximizing profits by scientific investigation and improvement of workers' productivity)*, Sheldon warned British and American managers that business's first duty is to the society within which it is privileged to live and operate profitably, not to maximized profits at any cost to society. Several of his principles for business are worth quoting, written, as they were, 60 years ago:**

> "It is important, therefore, early in our consideration of Management in industry to insist that ..... its primary responsibility is social and communal." And "the governing principles of an industrial management must be based on the concept of service to the community." And "while management must be concerned with profit, it must also achieve efficiency in the human elements of the factory." [4]

Sheldon was not alone for long in his new view of the social duties of business. Increasing numbers of writers from every social field (philosophy, religion, political science, sociology, etc.) urged limits upon capitalism, more social responsibility of business, some even to the point of eradicating capitalism entirely in America and replacing it with society-oriented socialist arrangements -including Russian and Marxist communism.

A Definition of Social Responsibility (of Business)

"Social responsibility" is defined in as many ways and degrees as there are writers using the term. The term, therefore, is hardly exact. However, in general, social responsibility refers to a business's action performed in the interests of society's needs over and above its basic

---

* A detailed explanation of Taylor's "scientific management" can be found in this author's The Theory and Practice of Managing (1982, pp.45-48).

** Sheldon was not an impractical academic theorist, idealizing in an "ivory tower." Oxford educated, he spent his entire career in industrial management, rising finally to top corporate management and the board of directors.

functions of producing and/or distributing economic goods efficiently and profitably. Many such actions are now required by law (fair advertising and pricing, product guarantees, non-discriminatory hiring, contribution to society's needs through corporation taxes, compliance with pollution-control norms to protect the environment, etc.). This is the kind of social responsibility, required by law, that started about 1900 with the public outcry for antitrust laws. Today, many writers regard such business actions (required now by law) as minimal and not at all genuine social responsibility. Genuine social responsibility of any business, judged by many American writers and voters, means business actions in society's (not merely business's) interests beyond the mere minimum requirements of law.*

For example, hiring a fair quota of minority employees (even if many are not really qualified for the job and the hiring is done just to "meet quota") is no longer regarded as genuine social responsibility - since this contribution to society's problems is a minimum requirement of current law. An example of genuine social responsibility would be a business starting a program of training for hard-core and uneducated "unemployables," at usually high company costs, paying them while in their classrooms and "carrying" their inefficient work performance for years afterward, all of which is (as yet) a social contribution beyond the requirements of law.

A (Partial) Force-field Diagram of Three Economic Systems

Now that we have before us the concepts of capitalism, socialism and social responsibility, let's contrast their values (ethical and other) by the convenient method of force-field diagramming. We will use the shorthand (outline) version of force-field analysis (review p. 169 above) with plus lines and lengths (+++++) for positive factors and minus lines and lengths (-----) for negative factors, except here we will permit all line lengths (representing strength of the factor) to be the same. The reader, if he wishes, can increase or decrease line lengths based on his own value preferences as to the significance of each factor. Note, too, that it is a partial, not complete, analysis; for purposes of initial clarification and appraisal of the values in each of three economic systems. The reader might wish to complete this

* For a full-length review of current definitions of social responsibility, see Thomas Zenisek's "Corporate Social Responsibility: A Conceptualization Based on Organizational Literature," Academy of Management Review, 1979, Vol.4, No.3, pp.359-368. The author concedes there is much confusion about a specific definition of social responsibility of business -and attempts his own.

analysis after reading the remaining chapters of this book. The partial force-field analysis is as follows:

Option 1 Pure Capitalism (America - 19th Century)

+++++ Individual human freedom unrestricted (individual pride)
+++++ Personal ownership of property (the right to use it freely)
+++++ Equal opportunity for all to reach highest potential based on how hard they want to work (profits as the reward)
+++++ Economic supply of goods regulated by demand (free market forces control production and distribution efficiently)
+++++ Maximum abundance of production, productivity, living standards and national wealth (fueled by profit motive)
----- Uneven distribution of profits, wealth and purchasing power (raw competition channels riches to the successful and poverty, often abject misery, to the unsuccessful)
----- Winners in pure competition win big; losers work & starve
----- Insecurity for all (even the rich); no government help at all when misfortune strikes (capitalism's typical swings from boom to bust, high to low employment, etc.)
----- Individual freedom creates disorder, instability, anarchy

Option 2 (Democratic) Socialism (Sweden 1980s - See Case # 11)

+++++ Government guarantees distribution of goods equally to all
+++++ Security for all: Government provides welfare equally for all independently of any individual's age, health, ability to work, skills, effort or personal circumstances
+++++ The Marxist principle: "a communal spirit in which each contributes to the community according to his ability and receives from it according to his needs."
+++++ Government, by its decisions, cares for all (cradle to grave)
+++++ High degree of order, stability and discipline in a society (little danger of anarchy or disruption caused by men bent upon asserting their individual freedoms, etc.)
----- Very little individual freedom, pride, initiative or personal development of individual potential (any assertion of such is viewed by the state as suspicious or disruptive)
----- Very little incentive to work hard (no proportionate reward -profits - for extra individual effort; extra production by outstanding effort goes to the state and is given to all equally, whether they work hard, easy or not at all)
----- There is, as above, no profit motive for personal incentive
----- Minimum national production to be distributed (equally)
----- Great incentive of people to cheat the welfare system
----- Most citizens passive, do little, wait to be fed by the state

Option 3 Modified Capitalism with Social Responsibility (USA 1980s)

+++++ Considerable degree of freedom but limited by many laws

+++++ Personal ownership of property but uses limited by laws

+++++ Economic demand regulates supply, with some control of both by government intervention (by means of taxation and welfare spending)

+++++ Profit incentive still at work but limited (high taxes take much of one's extra effort but one keeps some of it)

+++++ Abundance of productivity, wealth and GNP not as great as under pure capitalism, but very good, not excellent

+++++ Government taxation and welfare programs distribute goods and money more evenly than under pure capitalism (whether one is healthy or not, works or not, all have a "right" to food, housing, education, "dignity," etc.

+++++ High security for all (the Government will provide)

----- Many professional and talented people, who could contribute much more to national resources, don't (taxes take most of it; not worth the extra effort for the little left)

----- The efficient law of economic supply and demand is manipulated by government and no longer works well

----- For many non-workers, there is little incentive to find or keep jobs (they get equal income from welfare benefits)

----- Great incentive for non-workers to cheat on welfare system

----- With large proportion of adults motivated to live on welfare rather than work, this non-productive (useless) burden of consumers (but not producers), a gigantic "overhead accounting" charge against the national net economic and financial condition, reduces the nation's financial health and ability to compete successfully with more capitalist-oriented economies such as Japan's (whose higher productivity by all its people results in better products and lower prices - and even Americans buy them)*

----- With universal suffrage (see pp. 41 & 82 above), now a reality in America (explicitly rejected by America's founding fathers as absurd and self-destructive for the nation's survival), millions of self-perceived "poor," "disadvantaged" or otherwise dissatisfied voters can "modify" American capitalism by new laws all the way to complete socialism, if not dictatorship (see p. 13)

---

* America's new annual debt, mainly for social welfare and interest on old debt, now averages $100 billion; total debt $1 trillion; interest on it annually $18 billion; number of Americans getting welfare: 30 million on medical aid; 22 million on food stamps etc.

Although we will not consume the space for it, one could easily add many more options to the three illustrated. For example, Option 4 could be Communism (Russia 1980s), Option 5 South American dictatorships, and many variations of Option 3 increasing or decreasing either the capitalist or the socialist components of it in infinitely varying degrees (which is what American politics is fiercely debating right now).

Social Responsibility as the "Internalization" of External Costs

The terms in this title need defining with an example. Keep in mind that business costs are all resources (money, labor, utilities, etc.) used or destroyed in the process of making a product for ultimate sale. Such costs, of course, are itemized and deducted from final sales price as gross margin which determines ultimate net profit after all costs. As we shall see, identification and recognition of costs are essential to any calculation of net profits. In a food supermarket, for example, average costs (products bought, labor, all overhead, etc.) are 99% of final retail price, leaving 1¢ net profit on each dollar of sales (and that is before income taxes which take 1/2 of each cent profit).

But consider the case of Apex Chemical Co., which produces tons of industrial chemicals for other manufacturers of paints, black-top highway materials, roofing sealants, etc. and has all the ordinary internal costs of labor, materials bought, overhead etc. Apex, of course, itemizes these costs and, on a cost-plus routine basis, sets final prices accordingly. But, while Apex Chemical is using labor and other internal resources, it is also dumping several million tons of waste into its adjacent river (which is the drinking water source for many downstream cities). These downstream cities spend tax funds to purify the contaminated river water to make it safe to drink. It is a cost, but a cost external to Apex Chemical. Several of the cities downstream complain that they (their citizens) are paying costs of removing dangerous wastes created by another (Apex) and insist that Apex Chemical begin to pay these costs (external to it) by direct tax on amount of waste dumped or by internal mechanisms to remove the waste before it is dumped into the river. Apex agrees (or is forced to) and "internalizes" into its routine costs the "external" effects (wastes) it causes.

America is full of cases like this where manufacturing companies pollute water sources, expel poisonous substances into the air people breathe or otherwise damage the physical (and social) environment which are all costs someone somehow someday must pay. Social responsibility implies that companies that cause the damage internalize the costs of eliminating or correcting the damage. The auto industry has begun to internalize pollution costs by pollution-control devices and low-pollution gasolines which are now internalized costs built into the original price of the new automobile.

Garrett Hardin (Exploring New Ethics for Survival, 1969, p.81) has been as interested in this issue as any major environmental scientist for many years (see Case 11 below) and has charted business's internalization of external costs as follows:

Specific External Cost	When Internalized
Cost of raw materials	Before Christ
Cost of labor	From about AD 1000 to 1862
Cost of raising and educating labor	From about 1800 to 1900
Cost of industrial accidents	From about 1875 to 1925
Cost of industrial diseases	From about 1900 onward
Cost of cleaning up pollution	Yet to be internalized (fully)
Cost of preventing pollution	Yet to be internalized (fully)

Pure (perfect competition) capitalism, attempting to literally maximize profits in every way possible, internalizes no external costs; socialism, by its definition, internalizes all external costs; modified capitalism (America 1980s, as above in the force-field analysis) prefers not to internalize such costs but gradually does so as public pressures, laws and the demands of social responsibility in a democracy make this new policy either necessary (by law) or advisable (to avoid more restrictive laws and regulations upon business).

The Case for Increasing the Social Responsibility of Business

In the atmosphere of the modified capitalism of America today, a wide and vocal division of opinion exists over whether -or the extent to which- increasing business social responsibility is valid, nationally useful or realistically wise. Let's look first at the arguments advanced in support of increased business social responsibility.

1. If business does not anticipate and assume a degree of social responsibility that satisfies the public, the public will force it upon business by restrictive laws and government regulation. This is the supreme practical reason why business, in its own interests, must be sensitive and effective in meeting its social responsibility. Antitrust laws, precipitated by blatant profit-maximizing of the "Robber Barons" and followed by a century of increasingly restrictive government regulation, dramatically illustrate this practical reality in a democratic America (see pp. 16-21 above).

2. The American public will not tolerate business's failure to internalize external costs which business causes (as explained in the section immediately above).

3. Any person, individual or corporate, must accept a degree of responsibility commensurate with his or its power and authority. In the case of giant corporations, power and authority to influence society arise from their financial resources by which they can open or close plants, create or eliminate jobs in one community vs another, affect elections by financial support of chosen candides, invest in capital equipment or projects, influence supply and prices, and so on. The more power a corporation exercises over a society, the more its basic responsibility to the ultimate good of that society -as a whole.

4. Reciprocity: Large firms like Exxon, IBM, etc. take so much money and resources from society by their operations and sales, from which they profit, that they owe some of it back to society in the form of contributions to benefit society.

5. All organizations are run by people at the top and corporations are legally persons subject to law and to the same ethical norms that should bind every person in a society. Therefore corporations owe society as much service and sacrifice as individual citizens (in military efforts for national defense, keeping the environment clean, aiding the disadvantaged, training citizens for productive work, etc.).

6. People, including corporations, are responsible for shouldering and solving the problems they create (this is similar to #2 above -internalizing external costs).

7. Corporate management as trustee: A large proportion of the resources of America and its society is, in effect, entrusted to the managers of corporations in a manner similar to a bank acting as the trustee for a customer, manging his funds in his ultimate interest but with a fair fee (profit) to the bank. Like the bank, all corporations should regard themselves as trustees of society's resources, acting in society's interests as primary objective with personal profit secondary. Robert Brookings advanced this thesis as early as 1925: "Management is thus coming to occupy the position of trustee.....This change is not yet complete. It is a trend rather than an accomplished fact, but it is a very promising trend."[5] (Already a trend in 1925; now it's 1982.)

8. "Business can profit by filling unmet social needs." William Norris, chairman of Control Data, rather than an academic or government theorist, made that statement in 1981.[6] Paraphrasing his reasoning, government is running huge deficits trying -and failing- to meet social needs (poverty, unemployment, etc.), which deficits force government to keep borrowing, driving up interest rates and damping business ability to raise capital and operate at maximum productive capacity. If business stepped in, assumed many of the social responsibilities, deficits would shrink, business activity increase, more workers would be needed and have jobs, demand to buy would rise, business revenue and profits would follow -and all would gain.

9. Corporation management (its uniquely skilled and successful managers, so talented as to be worth in many cases near and over a million dollars of annual income) are far more capable than government bureaucrats of finding solutions to social problems and cutting through "red tape" to get it done. American government is notoriously ineffective and inefficient in achieving established objectives (for example, the current fiscal mess in the Social Security program, wild degrees of blatant fraud in administration of food stamp and others of the hundreds of uncoordinated social programs, the Postal Service - imagine what telephone service would be like if the government were in charge of it!). Obviously, the bottom-line-orientation, reality- and market-tested top talent of America's corporations could work a miracle as compared to government's past track record.

10. Pragmatism and Long-range Utility standard (p.70): In the long run, business will be far better served (in terms of its own profit interests) by serving -rather than fighting- a democratic society which -by its voting- is the ultimate determinant of the fate of business in America. The "old days" of "let the public be damned," as voiced by the robber barons of yore, have yielded to a dangerous (to business) public attitude of "let business be damned" unless it can show that it's a good citizen, contributing greatly to society, excelling in its consistent record of imaginative social responsibility and a (perceived) net asset rather than liability.

11. Public Image of individual corporations - in "capitalist" competition: the time will soon come -many say it's already here - when a corporation's present and future prospects for survival and profits will depend critically upon how competing corporations in the same or diverse industries are perceived by the public as socially responsible or not, good citizens or not, "good guys or bad guys." The public's key buying decisions, investment decisions and voting on matters affecting regulation of business in general and punishment of specifically targeted firms will all be based on each individual corporation's perceived public image. Corporations will -or should- find themselves in classic capitalist competition for the most "socially responsible" and attractive public images - no longer as a fringe element in corporate policy but a bottom-line "survival" business strategy.

12. "The Iron Law of Responsibility:" Well known in the history of governments and political science, this ultimate and practical law states that "ultimately, and inevitably, those in power who abuse it -the perennial human tendency of men when they finally achieve power- and ignore their responsibility to the people, soon lose it," either by societal rebellions and revolutions, economic sanctions or killing restrictions imposed by law. No one ever escapes the "Iron Law."

The Case Against Increasing the Social Responsibility of Business

1. The specific (internal) objective of a business as "profit and the maximizing of it:" Although occupied recently with monetarist economic theories (for which he won his Nobel prize), Milton Friedman is still the national champion of free market economics with the absolute minimum of government interference (such as regulation) and virtually no so-called social responsibility. Friedman's works, especially his Capitalism and Freedom, constitute the modern "bible" for opponents of the social responsibility movement.[7] (Needless to say, they dislike the semantic wording of the issue which verbalizes them as "against social responsibility".) In their view, the exclusive social responsibility of business is to perform its business function efficiently and better than any other nation on earth; in this way, as in the past, American business's contribution to society, in terms of astounding feats of production and fast-rising standard of living for all, is the best and only possible contribution an efficiently functioning business system can or should attempt. To contaminate the essential functions of American business (efficient production and profit to the producers) is to destroy the business system as the unique and complex engine that has driven America, in less than two centuries, to the most prosperous people on earth. Why tamper with, or tear apart, a mechanism which works - as no other economic system, especially socialism, can do? Friedman's best recent presentation of his case sums up his view in the title, "The Social Responsibility of Business is to Increase its Profits" (The New York Times Magazine, 9/13, 1970). If business fails to make a good profit, the functions of profit (below) cease to operate (as occurs in socialist nations) and the unique economic engine that has made America an unprecedented success fails as well. The best contribution business can make to American society is to keep on being the most efficient producer in the world and generating the profits needed to sustain and motivate people to that high level of effort.

2. The Functions of Profit: As mentioned often above, the key and miraculously simple magic underlying America's economic success is enormous human incentive to work and produce at each person's highest potential for the rewards (profits) equally available to all who set their minds and wills to high levels of effort and productivity. As personal profit from hard work is eroded by taxation and other social costs demanded by law or "expected" by the public, the critical factor of incentive to work hard and well is eroded as well. The result (appearing already in America) will be -or is- the lethargy and "do-as-little-as-possible" work attitude common today in socialist nations (review Case 11 below). As profits decline, business has less money to reinvest in plants and equipment which create jobs, payrolls and

demand by consumers -with money- for products, all of which in continuing sequences keep the economy running in high gear; and the entire productive process is fueled and sustained by profits and each person's natural desire for them. The solution to social problems such as poverty and unemployment is not to bankrupt business and government with welfare programs that reward indolence but to cut such waste to the bone and encourage everyone to work his way back into a profit-oriented, high-production and high-motivation capitalist system.

3. Corporate managers, who give away profits to society, are violating the rights of owners and stockholders. Friedman, in the article cited above, says: "What does it mean to say that the corporate executive has a 'social responsibility' in his capacity as businessman? If this statement is not pure rhetoric, it must mean that he is to act in some way that is not in the interest of his employers. For example,.....that he is to make expenditures on reducing pollution beyond the amount required by law in order to contribute to the social objective of improving the environment. In (this) case, the corporate executive would be spending someone else's money for general social interest. Insofar as his actions in accord with his 'social responsibility' reduce returns to stockholders, he is spending their money." He might have added that most of the stockholders are not the "rich" but ordinary hard-working citizens whose life savings are directly or indirectly invested in corporations through annuities, pension funds and other securities. In strict legal terms, such executives, spending other people's money unnecessarily, are violating their <u>fiduciary</u> obligations; that is as illegal (or should be) as a bank trustee spending his customers' funds whimsically.[8]

4. The fundamental assumption underlying the semantically luring expression "social responsibility" is purely socialistic and subversive. That socialist (Marxist) premise is that private ownership and profit-making should be eradicated (as they are in Russia today), all economic control of production and distribution ceded to a powerful central government and that all will work and contribute to the state according to their abilities and receive benefits (from the state) according to their needs. See page 186 above for more detail. All agree that America has in no way reached the ultimate of socialism as now pervasive in Russia, China or Sweden; but the popular yearning for more and more government "goodies," implemented into law by congressmen and state legislators in order to get reelected, has set a clear trend and direction toward socialism - and operates upon its fundamental assumption (only vaguely recognized by most Americans). The current American tilt toward socialism is, of course, aggravated by the dangerous American policy, now law, of universal suffrage.

5. The costs of social programs and social involvement: As is obvious, social programs (welfare, food stamps, subsidized housing, pollution controls, safety regulations, product liability and so on) constitute consumption without commensurate -or usually any - net production of goods or services, i.e. overhead costs that somebody must pay somehow. ("There's no such thing as a free lunch; somebody pays for it.") The American taxpayers, including businesses, already pay to a point where incentive to work at maximum capacity is fast eroding (see #2 above on the Functions of Profit). If businesses are required or expected to pay even more of such social costs, these costs must be passed on to consumers in the form of higher prices, sales decline, production is decreased, workers are laid off and the entire fine-tuned economic system begins to collapse. Marginal firms, usually small businesses operating on a thin profit margin, cannot absorb the additional costs and simply go bankrupt. Even corporations that survive (for a while) must absorb the social costs in higher prices which drives consumers to more efficient and lower-priced foreign competitors. In this sense, social involvement is destroying the American economic system and outright socialism may become the only alternative remaining.

6. The Iron Law of Productivity: People will naturally buy from the producer with the highest quality goods at the lowest prices. Today, millions of Americans buy Japanese cars because Japanese productivity is simply higher (a better product for a lower price). Their buying decisions just follow the "iron law of productivity;" all the rhetoric about 'social responsibility' and 'social ideals' will not alter such market realities. As American businesses add more and more costs of 'social responsibility' into higher and higher prices, productivity decreases, sales are lost to competitors and the system stalls. Those who, by law or public pressure, insist on burdening American business with more social costs threaten to keep reducing American productivity as a result -and with it the entire economic system. All Americans would lose if American business is forced to diverge from its inherent economic purpose (see # 1 above).

7. The major cause of destructive inflation is government deficit spending for social programs. If business, as well as government, adds in similar social costs, prices must rise even further, meaning even more inflation. Inflation is the cruelest cost of all to the average American worker, a hidden tax for past social spending in the form of ever-rising prices for essential goods, crushing especially those on fixed incomes from life savings (such as old and retired workers). The only gainers in inflation are debtors (who pay back in devalued money) and non-workers (welfare is indexed to rising inflation). The moral

significance of this is obvious by any of the fundamental ethical tests (p. 155 above) such as justice, long-range utility, the general law standard etc.: the (probably) well-intentioned movement toward more government social spending and more "social responsibility" for business (however nobly sounding the semantic expressions chosen for it) is fundamentally unethical in a still-free society and patently unwork-able and impractical upon any long-range analysis of consequences;* in simplest terms, lifetime hard workers lose what they earned while non-workers prosper and live increasingly better (due to protests, etc.) -all of which is clearly unethical.

In purely ethical terms, both socialism and capitalism pass the ethical tests. Capitalism justly rewards the hardest workers with the highest profits for their effort; socialism justly distributes to all equal proportions of the nation's production based on equal, and usually minimum, work effort by all. America's current and ambiguous system, deceptively tempting hard workers with rewards which taxes and inflation take away from them (gradually but surely) while actually rewarding non-workers and non-producers with abundant welfare for a lifetime, violates every ethical test. This hard reality, underlying all the semantics and euphemisms (especially the adroit and deceptive term "social responsibility"), poisons the current American system and must inevitably drive it either to the full ethical and practical integrity of traditional American capitalism or honest socialism.

Social Audits - Measuring Corporate Social Responsibility in Action

Whichever of the many positions one advocates on "social responsibility" (the extreme views, as above, as well as the many intermediate options), the trend toward business social responsibility and some significant degree of it already exist as facts in today's America. The proponents of social responsibility, in the 1970s, have even begun to try to measure it in large corporations. The effort to measure a particular business's social responsibility is called a "social audit." Being a very new discipline, social audits are thusfar, of course, very rough in their methodology (surveys of corporations' socially responsible actions and plans, etc.) and will need much refining. But even these embryonic versions of social auditing create the beginnings of public

* The massive example of impracticality of a social program and grossly misjudging its long-range consequences is the Social Security program in America, begun in the 1930s as OASI (Old Age Survivors Insurance). The program is now virtually bankrupt and is not insurance at all (benefits based ultimately on invested premiums), but current taxes on the young to pay benefits to the old. It's simply a social program; and many aren't counting on it.

documentation and thus increased accountability for social action by named corporations in such specific categories as pollution control, product safety, minority employment, training of hard-core unemployed, personnel counseling, public health, etc. (see the recent study by W.F.Abbott and R.J.Monsen, "On the Measurement of Corporate Social Responsibility," Academy of Management Journal, 1979, Vol.22, No.3, for details).

REFERENCES

1 Heilbroner, R. & L.Thurow, Economics Explained, Prentice-Hall, 1982
2 Graphics are from Davis, K., et.al., Business Society and Environment, p.20
3 Josephson, M., The Robber Barons, Harcourt, 1934, p.10
4 George, Claude, The History of Management Thought, Prentice-Hall, 1972, p.134. And see Sheldon's book, p.xv.
5 Brookings, R.S., Industrial Ownership, Macmillan, 1925, p.23
6 U.S.News & World Report, 9/21/81, page 74
7 Capitalism and Freedom, U.of Chicago, 1962
8 See also Theodore Levitt's critique in "The Dangers of Social Responsibility," Harvard Business Review, Sept.-Oct., 1958.

For Further Reading

Davis, K. & R.L.Blomstrom, Business, Society and Environment, 1971
Hay, R.D. & E.R.Gray, Business and Society, Southwestern, 1981
And, see appropriate titles in the Bibliography at end of book.

QUESTIONS AND PROBLEMS

1. Define and illustrate (a current example) the following concepts:

(a) Business	(b) Economics	(c) Democracy
(d) Dictatorship	(e) Capitalism	(f) Socialism
(g) Marxism	(h) Communism	(i) Laissez faire
(j) Political system	(k) Economic system	(l) Free market
(m) the Lockean Five	(n) Freedom vs Order	(o) Profits
(p) Maximizing profits	(q) Satisficing profits	(r) Business purpose
(s) social responsibility	(t) Force-field diagram in outline form	
(u) Democratic socialism	(v) Internalizing external business costs	
(w) universal suffrage	(x) Government regulation of business	
(y) Iron laws of "responsibility" and of "productivity"		

2. List and explain the functions of profit in America's capitalism.
3. List and explain the (a)strengths and (b)weaknesses of capitalism.
4. List and explain the (a)strengths and (b)weaknesses of socialism.
5. Are you for or against "social responsibility" of business? Why?
6. Since only 10% of American drivers use seat belts in cars, government may soon mandate air bags. Do a force field diagram of this.

7 Consumerism

By its nature, any business's primary and fundamental relationship is with consumers, those who decide to buy and continue to buy the products (or services) of the business. Consumers' purchasing of its products is a business's sole, and essential, reason for even existing. (Jobs it provides, taxes it pays, social programs it supports, etc. must all be secondary to a business's inherent function of producing products people want and will pay for; if a business fails to satisfy consumers as to quality, price and other aspects of product delivery, they just don't buy and the business ceases to exist - the consumer relationship is just that basic.)

In a socialist nation, this relationship between producer and consumer is controlled by the state: producers make products, in kind, quality and quantity, according to central government annual plans; consumers buy it,after long waits in lines at stores, with little or no consumer choice - they buy what's available, if it is. A "consumer movement" in a socialist state like Russia would be a joke, a sad one, unless accompanied by a violent mass uprising like the Bolshevik or French desparate revolutions. In a free, democratic and (somewhat) capitalist America, a consumer movement for better products, quality, prices, and general consumer satisfaction is not only possible but a major fact of life for businesses in the 1980s. In America, a free and competitive market (to a substantial extent, despite socialist trends), not central government planning, determines what is produced: if a business produces anything other than the products, quality,prices, choices of color and style, etc. demanded by consumers, the latter just buy from a business that does satisfy and, by "natural selection," dissatisfying businesses quickly die while satisfying businesses thrive. This is essential capitalism and free market economics at work.

The Consumer Movement in America

But American consumers have suffered and been cheated often in their relationship with businesses, especially in the last century (see p.28-30 above). Which led to the first "consumer movement" about 1880. At that time, groups of consumers began organizing to communicate various consumer dissatisfactions to businesses and legislatures on such matters as misrepresentation of products, product defects and complete breakdowns, safety problems involving often danger to the life of the user, and especially the wild and exploitative trade in all "medicines," sought desparately by the sick (expecting the promised miracle cures) but often providing in reality nothing but ordinary erbs, vegetable oils and opium to suppress pain but hardly cure -and salesmen's profit margins were gigantic. Between 1880 and 1910, according to Beard's history of the period, over 100 laws were passed to control and regulate food and drug businesses and the Pure Food and Drug Act was enacted.[1] These consumer efforts were the beginnings of the "consumer movement" in America, now usually termed "consumerism." Since then, hundreds of consumer organizations have formed and gained political influence such as the Consumer Federation of America, the Consumer Union of the USA, the National Consumers League, Better Business Bureaus in most cities and states, etc. All are wielding enormous consumer pressure today upon businesses either directly or by means of political action affecting businesses. And with obvious firm effects: Borax Inc, a highly ethical advertiser of soaps today, ran early American advertisements claiming its "20-Mule Team Borax" would surely "improve one's complexion, remove dandruff, cure epilepsy, remove bunions, etc." as well as clean things as soap is supposed to do -which it did and does.[2] Borax's ads are much more conservative and factual today. (The Borax case is just a single, but typical, example of business life in early America. Even today's ethical and dependable Sears-Roebuck Co. would provide another example of changed views by businesses of consumers - see p.29 above.)

Let's examine, briefly, some of the main consumer issues today.

Product Reliability, Safety - and Liability

On March 3, 1974, a Turkish Airlines DC-10, with 346 passengers aboard, crashed into the outskirts of Paris, France killing all aboard. The DC-10 was built by McDonnell-Douglas Corporation with major design sub-contracts to the Convair Division of General Dynamics.[3] It was Ship 29 of the DC-10 line. And it was no accident in the usual sense - design engineers knew it was bound to happen. Ship 29 fell from the sky when its cargo-hold door blew open causing the floor of the passenger compartment to collapse, which tore apart the hydraulic and electrical control lines installed just under the floor. With complete loss of pilot controls, the DC-10 just dropped 10,000 feet to the earth. A similar incident had occurred in 1972 over Windsor, Ontario but enough below-floor lines held long enough to land safely. But, even as early as July 1970 when Ship 1 of the DC-10 line was being tested the same failure of the cargo door occurred. There can be no question that many engineers and managers at McDonnell-Douglas knew, before the Paris and Ontario crashes, about the high potential for a Class IV hazard (i.e. a hazard directly endangering life). The fatal management decision was to adhere to cost-cutting policies in every possible design option, still mindful of the severe financial crisis McDonnell-Douglas had weathered in the 1960s. An option in the design of the cargo door and passenger floor was available (i.e. not to run the critical control wires under the floor but through the ceiling so that a floor collapse would not make the plane unflyable) but was rejected as involving radically higher costs. An engineer (Homer Sewell), who has studied carefully the evidence from hearings and investigations following the Paris crash, categorically blames the McDonnell-Douglas engineers and managers:

"I believe that the engineers/managers at McDonnell-Douglas who were aware of the safety implications of the original floor configuration should have been charged in the DC-10 no.29 case with criminal negligence and prosecuted to the full extent of the law. They are, in my opinion, guilty, prima facie, of manslaughter, at the least.

It is nonsense to assert that, in an organization as large as the McDonnell-Douglas Corporation, it is impossible to distinguish the responsible parties from their fellow employees. In any aerospace company, a clear hierarchy of responsibility for basic product-design decisions begins with first level engineering supervision and would, in the case at issue, reach up to and include, as a minimum the individual executive in charge of the design engineering function in the company."[3]

A force-field diagram in outline form (p.169), ignoring many of the less important details, would look like this:

Option 1 Install electrical and hydraulic control lines under floor
+++++ Reduce a manufacturing cost relatively small in the plane
---------------------------------- Accept a Class IV hazard

Option 2 Install the control lines elsewhere such as in the ceiling
++++++++++++++++++++++++++++++++++ Avoid a Class IV hazard
----- Incur a relatively small increase in cost and price of plane

The ethical tests (p.155), especially the tests of justice, golden rule, long-range utility and the general law -and the no-harm test, clearly demand huge differences in the plus-lines and minus-lines, demonstrating Option 1 as clearly unethical. Once the real choices - and what they mean ethically - are set down in black-and-white, as a force-field analysis requires, anyone with any ethical sensitivity has to discontinue rationalizing and face the clear reality of the grossly unethical nature of Option 1. Apparently, the McDonnell-Douglas managers did not stop to do a force-field analysis and think it through.

Closer to the average consumer's interests is the Pinto case of the mid-1970s in which Ford's engineering managers saved $6.65 per car rather than add a protective device to prevent gas tank explosions in rear end collisions. Many deaths have since been attributed to this design defect (see Case #1 below for details).

The Costs and Prices of Product Reliability

The DC-10 and Pinto cases, at least by hindsight and probably at their design origins if a force-field analysis had been used, are clear-cut cases of consumer abuse by corporations. A force-field analysis, like the one on the previous page regarding the DC-10, would quickly show the ethical absurdity of saving a $6.65 cost vs the clear prospect of deaths by explosion and burning. Without, however, a force-field analysis, sharply drawn black-on-white for all to see and thus forcing all to explicitly face the facts and ethical issues really there, it is easy for daily business pressures upon managers to prevail thoughtlessly while quickly rationalizing profit-oriented decisions that emerge ultimately as blatantly unethical. When the "truth" of it finally rises from private corporate planning meetings (and decisions there) into the bright light of public knowledge and national media coverage (after, for example, the DC-10 and Pinto sensationally newsworth incidents), all, including the busy and quick decision makers, acknowledge the wrongness of the action. But it's too late; public outcry against abuse of consumers leads quickly to even more restrictive regulation of all businesses in an industry, including those consistently making sound, ethical decisions. As well as new laws regulating all businesses in all industries, because of unethical action by one or a few. This is just another example of the practicality of business ethics (see Chapter 1). The American businessman or corporate executive today, who is consistently insensitive to ethical issues and the "right-vs-wrong" of his decisions, is simply a net business liability, not to be tolerated if the business is to maintain its (practical) success in the markets and with the consuming public. Unethical decisions (like the DC-10 and Pinto cost-oriented decisions) usually end up as major, and unnecessary, business costs in terms of national press revelations that cancel out millions of dollars of advertising efforts, financial compensation in the millions for injured consumers, and usually huge legal expenses.

But let's consider the more usual cases, the "gray area" cases, where managers must make decisions about high added costs to insure the reliability and safety of products against increasingly minor risks. For example, suppose a manufacturer of rotary lawn mowers could decrease consumer accidents with lawn mowers by 1% (100 fewer injuries) by designing in safety devices which raised the average price for the mower 100%, from $200 to $400. Would you pay the extra $200 for safety devices which reduce your accident risk insignificantly from 2 to just 1 chance out of a million users experiencing accidents while also suffering the inconvenience of the safety device (the mower stops automatically whenever you leave it for a second to remove a piece of debris in its path, requiring great -and sometimes unsuccessful- efforts to restart it with many sweat-producing yanks of the starter cord), when, as is usually the case, sensible caution in the use of the mower, without the idiot-proof safety devices and the extra $200 for them, is almost perfectly safe? A hint as to the answer for most consumers: (a) market research studies show conclusively that consumers buy the lowest-priced item and reject insignificantly-extra safety devices and their added costs and prices; (b) safety seat-belts, installed by law in all American cars -at added costs and prices, are actually used, "strapped on," by only 10% of drivers (for the other 90% the added seat-belt cost is a waste of money). Nevertheless, or because of consumer refusal to use seat-belts which require a safety-oriented action (actually "strapping them on"), government is about to require by law that all cars be equipted with "air bags," installed under the car dashboard and automatically expanded into a safe cushion in case of accident, a "passive" device requiring no voluntary action by the car driver (but all drivers will pay the added cost built into the car).

Thus there are many degrees of reliability and safety producers can design into a product, each a managerial decision and each a trade-off between added cost and price on the one hand and degree of reliability and safety on the other. Clearly, decision makers who opted for the unsafe DC-10 cargo door and the Pinto explosion-prone gas tank excessively and unethically favored cost considerations over reliability and safety considerations; but, just as clearly (at least in the consumers' minds), the highest possible degrees of reliability and safety -along with their necessary costs and prices- are consistently rejected by buyers, who prefer lower prices along with good, but not perfect, degrees of reliability and safety. That is, until their product breaks down or causes an accident; then they're off to the courts for a product-liability suit, ignoring at this later moment their earlier option for a bargain price with slight, but some, degree of product failure possibility or probability. So, after all, product problems with absolute reliability and safety are partly caused, in a free market, by price-conscious consumers as well as by sales- and profit-minded business managers. Force-field analyses of these subtle degrees of trade-offs would, of course, vary greatly among different individual interpreters, whether product managers or buyers, and whether they were at the design or buying point, respectively, vs the occasional product breakdown point.

Reasons for Manufacturers to Stay on the "Safe Side"

The intensity of consumerism, over the past several decades, in its many forms of consumer protest and political action, has virtually replaced the caution "caveat emptor" ("let the buyer beware") with "caveat venditor" ("let the seller beware"). A quick review of sales tactics and shoddy products in 19th-century America (pp.28-29) will underscore the wisdom of "caveat emptor;" recent victories of angry consumers in the courts and congress dictate the wisdom of "caveat venditor" for manufacturers and other businessmen. And for good reasons, at least in the minds of consumers. About 20 million Americans annually suffer injuries in product-related accidents (and these are only ones reported by hospitals and doctors), about 30,000 die while over 100,000 are permanently disabled, the cost to the economy about $5.5 billion.[4] And thousands of these victims sue the manufacturers -and win large awards, sometimes in the $millions.

Ralph Nader's book, Unsafe at Any Speed (1965), highlighted the safety problems of automobiles (see the Pinto Case # 1 below also) and documentation by consumer groups shows the most dangerous products to be (other than cars) bicycles (372,000 accidents), stairs and ramps (356,000 accidents), nails, tacks etc. (275,000 accidents), sports equipment (750,000 accidents) etc. These figures are for 1973.[5] Many of these accidents, of course, are the user's fault, not the producer's or retail dealer's. But, the clout of consumerism is becoming so powerful that product liability laws increasingly favor the product user and penalize makers and distributors for products containing a "proneness" to being misused by the "average, reasonably careful" user. Not many years ago, a manufacturer was liable and could be sued only for negligently unsafe products provided they were bought directly from that manufacturer - and appropriate warning labels were usually sufficient defense against a legal suit. Today, these laws are radically expanded and court decisions increasingly favor injured users both in verdicts and dollar award amounts: in a product liability case today, a user can sue anyone or many in the entire chain of distribution including the manufacturer, all distributors and retail stores handling the product and even celebrities endorsing it in ads, whether or not the product was bought from the manufacturer directly - and there is no longer any need to prove negligence (the fact alone of a defect or "avoidable" injury is sufficient to sue -and probably win). Obviously, consumerism has advanced its interests by quantum leaps in recent decades and, just as obviously, "the vendor best beware."

Even huge warning labels (PLUG THIS ONLY INTO A WALL OUTLET -NEVER INTO AN EXTENSION CORD!!!!!!) provide little legal protection for manufacturers in liability suits, even if the user was injured putting out a fire caused by plugging an appliance cord into an extension cord, despite the WARNING, and despite defeating his protective circuit breakers by bypassing wires to avoid irritating power cutoffs. The fact that he was injured using the product is enough to sue the manufacturer or distributors - and probably win.

The consumer message in the 1980s to product manufacturers and retailers is clear: for both ethical, and legal, reasons, consumer safety, in every way possible, must be a critical factor in management force-field analysis and decisions.

Has Consumerism Gone Too Far?

Businessmen and many economists obviously worry that consumer activism is exceeding its reasonable goals of reasonable product quality, reliability and safety as these are inevitably related to costs. Especially as costs of uneconomically high reliability and safety (see p. 201) drive prices up (and fuel the very real danger of inflation) and decrease national productivity (lower productivity means sales and jobs lost to international competitors) because of the added costs of "defensive" manufacturing, which is inefficient, and million-dollar product liability awards which become simply "overhead costs" built into product prices.*

When the appliance user (above), who was injured by stupid or reckless disregard of clear instructions in the use of the appliance, wins, say, $100,000 in his product liability suit, the manufacturer must naturally add this overhead cost into his product prices - as well as payments for product liability insurance and sophisticated, but very costly, idiot-proof safety devices to avoid liability suits. Nothing is free, neither a free lunch nor a windfall court award like the lucky $100,000 injury award; somebody has to pay and that is the consumer himself in higher product prices. What happens also, increasingly, is that American consumers, despite the rhetoric of consumerism, avoid the high prices of American products and buy products from Japan and Korea. Businessmen (rightly) view this phenomenon as ironic and self-defeating for American consumers, workers (those who still have jobs), retirees on fixed pensions (crushed by inflation), even welfare recipients whose programs are cut by lower tax revenues from unprofitable

---

* "Defensive" manufacturing is an attitude similar to "defensive" medicine, law practice, consulting or even university education by which practitioners purposely incur added costs, many quite unnecessary (such as lab tests), to avoid or defend in court suits.

businesses whose "overhead" costs are too high to compete well, and the national economic health as a whole upon which all Americans depend.

Space does not permit it here, but the reader might be interested in working up a detailed force-field analysis (p.169), citing and evaluating all the pro vs con factors -and trade offs- on the issue of consumerism and how far it should go. Key factors will be degrees of product reliability and safety as well as related court costs to get it versus nation-wide effects upon productivity, American jobs, resulting inflation, American corporations' international competition for sales, net national GNP and other bottom-line indexes of economic health. Every responsible American citizen should be thinking through such a force-field analysis of this consumerism -and other- issues constantly; decisions about them, reflected in laws and the courts, can make or break America as a viable social and economic system.

Why It's So Hard to Get Things Fixed Right

This is the title of a U.S.News & World Report article (6/28/82) -The Wall Street Journal ran several similar articles in the same week- documenting consumer irritations about products that fail soon after purchase and repairmen ("vultures," some angry consumers say) who, when called and then arrive at the scene of a buzzing but failed unit, charge a $30 service charge just to look at it and then either tell the owner it's hopeless and leave in five minutes with their $30 or fix it (the bill then usually doubles or more to $60 to $140 with "parts and labor") so that it lasts another week or month, then again breaks down and the repairman-cycle starts all over again. Understandably, the average consumer resents both the interruption of the product's service and the repairman's cycles of high-dollar charges to resurrect the unit periodically. And such consumer resentment fuels consumerism to new highs of justified activism -and the costs associated with it.

In the repairman business, this is called "repeat repairing," very profitable considering high service charges just to arrive each time. For some businesses, the "repeats" are the core sustainers of the firm and the policy is to welcome, if not actually "arrange," them-until the consumer gets wise to it, shifts to another repair service which, a bit more subtly, plays the same "repeat repair" game. But, according to some consumer groups, it is manufacturers' cheaply made products that create this delightful wonderland for repairmen. For example, a freezer bought by a Wisconsin man developed cracks in the housing in just two months; the local repairman fixed it but the cracks started again a few weeks later and, this time, the repairman, after a charge of course, said it couldn't be fixed; after complaining to the maker's home office, his claim was denied for "insufficient information."

Each such dishonest act by business, in its short-range interests but long-range net loss, adds one more angry consumer to one or another rabid consumerist group, determined to saddle business with more laws and more regulation. Everyone, even consumer group members, know such efforts are time-consuming, cost-producing -or just sport; but business has yet to act effectively against its minority of members who create the consumer and legal problems for all. Effective and specific codes of ethics (dealt with in detail in a later chapter) can be an easy and substantial answer, but business is still slow to act effectively on such codes. (Most businesses and industry associations have such codes, but most are noncommittal generalities and generally, therefore, quite meaningless - as probably intended.)

Expressed and Implied Warranties (Guarantees)

A manufacturer's or other businessman's warrantee is a moral, and now legal, promise to perform certain actions, usually reparations such as product replacement or money rebates, or at least no-cost repair, in the event of product failure and within specific conditions stated in the warranty claim. For example, Apex Electric Co. might provide a firm warranty in writing that any of its TV sets, after unpacked and installed in a consumer's home and then malfunctioning in any way, will be repaired or replaced within 5 days - provided the user has unpacked, installed and handled the set properly and in accordance with a list of several dozen warranty-related stipulations, often in very small print (for later legal use) but most of them reasonable (such as "if the set is carelessly dropped and crashed onto the floor, the warranty is null and void"). Ethical companies strictly honor such warranties and, by such action, gain and retain customer confidence and customers over entire lifetimes (millions of Sears-Roebuck customers buy Sear's products for peace of mind and without even comparison price shopping); many companies, however, renege on their warranties by either downright default or by legal loopholes in their warranties' small print - and they also spend much time in court, lose customers and fuel up the energies of dedicated (and professional) consumerists.

Some warranties are expressed (explicit) but many others are only, but importantly, *implied*. Expressed warranties are written and virtually legal documents, as illustrated above. Implied warranties, certainly of ethical significance -and sometimes legal- as promises or obligations to another, are based on more general and public statements by manufacturers and other businessmen such as in their ads and their claims in literature or labeling packaged with a product. If a product fails to even approximate the performance promised and expected by such ads and claims, the consumer has an ethical right to a fair reparation - and, often, a legal right as well. For example, Brit Paints Inc. widely advertised its Quick-dry brand on TV as "sure to dry hard to the touch in two hours on any average sunny day;" one consumer painted his entire house with it, planning to avoid pollen and insects getting stuck in it and marring the surface, and found the paint still wet and collecting debris after seven hours; a waste of 12 hard hours of painting, the price of the paint and an ugly, spotted surface. Brit's ads constitute a clear, implied warranty which the painter counted on. In ethical, or legal, terms, what should the reparation be?

Planned Product Obsolescence

Vance Packard's bestseller, The Waste Makers, popularized the concept of planned obsolescence in 1963, the term referring to manufacturers' deliberate design of products with limited quality and durability. The reasons for such "design-down" practices are twofold: costs can be cut drastically providing attractive prices, sales and profits; and, as products such as appliances break down more frequently, they need to be replaced more frequently (more new sales). Most consumers are angry when a product breaks down, even though they chose the least costly model at the time of purchase. Many believe that Packard was somewhat naive in his attack on businesses and their marketing strategies as well as somewhat ignorant of how free market supply-and-demand forces work: if one manufacturer produces a highly-durable refrigerator at a high price but finds consumers actually buying competitors' low-durability models at bargain prices, he designs his products according to customer demand. A clothier could make a man's suit to last 20 years at $500 instead of $150 for a suit good for about three years. Who wants to wear the same suit for 20 years - and pay that higher price? Very few purchasers. Therefore, it is the market that demands particular trade-offs of durability, price and "obsolescence" and manufacturers who respond quickly to it or else lose all their business. "Planned obsolescence" certainly exists, as Packard documented it; but he seems to have confused cause and effect: the consumer's demands are cause, manufacturers' action is effect and, in itself, it seems a marketing phenomenon in a free market, not a serious ethical problem (unless, as above, deception, safety, etc. are also involved).

Is Advertising Unethical?

The question implies that not only dishonest advertising but also advertising per se may be unethical - and the question is not posed facetiously. Everyone now acknowledges deceptive advertising as unethical (and, in most cases, even illegal) but many also question the ethics of any kind of promotional advertising (which tries to create consumer "needs" and desire to buy) as distinct from purely factual information-type announcements about goods or services available. A well-known economist, along with many well-credentialed colleagues since, launched an attack upon the advertising industry *per se* in his popular 1967 book, *The New Industrial State*, his main theme being that powerful (hard-sell) advertising has become a way of life for giant capitalist corporations in which they constantly fire up people's desire to buy things they don't need (thus increasing sales and profits); "...advertising and its related arts thus help develop the kind of man the goals of the industrial system require - one that reliably spends his income and works reliably because he is always in need of more."[7] Thus consumers spend all they earn, save little or not at all, often go into deep debt with plastic cards that lure, and many even into personal bankruptcy and poverty, all because of the "evils" of advertising.

Two basic lines of argument have been advanced against this attack on advertising. One develops evidence that inherent needs of consumers (food, drugs, shelter, insurance, etc.) are appealed to more often in advertising than so-called "created" needs such as cosmetics, candy, cameras etc. and cites the key flaw which is the mere assumption that psychological desires are not human "needs" while (only) physical desires are.[8] Quite apart from advertising, many a woman would gladly substitute hot dogs for steak to afford a weekly hair-do that does much more for her ego and social enjoyment than a steak; many a man makes similar substitutions to buy a small motorcycle and the excitement of travelling the country on weekends and holidays. The critics thus have cause and effect confused again: it is the market (of both physical and psychological consumer desires) that causes producers to make and advertise what they think people want; advertising is mainly a response, an effect, reacting to market forces.

The other line of argument worries that advertising (and selling) may not be sufficiently effective in creating consumers' desire to buy, thus slowing down the higher potential prosperity and standard of living generated by sales which generate production which generates jobs which generate purchasing power, an economic cycle that benefits all -and the interruption of which usually causes the misery of depression. "Nothing happens in a market economy until somebody makes a sale;" a sale is the first domino activating a free-market economy's "magic" of abundant production and distribution of goods and services for all (see p. 176 above).[9]

The attack on advertising *per se* seems prompted mainly by an economic preference for a socialist system (p.180) and is hardly a serious ethical issue in a free market (capitalist) economy.

Deceptive and Unfair Advertising

But, even if advertising per se is ethical, many of its methods and purposes are not. Or, at least, are on the borderline between the ethical and the unethical. And sometimes on the edge or beyond the law also.

In 1975, Dr. Margaret Mead was quoted as saying "most advertising people don't believe in the products they advertise or the words they are writing about their clients' products." In a 1978 survey done for Advertising Age, almost half the respondents (not occupied in the advertising business) rated advertising as the one "with the lowest ethical standards." A 1977 Gallup poll asked a sample of Americans to rank 20 occupational groups from "highest" to "lowest" in honesty and ethical standards; advertising practitioners were ranked 19th, just after labor union leaders and state officeholders but ahead of car salesmen.[10] Frederick Wakeman's popular novel (1946), The Hucksters, and the Clark Gable movie of the same title pictured admen explicitly -and without redeeming features- as fast-talking, scheming, frankly unethical, unprincipled and even amoral, any and all ethical norms to be sacrificed to the gods of "new accounts" and money. Since then, this has become the accepted stereotype of the adman (and also the salesman). The stereotypes of both the adman and the salesman are justified based on advertising and sales practices of the past century (p.28) as are the more general stereotypes of businessmen of that time (p.23). Government regulation of advertising and sales tactics in this century has reduced or eliminated the most blatant of the "old" tactics assisted by the voluntary effort at self-policing by the industry (its recent codes of ethics). But let's consider some current advertising practices and issues that still raise questions of ethics.

The Role of Advertising as Information for Consumers

Over most of human history, buyers avoided deception by sellers through the simple device of personally "inspecting the goods" before making the purchase. Even a minimally experienced and intelligent adult purchaser could judge the worth of goods by simply looking at a cow to determine its health or age, feeling vegetables or grains to detect the rotten among the firm, smelling or tasting wines to distinguish the sweet from the sour, and so on. (Knowing the right price was quite another matter but does not concern our issue here of correct information about a product - the issue of pricing, fair or otherwise, is dealt with in a later section.) However, with the radically advanced products of the 1980s, with their underlying scientific sophistication and ever-advancing technologies in chemistry, electronics, etc., average buyers are utterly unable to judge a product by "inspection" (indeed, in most cases, the product is carefully packaged and won't even be seen until unpacked at home after the purchase). For example, an average purchaser could look at, i.e. "inspect," a personal computer or Hi-Fi set for hours and never know a thing about its integrity or reliability.

Thus, today's buyers depend upon information provided by advertising and salesmen in order to make correct buying decisions. Product information of maximum accuracy and credibility is so vital that today hundreds of information and even product testing services, independent of sellers, thrive on the consumers' need for sound information; examples are Consumers Union, Buyers' Guide to Products, automobile magazines which test new cars and report, and similar magazines covering almost every product category (computers, HI-Fi sets, etc.). Therefore, virtually all ethical questions about advertising involve the moral obligation to tell the truth and refrain from lying in dealings with customers who have a right to know what they are buying.

The Many Arts of Lying – or Avoiding the Truth

Lying seems to be a simple concept and the act of it clearly unethical. But even a cursory reading of any basic text on ethics will quickly reveal severe difficulties in defining what lying really is as well as many kinds, shades and degrees of lying.

What is a lie? A superficial, and wrong, even naive definition would be "telling someone something that is not true to the facts." If this be lying, then all men have been, and are, liars; especially in the functional categories of politics, love relationships, job resumes, stories told about past accomplishments (size of fish caught, etc.) and convincingly read fairy tales told to young children, even one's own. Is it lying (i.e. unethical) to tell a child a fairy tale or insist on promulgating a geocentric view of the universe (as the medieval church did) or "recall" that the fish caught on vacation was a full 36 inches when really it measured 34 inches which is almost 36 inches? Or tell a very average wife she's the most beautiful woman in the world? Or a salesman cold-canvassing by phone that you're moving to the west coast in a month and therefore don't need his storm windows (when, of course, you have no intention of moving at all, just intend to dismiss the salesman politely but for good)? Most of us would evaluate the above statements, not as unethical lies, but as fun-intended fantasy or as sincerely believed error (the geocentric universe view) or as harmless and natural exaggeration or as ego-building flattery, etc.

And, of course, lying can be confused with intentional ambiguity, avoidance of direct response to a question, suggesting without stating and so on.

Lying is, thus, better defined as misrepresentation of information given to another who has a right to the truth based on such grounds as fairness, possible harm to another, the general law standard and other ethical tests (p. 155). For example, a salesman trying to get an appointment with me next week, when I prefer it two or three weeks hence, has no right to know why or what I am doing next week; I can be quite ambiguous in my explanations for the postponement with no risk of unethical lying. On the contrary, if I have purchased a product from the salesman and he needs to know what days I'll be home to accept his delivery of it, ambiguity or misinformation could cause a wasted trip to my home to deliver, necessity for another and a loss of money, all harmful to the salesman - and thus unethical; in the latter case, the salesman has a right to know based, not on whim, but on a substantial ground. Similarly, a potential purchaser of a product has a right to accurate information from the manufacturer and salesmen of that product on the ethical grounds that wrong information, no matter by what methods it becomes accepted by a purchaser (lies, ambiguity, exaggeration, suggestion, etc.), can and probably will cause harm to the purchaser, financial or otherwise. As usual, in ethical matters, there are many degrees between absolute truth and absolute lies based on degrees of actual deception, and their consequences; often a force-field analysis is needed to sort out the issues when one person's right to information conflicts with another's right to withhold or guard information.

Examples: consider the common case of a medical doctor, completing a physical examination of a patient in which terminal lung cancer was discovered, now face-to-face with the patient who is totally unaware of any problem with his lungs and asking "well, what does your battery of tests show this time, am I still fit as a fiddle?" Some would argue that the technical right of the patient to the exact information known by the doctor is offset by the right (even the duty) of the doctor to try to avoid as much traumatic shock his information could cause the patient, even depriving him of any hope and will to cooperate with efforts to make his last months or year as self-fulfilling as possible. The doctor would thus, not "lie," but understate the facts, withhold some details (especially about cancer pain), create ambiguities about the patient's true state, cite almost irrelevant cases of unexplained remissions of cancer or new medical breakthroughs just in time to save once-terminal victims, etc., any or all of the above to tell the patient the "essential" information truthfully but not quite all of it. Cases like this, whether occurring in medical, legal, national security, financial or other fields, are not black-and-white ethical issues;* and usually require force-field analysis, outlined or implied, to determine the most ethical course possible under difficult circumstances.

Or, consider a case containing misrepresentation of facts but in no way deception: a salesman on leaving for work tells his wife, in a joking mood, that he's going to make a million dollars today; he is exaggerating, he knows it, she knows it, and no one is deceived by the fun-intended repartee - and certainly no unethical "lying" occurred. Deception, intended or not, is of the essence of "lying" as an unethical act. TV advertisers often put their messages in the mouths of entertaining animated images of animals (Exxon's Tiger, Smokey the Bear) which is a misrepresentation of fact (animals can't talk in words) but deceives almost no one as to that fact. The qualifier "almost," used in the previous sentence, is, however, critical as related to ethics in advertising. Suppose an ad, directed on TV at children, portrays a doll talking humanly and playing competitive and interesting card games to the delight of a small girl (which watching parents know the doll can't do) deceives a child into believing the doll can do all that she is watching so that she insists on it for Christmas despite all the parents' explanations about the deception, all of which are beyond her young mind? In this case, no adults are deceived but the target audience (children) is - and, therefore, it's a "lie" and deceptive advertising. A more ambiguous case is the typical advertising of new cars to young men by portraying beautiful women surrounding the car, attracted to it and, therefore, by suggestion, attracted also to the man who buys one (the male viewer wants the women more than the car and might buy the one to get the other). Is this deceptive advertising? Not if, indeed, some women choose dates partly based on the kind of car a man drives. But, quite deceptive are many ads exploiting peoples' natural inclination to infer conclusions that go beyond a literal statement, the conclusions encouraged and expected by the use of key "qualifying" words such as "help" as in: "it can help restore that youthful energy you need on the job;" key qualifying words permit the advertiser to suggest almost anything without literally stating

* Is it unethical for the defense department or its intelligence arms to withhold or distort information to the public press when such information would benefit an enemy during war, an investigation of organized crime activities, or a threat from a foreign power? Suppose the national health service withholds information about a public health threat, quietly being investigated and almost under control, which, if known, would cause panic and ruin the control plan?

it to be so, with confidence that many will overlook the qualifier and accept the suggestion as a firm conclusion in their purchasing choices. Other common "qualifying" words are "can" (it can keep your home germ-free), "normally" (it is normally trouble-free), "as much as" (it can cut repair bills by as much as 50%), and so on.

If an advertiser intends to lie, there is almost no limit to the subtle and imaginative methods for deceiving purchasers. But, no matter the method, a lie is a lie - and unethical.*

Packaging, Labeling and Selling

The ethical issues involved in how sellers package, label and sell products are essentially similar to the issues discussed above regarding advertising. The critical one is the handling of information, which consumers need for correct buying decisions, and whether the information provided is genuinely true or really a lie in terms of the intent of the information (to inform or only to sell), linguistic methods used (to be clear vs devious), ultimate result of the information effort in the mind of the average consumer (accurate knowledge vs wrong impressions and conclusions).

Like advertising a product, the ways in which it is packaged and labeled as well as the things a trained salesman says about it provide information to consumers as to whether to buy it or not. Packages, labels and salesmen, as much as advertisements, can convey truth or lies -and are ethical or unethical accordingly.

For example, a large box of breakfast cereal by its size alone suggests a generous quantity of the product while the consumer is unaware of the false bottom and sides of internal paper-ribbing, used for unnecessary protection of the product and less actual product to fill it (each unit cutting product costs and increasing profit margin); the package "lies" and is unethical, despite its very small print note about the quantity of product in ounces which few consumers can read or will even notice as they busily shop through a supermarket. Candy-producers in the 1970s, afraid to raise familiar candybar prices, retained profit margins by keeping price the same but cutting the amount of candy in each bar by 5% but "paper-puffing" the package to look the same as always. By both intent and effect, the package lies as much as any advertisement suggesting the same conclusion to buyers. Clever labeling of products, especially suggestive words used, can achieve the same false- or non-information effect, again unethical.

---

* One of the finest articles, addressing this issue in both a practical and philosophical manner, is Theodore Levitt's "The Morality of Advertising" (Harvard Business Review, July-August, 1970).

Salesmen and Salesmanship: Selling is essentially persuasive communication comprising two purposes, to give a prospective purchaser (prospect) information about a product and additionally to persuade the prospect to buy it. (As noted above, both of these purposes are also involved in advertising, packaging and labeling in many instances and, insofar as they are, this discussion of selling applies to those business practices as well.)*

The two purposes and practices (informing and persuading) often conflict, the desire to persuade overriding the ethical obligation to provide complete and accurate information. Virtually all unethical advertising and selling can be attributed to this natural conflict between the seller's main goal (persuading the prospect to buy) and the prospect's main goal (getting sound information for a buying decision). All of the deceptive and misinformation tactics discussed above concerning advertising (exaggeration, suggestion, etc.) can be used as well by salesmen - and are also unethical for the same reasons. But the two purposes need not, and should not, conflict if a salesman adheres strictly to ethical standards and tests (fairness, general law, etc. as on p. 155 above). And, for all the practical reasons outlined in Chapter 1 (especially pp. 19-21), unethical salesmen and other business men are gradually eliminating themselves from business as their tactics become publicized and they forfeit credibility with customers who no longer do business with them and communicate the unethical practices to millions of others through the media. Often, indeed, it is the unskilled, unprepared and unprofessional salesman who must resort to "easy" and deceptive tactics to make a sale (his "hit-and-run" way of business usually catches up with him); the professional salesman, who does his homework, knows his product and its benefits well, knows his customers' needs, knows competing products thoroughly and thrives on "repeat business" from satisfied customers, avoids unethical tactics as self-defeating and has no need or desire for them.[9]

But unethical salesmen and sales practices still persist, despite progress made by government regulation and business's own self-regulation. Some of the unethical tactics, not covered above in discussing advertising, are as follows:

Bait and switch: This is a two-step process involving both advertising and face-to-face selling. An ad offers a dishwasher at $100 less than most good dishwashers and, of course, draws many buyers

* In all of these business practices (advertising, selling, etc.), we must distinguish between what is unethical and what is merely, but irritatingly, tasteless or crude. Hundreds of TV ads for soap, deodorants, medicines for colds and hemorrhoids, etc. are crude and offensive (especially while eating) but not deceptive or unethical. They should be banned, but not for being unethical.

who, when they arrive at the store, learn from the salesman that the model advertised has many limitations (it washes but doesn't dry, etc.) but that his standard heavy-duty and higher-priced model is also on sale. The advertised model was the bait; the salesman executes the switch to the regular high-profit model. The ad is more unethical (deceptive) than the salesman but both are involved in a conspiracy to lie. (Today, by law, the salesman must have the advertised model in stock and sell it, if the customer insists; in the "old days" the advertised model didn't even exist, except on paper as bait.)

Telling part, but not all, of the story: for example, a salesman sells a pony to parents, by appealing to the child's desire for it as a birthday present, stressing that it's only $150 (he says nothing about the $1000 per year to feed, house, exercise and care for the pony). Given the inexperience of the parents and their ignorance of the facts about owning a horse (ponies grow up!), even though it did not occur to them to ask for critical details, does the salesman have an ethical obligation to volunteer all of the critical facts before the purchase - even if he thus risks losing the sale? A reasonably objective force-field analysis of the choices (p. 169) will show, for most salesmen, that the answer is clearly affirmative. Kodak sells cameras at virtually no profit, its real profits secured by high-profit sales of the film for the cameras; the average purchaser realizes the film will cost far more in even one year than the original price of the camera, there is no deception and generally no breach of ethics. A store advertises a giant antenna (for TVs) at a bargain price but says nothing about the $100 installation charge until the prospect arrives, has decided already to buy, resigns himself to the unexpected charge, and buys (if he had known about the extra $100, which could have been noted in the ad, he would have discarded the ad and never bothered making the long trip to the store). Ethical? Try a force-field analysis on this and other similar examples.

Exploiting the customer's weaknesses or subconscious: many salesmen are "practical psychologists," quick to detect personality weaknesses and subconscious needs that can be used to pressure a prospect emotionally into buying even though his rational judgment is strongly opposed to it. The pony salesman above, apart from his incomplete information, was exploiting the parents' emotional need to please their child and, especially, to avoid the emotional pain of her disappointed tears. The salesman, in expert control of both these factors, easily made the sale. His "incomplete information" tactic was judged clearly unethical (above); is his use of the parents' emotions about the child good hard selling or unethical also? It seems complicated and confusing until you outline a force-field analysis, using the ethical tests (as on p. 169 and 155, which should be reviewed). Roaming photographers are adept at "working" the emotions of young men (without wedding rings) with a female companion, obviously not his wife and to be impressed at all costs, in swank restaurants and similar places (nite clubs etc.) by simply saying something like "I'm sure you won't deprive this so lovely lady of a picture to remember this night - with you," and he instantly buys at an extravagant price rather than look cheap by discussing or rejecting the price. Some life insurance salesmen play on the irrational fears of the wife (for her children) to sell the husband, in her presence and emotional state fueled by the salesman's pictures of potential doom, insurance policies which the family rationally does not need and can't afford. Cars are advertised surrounded by attractive women to appeal to a man's subconscious desire to meet and have the woman of his dreams. Overpriced cosmetics are advertised to women who buy to meet and have the man of her dreams. And so on. Are emotional appeals such as these ethical? Should we condemn the salesman, who works hard and imaginatively, because the young man in the restaurant lacks the gumption to ask the price of the photos and reject them if overpriced or the husband is too meek a personality to reject or modify the insurance he is being sold? So long as the salesman provides complete information and does not deceive, what is wrong, if anything, about him making his best case for his product, including appeals to emotion as is commonly done in great literature and TV "soaps" to elicit viewer interest and emotional identification with the theme? On the other hand, are such high-pressure selling tactics the unethical rape of a weaker mind by a stronger one?

No one (I hope) would advocate banishing salesmanship, the art of persuasive communication, from the world, especially from the free world of America. It couldn't be done anyway since it's inherent in the human species and its history (even children stage tantrums -adults often do too- to "sell" parents or others into actions desired such as being fed, picked up and hugged, given a fur coat or sex, the latter usually involving a male tantrum). Thus, some, but few, of the complex mental and emotional processes called "salesmanship" can clearly be labeled "ethical" or "unethical;" an intelligent adult "conning" a child into an act harmful to the child is clearly unethical while an industrial salesman selling hard to an equally knowledgeable corporate purchasing agent is usually -and must be- carefully ethical. Most acts of hard selling and persuasive communication fall in between the extremes of "ethical" and "unethical" and must be judged on a case-by-case evaluation, usually an expicit or implied force-field analysis. Cases at the end of this book provide the reader abundant opportunity for such evaluations and force-field analyses.

Pricing – How Businessmen Set Prices for Products and Services

As an exercise in capitalistic micro-economics (economics of the firm as distinct from the macro-economics of an entire nation), setting a price for a product is a simple calculation: all actual costs incurred in producing the product or service (material, labor, utility bills, etc.) plus a profit margin for the producer, his personal income from his job, determined by limits imposed by the prices of his competitors. If his price and profit are too high, consumers shun his products and buy instead from his competitor with similar-quality products at lower prices. Thus a producer is motivated to maximum efficiency in controlling all costs to produce a quality product, competitive in price with other producers, and, in the end, generating a personal profit that justifies his business effort. This is the essence of capitalism (see p. 176) and, even today, generally works well in the free-market control of production and its pricing. But it doesn't always work, for reasons both of macro-economic conditions (inflation, interest rates, etc.) and the natural human drive to maximize profits -by means of high prices- if and however this can be accomplished, such as by cartels, price-fixing, administered industry-wide profit-assured prices and other sorts of collusion.

Cartels and Product Monopolies

A monopoly exists when only one producer of a product or commodity owns or controls all of it so that he can set production quotas and prices at any level he wishes without any interference from (non-existent) competition. An oligopoly exists when just a few producers own or control all of a product or commodity in which case they might compete strongly and fairly (maintaining the essential competitive nature of capitalistic free markets and prices) or, being just a few, meet together and agree not to compete with each other but to cooperate toward optimum profits for each member of the oligopoly. This can be done by "dividing up" markets (for example, each of three companies of an oligopoly might operate only in its agreed-upon one-third of the nation and therefore, in effect, a monopoly in its section) or by agreeing on minimum or identical prices charged to all consumers, thus removing any mutual competition, whether in posted prices or bids for contracts.* Such production and pricing agreements, especially when among a few or even many producers in different nations, are called cartels.* Although the variations are as many as imagination can conjure, the essential intent and effect of monopolies, oligopolies and cartels are to avoid genuine market competition among the members

* Non-competitive, agreed-upon bids were the method used by the 1950s' electrical companies. Today's OPEC is a cartel (see p.26).

by agreements to set mutually beneficial production schedules and/or prices for the controlled product or commodity. In the "robber baron" days in America (pp.24-29), such arrangements were called "trusts."

Trusts and cartels are illegal today in America (although quite legal in other nations such as the oil-producing nations' OPEC) but occasionally the business yearning for price "stability" surfaces in the form of price collusion, i.e. competing companies agreeing somehow on prices mutually profitable to all parties to the collusion agreement. For example, in a mid-sized American city, two cement-mixing firms have grown large enough to be able, by economies of scale, to win all commercial and government contracts for building, roads and other construction projects, their smaller competitors now driven out of the market. But, as each of the two surviving "giants" lowers prices to win contracts, each firm's profit margin is minimized. Preferring to maximize these profit margins, the two firms meet and agree on contract bids and prices such that each gets sufficient business at high prices and profit margins. Their collusion results in higher profits for both firms as well as higher prices paid by commercial and government consumers. This is unethical and illegal, but it is not uncommon.[11]

"Administered Prices" - Are They Unethical?

In a general sense, all producers administer the prices for their products insofar as they determine by decisions what they shall be, based upon information feedback from the market, optimum supply-and-demand analyses, realistic cost structures for production and desired ultimate rate of profit return. More specifically, "administered pricing" refers usually to oligopolies in which a few major producers in the same industry, with the same cost and profit problems, arrive independently at a "right" and virtually identical price for similar products - without any collusion. Each firm closely monitors the price changes, usually small, of its competitors and, within days or even hours, adjusts its prices to match. No collusion is involved - it is not necessary since all such prices and price-changes are widely publicized instantly in the public media for all to monitor. Often one of the firms emerges as the "leader," exercising "price leadership," i.e. it sets correct prices from the firm's viewpoint (while, of course, fully recognizing the realities of the market and avoiding excess prices and profits bound to invite unwanted government interference); the price leader announces prices and price changes periodically, and the few other firms in the industry do essentially likewise, usually within a day or two. No collusion has occurred, no cartel is at work, but all know that a subtle and wordless "price-fixing" dominates such price-administered industries, usually -almost necessarily- oligopolies.

Historically, in America, the steel industry is an example.

The purpose behind such undiscussed (no collusion) price administered tactics is simply to avoid mutual cut-throat competition in which each firm would cut prices to a point where no reasonable profits would remain to finance plant improvement, R & D for new technology, overhead for subtly-mandated social efforts such as hiring and training minority members and others "disadvantaged" but net added cost factors to firms, and survival of the firm itself - and the jobs it provides. It is interesting to note that, over the past half-century, firms in price-administered industries (such as steel) have earned a bare minimum of profits, both in absolute and rate-of-return terms, deciding consistently upon low profit margins under government pressure (acting, in effect, as if tightly-monitored utility companies under local community rate controls) and, today, many such firms are being overwhelmed by realistic foreign competition, especially from (for example) German and Japanese high-profit, high R & D oriented and high technology firms, such as steel producers (over the last decade, thousands of American steel workers have lost jobs while German and Japanese workers gained them). This seems less a question of ethics and more a matter of political naivete by government and its rising control of American business (in Japan, for example, there is a cooperative and mutually-supportive relationship between business and government as opposed to the mutually self-defeating and adversary relationship in America).

Predatory Pricing

If you and I own the only two drug stores in town and I have enough financial strength to cut my prices below cost, absorb the losses and "wait you out" until you go bankrupt (by losing either your profits or your customers) after which, now a monopoly, I raise prices to a high-profit level, I am engaging in "predatory pricing." My strategy is simply to first drive you out of business and then enjoy complete control of the market as the "only store in town."

Predatory pricing was a common practice in the past century, used often by the robber barons and local businessmen in small towns. It is clearly unfair and unethical, and, in America, now illegal (as a form of conspiracy to restrain competition and create a monopoly).

Prices and Profits

In the arithmetic of business, the price I receive for a product, less all my costs in making and selling it, equals my net profit before taxes. I can increase my profit by either raising my price or lowering my costs,or both. In the pure theory of capitalism (free and open competition among many producers), maximum efficiency in keeping costs at a minimum is needed to make a profit because I cannot raise my prices above my competitors' or I'll lose sales. The market keeps prices low and, if I am to receive a profit, I must keep costs low as well. (As we have seen, this market mechanism is defeated under conditions of monopoly, price-fixing in an oligopoly, cartels and predatory pricing, and, to some extent, administered pricing.) It is obvious that a businessman, having already cut all costs to the bone, can reach a desired profit margin only by raising his prices - if he can and still keep his customers and avoid breaking laws against price-fixing and other acts in "restraint of trade and fair competition." But the urge to raise prices is always there, for the obvious profit reasons. For example, under conditions of inflation, where all competitors in an industry face equally ever-rising costs, all tend to raise their real prices together, not by colluding, but by the simple arithmetic of cost overtaking and exceeding price, a no-profit and intolerable condition for everybody in the industry.

What is a Fair Profit?

This is like asking what is a fair wage for a worker. The answer, in both cases, depends upon a combination of market forces and our ethical tests (p. 155) and is never a very exact answer. First consider the market forces of supply and demand. A producer naturally wants the highest profit he can get when selling his product and the buyer naturally wants the lowest price he can get (which translates to a minimum profit to the producer from a lowest price). The opposite tendencies and tensions in the transaction between producer and seller are obvious and, indeed, the essence of a free market's "invisible hand" or natural market mechanisms in a capitalistic economy's allocation of production resources most efficiently in the direction of consumer demand (i.e. what the consumer really wants and the prices he will -and won't- pay for it). If a producer makes products people don't want or in greater quantity than they want or at prices they will not pay, his products simply don't sell and he receives no profit at all. If a worker becomes skilled at a craft which no longer interests people -or which already is oversupplied with such craftsmen-, he can not get a job (it's not needed in the supply-and-demand economy) or, if he does, his wage will be minimum because supply of such craftsmen exceeds the demand and each is willing to accept low pay rather than no pay at all ("education" and "sociology" majors graduating from college today face this dilemma, and should have been advised to concentrate in high-demand fields such as engineering, computers).

These market realities can seem harsh to both the profitless producer (who goes bankrupt) and the not-in-demand worker (who goes jobless), while consumers buy from efficient producers at low prices but "some" profit to producers and producing companies hire and pay well those workers with skills needed by the market. A market (as distinct from socialist) economy drives all, producers and workers and consumers alike, to squarely face realities (quantity of food and other necessary commodities and products, and the human incentives to produce it); all of which is ultimately hard, but healthy, since "realities" are all that really "is," whether in a capitalistic or socialistic, a totalitarian or democratic national system. Capitalist nations face such realities as socialist systems avoid -or at least postpone them, as is clearly the case in America over the past fifty years.

So, what is a fair profit? From a producer's viewpoint, a fully maximized profit. From a consumer's viewpoint, virtually none at all as he seeks the lowest price he can get among all competing firms. A fair profit, therefore, is a compromise worked out constantly between producers and consumers and workers operating, as best each can, amid ever-changing free-market forces and the "realities" emerging from the interaction of these forces daily. To make all this more specific, imagine that you are a businessman, owner and manager of a small appliance store, working 12 hours a day running the business, with $90,000 invested in the business to start it up and run it, working 6 full days a week -and some Sundays at home- to handle the business, and, at year end, with a net profit (allowing no wages or salary to yourself) of $18,000 before taxes. Using your calculator, you'll find that it's not enough profit incentive to keep up the daily effort of running your business: after you deduct from the $18,000 your year's personal work hours at $3 minimum wage (4000 hours x $3 = $12,000) and note that the remaining $6000 is just half of what your $90,000 investment money would earn annually at a typical 13% rate in a bank's money market fund, you realize that you would be better off working for a competitor, as a wage-earner at normal $6 or more per hour, and putting your $90,000 into a bank's money fund for an annual earnings of $12,000, thus doubling your actual income (profit) from $18,000 to $36,000. Clearly, your profit margin from the business is less than half of what is necessary to motivate you to stay in the business; and so you leave it to join another business which is able to earn a rate of return (earnings on invested funds) at least equal to or slightly better than "just putting the money in the bank for interest earnings" and also able to provide a normal, rather than mere minimum, wage for the 8 or 12 hours of hard work you can, and will, do in your, or another's business - provided that you receive "fair" return on your work.

So, again, what is a fair profit? It is simply the rate of return on personal effort and invested funds sufficient to keep a businessman motivated to stay in business or a stockholder attracted to invest -or withdraw- his money as he examines the various rates of return, profits and dividends among various businesses competing for the funds he has to invest.*

But, then, consider the ethical tests (fairness, long-range utility, the general law, etc.). Note that the first test, fairness, has been implied throughout the above examination of market forces, interest rates on money invested in banks suggesting what is "fair" return on money invested in a business, or the prevailing wage for a particular skill (in high demand in the job market) suggesting what is a fair wage for a man working in his own business.*

The general law standard (p.68) also pervades our judgments about what is ethical in a free market economy. Can we regard it as a good "general law," and therefore ethical, that skills in high demand (such as computer programmers) earn higher hourly wages than skills in low or no demand (high school teachers)? Of course; since, by that law, people will be generally motivated to choose careers more useful to society and themselves and to avoid those which are useless to society and render people jobless and a burden on society. These are ethical market forces determining the prices (i.e. wages) of work just as they determine relative values of property (rents etc.) and a fair ROI.*

But, often, the ethical tests should override purely market considerations when, for a variety of reasons, free and fair market forces become suspended or clearly distorted by temporary economic circumstances. For example, in a small town, I might be the only plumber available over a holiday weekend when many townsmen, including all the other plumbers, are away at the beaches. When you phone for emergency service for a clogged toilet, your only one, I come over immediately on the Sunday afternoon, say nothing in advance about my rates but charge you twice my regular "weekend emergency" rate. Even if I had told you in advance the amount of my exorbitant rate, you would have little choice but to pay it, with no other options.

* For example, in 1982, money invested in a bank's insured CD (Certificate of Deposit) would earn about 14% annual rate of return; thus a fair rate of return on money invested in one's business (apart from a fair wage for his daily work) must be at least 14% and probably considerably higher, considering the risk, say at least 20% rate of return. This ROI (return on investment) is not tc be confused with "profit on sales," which can range from 1% to 100% or more depending on product turnover and other operating factors. The true "botton line" is ROI.

Is this ethical? Many, certainly you, would say the plumber was taking unfair, i.e. unethical, advantage of the situation to "charge all the market can bear." His action also fails the golden rule test, the general law test and, even, the long-range utility test (he lost a repeat customer for the future, you). If I, the plumber, had done a quick force-field analysis, the ethical and practical decision would be to charge regular weekend-emergency rates and explain them in advance. (The weekend-emergency rate is higher than weekday rates but that's fair and understandable, considering the added inconvenience of interrupting weekend activities to service a customer.)

There are many such pricing actions facing businessmen, which are either unethical or questionable, and require force-field analysis (p.169) to determine whether they are ethical or unethical. This is as true for executives in large corporations as for small business owners like the plumber. And many of the unethical actions are not covered by state or federal laws. But, nevertheless, unethical actions, even if not yet illegal by statute, impose their own practical consequences (such as the plumber's lost customer and future business).

Consider several other examples which raise ethical questions - and test them against force-field analyses. A furniture manufacturer sets a "list price" (often called "manufacturer's suggested price") at about twice the price needed for a good profit, so that retailers can advertise the furniture at huge 50% discounts for quick sales to people who can't resist such huge discounts, thinking such "big sales" a genuine bargain. Unethical? A car manufacturer establishes similar unrealistic list prices so that his dealers can lure customers in with tempting dealer discounts along with manufacturer "rebates." Are these deceptive tactics? Unethical? What about a retailer who designedly "loses his lease" and moves elsewhere every year or two in order to announce irresistable "clearance sales" and each time sell high volumes of merchandise at a very good profit? Unethical? Are such tactics, as illustrated in these examples, likely to deceive the average educated and experienced consumer? Are such tactics just good, hard, imaginative American selling, good for merchants, consumers and the health of the economy - or deceptive and unethical?

There are no easy or universal answers. Each pricing situation must be evaluated on a case-by-case basis, using force-field analysis.

Government Regulation and the FTC

Locke's and Smith's capitalistic ideals of "no government interference" in business and free market mechanisms (p.176) have become almost completely abandoned in modern America. Today, Government is as much the not so "invisible hand" controlling business and the economy as the truly "invisible hand" of a free market. We called this earlier "modified capitalism" (p. 187). Many lament the intrusion of government controls and regulations into the business system; but no objective observer, even an ultra-conservative one, could deny that American business's naively crude and unethical practices in the past century demanded the corrective -albeit stifling and costly- acts of government, driven by an outraged public determined to redress the evils of the then rapacious and irresponsible men who made business decisions. So, beginning about 1890, Government, driven by angry and voting citizens, marched into business with laws and regulations that now number in the thousands -or millions- and control almost all aspects of American business today. Most such laws established new, and costly -and usually inefficient, government agencies as regulatory arms of the government. Here's a small sampling of just a few of them (date established, recent number of employees, recent budget, and regulatory functions indicated in parentheses):[12]

Antitrust Division of Justice Dept. (1890, 900, $27 million, antitrust)
Securities & Exchange Commission (1934, 2000, $56 million, securities)
Federal Reserve Board (1913, 26000, $700 million, regulation of banks)
Civil Aeronautics Board (1938, 800, $22 million, airlines, rates & routes)
Federal Communications Commission (1934, 2100, $60 million, radio, etc.
Federal Trade Commission (1914, 1700, $55 million, selling practices)
Interstate Commerce Commission (1887, 2100, $57 million, railroad rates)
Equal Employment Opportunity Comm. (1964, 2500, $70 million, hiring)
National Labor Relations Board (1935, 2700, $83 million, unions & labor)
Federal Energy Administration (1973, 4000, $156 million, oil prices)
Federal Power Comm. (1930, 1450, $42 million, electric utilities)
Nuclear Regulatory Comm. (1973, 2500, $256 million, power plants)
Consumer Product Safety Comm. (1972, 890, $39 million, products)
Federal Aviation Administration (1958, 5000, $228 million, aircraft)
Food & Drug Administration (1931, 7000, $240 million, foods & drugs)
Occupational Safety & Health Admin. (1971, 2400, $128 million, health
National Highway Traffic Safety Admin. (1970, 800, $100 million, etc.

The above are just a few (there are hundreds more at federal <u>and</u> state <u>and</u> city or local government levels) government agencies whose sole business is to produce no products or economic value of their own but to monitor, investigate and control private businesses and corporations that do produce products and services. The "overhead" cost of such non-productive government agencies is in the <u>billions</u> of dollars today - and growing annually. Must it be so high a cost -and so high a damage to American productivity, as Americans try futilely to compete with Japan which suffers from far less such non-productive government regulation costs? Yes, unless business regulates itself ethically and responsibly. This notion and message to current and future managers of American businesses are, of course, the entire point of this book. Past-century American businessmen drove the public into this current self-defeating sinkhole of high-cost government regulation of business; current and future businessmen can -and should- correct this inefficient system by means of effective self-regulation based on increased ethical sensitivity and industry ethical codes.* This can be done, should be done and is far to be preferred to inept government regulation. Such ineptitude is illustrated by the FTC.

FTC - The Federal Trade Commission

For over half a century, businessmen have watched the FTC with terror about what its next move against business might be. The FTC seemed more directed by the whim of its academics (many Ph.D.s in marketing, etc.), with obviously little real business experience, than by market realities. And, with little reason and much whim, the FTC ax could fall upon, and destroy, any business. As it often did.[13] In 1914, FTC was established, for good reasons as we have seen, with a (too) general mandate to monitor, investigate and stop, by its powerful government decrees, any and all business trade practices which it regarded as either "unfair" or "in restraint of trade." That's quite a huge, and vague, charter for government operations; and FTC took a full advantage of both its size and ambiguities. Real businesses thrive upon planning and some degree of certainty about what they can and cannot do; FTC thrived upon just the opposite: uncertainty for all, including its everyday working academics, as to the next business target as well as the reasons for the new targeting. For example, FTC is a sharp (and costly) watcher of pricing mechanisms, along with the Justice Department's Antitrust Division (the two agencies, and others, duplicate each others' efforts, as is typical of government with no profit incentive but plenty of tax dollars), selling tactics, TV ads, and almost everything else occurring in the business world. Take TV ads, for example. FTC made Campbell Soup Company change its ads because the company used marbles in the soup to force the vegetables in it to surface to the top and thus be viewable in the ad. FTC watchers caught this "deception" (Campbell called it realistic representation of the soup as a consumer moved a spoon through the product) and, by its power of government decree, stopped it immediately. FTC

---

* Such codes will be dealt with in detail in our last chapter. They are the nation's best hope for renewed national productivity by means of intelligent and ethical business self-regulation to replace at least some of the non-productive cost burdens of ever-increasing government regulatory bureaucracies.

routinely orders manufactuers to prepare costly reports for FTC proving every aspect of every claim made on their TV ads (Sears, Roebuck Co., for example, had to provide proof, to FTC's satisfaction, that its radial tires were good for 100,000 miles of service, as advertised).

Some of the regulation of the FTC is probably necessary and cost-effective for society but many are convinced that (a) FTC's goals are unclear, (b) its regulating is vaguely targeted and duplicative, (c) its operations are wasteful of tax revenue and (d) it has generally been poorly administered.[13]

The Present and Future of Government Regulation of Business

As already noted, few would doubt that, sixty years ago, American business had excessive freedom and legal opportunity to abuse the ethical rights of consumers and society at large. Given the blatant pattern of unethical practices by business, then and before, it was inevitable that weak government control of business would, by public outrage, become greater and stronger. And it did, rapidly (see partial list and dates of establishment of agencies on page 223).

And, once started, the momentum of regulatory agencies drove them to ever larger size, power, budgets and controls – as if by an inner organic life-and-growth mechanism of each agency. Two decades ago, in the aftermath of the famous electric company cases (price-fixing on a massive and conspiratorial scale),[14] the number, size and control powers of regulatory agencies, especially the FTC, escalated by quantum leaps. At about the same time, incidents such as oil spills and other frightening damage to the air and water environments, caused by big business manufacturing operations, fueled the creation and growth of new regulatory agencies to protect the environment from pollution by business. Some idea of the growth can be gained by a look at budget increases for all (or most) government regulatory agencies over a typical recent four-year period: from 1974 to 1978, such government costs rose from about $2 billion to almost $4 billion, almost doubling in just those four years.

One of the best balanced summations of the situation today is George Steiner's: "Regulations have protected and subsidized business interests as well as consumer and general public interests. Regulation has helped society achieve economic and social goals. It has helped to improve the position of minorities, achieve cleaner air, hold business accountable, prevent abuses of the market mechanism, prevent monopoly, reduce industrial accidents, and so on. The list of pluses of government regulation is long. On the other hand, there are substantial costs of regulation, using cost in a broad sense. Many, but by no means all, have been discussed here (in the article). In the (net) aggregate, the costs of today's government regulations seem greater than the benefits. Twenty-five years ago the power scale between business and government was balanced reasonably well. Five years ago (about 1970), the balance seemed to be reasonable. Today, the overall balance is significantly upset in favor of government."[13]

REFERENCES

1 Beard, M., A History of Business (2 vols), 1962
2 Adams, V., "Why The Old Products Last," Duns Review, Apr. 1965
3 See for details Peter French DC-10 article in Business and Professional Ethics Journal (1982, vol. 1, no. 2) and Sewell's Comment.
4 Luthans, F., et. al., Social Issues in Business, Macmillan, 1976, p.362
5 Consumer Product Safety Commission 1973 Report
6 See C. Berenson's "The Product Liability Revolution," Business Horizons, Oct. 1972
7 Galbraith, J.K., The New Industrial State, Houghton, 1967, p.210
8 Ayanian, R. "Does Advertising Persuade Consumers to Buy Things They Don't Need?," Attack on Corporate America, B. Johnson (ed.), McGraw-Hill, 1978, p.236
9 Owens, J., Achieving Success in Selling, Mgmt. Ed., 1976, Ch. 11
10 O'Toole, J., "What Advertising Is -and Isn't," Across the board, 4/82
11 Johnson, B., "Can Corporations Collude?," in Attack on Corporate America (as above), p.261
12 Business Week, April 4, 1977, p.52
13 Liebeler, W.J., "Should the FTC be Strengthened and Enlarged?," in Attack on Corporate America (as above), p.289. And see G.A. Steiner "New Patterns in Government Regulation of Business," Business Topics, Fall 1978.
14 See J. Fuller's The Gentlemen Conspirators, Grove Press, 1962

For Further Reading

- Ackerman, R.W., The Social Challenge to Business, Harvard, 1975
- Bailey, E., Economic Theory of Regulatory Constraint, Heath, 1973
- Comanor, W., et. al., Advertising & Market Power, Harvard, 1974
- Eicher, A.S., The Megacorp & Oligopoly, Cambridge, 1976
- Luthans, F., et al, Social Issues in Business, Macmillan, 1980
- Strickland, A.D., Government Regulation & Business, Houghton, '80

QUESTIONS AND PROBLEMS

1. Define and illustrate (current example) these concepts and issues:
   (a) consumerism (b) product liability (c) warranties
   (d) planned obsolescence (e) "repeat repairing" (f) sales tactics
   (g) oligopolies (h) a "fair profit" (i) cartels
2. Do a detailed force-field analysis of "advertising" (pro and con).

8 Quality of Life in Business

The previous chapter examined business's ethical (and legal) obligations to consumers - as well as the scope of government regulation of business. This chapter examines business's obligations to the workers employed by businesses. Later chapters will address similar business obligations to others of its publics such as investors, stockholders and society at large in terms of environmental effects (ecological issues), international relations (multinational corporations) and the practical need for business's self-regulation by means of realistic and effective ethical codes.

Human Misery in the Workplace

About two centuries ago, as the capitalistic spirit combined with dramatic new technologies such as inventions of mass-production machines and methods, English and American factories of increasing size became the typical workplace for most workers. Charles Dicken's novels are classic dramatizations of the severe misery of the average factory and office worker (review p.38 for details of this economic transition). Workers, many 10-year-old children, at wages barely enough to buy minimum scraps of food to live on through the next day, worked 14 and more hours a day (literally worked and slept only, often too tired to eat) in dirty and dangerous factories (it was taken for granted by all, managers and workers alike, as just a "fact of life," that a large proportion of workers would die young from accidents, disease or exhaustion). Owners and managers were not unsympathetic about this, just realistic: minimum costs equal maximum profits in the manufacture of textiles, coal products, and other economic necessities -provided one's price remains competitive with national competitors as well as foreign competition (see "mercantilism," p.36 above). The movements of the "invisible hand" of capitalism were at once subtle, unrelenting, complex and even governed by the effects of far-flung international market realities. There could be no room for sentimentality or unrealistic "mercy" for anyone of any age or health condition -and all, even dying workers, accepted these realities as merely the harsh price for surviving rather than starving. Sad folk songs of these years, as well as sardonic and robust songs of humor and merriment, are still sung by today's folksingers (without probably understanding the history and realities the songs tell of).

By contrast, today's American workers fare better (8-hour workday, abundance of vacation leave, including routinely weekends, safe and disease-free factories and offices -usually air conditioned, with coffee and cafeteria always available, medical and retirement benefits, and so on) - but they are still not satisfied with the "quality of life" in their workplaces.

Quality of Life in the Workplace

"You'll be hearing more about 'QWL' in business" was the terse advice of U.S. News Washington Newsletter (6/25/82), explaining the acronym as meaning "Quality of Work Life," "bottom-up" philosophy in business whereby businesses listen to workers' ideas and needs, build these into policies decided at the top, and, generally, respect and involve workers in the day-to-day life of the business. (The Japanese call this involvement of workers "quality circles.")* "Working smarter" is the essence of QWL, and many big corporations are using it, claiming big productivity benefits to the business (AT&T, Westinghouse, TRW, GM, Kodak, etc. -although many unions still resist the idea as shifting power from unions to management). But QWL has arrived, is working in Japan and now growing in America. It is as much a new attitude by and toward workers (as responsible and potentially innovative contributors to their business and workplace) as it is a system of monetary gains and employee benefits. (Unions don't like it, generally, since QWL could make them unnecessary and obsolete.)

QWL exhibits two different faces, one from the workers' point of view and the other from management's. Let's examine both of these.

A "Bill of Rights" for Workers

America is a political democracy in which the people have rights and votes to elect their rulers (president, senators, etc.). America's businesses and corporations, however, are not democracies (workers do not "elect" corporation officers and managers; company owners do); a corporation is essentially a dictatorship or oligarchy in which one or a few owners dictate all rules and rights (if they decide to) for all workers.

* The new attitudes of today's workers, including the problems and potential of these new attitudes, are analyzed in detail in a section of this author's book, The Theory and Practice of Managing (1982), entitled "The New Breed of Workers" (pp. 228-239). "QWL," and the idea of "quality circles," will be found to be not very new but still generally unused ideas.

If a worker dislikes the rules or practices of his company –or its wage or other treatment of him, he has no voice or vote in changing such, as he does in his political role as a citizen of the United States, affecting the form and existence of the nation's laws governing everyone. A one-man owner of a small business, with three employees, even though all (politically) are citizens with rights and the power to vote, is absolute *dictator* of that small realm which is *his* business firm: nobody votes or helps to make rules or violates *his* rules, no matter how wise or whimsical, no matter how kind or harsh, no matter how helpful or hurtful of an individual; just as in early European kingdoms ruled by monarchs, any dissatisfied subject (or worker) has the simple choice of staying and obeying the business owner's (or monarch's) rules, or leaving and going elsewhere. Whether a small business, like the three-employee one just illustrated, or a giant corporation (owned by thousands of stockholders), even though operating in an American political democracy where all citizens have rights, a business and its owner(s) exist as a total dictatorship over all workers within its jursidiction, so long as they stay. The corporation's workers have no rights, except as unilaterally granted – or withdrawn– by corporation owners and management.

Somewhat ironically, John Locke's (Lockean "five", p. 175) principles of political freedom *and* personal property rights, the conceptual foundations of the American constitution, collide today: a citizen of a state should have freedom, vote and rights; and any man (or corporate group of men) should likewise have unimpeded ownership and control of his or its property and all rights adhering to and bound to it. Which sums up today into the situation of the average worker being politically free to vote in national elections but with no vote or voice in the decisions of the corporation that employs him.* Although some European nations are experimenting with "industrial democracy" (workers with vote on corporate boards of directors, etc.), the workers' democratic representation is very limited and so far reviews of results are mixed. In America so far there is virtually no such experimenting (nor in Japan) but corporation managements are seriously examining the need and value of giving workers a more genuine voice as advisory input into final decisions and of voluntarily establishing "rights" for workers, called today a "Bill of Rights" for workers. Management's motivation in this is not

---

* The idea of significant voting representation by a majority of workers in a corporation (or by *all*, "universal suffrage"!; see p. 187) in decisions about prices, wages and pay raises, cost-cutting and productivity, work hours and scheduling, etc. is interesting speculation – but, of course, a nightmare to owners and managers. If, as occurs already in the political realm with universal suffrage, workers voted themselves unrealistic benefits, businesses would go bankrupt.

softheaded sentimentality but realistic anticipation of such workers' rights (before government or unions take action, clumsily) and the prospect of more highly-motivated workers with resulting higher productivity.* Although the Japanese do not use the QWL or Bill of Rights terminology, they have made substantial progress in these directions with unquestionable success results.[1]

Let's look at some of the worker issues being considered for such a Bill of Rights.

The Worker's Right to Privacy

Every American citizen is protected by the Constitution from unlawful search of his home or invasion of his privacy by the government or by anyone. But it is still common for corporation managers, on almost any excuse, to search through a worker's locker, files, desk, either in his presence or absence and with or without informing him of the search. Employers also collect huge quantities of personal information about workers as a condition of being hired or staying hired; detailed and long questionnaires are used for these information banks along with psychometric tests, aptitude tests and even polygraphs (lie-detector tests). The worker, of course, is not forced to submit to such self-reporting; he has the other choice of withdrawing his job application or resigning his job. But the worker has little choice about another form of invasion of his privacy: information gathered by questioning others, especially those with substantial financial information (credit bureaus, banks) or health information (hospitals, health insurance firms). In our mushrooming computer world of giant and instantly-accessed data banks, such information is easily available and, indeed, is a for-fee and for-profit large industry today. And information businesses, selling information much of which is personal and even damaging, are growing rapidly along with their computerized data banks. (It is technically possible today -and has been for a decade, at least- to develop a single, giant, Orwellian data bank of all information on everyone in America; Congress has thusfar balked at permitting this, for fear of its possible abuse, including possible embarrassment to congressmen.)[2,3]

Other examples: Maislin Industries has developed its "Personnel Occurrence Profile," a computerized device installed in trucks to record (for later inspection by management) every move, speed, stop and

---

* The obvious notion of government legislating worker QWL rights has precedents pervading the American labor movement and is being seriously discussed. See Edward Lawler's "Should the Quality of Work Life be Legislated?," Personnel Administrator, Jan. 1976. It will be in management's self-interest to anticipate these moves.

time of a truck on duty; management says "we make the employee fully aware that we know everything he is doing and has done,....people are constantly creating their own record." Electronic cash registers record every aspect of a sale (product sold, by name, price, time, amount) so that a manager can exactly compare performance among sales clerks, what "specials" and in what quantity are being "pushed" by waiters in restaurants to determine managerial reprimands vs bonuses, etc. (If you do most of your purchasing by credit card, big data banks will soon have systematized purchasing profiles, from your credit card numbers, detailing what and how much and when you buy, including medications, alcohol, sex and hobby magazines, foods, all of which tell a lot about your mental set, physical health, habits, etc.) Many companies are installing computerized access-control systems whereby an employee routinely uses his numbered plastic card to enter the front door and every other door in the workplace, including the rest room; from these entries, the computer instantly maintains a real-time trail of every employee's motions and whereabouts at all times. In other companies, managers' appointment calendars are electronic calendar pads recording all appointments by time, duration, persons, nature of business, for higher management review if and when necessary (to fire someone?).[4] Research is rapidly advancing computer technology by which plastic ID cards can be obsoleted and replaced by any individual's thumb print on sensitized paper for entry into a computer data bank. Convenient. Or dangerous?

The government is, of course, also deeply engaged in the storage and uses of data bank information, especially intelligence services (the CIA, etc.), tax collector (IRS) and the Social Security Administration (lifetime wage records). It has been estimated that, in 1977, the government operated about 900 federal data banks with over a billion records containing personal information on citizens (and it's an open secret that the various agencies exchange information, the Pentagon with information about dishonorable discharges or the FBI with its criminal files and so on). Similarly, universities and all schools maintain student files with grades, dismissals, cases of cheating, moral scandals, courses dropped, all very personal information, especially for a middle-age man applying for a job and hoping his bad college record was now behind him.[3] In a data bank age, all information is recorded, none forgotten (people forget, computers don't) and it's all there, available.

Employer's and Other's Right to Information

As grim as seems the above invasion of privacy, there are no <u>absolute</u> rights. My right to swing my arm around as I please is limited to where your nose begins, at which point my arm-swinging freedom must be set against your right to a reasonably-shaped nose. My right to privacy is also limited by your equal and fair right to self-protecting information.

Examples: you are a small business providing security guards to other local businesses to protect their property, office files and employees; if you hire just one "wrong" person into your ranks, who might use his new position of trust to steal, gain information for extortion, or otherwise be of dangerous and untrustworthy character, you would lose your entire business -along with customer confidence- by just a single incident of security failure, not to mention the possible destruction of your client's business by your hired employee; thus you use questionnaires, polygraph tests and all information sources available (as described above) to avoid the accidental hiring of thrice-convicted burglars or drug-pushers, unstable or "emotionally disturbed" personalities (like Hinckley who tried to kill President Reagan), or others of the many incompetents living on habits of theft, lies, violence, street crime or even just fraudulent uses of welfare. Do you have a right to such information for such reasons?

Should the government intelligence services (CIA, FBI, NSA, etc.) be permitted to spy on Americans? Sounds awful - what an invasion of a citizen's privacy! Recently, Senator East (Republican, No. Carolina) and Congressman Edwards (Democrat, California) debated this issue, with clearly much to be argued for the ethics of both sides of the question (Americans' right to privacy vs other Americans' right to protection from organized crime, muggers, assassins, extortionists, pimps and habitual murderers routinely free on "personal recognizance" while prior court convictions are appealed and they are free to do it, as they always do, again and again). Hinckley shot a president (Reagan) with impunity - he will probably be freed from his mental hospital quarters within a few years - with the opportunity to do it again.[5] Hinckley's release from confinement is typical today, only noteworthy because his crime involved a noteworthy official. Does Hinckly have a right to privacy? Should his assassination attempt on a human being be expunged from his records so that he has a fresh opportunity for employment? Would you hire him, if you had access to information about his qualifications, past habits and activities? Do you have a right to that information before you make the decision to hire him? Many ethical analysts would rank your right to information as more ethically compelling than a criminal's right to privacy. (Their view is well backed by all the ethical tests.) So, on balance, right to privacy for any particular individual in a complex society seems ethically much less compelling than the rights of so many others to self- and society-protective information about a person, before he is hired, trusted, given responsibility involving others' lives, or kills or rapes.

The two above sections, "The Worker's Right to Privacy" and "The Employer's and Other's Right to Information," are, I believe, fair and reasonably objective presentations of each case; and, if so, illustrate the ethical dilemma and ambiguity about most business ethics issues we will, and already have to, deal with: ethical judgments cannot be exact and most ethical decisions must be approximations as close to ethical good and as far removed from ethical evil as is humanly possible, given all, usually inadequate, information on each issue, on a case-by-case basis. This is not intellectually satisfying (the intellect wants certitude and exact definitions) but it is inexact, humanly subjective and typical reality, especially man's ethical issues and decisions requiring ethical judgment rather than computations.

A Sensible Compromise: How IBM Handles the Privacy Issue

But, balancing the demands of corporate safety with worker privacy, IBM has become a leader in a worker's bill of rights for its nearly 400,000 employees. Its privacy code is radical (and somewhat expensive) in its structure: two files are maintained for each employee, classified and divided into job-related information (positions held in IBM, performance ratings etc.) and personal information (medical insurance claims, life insurance beneficiaries, activities prior to joining IBM). IBM managers can inspect the job-related files but are barred from the personal files of an employee (only the employee himself or someone with his written authorization or a court order gains access to these personal files). More importantly, it is the IBM principle, now being implemented, that is radical: personal information about all workers is confidential, not to be revealed to managers or external information-seekers (for their data banks). Moreover, management can collect information and file it only insofar as such information is required by law or necessary to manage operations (thus IBM job application forms no longer ask for previous addresses, criminal convictions dating back to more than five years, prior mental problems or criminal charges not resulting in actual conviction of a felony). Compliments to IBM for its initiative in such a complex matter; far better that business anticipate it, and act on it, than that government be forced by public pressure into attempting to control such a subtle issue, probably inefficiently and ineffectively.

When the Issue is Tough, Use a Force-field Analysis

In this matter of employee privacy (as well as most other matters involving workers' rights), countervailing rights spring up on both the side of owner/management interests and the worker's interests. Only a force-field analysis (p. 169) can sort out and weigh all the issues in a specific case. To illustrate, let's take an oversimplified case of a retailer who insists on polygraph tests for all job applicants. The force-field outline (oversimplified) is as follows:

Option 1 Use polygraph (lie-detector) tests on all new employees
++++++++++++++++++++++++ Reduce pilferage enough to survive
--------- Invading employees' privacy

Note: In this case, the employer's right to survive as a business (by using polygraph tests to cut down his huge pilferage losses) is viewed as more compelling than potential job applicants' inconvenience. But, are there other options the employer might consider?

The Ethics of Screening and Hiring Job Applicants

Until recently, the attitude of business owners or managers about hiring workers was simple: it's my business and my property, and, therefore, I have complete freedom to hire or not hire anyone I please, on any basis that satisfies me. That is, the right of an owner to hire or not, as he pleased, was virtually absolute and based in his property rights. (This is the "Lockean Five" again, p.175).

There are generally two broad classes of reasons for hiring or not: one is job qualifications (can the applicant do the job well?) and the other is the group of non-job-related considerations, some simply whim or personal taste and people preferences, such as a long friendship with an applicant's father or the personal beauty of the applicant ("she's a beautiful girl, but can she type?"). Until the 1950s, hiring was done routinely and freely on either job-related bases or not. Many of the latter excluded from some businesses job applications from Irish or black or old or Jewish applicants. Since the "civil rights" movements of the 1950s and 1960s, such discrimination based on race, color, sex, age or religion has been declared illegal by both federal and state laws. A majority of voters came to regard such discrimination as unethical (i.e. unfair to those discriminated against) and the laws followed the ethical views of the majority.

Thus, today, any discrimination in hiring, based on any but clearly job related factors, is illegal and victims of it can sue for damages. Also, the federal government can and does punish violators, based on its own investigations and judgment, by withholding or withdrawing federal funds, grants and contracts from businesses found in non-compliance of laws.

"Reverse Discrimination"

Discrimination in hiring is today so severely monitored and punished by government that any ethical questions remaining tend to be in the area of excessive or unfair enforcement of anti-discrimination laws rather than securing the original objectives of such laws. Such abuse, if such it be, takes two main forms, both closely related: government setting or "suggestions" of "quotas" of minorities to be hired by businesses and other organizations such as universities; and so-called "reverse discrimination."

Although government authorities, especially compliance officers whose sole job is to monitor business compliance with civil rights laws, avoid the term, it is common knowledge that they think in terms of "quotas" of minorities (blacks, hispanics, ethnics, women, etc.) to be hired by particular business and other organizations based on criteria such as the proportions of each minority group residing in a community. The proportions existing in a community cannot, of course, be exactly matched with proportions of people hired (if so, few whites could be hired in Washington, D.C.). But, government authorities set quotas based on approximate or feasible proportionality and first warn, then punish organizations failing to meet them. In many cases, enforcement of such quotas damages a business's opportunity to hire the best talent for the right job (as they are forced to hire the "right" color or sex to "meet quota") and its chances of competing profitably -especially with international competitors not burdened with such social quotas.* In many cases, such enforced quotas can amount to unfair (unethical) treatment of business owners who lose fair profits -or even the business itself - by hiring to meet quotas rather than essential company work needs.

"Reverse discrimination" is a recent term to describe the hiring of a minority member (to meet quotas) when (usually) an average white, male applicant was far more qualified for the job, but was denied it by enforced government preference for the minority member instead of the white, male competitor. In such cases, the white, male applicant, as an individual human being, is unfairly discriminated against (reverse discrimination) and, although the act against him was mandated by law, it was unethical. (Not the first time a state's laws were in conflict with basic ethics.)

Job Security and "Seniority"

Fifty years ago, the idea of job security did not exist. No matter how many years a man had worked for a company or in a factory or a mine, his next day's work(and pay) depended upon his here-and-now ability to perform that day's work as well as any competing job-seeker. Every day was a new day for everyone, the past ignored, loyalties irrelevant and each employer and worker alike assessing each other for

* Many analysts fault such quotas and other inefficient social costs as a major and pervasive cause of low American productivity and loss of sales and jobs to foreign firms which are unburdened by such huge overhead costs. T. Sowell, noted economist and a black, put the issue well and realistically in a recent U.S. News & World (10/12/81)

what advantages each could gain from the other on that particular day. This was free-market efficiency, in the use of resources, at its best. It did, however, cause personal tragedies in individual lives as the old and the weak -or sick- were quickly replaced with the young, strong and healthy; and, of course, the loser's family and children suffered as well.

Today, the "rights" of seniority have been built into most workplaces by the efforts mainly of American unions over the past fifty years ("first hired, last fired"). Not only the idea but the reality of lifetime job security dominate the workplace. Japan has gone so far (America has not) as to establish virtually guaranteed lifetime employment in its large corporations.* In most American corporations, a worker cannot be fired at will but only for cause, carefully documented in accordance with near-legal due process statutes. Then what are the ethical issues today?

One is the issue of fairness to younger and more productive workers who, with growing families depending on them, are laid off, during cut-back production periods, while less productive men with seniority (and often higher wages for the same work) have "rights" to be laid off last, if at all. A detailed force-field analysis (p.169) of a typical case of this is quite revealing about the ethics of such "seniority" preference (or is it a form of unethical discrimination?); the reader might wish to stop for a moment and outline such an analysis - and marvel at the probable results of it. And recall that the purpose of this book is not to indulge in the author's particular ethical conclusions (he reserves this for thesis-oriented articles in journals and magazines) but to urge the need for ethical sensitivity to issues and, most importantly, the methods of ethical analysis of such issues.[7]

Another is the issue of promotions from lower- to higher-paying jobs, which, from the standpoint of ethical analysis, is essentially the same as the issue of "hiring," as already discussed above.

Still another is the issue of discharge or dismissal of a worker from his job (in true English, "firing"). In the old days of Lockean property rights, firing workers, like hiring them (p.175 & 234), was the absolute right of the business owner, based upon his property rights. In effect, an owner was exactly that: he owned absolutely his property, his business and his right to admit or bar anyone from his property, hire at will anyone, for any reason, seeking a job or fire a person for any reason, even whimsical or discriminating, as he, owner, "saw" the issue. Those

* Guaranteed lifetime employment is a national policy in Japan today. It is possible through national planning, assuring every Japanese who wants a job that he will have one for a lifetime, by two methods in combination: a strict national norm of lifetime employment with the same firm and government subsidy to sustain this when necessary.

days are gone (forever?). A labor lawyer, writing in Harvard Business Review as recently as 1980, notes that, strictly speaking, the common law still holds that an employer may fire an employee "at any time, for good cause, for no cause, or even for cause morally wrong;" but that this body of law is rapidly changing, under public pressure, to require an employer to show fair and just cause for dismissal.[8] For many years, government workers, after completing a short probationary period successfully, have been protected by "status," i.e. a virtual "right" to their job with no threat of dismissal except for good cause. For many decades, for reasons of "academic freedom," university professors have enjoyed a similar right, called "tenure." Even in corporations, watched closely for compliance with civil rights laws (p.234), it can be reckless for managers to fire anyone except for documented and demonstrable cause, not yet for reasons of labor law but civil rights laws.

For reasons of both ethics and emerging law reflecting them, a wise employer today will avoid firing "for no cause or even for cause morally wrong" and approach the decision to fire with "good cause," and that reasonably documented. The right of "due process" is coming.

Discipline

Even under the best of circumstances, all workers (or anybody else) are not always good either in character or in performance. Thus sometimes managers must discipline workers for such things as pilferage, unexcused absence, lateness, abuse of medical leave (lying about it, for example), slow or sloppy work and so on. Discipline (punishment) can range from fines and warnings to suspension and dismissal. Essentially, everything said above about firing a worker applies also today to the administration of discipline.

Whistle-blowing

A common cause, not necessarily "good," for firing an employee in the past (and it's still done often) is an employee's critical attitude or actions against company practices, popularly called "whistle-blowing." Such criticism usually pits one ethical value, loyalty, and often another, long-range utility or self-interest, against many other ethical tests (golden rule, honesty, justice and the general law; see p.155). In the famous DC-10 case (p.198) and the Pinto automobile case (see Case 1 below), where engineering managers knew of life-threatening defects but did not blow the whistle, a force-field analysis made it clear that, in each case, the ethical would have been to notify top management or, if ignored, an appropriate government regulatory agency (FAA or NHTSA as on p.223 above). Consumers' right to life would outweigh the lesser ethical consideration of company loyalty.

A force-field analysis, from the potential whistle-blower's view, is almost heroic to act upon, but is certainly clear as to knowing rather objectively which options are ethical or unethical:

Option 1 As an engineer, blow the whistle to top management or others
-----------------Risk losing my job and references for another
------Loads of time and work documenting and proving my case
++++++++++++++++++++++++++++++++++++++Avoid high risk to lives
++++++++++++++++++++Peace of mind for me, wife and children
+++++++++++++Etc.Etc.

Option 2 As an engineer, say nothing about the DC-10 or Pinto defect (the plus and minus lines will be essentially the opposite of the above for Option 1)

Suppose the engineer informs just his own boss, who decides to say nothing? Can the engineer now, ethically, say nothing, having shifted the responsibility elsewhere? What would a force-field look like?

Fortunately, many ethically sensitive firms are establishing policies that not only protect a company critic or whistle-blower from dismissal but positively encourage employees to report "all the way up" information about product defects or other practices that could ultimately hurt the company's reputation or lead to a damaging court suit. Some such firms are Cummins Engine (a leader in business ethics for years), Atlantic Richfield, GE, New England T&T, Dow Chemical, American Airlines, Pitney Bowes, Delta Air Lines, and others.[3,9]

QWL and Job Enrichment

Most of the QWL (Quality of Work Life) issues discussed so far are in the area of "negative" ethics, i.e. avoiding unethical actions in hiring, firing, etc. The advanced sensitivity and progress being made in this area alone are essential and encouraging in the business world. But, fortunately, many businesses are also getting increasingly involved in the area of "positive" ethics, i.e. installing positive QWL human systems that enhance the good rather than only avoiding evil. Again, business's reasons for this are usually practical and enlightened self-interest for the long range. Positive QWL systems are proving that they not only increase workers' job satisfaction but, because they do, they also increase (often dramatically) the productivity businesses need desparately. Job enrichment is a now well-known example.

A host of research studies since the late 1920s in America and the experience of worker attitudes in Japanese companies prove that, in many cases, productivity soars when workers' psychic needs are satisfied by humanly interesting work, enhanced challenge and responsibility, recognition of their worth by managers and a genuine sense of being involved, needed and participating in decisions.* The research shows that, in the absence of these psychic factors, no matter how acceptable physical factors such as working conditions and wages, modern workers become bored, clockwatchers, sloppy in their work, resentful of the "dehumanized" quality of their workplace, all of which creates poor productivity and quality in the work done. Which ruins profits!

Job Enrichment, Quality Circles and Productivity

It is beyond our scope here to describe the many methods being used to enrich jobs for greater productivity; they are covered fully in the books below.* We will only suggest the direction and thrust of such efforts, in three major areas: work attitudes, job enrichment methods and quality circles.

In a Special Issue entitled "What the U.S. Can Learn from its Rivals," Business Week (6/30/80) summed up America's greatest long-range necessity as productivity, supported enthusiastically by a renewed attitude throughout American society at all levels (in essence, the "work ethic" attitude as discussed above on pp.72-3,80,115 & 177). The attitude is expressed well in Milton Friedman's recent Free To Choose: "Nothing is more important for the long-run economic welfare of a country than improving productivity." American society and workers must renew the once-American respect for the work ethic as that national attitude now thrives in Japan (with obvious results); so must business management begin again to invest in the high-technology plant and tools workers need to reach international-class competitive status again (this will mean, of course, more government cooperation, less taxation and social overhead costs, diverting national income from consumption into production). In macro-economic terms, the new attitude must translate into higher rates of American productivity, saving and investing at lower rates of waste, consumption, spending and liquidation of national assets by debt. And it all depends upon attitudes, always at the root of individual or national achievements (or failures).

Substantial, even radical, job enrichment progress is being achieved in today's American workplaces, mainly by re-design of jobs and production processes to make human jobs more "humanized," challenging, interesting and meaningful. Even a decade ago, AT&T began to give employees, who used to handle narrow and minute functions like typing or verifying telephone book entries, far broader responsibility for even all functions of entire sections of telephone book production. Job satis-

* All of this research is described in detail in the author's Theory and Practice of Managing, 1982, especially Japanese Quality Circles (pp. 197-8), Hawthorne studies (pp.214-18), Herzberg studies (pp. 218-27), Job Enrichment (pp.229-236). See also Pascale's book and Campbell's six-year study (suggested readings on next page).

faction increased as well as productivity. Many companies are now redesigning jobs and production structures in a similar manner (IBM, Eaton and Volvo of Sweden, for example).[11]

Japan's production methods and quality circles thrive in the U.S., reported Business Week, even five years ago (12/12/77). Matsushita took over Motorola's American-run television operations (losing money and almost bankrupt) and soon began showing a profit. One of the reasons was renewed interest of workers and lower-level managers invited into "quality circles," i.e. committees charged with developing new ideas for better quality and productivity, these ideas being recognized and often part of final top-management decisions. Quality circles delight workers with their genuine sense of participation and managers as they watch productivity and bottom-line profits soar.

These are major directions of positive ethics in American business.

REFERENCES

1 Pascale, R.T. & A.G. Athos, Art of Japanese Management, Simon, 1981
2 Cary, F., "IBM's Guidelines for Employee Privacy," HBR, Sept., 1976
3 Ewing, D.W., "A Bill of Rights for Employees," Across the board, 3/81
4 "Bid Privacy Farewell," Next Magazine, July 1981
5 U.S. News & World Report, Nov. 16, 1981, pp. 33-34
6 See R. Zager's "Managing Guaranteed Employment," HBR, May 1978 and Business Week on same topic, July 17, 1978.
7 IBM and Lincoln Electric are noted for "lifetime employment" efforts.
8 Summers, C.W., "Protecting All Employees against Unjust Dismissal," HBR (Harvard Business Review), Jan. 1980
9 Brenner, S. & E. Molander, "Is the Ethics of Business Changing?," HBR, Jan. 1977
10 See for details U.S. News & World Report special report "The Coming Industrial Miracle" (11/30/82) and Business Week special issue "Reindustrialization of America" (6/30/80).
11 Ford, R.N., "Job Enrichment Lessons for AT&T," HBR, Jan. 1973

For Further Reading

- Campbell, A., et al, The Quality of American Life, Russell Sage, 1976
- Pascale (as in Ref. 1 above) and see Bibliography for pertinent titles.

QUESTIONS AND PROBLEMS

1. Define and illustrate (current examples) these concepts and issues:
   (a) mercantilism as capitalism (b) "invisible hand" of capitalism
   (c) QWL (d) Bill of Rights (e) "work ethic" (f) Lockean five
   (g) "industrial democracy" (h) "universal suffrage"
   (i) privacy rights (j) data banks (k) Force-field analysis (p. 169)
   (l) social overhead costs (m) productivity (n) Quality Circles
2. Prepare a force-field analysis (with examples) on (a) discrimination and (b) "reverse discrimination" -or (c) FBI tapping criminals' phones

9 Ecology and International Issues

"An activist is the guy that cleans up the river, not the guy that concludes it's dirty," said Ross Perot, an American billionaire and patriot.[1] A fair summary of some stark realities and attitudes regarding ecology (the study of organic systems and how they are affected by changes in their environments). Fifty years ago, everybody, most scientists included, assumed that Earth's resources and living species were so many and firmly established as to be practically immune to man's constant destruction or use of them. So, routinely, human waste was discharged into rivers and oceans, new machine exhausts poured into the air, whales were harvested from the seas to light lamps (with their oil) and most of the world's forests were cut into homes and heating fuel. Hints about the real significance of the human use (or waste) of Earth and its species abounded in the form of strange incidents (the near-extinction of whales a century ago) and speculations of theorists (like Malthus on the effects of excess human procreation and population sizes -see p.136) but were generally ignored, especially by established institutions with high stakes in the status quo (state treasuries always needed more money from whaling, fur trade, etc. and the church always insisted on maximum number of children to increase its constituents and power). Because of the giant scientific and information explosion of the past few decades, thousands of researchers discovering facts and computers to organize them, man is becoming frighteningly aware of how his brain (technology and its uses) could easily destroy the Earth and its species upon which he depends for life itself.

Evolving, over millions of years, man's brain (developing unique intellectual powers for abstact thought) gained his survival against far mightier predators whom he learned to outwit, hunt, catch and eat; his superior brain, inventing the chemical and nuclear means of literally destroying his Earth (as we know it), can, quite feasibly today, destroy him as a species, probably not forever - man would evolve again in a few million years. Man, with his new machines (technologies), faces a self-inflicted extinction - unless his capability for ethical judgment soon catches up with his brain's technological powers. Man's survival itself depends on this equation.

The "Tragedy of the Commons"

In 1968, Garrett Hardin, a noted biologist, published his classic article called "The Tragedy of the Commons" (it's easily available as an appendix in his Pelican book Exploring New Ethics for Survival). In it, he compared today's earth and its resources to the common pasture (called the "commons") used by all farmers in a community to feed their cattle and sheep. Invariably throughout history, a self-destructive use pattern emerged: while each farmer would use and care for his own land carefully (the property immediately surrounding his home and barns), he was tempted to exploit and overuse the commons by breeding and feeding as many cattle as possible in the common pastures; and, of course, all his neighbors did the same, each motivated to "get his fair share of the commons, and a bit more," each over-breeding and overusing the commons until it was barren and useless to all. Hardin termed this the "tragedy of the commons." His point, of course, is that men tend to protect and use properly their own property but to waste carelessly what is owned by others or everyone or no one (watch someone litter a park or hotel room which he would never do in his own backyard or living room); and that, since the industrial revolution, men have been wasting and polluting the most essential "commons" of all, i.e. the very air, water, earth, vegetation and animals all men depend upon for survival. When man has finished destroying this "commons," we will see - or already are beginning to see - a cosmic version of the "tragedy of the commons." Stahrl Edmunds' national (and international) policy analysis in 1978, Alternative U.S. Futures, strikes the same theme with a chilling, almost clinical, objectivity and logic. Hardin entitled his book well: is there any more pressing ethical issue than man's voluntary participation in the destruction of his species?

How Man and Business are Ruining Their Environment

- Item: World-wide oil spills are killing fish, birds and some entire species. At present rates, many species will become extinct.
- Item: As human population expands and technology pollutes the wilderness, wild animal species become extinct - some scientists calculate, at present rates, most animal species will be extinct in 100 years.
- Item: Garbage from cities, chemical waste from factories, air pollutants from auto exhausts and smokestacks, nuclear wastes, etc. have already made some major cities often unfit for human habitation ("smog" in Los Angeles, poisoned rivers as water sources, vegetables and vegetation contaminated by chemical pesticides and destroying all animals in the "food chain" of animal feeding leading even to man).
- Item: And, as Malthus foresaw, the "tragedy of the commons" in the form of human population explosion depleting unrenewable resources

at ever-increasing rates - until few resources are left, and fewer men. (Population and resources research, and policy formulation on these two issues, is Garrett Hardin's special field, and his book, cited above, contains essential information for anyone concerned about these issues.)* But, still, nations (for increased tax revenue and military power) and most major religions (for increased power- and influence-base) pursue high-population policies such as tax deductions for children born, welfare increments (money, foodstamps, etc.) encouraging procreation, religious prohibition of most forms of workable birth control, and so on.

Ecology and Ecosystems

Ecological research today always examines carefully as many relevant ecosystems as possible (an ecosystem being simply the ways all living and non-living things in a system affect each other). It used to be called the "balance of nature" by which, for example, in Darwinian terms of survival of the fittest, an excess population of rabbits in an area would naturally decline to proper size by deaths due to eating up their "common" pastures and to predators thriving and increasing by the abundance of rabbit food; as the rabbit population declined, so did the predator's until a sustainable "balance" was reached (and vegetation rabbits feed on was given a chance to grow again). Multiply this simple rabbit example by millions of species of animals, insects, birds, plants, trees, humans, along with their interactions with their physical and chemical environment, and you have the Earth's miracle of thriving - and "balanced" - ecosystems. Man, as just one of the millions of earth species, is deep within thousands of these minutely-detailed ecosystems, but he has alone the technological power to alter them radically and permanently, "unbalance" them and, inadvertently, wipe out his own life-sustaining ecosystems. Using the rabbit example, Malthus saw man in misery from increasing famine, disease and wars for scarce resources; quite differently, today's ecologists see man technologically capable of - and bent upon - destroying the "commons" (the ecosystems) on which his own survival ultimately depends. (Rachel Carson's classic research work Silent Spring, detailing the unanticipated and destructive effects of chemical pesticides, is decades old but more valid than ever in its warnings about tampering with the "balance of nature.")

So, what should business and society at large do about this new threat to man's very survival as a species?

---

* Thomas Malthus, an early economist who called his field the 'dismal science' (because of the realities it had to face), published the first analytical study of the population explosion (Population, 1798). He forecast only human misery, in gigantic proportions, unless population explosion was controlled. In Malthus' times, population was increasing slowly; today it is doubling every 30 years, using up resources

Environmental Costs Must be Avoided, Limited or "Internalized"

Until very recent times, businesses and society at large have viewec the environment (air, water, earth, fish, animals) as a "free resource," available to all equally, with no restraints, no personal ("internal") costs, to be used freely as anyone pleased. Like a "commons." Despite what we know today about man's rapid destruction of his environment, this is still the case. There are five things, depending on the nature of the environmental problem, that society and businesses can do:

(1) Renew resources as they are used: lumber companies can plant and grow on their properties a new tree to replace each one harvested.

(2) Clean up the environment (or protect it) from pollution as – or before – it is ruined: develop devices, for use by all polluters (cities, suburban homes and business factories alike), which neutralize or convert chemical wastes into harmless or even useful forms before or as discharging them into the common atmosphere, rivers, oceans or earth. In each of these first two options, external (environmental) costs are being "internalized," i.e. recognized as true "costs" to society (not a "free resource") and handled by "internal" monies spent to maintain the common environment (therefore appearing on internal company statements as actual overhead costs). Such "internalization of external costs" was discussed in detail above, pp. 188-9 and should be reviewed.

(3) Stop, or at least limit, any use of the environment which ruins it without possibility of protecting or renewing it. Slaughtering elephants for a bit of ivory jewelry or exterminating the few remaining ocean whales for a bit of whale oil (or profit from it) are examples of human rape of the environment that, both ethically and legally, should be stopped. So should the hunting (utterly unnecessary for any genuine human use) of many species of birds, eagles, buffalo etc., now near extinction after once being abundant across the land and waters of earth –and, once gone, forever gone.

(4) End the human population explosion. As human populations double every 30 years, because of modern medicine's control of disease and famine (man's age-old population controller), it is obvious that such geometric increases of the species must soon exhaust Earth's resources, no matter how resourceful modern technology becomes.

(5) All of the above four kinds of actions will depend upon degrees of human cooperation, unprecedented in human history, at both national and international decision levels. Fundamentally ethical action, never accomplished before in human interactions among provincial, ethnic and national communities of people, will become necessary for human survival – not merely desirable in the usual form of platitudinous moralizing. Fundamentally ethical action, instead, must be specific and

reasonably pass the hard ethical tests (p.155) of long-range utility for man's survival as a species, the general law standard, the lesser-evil standard and so on. Man's solutions to the problems and threats of the rising destruction of his ecosystem depend far more upon progress in the human "sciences" (especially ethical awareness and action) than upon even greater advances in technology. Man's exponential advances in sophisticated technologies must someday begin to be matched by similar advances in interpersonal competence, the human ability to live in mutually effective ways with other members of his species; as noted so often in this book, these practical life-and-death objectives depend basically upon rapidly improving ethical awareness, sensitivity and action.

Fact-oriented and objective scientists also, often, stress this same theme. Man's technological competence built the nuclear arsenals that can now destroy world-wide ecosystems, millions of living species and man himself as a species; only his human (and ethical) competence can bar his catastrophic use of this technology (that's a human, not a technical, decision!). (It seems naive, even to this author as he writes the above paragraphs, to really expect -rather than merely hope- that man will be able to develop soon the human competence of constructive co-operation which he has never been able to do before in his long history; but, still, he must - for obvious reasons just described.) Even twenty years ago, a team of scientific writers said after a thorough analysis of the nuclear arms race: "It is our professional judgment that this dilemma has no technical solution; if the great powers continue to look for solutions within science and technology only, the result will be to worsen the situation."[3] Garrett Hardin, a decade ago (in Exploring New Ethics for Survival), emphasized the same kind of warning:

> "An implicit and almost universal assumption of discussions published in professional scientific journals is that the problem under discussion has a technical solution, defined as one that requires changes only in the techniques of the natural sciences and technology, demanding nothing in the way of change in human values or ideas of morality (ethics)......We are confronted today with a whole class of human problems which can be called 'no technical solution problems.'..An example: the population problem has no technical solution; it requires a fundamental extension in morality... The real difficulties, as Shakespeare's Cassius said, lie not in the stars but in ourselves; our minds are trapped by unexamined assumptions and subconscious resistances. We hope for easy solutions....As a scientist, I wanted to find a scientific solution (to the population problem), but reason inexorably led me to conclude that it cannot possibly be solved without repudiating

> certain ethical beliefs and altering some of the political and economic arrangements of today." (Emphasis added.)[4]

Perhaps Herbert Spencer, Darwin's contemporary and the philosopher of evolutionism as a generalized concept (p. 127 above), was correct: like animal and plant species, man's brain and his very ethics must evolve and adapt to new circumstances if he, as a species, is to survive as 'fit.'

A Note on "Futurism" and "Futurists"

Confronted, for the first time in human history, with problems affecting his very survival as a species, man (scientists, philosophers, etc.) has recently developed a new discipline called "Futurism." Futurists (including this author) attempt to project current trends into their future consequences, change the trends and their implicit goals when future consequences are analyzed to be intolerable for man as a species, develop alternative human strategies for survival in a variety of areas (directions being pursued in various industries, societal arrangements, religious and other institutional prejudices of the past, political values, and military as well as social programs) and, most critically, examine innovative social concepts and ethical alternatives (based, not on historical patterns of the past only, but the hard ethical tests –as on p. 155– applied to today's unprecedented actual realities).

A major rallying point and coordinating center for futurism studies is the World Future Society (Washington, D.C. 20014). Its members, most of them with doctorates in the sciences or similar credentials in business and other professional fields, share research through The Futurist, the Society's monthly journal, and increase greatly in number annually as more "concerned and thinking" people –from many nations– take very seriously the serious questions facing modern man.

Critical Agenda: International Ecological Norms

An implicit human law of life, known by all historians, runs like this: if all, except one, cooperate with each other, none can or will. If, for example, all members of a cartel (like today's OPEC –see p. 26) agree to charge a minimum and set price to sustain the profit margins of all and if just one of the members reneges by lowering his price below the minimum set, thereby gaining customers while other members lose them, all members must soon break the cooperative agreement, set new prices and fight for customers, each in his own interests. This is simply human nature –and why cartels usually don't work for long!

Another case: suppose Apex Co., a U.S. chemical manufacturer, decides to install costly anti-pollution equipment, either because of its ethical sensitivities about the ecosystem or newly-established U.S. law, while a Japanese competitor avoids the anti-pollution costs, is able thus to price lower with still a good profit and gain customers who abandon the U.S. firm and its higher prices. Apex has two choices: eliminate the anti-pollution equipment and its costs (if it can) to restore prices competitive with its competitor - or just keep losing sales, profits and go bankrupt. This is an over-simplified scenario but essentially accurate for an increasing number of U.S. firms competing (under U.S. laws) against foreign firms unencumbered with such additional environmental "internalized" costs. Or suppose Apex, with no laws requiring it but because of sincere concern about ecology, installed the same equipment while a competing American manufacturer did not: the same end result, as above, as Apex's higher costs and prices drive its customers to its competitor. The point is obvious: if one competitor violates such a norm -and is permitted to do it with impunity, all others in the same "game" must do the same, or lose. Equally obvious: anti-pollution and pro-ecology norms, both national and international, are possible only if all cooperate with and abide by them together, all at once, without a single individual violation of the norms (if one does, all must).* Can a nation -or world- of competitors achieve this kind of cooperation and enforce it? Or should national governments (for national competitors) or nations together and jointly, by some kind of international compact (for all international competitors), regulate these issues by norms established by laws? But, then, think about the resulting bureaucracies.

If our current maze of regulatory agencies is becoming absurdly inefficient and fraud-laden, what would similar international agencies be like? Could competing firms in the same industry, both national and international, meet together "in a hotel" to agree on such ecological norms, imposed upon all equally and thus with neither benefit nor net loss to any?* But, if they all could -and did, by constructive, mutual cooperation, such world-wide industry agreements would simultaneously (a) solve all human ecology problems by mutual use of anti-pollution and pro-ecology methods (as on p.244) and (b) accomplish this by equal absorption of ecology costs, all firms "internalizing" them equally, thus all maintaining equal cost levels for ecological overhead with no gain or loss of competitive advantage in this specific element of operations. Theoretically, voluntary pacts of this kind are obvious ethical goods - by any kind of force-field ethical analysis; but are they yet humanly realistic? If not, international governmental regulation is necessary (is that any more realistic?). Man must hope that one or the other is!

---

* Ironically, current U.S. antitrust laws prevent competing firms from meeting "in a hotel" to establish agreements about anything. This is, of course, excessive (and typically bureaucratic) reaction to business sins of the past (trusts, oligopolies, cartels, etc.). Can government bureaucrats ever distinguish such good vs bad agreements? I guess not.

Ethics and Multinational Firms

A business firm operating in more than one nation (a "multinational") has special ethical problems, some of them tortuously ambiguous because of the differences between any two nations in their cultures, religions, specific ethical codes, taxation systems and laws. We will confine ourselves here to American multinationals.

It is to be expected that most of the major "scandals" about business have involved multinationals. Compared to relatively clear standards and laws in America, standards and laws in many other nations, especially developing countries in Africa and Asia, on such issues as payoffs, human rights, antitrust, pricing, advertising etc. are not only unclear but also much different from America's when they are clear. On many of these issues, a multinational is "damned if it does and damned if it doesn't." No matter what action it takes, different people will view it and measure it with different yardsticks.

Moreover, a multinational is faced with a group of postures in the host country (for example, Apex Co., an American firm, operating in South Africa as the host country) ranging all the way from passive noninterference in the political and moral practices of the host country to extreme and active persuasion or intervention. Let's look at a sampling of such issues and alternative postures for Apex.

Payoffs to Officials for Business Opportunities

In America, the law is clear about any sort of payments of money or equivalents by Apex to government or other organizational officials for favors (other than normal buying and selling of economic goods and services in the open market). Such payoffs, bribery or "under the table" money have been outlawed in America since the days of the robber barons because of their damage to consumers, fair competition and the entire free market system. In America, payoffs are not only unethical but clearly illegal.

But in many foreign nations (in Africa and the mid-East particularly), payoffs to high officials, for the opportunity to do business and get contracts, are both legal and routinely expected. If Apex refuses to make such payoffs to those officials, its bids for contracts and other business won't even be considered and Apex will be unable to operate in that country. An irony is that many of Apex's competitors in industrial nations like West Germany, Japan and France, which outlaw payoffs in their own countries but permit them as legal and necessary business practices for their own multinationals operating in another country, can pay off foreign officials and get business while Apex loses it (and its home country, America, loses tax revenue, jobs and favorable balance of trade payments). The American law, prohibiting Apex from payoffs to foreign officials, is a very recent law (and many feel it should be repealed). But, prior to passage of the American law, the ethical choice of action for Apex raises a host of conflicting "rights" and "goods;" a force-field analysis, under the ambiguous internationalcircumstances, would be very complex and loaded with offsetting ethical tests, probably with liberal resort to the general law standard and the lesser-evil standard.[5] Despite the semantic tone of the word, is "bribery" or a payoff for a favor inherently (per se) unethical (like murder or rape) or can it be ethical under particular circumstances if it passes the ethical tests of the golden rule, long-range utility, general law standard or, at the very least, the lesser evil standard? Can a law be ethical in one nation and unethical in another, given enormous differences in cultural views, beliefs and lifestyle preferences? For example, a law in India (or some of its provinces) barring the killing of cows would reflect and support a strong religious belief of the people and, probably, be quite ethical (by the tests); a similar law in America would violate the right of many beefeaters to pursue their own lifestyle so long as it harms no one else. Finally, resorting to the lesser-evil standard, do the ethical pluses of an Apex payoff to a foreign official (more American jobs, etc.) outweigh the American technical distaste for the action (again by the ethical tests, including the lesser-evil standard)?

International Cartels and Price Collusion

Cartels, monopolies and price collusion (already discussed, p.216) are illegal in America; antitrust is taken very seriously. But, cartels and varieties of pricing arrangements (collusion) are common in many foreign countries. Within many nations, especially socialist ones and dictatorships where the economy is dictated by government, there is no free market anyway, so that production and prices are simply set by the central government, a kind of government monopoly in which price or other competition -and antitrust- are irrelevant. (Most such nations, including Russia, have thriving free market "black markets" but these are very limited, illegal and unofficial.) Among many nations, which produce similar products for export such as wheat, oil or minerals, a free international market (based on supply, demand and buyers searching for minimum prices) controls prices in a generally fair manner, as in America's internal economy. Unless all nations producing a similar product form a cartel and agree to enforce identical prices. OPEC (p. 26 above), controlling international oil prices, is the current classic case. Using the principles and ethical tests which led America to reject cartels and price collusion as unethical -and then illegal, international cartels fare no better and should be viewed as unethical.

Investing in or Trading with "Unpopular" Nations

Is it ethical for American corporations or investors to deal in or with so-called "pariah" or unpopular nations, whose national practices violate the human rights of its citizens? For example, nations that discriminate against blacks (South Africa), torture political dissidents (many South American dictatorships) or deny rights (Russia, China and most communist dictatorships)? Before answering, consider that, without such American investment, the citizens of such nations would be even more miserable in terms of jobs available, production of necessities of life and opportunities for better political status in the future.[6]

REFERENCES

1 See C.S.Wren's "Ross Perot: Billionaire Patriot," Look, Mar.24,1970
2 See H.Hayes' article on Hardin's views, Atlantic Monthly, May,1981
3 Wiesner and York, Scientific American, No.4, 1964
4 Exploring New Ethics for Survival, Pelican, 1973, p.251
5 See J.R.Basche's "Unusual Foreign Payments: A Survey of Policies of U.S.Companies," Report #682, The Conference Board, New York. See also J.G.Kaikati's "The Phenomenon of International Bribery," Business Horizons, Feb. 1977.
6 Logue, D.E., his article in Attack on Corporate America, 1978, p.71

For Further Reading

- Edmunds, Stahrl, Alternative U.S.Futures, Goodyear Co., 1978
- Hardin, Garrett, Exploring New Ethics for Survival, Pelican, 1973
- Johnson, B.(ed.), Attack on Corporate America, McGraw-Hill, 1978
- Walton, C.(ed), Ethics of Corporate Conduct, Prentice Hall, 1977

QUESTIONS AND PROBLEMS

1. Define and illustrate (current examples) these concepts and issues:
   (a) "Commons" (b) Futurism (c) Population trends
   (d) Ecology (e) Ecosystem (f) antitrust laws
   (g) Internalizing costs (h) International ecological norms
   (i) Technological vs human (and ethical) competence
   (j) Multinationals (k) Price collusion (l) Cartels
2. Prepare a force-field analysis on whether or not an American firm, say Apex Co., can (ethically) set up a business operation (invest in, manufacture products for, sell and make profits) in (a) South Africa or (b) a South American dictatorship nation or (c) Russia.
3. Prepare answers, in the form of a brief report for each, to the series of questions on the top half of page 249.
4. Prepare an outline, for discussion, of the pros and cons of a world international regulatory agency to regulate all nations' ecological destruction of the environment (air, waters, oceans, wildlife, etc.).

10 Other Contemporary Issues

Although the scope of this book excludes consideration of all current issues and even full discussion of some of the major issues selected for brief ethical analysis (our purpose being always to stress the practical importance and the methods of ethical analysis for business decision-makers), our sampling of issues should include several others. The main claimants of ethical obligations from a business are its customers, its employees and the broader society -both national and international- affected by the business. These groups and a business's ethical obligations to them have been discussed in the last four chapters. In this chapter, we will consider issues involving a business's stockholders (owners) and career managers.

Stockholders and the Stock Market

Most large and even mid-sized businesses are no longer owned by an original founder as a sole proprietorship but are organized as corporations (with limited liability) whose ownership consists usually of a large number of stockholders, each with a relatively small share of the stock. These stockholders, in effect, invest their savings by buying a certain number of shares of stock in a company in expectation of a fair return in the form of dividends and capital appreciation of the value of the stock. Although any such investor realizes there is some risk in buying stock (stock prices rise and fall, unanticipated market and world events can drive a firm into bankruptcy, etc.), still the top management of a business (Board directors, chairman of the Board, president, vice presidents, etc.) have a fiduciary obligation to use the business's assets and stock responsibly and fairly.

If, for example, directors of a business made decisions as reasonably as anyone could expect but the business went bankrupt due to unique and unforeseeable circumstances (a Russian takeover of Saudi Arabia or similar event), investors would have risked their money and lost it. But this would be misfortune, not unethical action by the directors. If, on the other hand, the directors secretly conspired to risk business funds in a wild-chance venture from which they, but not other stockholders, would profit, the action would be unethical by most ethical tests (p.155) -whether the venture succeeded or failed. It would be an irresponsible and unfair use of the stockholders' property (assets and stock value).

Management Information to Stockholders

An entire class of ethical problems involves the information directors and managers of a corporation provide stockholders: the amount of such information as well as its accuracy and intent.* Based on the ethical tests, such information should be sufficient, essentially true (accurate) and for purposes that are fair to stockholders, whether actual holders of stock or investors contemplating purchase of stock.

During the past century's robber baron days, some of the most blatantly unethical actions of business's owner/managers involved false information with the intent of deceiving and "robbing" stockholders - usually then legally and just within the edge of the law. These robber tactics led belatedly to the establishment of the Securities and Exchange Commission in 1934 to regulate the stock markets, transactions in stock and other securities (bonds, etc.) and, especially, information provided, such as in annual reports to stockholders, advertisements to potential investors for purchase of stock, and so on. Before 1934, and to some extent even since then, the ingenious and unethical methods used to deceive stockholders, "manipulate" securities' prices and "water stock" (see second footnote below)** defy imagination for their variety, complexity and deviousness. Today, greatly due to SEC regulation, the more crude forms of misinformation to stockholders are under control, but the problem still exists in more clever and subtle forms.

"Insider" Stock Trading

One of the issues constantly raised in the legislative debates leading to the 1934 SEC final legislation was "insider trading" (i.e. the

---

* The terms here are important and to be distinguished carefully. In a small sole proprietorship, a man was both owner <u>and</u> manager of the business. As a large corporation, ownership is represented by stock owned (stockholders) as distinct from management (directors and managers who might or might not own stock). Typically, directors and top managers <u>also</u> own stock but the two roles are different.

** "Watering stock" arose from cattlemen's practice of stopping a herd, being driven to market, at a river to drink its fill just <u>before</u> being sold by the <u>weight</u> of each head of cattle, an extra <u>margin</u> of profit while the tactic lasted. Today's (paper) stock is "watered" by false claims and other deceptive information (usually to stock purchasers).

buying or selling of a corporation's stock by managers and directors of that same corporation who, as "inside" officials, knew first any good or bad information potentially affecting the value of the stock). For example, suppose a director learns at a board meeting about final government approval of a large contract certain to drive the corporation's stock price up as soon as the news is released to the press, and, before that information release, buys a block of his corporation's stock at its current deflated price (deflated while everyone waited for the big government decision). When, a day or so later, the price soars, he makes a substantial profit (in cash, if soon after he sells to those late getting "on the bandwagon"). Or, the same director might have heard early bad news, as an insider at a board meeting, and sold quick before the stock prices collapsed. Obviously, trading with "inside" information can be easily and substantially profitable. But, is it ethical? The framers of the 1934 SEC legislation generally agreed insider trading was unfair (unethical) - but that issue was excluded from the legislation as being too subtle and undetectable to regulate realistically. It would be difficult to <u>prove</u> that information someone happened to have as an insider was <u>the</u> reason for a particular stock transaction (even if it seemed obvious that that was the case).

In today's "age of instant information" (p.20 above), with minute-by-minute investigative reporting through electronic and computerized media, the information advantage of insiders is far less substantial than in the early decades of the century. But, to the extent that insiders still have the early-information advantage in stock transactions, very serious ethical questions remain.

Conflicts of Interest

In the world of owners and/or top managers of organizations, not only business but political and other organizations, conflicts of interest are probably the largest class of ethical problems. The potential for conflicts of interest is almost infinite for top people at the center of hundreds of key events and decisions, many of them related to each other <u>and</u> to the personal profit of such top people. An American diplomat finds that a favorable decision (or recommendation) for arms aid to his host country will also indirectly gain him access to profits in the oil industry. A professional real estate appraiser, employed by a firm managing pension funds, finds that his superiors prefer appraisals of property in the firm's portfolio "tilted" slightly upward to "puff up" somewhat the asset side of the balance sheet - and such "tilting" seems correlated with his own excellent salary increases. The appraiser can easily rationalize his "upward" thinking since, quite truly, such appraisals of real estate vary among appraisers anyway by 20% or more. Consider a bank president who permits overdrafts (checks that should, but don't, "bounce") in his own personal account and those of other board directors to maintain interest-yielding -or speculative and risky- investments elsewhere than in his bank and the interests of its other stockholders. (Bert Lance, president of Georgia's Calhoun bank and soon after a top official in the Jimmy Carter administration, is a recent example: between 1972 and 1975 Lance's account was typically overdrawn by $50,000, his wife's often overdrawn up to $110,000, and many Lance relatives overdrawn in amounts totaling $450,000; all for personal interests, not those of the bank's stockholders.)

Conflict of interest is difficult to define. But the above examples illustrate it as generally the use of one's official position to gain a personal goal independently, or at the expense, of one's organization or contractual client. There is more, in this attempt at the definition of conflict of interest, than first meets the eye. First, use of a position for personal gain is the major motivation for anyone seeking a job or position (for income, status, etc.). Therefore, the definition makes it explicit that such official use is not conflict of interest so long as one is advancing personal interests by means of first advancing and adhering to goals of one's organization or client, i.e. not risking or damaging the interests of the latter for one's personal interest. Only then is there conflict of interest. Next comes the question of whether the conflict of interest is ethical or unethical (or legal or illegal). It would be not only superficial, but wrong, to suggest, in the abstract (often done in texts) that all conflicts of interests are unethical. Such a conclusion is simplistic: the top engineering manager OKing the defective DC-10 design (resulting later in hundreds of aircrash deaths -see p. 198 above) was in a conflict with, but fully supported, his company's cost-cutting goals and specific decisions insisting on the defective design - despite his own personal desires for professional integrity and moral concern for aircraft safety and protected human lives. In this case, conflict of interest was ethical (by all tests) and the engineering manager should ethically have fought for his position on the final aircraft design - or even "blown the whistle" to warn a government agency (FAA) about an unsafe aircraft. Conflict of interest, therefore, is not per se unethical at all. Each case of it must be evaluated by the ethical tests (p. 155) to determine its real ethical value. By such tests, the diplomat, appraiser and bank president above were surely acting unethically; the diplomat and banker by unethical conflict of interest and violation of their organizations' good aims, the appraiser by unethical cooperation with his organization's intent to deceive. Such "conflict of interest" situations cannot be neatly "formulized" as ethical or unethical; each must be subjected to hard and specific force-field analysis (p. 169) using the ethical tests (p. 155).

A good number of cases, involving conflict of interest, is provided in the Case section at the end of this book for further ethical analysis.

Board Directors and their Ethical (and Legal) Responsibilities

Only recently have board directors of corporations come under any kind of law-imposed sanctions for their actions (or omissions, conflicts of interest, or negligence - such as showing up at the meeting but without doing homework and preparation they were responsible for). But, so far, these laws covering board directors and attached sanctions are too vague to be useful. In the meantime, board directors are bound mainly by ethical norms to the extent they choose to be.

The traditional function of corporation board directors has been to protect the interests of the stockholders who, directly or indirectly, are to "elect" each member of the Board of Directors, including the chairman of the board. The latter is often the CEO (chief executive officer) for decision-making on general policy and specific operations of the corporation. Or, the chairman, with consent or majority vote of the other directors, appoints a president as CEO, while he, the statute chairman and chief representative of the stockholders, acts (usually) as a figurehead and recognizable symbol with which stockholders can confidently identify. Or, in bad times, the chairman and/or president, no matter which is functioning as CEO, are discharged (as scapegoats to remove company problems into whatever wilderness they go -but away from the boardroom). Or, today, arrangements are made to "elect" to the board "outside directors," people who (a) are not corporation managers or employees and (b) represent often and explicitly interests other than stockholders' (such as employees', minority groups', the local community's, etc.). So, today, board directors come in many colors and stripes, with many different interests, and many -or few- functions. Similarly, the true (ethical) responsibilities of directors, with their new and diverse intents, create ambiguity of direction and accountability at the highest levels of the corporate structure.

As in the case of "insider trading," Congress has addressed the issue of directors and their responsibilities but found it difficult to formulate laws specific to their functions. The reason is that the evaluation of a director's actions falls within ethical norms related to conflict of interest (above) or "influence peddling" (below), not to the director's functions *per se*, and they must be determined as ethical or not on a case-by-case basis using the ethical tests (p. 155).

Influence Peddling

Often indistinguishable from conflicts of interest, selling one's "influence" or ability to arrange "favors" for favors in return deserves special treatment. First let's remove the semantically "loaded" part of the common term (used recently even in Harper's[1]) and discuss here the "use of influence," which can be either ethical or unethical; the loaded term, influence peddling, obviously is meant to refer to the unethical use of it.

The use of influence, including personal, financial, official or other, is best defined by examples. Your doctor uses his rights to admit his patients into a prestigious hospital and this privilege for his patients is part of his higher-than-average fee all of his patients pay. He also refers patients to specialists who routinely refer their patients to him for his specialty, surgery. A lobbyist, whose reliable economic research on issues is highly respected by congressmen, easily gains access to key congressmen to explain or "make the case" for legislation very much desired by particular corporations, which, of course, pay him a high consulting fee for his time and services. A professor, whose judgment is highly respected by his dean, is able to get instant access to the dean in behalf of a student who needs a special exception in order to graduate. Joe's son is able to get a prompt job interview because the interviewer happens to be a good friend of Joe's. Joe's son is also able to get a date with a girl, who seems less than anxious about it, because the girl's father and Joe are lifelong friends. And so on. In a broad sense, human life and interactions are built largely upon people "influencing" each other - for a host of reasons and in a host of ways, some ethical, some clearly unethical and some very difficult to judge.

Most of the examples just cited are probably ethical uses of influence, provided all relevant facts in each example involve no violations of the ethical tests (p. 155). It is key facts or circumstances that determine the difference between ethical and unethical use of influence. Suppose, for example, that the doctor refers patients to another specialist because the latter is the best in town, even though the latter doctor rarely refers patients to him; suppose, however, that each doctor refers patients to the other independently of optimum qualifications for the patient services in order to insure maximum traffic for each doctor - or each doctor received 10% of the fee charged to any referred patient. These latter practices edge dangerously close to unethical conflict of interest (is this fair to the patient? would one of the doctors himself like to be referred on mainly marketing or earned commission bases? can you make a reasonable general law based on the doctors' practices or justify them against the "no harm" ethical test?). Suppose the expert lobbyist sells his client's case to congressmen by leaving out key information, developed in his research, damaging to his client's case and to his own retention of a good-paying "customer." Suppose both of Joe's "friends," who did favors for his son as above, work for Joe in his bank.

Suppose someone influences another effectively by plain blackmail or other stated or implied threat.

Quid Pro Quo

Quid pro quo is a Latin expression meaning what for what? or something for something, one "favor" in return for another. Good friendships, good marriages and good business relationships (between manufacturers and their dealers, retailers and customers, etc.) include a large proportion of such quid pro quo. Again, it's not per se either ethical or unethical, but depends on the facts underlying such human reciprocity, its intent, methods and effects, tested case by case against the ethical tests (p.155). Depending on the nature of these elements (intent, methods and effects) quid pro quo can range from human exchanges based essentially in justice and the golden rule norm (ethical) all the way to extortion (I'll say nothing if you pay me), "protection" (I'll refrain from destroying your store or home if you pay me), kidnapping, robber-baron-type business monopolies or oligopolies and international nuclear blackmail (we won't launch a first attack if you agree to....etc.). The Mafia's (criminal) mutual "favors" abound.

The variations on the themes of quid pro quo and use of influence proliferate as imaginatively as conflicts of interest (above), including the unethical or questionable ones. Only several recent variations, questionable or clearly unethical, can be cited here (although the cases at the end of the book contain many others).

The "five percenters" of the Truman years helped remove him in favor of Eisenhower (1952 election). They outraged the public by using their political "connections," congressmen or other officials who owed them "favors" from past election assistance, to get government business for corporation contractors -and received themselves 5% of the newly gained business.[1] Since about the same time, another phenomenon called the "revolving door" has irked the public sense of morality: prominent appointed federal officials move back and forth, every few years, from government into business, use their former connections to profit in business, join government again, cultivate more connections, and so on. Much of this is probably unethical conflict of interest - or, at least, the public thinks so. Until recently, political quid pro quo with business interests flourished in the form of huge money contributions by business (or unions or other favor-seekers) to politicians for their campaign to get elected or reelected; after election, the favor was returned as favorable votes on key legislation needed by the contributors - usually, also, an unethical conflict of interest. Such practices are less blatant, with new election laws, but still exist; just more subtly, and with greater caution to be 'indirect' and avoid publicity.

CPAs (certified public accountants), especially in their auditing functions, are the essential guardians of the integrity of information used by most of us for most of our business decisions. The CPA's signed certification of the integrity (adequacy and accuracy) of company financial reports, and the information within them, is the information base for decisions investors make about investing life savings, banks make about loaning millions of dollars of depositors' funds, stockholders make about holding or shifting shares, pension funds make about financial investments for future retirees, and so on. These reportings of critical information, audited and certified as sound decision information bases, are the quiet foundation for most people's very lives.

Is such information always reliable? Are business's (or other organizations') reporting of facts always honest? Do business and other managers ever "fudge" figures in their own interests (sales, costs, expenses) or under pressure from top management? Two no's and a yes, of course. For example, recently JWT Group Inc., McCormick & Co. (Baltimore) and Saxon Industries admitted their employees juggled numbers such as deferring expenses falsely, altering invoices, inflating revenue, puffing inventory values etc. Other firms are admitting the same, including Flight Transportation Corp., Datapoint Corp., etc. "In all cases, the auditors accepted without qualification the accounting practices used by the companies."[2] Such cases are alarming CPA firms (the auditors and certifiers!) and driving them to renewed efforts to stop these embarrassing scandals, which hurt them as much as the unethical firms.

REFERENCES

1 R. Kaus's article in Harper's (Aug. 1982, p. 8) has many recent cases.
2 Wall Street Journal, July 9, 1982, p. 19

For Further Reading

- Heyne, P.T., Private Keepers of the Public Interest, McGraw, 1968
- Johnson, B. (ed.), Attack on Corporate America, McGraw, 1978
- Litschert, R.J., et al., Corporate Role and Ethical Behavior, 1977

QUESTIONS AND PROBLEMS

1. Define and illustrate (current example) these concepts and issues:
   (a) stockholder (b) Board director (c) investor
   (d) "Insider trading" (e) conflict of interest (f) quid pro quo
   (g) influence peddling (h) ethical tests (p.155) (i) SEC
2. Making reasonable assumptions as to the facts, prepare a detailed force-field analysis (p. 169) on any example used in this chapter, such as five percenters, Joe's son, doctors who refer patients, etc.

11 Codes of Ethics

In a 1962 address, President Kennedy emphasized that "in the last analysis, high ethical standards can be achieved only through voluntary effort."[1] Later in the same year, Chief Justice Warren said essentially the same thing in much more detailed terms (p.15 above). What each meant, when analyzed, is a critical theme of this book: if the only way publicly-perceived unethical actions of business can be controlled is laws, more and more of them, each more cumbersome and costly to administer than its predecessors, all draining national productivity by duplicative enforcement, paperwork, reporting requirements, armies of government compliance officials, etc., then the American free enterprise and free market system will collapse (probably into full-blown socialism) under the sheer weight of government regulation costs.

The need of the voluntary element in a free America, if it is to remain free, has many analogies: for the great majority of free Americans such actions as paying fair share of taxes by democratically accepted rules, refraining from criminal and other antisocial activities, maintenance of land and homes in a safe and sanitary condition, etc. are done voluntarily, with little or no need of government enforcement or armies of police (as in police states like Russia). A minimum, and low-cost, government force of tax collectors (IRS), local police officers and building inspectors is sufficient to maintain proper civil order (to deal with the small minority of irresponsible citizens violating the rules that make freedom possible). If the voluntary compliance of most Americans, including businesses, ever failed to maintain societal stability and civil order, then necessarily a powerful strong-man-type or socialist-type central government would quickly step in to restore and maintain order. (It's done almost annually in many African, Asian and South American countries, whose peoples lack the inner- and self-restraint necessary for democracy and quickly find it supplied externally by a strong central government. Democracy -workable and practical for any length of time- is almost unknown throughout most of human history.) We are back to Toynbee's "order vs freedom" theme (p.13 above). It's an iron rule of history. With no exceptions. Civil order is necessary;freedom is not.

Thus, free businesses in a free market and free democracy can stay free only by voluntary efforts at high levels of ethical action. Business ethics in America is just that starkly and "bottom-line" practical.

Ethical Standards and Ethical Codes

As explained in an earlier section (p.75), ethical standards are very general normative statements (essentially the ten tests as on p.155) subject to broad interpretations, while ethical codes are the very specific interpretations of these standards. Whereas standards are abstract and usually vague, codes are concrete, sharply detailed, unambiguous (or they should be) and leave little room for subjective interpretation – or "creative rationalizing" around, and in defeat of, them and their ends. Using an organizational analogy (soon to become essential in this chapter), standards are like policies while codes are like rules and SOP (standard operating procedures). Policies and standards permit widely diverse interpretations (sometimes stretching to near absurdity) while codes allow few or none, depending on their narrowness and pointed specificity. (Often, of course, excessively specific codes, and rules, adhered to blindly and mechanically, as is the case in many religions, and applied rigorously with no room for judgment, result in actions that violate the true spirit of the standards which the code was supposed to serve –as, for example, when a virgin refuses to "bend" her code for her fiancé who, at least subconsciously, needs to "know" her better before the major commitment of marriage, or when an executive flies at coach fares, by strict rule of a company, despite a special first-class rate, for promotional reasons of the airline, half the price of regular coach fares he will pay.)

Thus, codes can be too general to be useful or too specific to allow for intelligent and good-willed judgment. Effective codes are not easy to formulate, whether in the form of company rules, religious codes or national laws. (One national law, in America of the 1920s, the "prohibition" law, outlawing any use of liquor in a public place, intended for the good purpose of reducing alcoholism and drunkeness, had just the opposite effect, higher per capita consumption of alcohol along with the birth of massive organized crime syndicates to supply liquor illegally to otherwise law-abiding citizens who "occasionally needed a drink" – and, organized crime has since expanded into gambling, narcotics, prostitution and is still with us, probably forever.) Laws, and other specific codes, are necessary – but must be formulated carefully.

Voluntary vs Imposed Codes

A final, but critical, classification of codes: codes are either adopted and accepted voluntarily by groups who appreciate their value for the good of all concerned (these are generally abided by as a moral commitment by all and for all) – or they are set by a central authority and enforced by it (these are generally fought, resented and evaded). Codes imposed by government regulatory agencies are of the latter sort.

As a sustained strategy, American business has the choice of fighting government-imposed regulatory codes forever – or voluntarily creating fair, effective and cost-efficient codes of its own; codes that are fully realistic (government's rarely are), sensitive to consumer and other public concerns, and self-enforced by firms or their voluntary associations.

Professional and Trade Associations

Virtually all working Americans belong to associations centered around particular groups' professional, trade or other concerns. There are thousands of such associations, the titles usually suggesting the kind of membership and purposes; most publish monthly journals or news magazines and provide other services (for a fee) such as trade information, market trends, management and financial advice, consultants to help businesses in difficulty, management training tailored to the specific trade needs of members. For example: American Medical Association, American Association of University Professors, Industrial Launderers, National Association of Appliance Dealers, National Association of Retailers and similar associations of dentists, retailers, wholesalers, automobile dealers, printers, government executives, secretaries, etc. And, of course, there are labor unions, which are similar in intent to associations.

Many associations, in addition to their usual functions of aiding members with trade, industry or professional information, have begun to address the practical need for ethical codes (often called standards of conduct) for the self-regulation of members or member firms in strict accordance with the prescribed behavior canons of the code. The reason for associations' interest in ethical codes is not mere sentimental moralizing, but the practical concerns already discussed often above, specifically the aim of anticipating and properly handling ethical problems within a profession or industry before external (government) laws and regulations do –usually in a mood of public panic and "overkill." Although many ethical codes and "ethics committees" of associations originated early in the century, a new wave of association interest in ethical codes heightened in the early 1960s (and note the dates of both President Kennedy's and Chief Justice Warren's speeches cited above). What triggered this heightened interest in ethics and ethical codes was the notorious scandal of price-fixing among the major electrical manufacturers and their top executives, which filled the newspapers in 1960.

The Gentlemen Conspirators

This is John Fuller's description of the principals involved in the price-fixing conspiracy in which a number of major electrical manufacturers were indicted in a U.S. court (June 22, 1960) for alleged elaborate conspiracies to fix prices for large power generators and other electrical equipment for sale to public power utilities. As the evidence and convictions in the case developed, each day a "new scandal" for full press coverage and renewed public rage -which the public actually seems to delight in, a pattern of customer deception and illegal price collusion emerged: the gentlemen conspirators, often top marketing executives of the huge corporations involved, simply met secretly in hotels and elsewhere (after complex preparations to conceal personal identies and discussion agendas) and set agreements on prices in their bids for big electrical contracts in which the "low bid," and business, was rotated equally among the conspiring firms - so that each could get sufficient sales at high prices and profit margins.[2] The net result, from the viewpoint of the purchasing utilities and their power-consuming customers, was that all were being grossly overcharged in prices being paid for electrical power. (Which is why price collusion is both unethical and illegal.)*

The Strengths and Weaknesses of Ethical Codes

In the aftermath of the electrical conspiracies, as later following the Watergate scandals of the early 1970s, every association felt compelled to strengthen its ethical codes as protection for its members from the fate of the electrical companies (damaged public credibility, huge financial losses in court-ordered fines and customer rebates, lost future business, etc.). And so they did. But still with many weaknesses as well as strengths.

Despite weaknesses, a code of ethics, adopted by a corporation or association and publicized among members and external publics, has the important value of at least a public commitment by all to try to do the ethical thing in all business dealings and create peer pressure for all to try to abide by the spirit of the code. No code at all, reversely, is a public admission of little or no interest in ethics and its significance to customers, employees and the general community within which a business operates. Many such codes might, indeed, be just lip service with little real intent behind them; but they are a start, at least, in

---

* Price-fixing cartels are also difficult to maintain (see OPEC, pp. 26 and 249) as members quarrel among themselves for the best deal in the collusion agreements. After ten years of an iron grip on oil production and pricing, OPEC finally collapsed, at least for awhile, when its July 1982 meetings in Vienna ended with no substantial agreements on production or prices (to the delight of OPEC customers, including American oil consumers). (Washington Post, 7/11/82)

the right direction and begin to focus attention on ethics and the need for them in a modern business. As the Chinese philosopher put it: even a journey of a thousand miles must begin with a single step.

But, obviously, such feeble attempts at an ethical code are far from sufficient to meet a code's practical objectives (actual improvement in ethical business action - to create customer credibility and forestall counterproductive government regulation). Even very sincere codes, developed with clearly good intent and effort at enforcement, are, in most cases today, far from adequate to reach such practical objectives of a code.

The Usual Flaws in Codes: Too general, too Vague and Unenforced

In Ivan Hill's book-length discussion of ethical codes, containing an abundance of examples of codes as well as their history and values,[3] three central weaknesses seem still to mar their effectiveness: excessive generality; vagueness; and inability - or unwillingness - to enforce such codes. Let's examine each of the three problems briefly.

Excessive Generality: A code that states "all dealings with customers should be handled with the highest degree of fairness" is too general (and vague also) to be useful or enforceable. Useful versions of the spirit of the statement must address very specific and typical business situations and stipulate categorically what actions are ethical or not. And sanctions (reprimand, suspension, even dismissal) for code violations should be explicit and publicized; all of the above features in writing, of course. (Many firms, especially ones stung in the electrical conspiracies, require employees to read their codes and sign their names attesting that they have read and will abide by the codes.)

Vagueness: A code that states "all customers should be treated as members of our company family" conveys nice, and harmless, sentiments but is so vague as to admit of any interpretation (some people enjoy hurling obscenities at their family members). These flaws, both vagueness and excessive generality, can be remedied by specific statements such as "if an item is on sale and the customer seems unaware of it at the checkout counter, he is always to be charged the sale price, never the regular price." This statement of code pursues fairness to all customers as well as family spirit but in a manner that is clear, easy to comply with and easily enforceable.

Unenforced Codes: A code that is too general or vague cannot be enforced. The examples above about fairness and family permit everyone to interpret as he pleases and no one accountable for specific actions which can be interpreted as within or outside code, depending on such interpretations - thus, there is really nothing clear enough to enforce. So, a genuine and serious, enforceable, code must begin with specific code statements that remedy the first two problems of excessive generality and vagueness. Given, finally, clear and specific codes, the final problem is the one of genuine intent by a firm or association: the will and implementation to seek out code violations, investigate them and enforce them by substantial punishment for violators. A good example of this is the National Association of Realtors, whose code of ethics was adopted in 1913, which, after many revisions, now stands as very specific in many instances and actually enforced: violators are dismissed from the association and not allowed to use the name "realtor" (a now well-known trademark for confidence among home buyers and sellers who prefer to do business with "realtors") in their stationary, advertisements, etc.[4]

A recent (1977), and excellent, study of ethical codes in business, involving the Fortune 1000 top corporations, was done by the University of Virginia's Center for the Study of Applied Ethics. Anyone interested in the subject needs a copy.[5] One interesting finding was that a full 90% of the Fortune firms now have codes of ethics - and they take them seriously. There are still problems (essentially the three discussed above about generality, vagueness and enforcement); but, certainly, most American businesses now appreciate the practical significance of good ethics and promising progress is being made to develop effective codes of ethics for self-regulation rather than the counterproductive government regulation (which is inevitable unless forestalled by increasing ethical sensitivity and action by business itself).

REFERENCES

1 "A Statement on Business Ethics and a Call for Action," at a meeting of the newly-established Business Ethics Advisory Council, Jan 16, 1962, Dept. of Commerce, publisher, 1963, p.9

2 Fuller, J., The Gentlemen Conspirators, Grove Press, 1962

3 Hill, I. (ed.), The Ethical Basis of Economic Freedom, American Viewpoint Group, Washington, D.C., 1976

4 Hill, ibid., p.353

5 Write Graduate School of Business, Center for the Study of Applied Ethics, Univ. of Va., Charlottesville, Va. Title of the work is Standards of Conduct in Business (by P.M. Hammaker, et. al.).

Note: Recommended readings are the books just noted in References.

QUESTIONS AND PROBLEMS

1. Define and illustrate (current examples) these concepts and issues:
   (a) voluntary compliance (b) ethical standards
   (c) ethical codes (d) voluntary codes of ethics
2. Describe the three flaws in most ethical codes. How remedy them?
3. Outline the practical reasons for business's self-regulation.

12 THE Professional MANAGER

By way of concluding this book, let me indulge in a strong personal thesis: American managers of the future, in order to make viable business decisions and steer their organizations in ultimately successful directions, must –and will – become "professional" managers, in the strict sense of the term. (Otherwise, they, often along with their organizations, will quickly violate society's emerging and firm expectations, cease to be effective for their functions, and depart from the modern organizational scene.)

Management as a Profession

Although the term "profession" is still not precise, we have a useful idea of what it means in practice. With little practical ambiguity, we regard doctors, lawyers and university professors as professional people and, when dealing with them, fully expect to receive professional treatment. People who use the term seldom stop to analyze the elements constituting such professions; so, let's do that now. My analysis identifies six elements of a true profession (i.e. one accorded credibility, confidence and reasonable degrees of assurance of expected services as perceived by the general public). The six elements of a profession:

(1) Lengthy training and education, by means of course-work in accredited schools, intensive personal study, and practical experience. (For example, doctors spend all waking hours, for ten or more years, in college, medical school, textbook study and supervised internships in hospitals before anyone regards them as professional doctors, ready to practice that profession.)

(2) Certification: A professional* is never judged to be one merely by self-declaration as such. He must prove his competence and overall worthiness by a series of demanding tests of knowledge, skill and competence in his performance. If he succeeds in such tests, he is only

---

* "Professional," a much abused and ambiguous term in common usage, obviously is not used here to mean people for hire (vs amateurs); pay is not even one of the six elements above. Doctors and lawyers tend to make good incomes; but it's a byproduct of the profession, not its nature.

then, and because of such public proof, certified as competent to begin actual practice in his field (typical certifications are medical degrees from accredited medical schools, law degrees, university doctorate degrees).

(3) Peer Review: Professionals are the best judges as to the competence and continuing competence of the practicing members of their field. To protect and insure the integrity and high-quality performance of the profession, as well as its public image, members establish professional associations and committees to monitor members and even remove the licence to practice in cases of proven incompetence. Thus, the American Bar Association, American Medical Association and most universities have boards or committees of peers to judge, admit, reprimand or dismiss members. In most universities, promotions are determined mainly by rank and tenure committees of peers recommending or withholding such promotions.

(4) Codes of Ethics: Every profession has developed, often over centuries, strict ethical codes that are specific, enforced and generally very effective.

(5) Stress on Human Service: A professional doctor, dentist, minister, lawyer or teacher may in most cases (not all) earn a good to high income, but this is secondary to his dedication, as a true professional, to delivering a human service competently and ethically. It would be clearly unprofessional for a doctor to recommend surgery, not strictly indicated by the nature of the patient's case, mainly for the fee to be received. Similarly, a lawyer should not accept a case for which he feels less than fully competent (he should refer it to another who is); and a teacher should not teach a course for which he is not fully prepared. For a professional, whenever there is a choice to be made between income versus fully competent service, the latter comes first.

(6) Self-regulation: Although some government (external) laws and regulations must be established as mechanisms to control the practices of professionals, a profession keeps these at a minimum by effectively (usually vigorously) maintaining its own mechanisms for self-regulation – to forestall the need of much external policing. These mechanisms for self-regulation are mainly the ones above, especially certification, ethical codes (strictly enforced) and continuing peer review.

The above six elements constitute an idealized model of a true profession, which, in reality, will approximate the model in most respects but often not fully meet it. It follows, too, that the actions of professionals, to the extent to which they ever compromise or deviate from the model's norms, are to the same extent unprofessional and unethical. For example, it would be unprofessional –and unethical – for a professional peer to "fudge" and inflate a competence rating of a colleague for personal, financial or any reasons.

Thus, the issue of whether managers (or accountants, engineers, teachers, businessmen or any group of skilled people) are professionals must be restated as follows: to what extent do managers, as a group, pursue and meet the six elements of a true profession? The practical advantages, and significance, of the issue are, of course, that the closer management comes to pursuing the six elements of truly professional status, and reaching them, the more public confidence and credibility in management will increase, and the less oppressive government regulation (and business inefficiency) will be necessary.

To What Extent is American Management Today a Profession?

With, now, the question properly stated and the specific six tests to judge professional status identified as above, let's discuss how far managers as a group pursue or meet the six elements of a profession.

First, it is obviously impossible to generalize because (a) managers are not organized into a group of "managers" as such (as "doctors" are, for example, in a fully visible and institutionalized system of training, certification, associations and codes) and (b) managers, as a group, are widely heterogeneous, ranging from top officers in large high-technology corporations to foremen in used-car repair shops.

But, confining the discussion to middle and top managers in highly visible and sophisticated firms (like IBM, etc.), a good case can be made that management is rapidly advancing in the direction of a profession. Many industry associations (such as the realtors instanced above) are doing the same. On the first three tests for professionalism (training, certification and peer review), considerable progress is being made: most middle and top managers have college degrees, many MBA degrees (Master of Business Administration) and virtually all participate periodically in intensive management education seminars or courses, ranging in length from a week to several months; the degrees and certificates earned are an increasingly recognized form of certification; and elaborate performance evaluation systems (many built around specific MBO, i.e. "Management by Objectives," programs) place such managers under continuing peer and supervisory review as to competence and performance.

More progress is needed with regard to the last three tests (ethical codes, keener orientation to human service objectives, and self-regulation). The reasons for this assessment need not be repeated here; all the previous chapters have explicitly detailed them (codes too general, consumers and other publics still too often threatened by profit-seeking fraud, such as price-fixing, and still too much need for government- instead of self-regulation).

But, what is most significant and hopeful is the trend: there can be little doubt that enlightened managements are, like never before in American business history, advocating true managerial professionalism in general, and specific, enforced codes of ethics in particular, as sound and practical goals - to be insisted upon and ultimately achieved. As, in the 1980s and 1990s, this professionalizing trend accelerates and dominates more and more businesses (including fields such as computers, engineering, sales, purchasing, contracting, maintenance, etc.) -and as business's ethical codes develop into more effective forms, business self-regulation will be able to remove much of the costly (and usually inept and inefficient) albatross of giant government regulation. As this occurs, America can begin to become, as it was, the most productive and prosperous nation on earth -proud, again, of its unexcelled productivity.

REFERENCES

1 Newton, L.H., "Lawgiving for Professional Life: Reflections on the place of the Professional Code," Business & Professional Ethics Journal, Fall, 1981, pp.41-56

For Further Reading

- Hastings Center, The Teaching of Ethics in Higher Education, and Ethics in the Education of Business Managers, and Ethical Dilemmas and the Education of Policymakers, all 1980, Hastings Center, 360 Broadway, Hastings-on-Hudson, N.Y., 10706
- McGregor, Douglas, The Professional Manager, McGraw, 1967
- Owens, J., The Theory and Practice of Managing, Mgmt.Ed., 1982
- Silk, L. & D.Vogel, Ethics and Profits: The Crisis of Confidence in American Business, Simon and Schuster, 1976

QUESTIONS AND PROBLEMS

1. Define and illustrate (current examples) these concepts and issues:
   (a) profession (b) certification (c) peer review
   (d) ethical code (e) purpose of business
2. Outline a report on the major differences in business ethics today in America as compared to a century ago. Has ethical progress occurred? For what reasons? (The Index of this book will help.)
3. Using the six elements (tests) for a true profession, to what extent do you evaluate the following groups as "professional:" accountants, engineers, salesmen, university professors, air traffic controllers, congressmen, paramedic (rescue) teams, military officers?

CASE INCIDENTS IN ORGANIZATIONAL ETHICS

Case Analysis - An Introduction

The central purpose of this book is to improve the skills of ethical analysis and application of ethical theory to business realities. As noted in the Preface to the book (and on p. 149), knowledge alone, of the theory and history of ethics, is not enough. We are concerned here mainly with applying it. To be sure, a firm grasp of knowledge of the field is necessary; and fully half of this book is devoted to providing the essentials of that knowledge base as a needed framework. The second half has examined a number of current issues involving business ethics and applied knowledge and theory to each of them.

It is widely accepted, however, in professional schools (law, medicine, business, etc.) that the best way to master the skills of applying knowledge, analyzing it and using it, is case analysis in discussion groups -after thorough individual preparation beforehand by the discussants. Thus this section of the book provides a number of realistic case situations, covering many ethical issues typical of daily organizational life, for use in classroom discussions and the application of ethical theory.

It is important to note that case discussion is not necessarily the same thing as case analysis. Analysis requires the skills of orderly and disciplined mental processes and procedures, keen attention to actual details and facts, cool and rational discussion (as opposed to the common heated and emotional arguments) and the firm grasp of both the essential knowledge within and history of the field being applied. In many classrooms and conference rooms, case discussion is not rational analysis at all, but rather emotional (usually enjoyable, but useless) "bull sessions." This is inevitable unless the requirements for analysis (as just listed), especially the firm knowledge of a field's history and theory, are met, mastered, enforced and ever present in the discussion environment. Case analysis can -and should- still be enjoyable; but, first and critically, it requires hard mental work, preparation and the skill (and will) to confront issues by reasoning (logic) rather than deep emotionality (often mere fixations of beliefs and prejudices molded into the mind at an early age). These conditions for useful case analysis are true no matter what the field (legal analysis, medical analysis, business and financial analysis, etc.). In this book, it is ethical analysis. This means, specifically, that any discussant's position or opinion about a case must be supported by logical reasoning and explicit reference to the field's knowledge base (i.e. the Ten Tests, p.155, with a full understanding of the meaning of each, both theoretical and historical) and its methods of analysis (especially force-field analysis as on pp.163-9); statements such as "I can't explain it but I just feel like" (abortion is right -or wrong, firing a man from a job is just wrong, etc.) are the right of free Americans to express, but not in a college classroom or other professional discussion group where reasoning and analysis in support of opinions, not mere emoting and fixed feelings, are - or should be- the absolute norm.

The cases that follow are purposely short "case incidents," highlighting the essentials of a situation and the issue involved with as few necessary facts as possible. The advantages of brevity and quickly "getting to the point" of an issue often require that the reader make reasonable assumptions about other facts not explicitly stated (time, place, local laws, ages of people, organizational structure, ethnic composition of workforce, etc.) and include these assumptions in his analysis; or, often most interesting, use different assumptions in a series of them, analyzing the case on the basis of many different sets of assumptions with (usually) varying final conclusions or decisions.

Finally, case analysis is essentially decision making, the acid test of any manager. Academics in universities theorize, economists build abstract models, social scientists usually fantasize about utopian worlds, but managers must make here-and-now decisions about real situations, take action on them -and live with them. The reader should review a standard treatment of the process of decision making (one is this author's Theory and Practice of Managing, Chapters 4 & 5, 1982). And see page 164 above regarding force-field analysis.

The cases follow and are numbered for convenient reference.

1 THE PINTO

Over the period 1971–1978, Ford Motor Company was sued about fifty times as negligent in accidents involving rear-end collisions and gas tank explosions of its Pinto automobile. One case in particular, now called the Winamac case, was unique in that the State of Indiana charged Ford with criminal negligence (reckless homicide) and the case was decided by jury on March 16, 1980. The case involved a 1973 Pinto whose gas tank exploded and killed three girls when it was struck in the rear by a van.*

Briefly, seven witnesses for the state testified that the Pinto was moving in traffic at speeds they estimated to be from 15 to 35 mph and the van at about 50 mph when the van struck the rear of the Pinto. The gas tank of the Pinto exploded and burst into flames which were uncontrollable. Harly Copp, once a high ranking Ford engineer, testified that the Pinto gas tank was poorly positioned behind an axle bolt which would pierce the tank on collisions from the rear at 20 mph; a $6.65 mechanism would have positioned the tank over the axle bolts where it could withstand rear-end impacts of 30 mph, a relatively safe tank, but Ford executives rejected this additional cost per car in the interests of improving profits (or reducing final price for higher sales). Thus Ford executives acted negligently in sacrificing safety for profit; and the implication was that Ford engineers were also at fault for not insisting on the $6.65 part as a technically needed safety feature.

Ford's defense attorney, James Neal, developed critical evidence (from statements by the Pinto driver before she died) that the driver had just filled the tank, forgot to replace the cap and had stopped the car to check it and, at that point, was rammed by the van. Neal argued that no gas tank can be designed to withstand a 50-mph impact from the rear and prevent an explosion, especially with the cap off the tank. The accident occurred in August 1978 and it was only in the prior year that the National Highway Traffic Safety Administration (NHTSA) set safety standards for gas tanks in cars (standards higher than those met in the Pinto's design). But, Neal argued, the car involved was a 1973 Pinto. The jury agreed with Neal's arguments. Ford was "not guilty."

But, apart from the legal aspects -and findings- about the Pinto gas tank design, what is your e t h i c a l analysis of these questions:

(a) Was Ford Co. unethical in rejecting the $6.65 part? Why?

(b) Should Ford engineers have fought the safety omission? How?

* For more detailed facts in the Pinto case, see R.T. DeGeorge's article "Ethical Responsibilities of Engineers etc.," Business and Professional Ethics Journal, Fall 1981, pp. 1–17.

2 SEAT BELTS

By government mandate, seat belts are required safety equipment for all cars sold in the U.S.A. Also, government policy, based on studies claiming many lives saved in accidents by use of seat belts, is to gain the public's compliance in using seat belts (actually "strapping in") by strong advertising of this aim as well as compelling manufacturers to build in devices that "punish" drivers who delay or fail in using belts (flashing lights and irritating buzzing until the belt is properly in place -and it's illegal to remove or disable them).

There is nothing new about Washington influencing the public to embrace good moral habits and avoid bad (over and beyond, of course, the minimum constraints of established law -which is its major function). Washington encourages good (charity, for example) by tax deductions for it; and discourages evil by taxing it vigorously ("sin taxes" such as on purchases of cigarets or alcoholic beverages). (Interestingly, the government still provides huge <u>subsidies</u> to farmers who grow tobacco -but that's only because congressmen need votes to get re-elected; the "sin tax" is designed to fall upon and punish users, not the suppliers.) One is rewarded for growing tobacco or distilling whisky but, by huge sales taxes, punished (in one's pocketbook and checking account) by buying and using the products.

Some questions for ethical analysis are:

(a) Is it unethical for a car driver to refuse to use seat belts? (Recent studies show that most drivers do not use them and resent government telling them how to live life.)

(b) Is it unethical for government to "coerce" citizens to avoid "bad habits" (smoking cigarets, drinking alcohol, not using seat belts, etc.) by taxation, stiff safety regulations, etc.?

3 PROTECTING A CO-WORKER

Marshall and Len, both in their early twenties, have been full-time retail clerks in a large department store for two years, socializing often off-the-job and generally good friends. They work in adjacent, but different, departments and, calling across from one department to the other, usually time coffee breaks and lunch so they can share them together. During work hours, they often see each other moving about from one customer or chore to another -and wave a quick greeting. Both have excellent attendance and performance records; and both receive regular wage increases and will soon be routinely promoted to assistant managers of their respective departments.

On several occasions recently, Len noticed Marshall slipping a small item of merchandise into his pocket and later saw the same item in Marshall's home. Len hasn't mentioned any of this to anyone, including Marshall, although he feels uncomfortable knowing about it. However, Len finds himself glancing more often in Marshall's direction at work, and it seems that Marshall's small thefts are very infrequent.

But evidently Marshall's department manager has become suspicious. Meeting Len, as if casually, on the aisle separating the two departments, the manager said to him: "Marshall has probably told you he's up for promotion next month but one thing bothers me." Then, with a disarming smile, "do you know whether he's walking off with some merchandise once in a while?" Recovering quickly from initial shock at the question, Len just said: "I don't know, of course, but I'd be amazed; he's a great guy."

(a) Was it ethical for Len to protect his friend by "lying?"

(b) Was it ethical for the manager to ask Len the question?

4 OVERSTATING THE SALES RECORDS

The Washington Post reported (5/29/82, p.D8) that McCormick & Co., the large Baltimore-based spice maker, admitted to sales and other company records being adjusted to overstate sales and profits as ultimately presented to investors in the annual reports. The altered records created $46 million in phony sales and $4 million in unreal profits. No action by McCormick is planned against top executives, including the company's president, all of whom knew of the improper accounting practices. McCormick spokesmen said that the company has already taken action to eliminate such practices in the future.

How it was done: the grocery division usually worked overtime at the end of a fiscal quarter to ship still unsold merchandise (unordered) to regular customers (retail stores, etc.) so that these would appear as "sales" in the prior quarterly report; invoices were often pre-dated (i.e. altered from actual date of sale) for the same reason. Similarly, expenses were understated from actual accounting events to inflate the final report on profits. McCormick prudently reported all this, finally, to SEC (Security & Exchange Commission) along with explanations: it seems that the accounting irregularities must be attributed to over-zealous executives pressured to meet what they considered unrealistic sales and profit goals set by top management. In addition to the severe pressure for profits, McCormick's spokesmen said that "there was a team spirit which led persons to participate in practices they knew to be 'wrong'."

(a) Using ethical tests, why were they 'wrong,' if they were?

5 "OFF THE BOOKS"

Depending on who does the estimates, IRS (America's Internal Revenue Service, a euphemism for "tax collector") loses from $40-to-$90 billion each year in revenues (enough to balance the current U.S. budget whose deficits cause skyrocketing interest rates and bankruptcy for businesses and families) owed it, but uncollectible, from income received by citizens but kept "off the books." Economists call it the "cash economy" or the "underground economy" in which all transactions are in cash, no checks written or records kept of anything. For example, a plumber quotes you a price for a plumbing job of $80 if payment is by check but $60 if in cash (if in cash, he can avoid an average $25 income tax on a recorded $80, gaining $5 for himself and $20 for you; only IRS is the loser) or he and you avoid the taxman by the alternative route of bartering (he trades his $80 service for an $80-valued painting on your wall or a similarly-valued service from you, such as an eye examination if you are an optometrist). Whether by cash or bartering, the exchange of goods or services is not recorded anywhere as income for either party in the transaction and thus easily omitted as taxable income. By law, such "off-the-books" income is taxable and for the same reasons as is all recorded income of citizens (government costs to provide highways, protection from criminals, aid to blind or other disadvantaged citizens, national defense, medical research, etc.). It is assumed, in a civilized society, that these needed costs of government services will be shared equally among citizens who all benefit from them. But the temptation of man to avoid taxes is great.

(a) Is the plumber above, evading taxes by cash or barter, acting ethically? (His action is illegal but, no records, unenforcible.) (What about lawyers, doctors, farmers, prostititutes, teachers, etc. who evade taxes by off-the-books transactions?)

(b) Is it ethical for a man to evade taxes because he disagrees with tax laws (established in a democratic America) when IRS revenue is being voted into spending he opposes (wars, social programs for the "lazy," ethnic forced integration)?

(c) Is it ethical for you to cooperate with the plumber's offer of an "off-the-books" transaction (or should you write a check)?

6 PIRATING PROGRAMMERS

Good, even fair, computer programmers are in short supply, hard to get and harder to keep - because of corporate pirates. "Pirating" is an ancient custom by which needy humans seek, find and take what they need (ships at sea with valuable goods and insufficiently guarded, drunken sailors or any able body hauled to ship and pressed into service, beautiful women for their needed services - and today programmers).

American, and other nations', computer hardware is now abundant, even cheap, rolling off assembly lines chip after chip like Detroit or Datsun automobiles. But a computer is lifeless until a human programmer writes a suitable program (set of instructions in code) usually called software. It is the need for software –and the programmers who write it– that is escalating faster than the availability and training of programmers.

CompIn Inc, a computer software firm specializing in programs for large insurance companies, is desparately understaffed in several of its programming departments. Its personnel officer knows of a common technique for attracting programmers to the firm (and engineers and key executives too) but has been reluctant to use it –until now. He offers any of CompIn's programmers, who know many other programmers in the city, a $500 bonus if they can locate and "hire" new programmers into CompIn's ranks. The persuader: CompIn will match any new hire's former salary plus a $2000 cash bonus the day he's hired and begins work. CompIn's understaffing problem was soon solved.

(a) Are CompIn's bonus tactics unethical or just hard competition?

(b) Is it ethical for a programmer to accept his $500 for services?

7 PROMISES, PROMISES

George, suffering a severe but temporary cash flow problem in his young business, persuades a friend (Tom) to loan him $10,000, promising with right hand held high to repay it in full two weeks later. Tom himself would be in serious cash flow trouble without his $10,000 back when due. There are no legal documents involved in the loan, just a certified check, a handshake, a promise and a gentleman's agreement.

Everyone knows George is an honest man and he fully intends to repay the loan when due. But an incident, virtually impossible, destroys his plan: his best customer, who's never been late paying for George's products, phones to say he will be 20 days late in paying and there's nothing he can do about it, given the same tight-money and high-interest climate that prevents both from getting routine bank loans. Unable to borrow, the only way George could repay Tom on time would be to sell product at a loss to a large distributor –but for cash on delivery. This would set George's business back at least a year before he would again begin to generate a profit –if he ever did. Very despondent and humiliated by his necessary phone call to Tom, George musters the grit to make the call, explains what has happened and very apologetically tells Tom his repayment will have to be 20 days late. Tom, furious, hangs up on him. As Shakespeare said: "Neither a lender nor a borrower be."

(a) Is it ever ethical to break a promise? Is George's act ethical?

8 MEN NOT WANTED

Larry Johnson, owner and manager of the "Lovely Lounge," an always crowded and profitable cocktail lounge in a metropolitan airport, bases much of his success on a decade-long reputation for "the loveliest waitresses in the world" (as his somewhat exaggerated ad puts it). Tired and frustrated travelers, mostly men waiting for late flights, far prefer their time-passing drinks with some beautiful and distracting scenery, Larry reasons. Naturally, Larry is most demanding in his hiring and criteria for his waitresses. The most essential criterion of all, of course, is that the candidate be a young female. And Larry is proud of his record of never discriminating (excepting men and the over-forty group): his girls are white, hispanic, black, chinese etc. "Men enjoy variety" (again from his ad) and, he says, it's good for business. Larry's hiring policies have been a strong foundation underlying years of success in the "Lovely Lounge." He wouldn't change his "formula" for the world. Or would -or should- he? He's now trying to explain to a young man, a handsome and athletic one, why he can't hire a "male waitress" while the man keeps insisting he wants a job as a waitor and has a "constitutional right" to it -so his lawyer says at least.

(a) Is Larry discriminating? Is it unethical? Is it illegal?
(b) Is Larry's attitude toward women "sexism" (as you define it)?
(c) Suppose an airline owner hired only stewardesses for the same reasons as Larry's? Is that illegal? Is the illegal ever ethical?

9 EASY-DOES-IT BANKRUPTCY

About 1980, American laws permitting debtors to erase most of their personal debt (to stores, credit card firms, etc.), i.e. to declare personal bankruptcy, were made radically more lenient for debtors and risky for lenders. In brief, a person, who carelessly ran up excessive debts by buying on credit and with the so-convenient plastic cards at the so-convenient shopping malls, can erase all that debt with relative little personal distress. The law permits the bankrupt to keep most of their essentials (essential furniture, tools, housing equity, etc.) while non-essential assets (hi-fi sets, used, are not worth much) are sold to repay creditors usually a minor fraction of the money owed them. The rest is just charged off as a loss by the stores and other creditors. Of course, somebody pays this debt: the average consumer, who pays his bills regularly, in the form of higher prices stores must charge to cover the "expense" of bad debts as well as theft of merchandise, these line items listed on financial statements as "overhead" expenses. When a bankrupt elects not to pay a debt, someone else ultimately has to.

This is simple and inevitable economics; just as is inflation (ever-rising prices in a national economy) to compensate for government spending in excess of its revenue. (In the latter case, governments print more paper money for themselves -or debase coin-* and repay debt with lower-value money, an historical law of inflation and a common way in which governments cheat citizens.)

In a typical 1980s personal situation, Carl, age 30, single, skilled and highly-paid engineer, furnished his new apartment with lush carpets, gold-tinted draperies, foreign China dinnerware, several high-priced but "genuine" paintings, top-of-the-line finely-engineered hi-fi amplifiers and other audio equipment, a full-capacity micro-computer system to orchestrate all his apartment operations, etc.; all of this, of course, over a busy and creative purchasing period of three weeks and with credit cards. But, when the apartment was finally finished, it was unquestionably life absolutely first-class all the way - and never a visitor left his "place" unimpressed by the quality and sure tastes of Carl's lifestyle and sophisticated living environment. But, the costs and debts incurred were first-class too. He never really added it up and compared it with his income realities for about a year (drawing from a slight savings account to handle monthly irregularities), a common mental defense mechanism to avoid discovering and looking at "bad news." When he did, he found he was $27,000 in debt (unbelievable! - as he began to think about it), would need six years to pay it all, provided he moved into a much smaller apartment and drastically cut his life-style to daily meals of hamburger instead of top-steaks and cheap wine for visitors instead of his usual French imported "drinking adventures." This severe reduction in life-style was too much for Carl to face. The law allowed him to pursue his right to declare bankruptcy, erase all his debt, maintain his essential assets and start over without the debt burden for six long years of working and paying bills. Without that burden, he could start over, maintain his apartment, re-furnish with cash and probably soon even get more credit - if he wanted it. Excellent solution, thanks to the new bankruptcy laws. Carl reflected (briefly) on those he owed, how they would handle their losses, his essential style and inner character as a man avoiding an obligation and promise to repay those who honestly provided goods and services on his "word;" but,

---

* Roman emperors excelled in this technique (especially Diocletian). As spending of government funds greatly exceeded tax revenues (limited to that level beyond which rebellion occurred), debasing coin became the preferred method of raising cash. At one point, copper coins were melted down, recast with cheap metal and just 10% of the valuable copper, providing much new coin & inflation.

as a realist, made the decision to declare bankruptcy. Using inexpensive legal services for the purpose (advertised daily in the newspapers), he was delighted with how simple the bankruptcy process was, needing only his signature on a few papers prepared by the legal firm.

(a) Carl was quite capable of paying money owed, although over a six-year period. Although legal for him to do so, was it ethical for him to declare bankruptcy and avoid paying it?

(b) When a person or firm loans you money, to what extent do you incur an ethical (or legal) obligation to repay it?

(c) Are stores ethically at fault for providing people with easy credit and tempting plastic credit cards?

(d) A loan is essentially a human promise to repay. Under what kinds of conditions, if any (examples, please), is it ethical to renege on a promise, a loan or an oath to perform on a given promise?

(e) Is this kind of easy bankruptcy law ethical and fair to all?

10 BOYS AND GIRLS HARASSING

Wallace is personnel director of Longjohn-Gold Inc., a stock market advisory and research service organization specializing in the ever-changing investment potential of precious metals, mainly gold, silver and platinum (and, for some true speculators, palladium). Many Fortune 500 companies' pension managers subscribe to Longjohn's weekly 'goldletters' (for pension money investment decisions) as does an even larger number of individual investors. Wallace is almost a stereotype of the ancient, brusque, mature male American. Aged 43, 210 pounds, a fair portion of it in the midriff, an achiever despite harsh discrimination and lack of education in early years, married (not particularly happily as is typical of American marriages), three children (and the costs of them), habituated to hard drinking after work and smoking big cigars always, Wallace is the self-made American man, done with no government welfare but with loads of learning from hard life-experiencing and patient hard work. Not untypically of the American male, he is loyal, helpful and kind, once risking his life to rescue a child from a stream swollen by a flash flood deluging through his mid-western town. In short, everyone would love Wallace, especially, in his view of himself, the new girls constantly recruited into his ever-growing clerical departments.

In old-fashioned American style, Wallace delighted in helping, "fathering," teaching, protecting and solving personal problems of his girls. And he did all this with no thought of taking advantage of any of them sexually. And he never did. But, he hugged his girls a lot and had a habit of placing a light slap on the rear of any he passed on the aisles of his department. It was his way of showing affection and concern for them as individuals –and never intended or taken as any sort of "sexual advance." Until Hilda got hired and routinely slapped on her rear as Wallace passed her one day.

Hilda filed a complaint of sexual harassment with government authorities against Wallace. The case, both within the company and in outside government agencies, has been pending for months. Wallace is confused by the complex (almost Freudian) interpretations of his actions as he listens in the complaint hearings, his executive style became utterly changed (he dared not hug anybody), the friendly atmosphere of the office was converted to stiff and impersonal business transactions - and these only, there are no smiles on Wallace's or his girls' faces, Wallace and his girls knowing he might lose his job (and all that means to him) because of his sexual harassment.

Interestingly, in the many hearings ("overhead" charges cutting bottom-line productivity as compared to Japanese firms which concentrate vigorously on productivity rather than sophisticated social issues), most of Wallace's girls testified that they liked his personal attention, genuine concern for them and didn't even mind his occasional slaps on their rears (a minor inconvenience in the total picture of the friendly, productive and "fun" office atmosphere Wallace maintained).

(a) Define and give an example of "sexual harassment" which you regard as unethical and/or illegal. Is Wallace's action (above) an example of it? Do women ever harass men?

(b) Are there other or better ways for a victim of harassment to put a stop to it –instead of or before taking legal action?

11 THE USA: A VERY BIG SWEDEN?

Sweden's great experiment with the welfare state is a human and ethical failure, according to recent commentators.* The welfare style of life has changed the Swedes, once a proud and honest people, into a nation of cynics and cheats. With most of one's income taken in taxes by the socialist government to run the government welfare system, there is little incentive to work beyond the minimum required and a pervading incentive for all to cheat on taxes and to get more

* Much of the content of this case incident or issue is drawn from Eric Brodin's article "Cynics and Cheats" (Reason, June 1982) and his quotations from Clarence Carson's article on Sweden in The Freeman. Brodin, a professor of business, spent eight recent years in Sweden, his birthplace, and is now a USA citizen. For the sake of brevity, mere excerpts and paraphrasing are used here.

than their share of welfare benefits by false reporting of needs and other fraud. Citizen uses (abuses) of the welfare system are riddled with cheating and the system actually causes such fraud: each consumer trying to get as much out of the common pot of government benefits as possible (since the pot is owned by nobody except the government). Very few Swedes own property (most of which belongs to government) and have little incentive to use it efficiently.*

Examples of "ripping off the system:" whereas in the past (pre-socialist Sweden), virtually all tax reports from earners were honest and without serious inaccuracies, now almost half of these reports are estimated to be dishonest (far too many to audit and thus a chaotic and unreliable revenue system for essential services, national defense, etc). The number of people "reporting ill" to avoid working is huge and rising fast (why work when taxes take your money and government feeds and houses you anyway?). Any government benefit offered to all who need it immediately increases the number of people who "need" it (workers with minor aches take advantage of medical services not at all needed but costly to deliver). "Mutual cheating" is everywhere: my school receives subsidies based on number of students attending while you get funds for enhancing your work skills by attending school; I sign your report validating your school attendance (while really you are relaxing and "vacationing" at home) and you sign my report certifying an attending student to help puff up my student numbers –you sign my report and I'll sign yours and we both gain; only an impersonal central government loses (i.e. the "commons," as Hardin notes below*). And so on. The variations of individual cheating for personal gain are limited only by imagination and the time to use it (as now in America, welfare cheats in Sweden avoid work and have all day daily to dream up ways to successfully "rip off the system"); while, without energetic productivity by all, national resources as a whole decline to a danger level and the nation becomes weak, dependent and vulnerable to takeover by a stronger neighbor (like Russia who's coveted her ports since Peter the Great built the first Russian Navy).

Over the past fifty years, America has adopted socialistic practices (like Sweden's) but so gradually and by disarming names such as

* The historical tendency of people to waste and abuse property that is not their own (i.e. held in common for use by all) is best described in Garrett Hardin's classic article "The Tragedy of the Commons," 1968, conveniently reproduced in his paperback book Exploring New Ethics for Survival, Pelican Books, 1968. The apt analogy is to common pastures overused by cattle-growers, each increasing his own herd to get most from the pasture; until too many cattle ruined that 'commons' and everyone's cattle died.

Social Security old-age "insurance" (which it isn't at all) that few Americans are even aware how far America has sunk into Sweden-like socialism -and its consequences. Brodin concludes sadly that "it is too late to save Sweden but not too late for the United States."

(a) If a citizen believes taxes are unethically high and unfair, is it ethical for him to cheat in his reports to avoid taxes? (Clearly it is illegal and punishable by the state, if detected.)

(b) Why is "mutual cheating" (signing mutually beneficial reports) unethical? What ethical tests apply?

(c) What is your opinion about the ethical character of Americans today as compared to a hundred years ago? (Review Chap. 2.)

12 BAD-MOUTHING THE COMPETITION

There are laws, of course, against false advertising in your own interest and libel or slander directed against your business competitor. But, legally, you can still "bad-mouth" a competitor in private conversations, such as your sales presentation to buy your product and not his, insinuating or even explicitly stating information either damaging or false or both.

Joseph Masters is an example. He owns a small computer store, retailing personal computers such as Apple, Tandy, Commodore, OSI and off-the-shelf software for each of them. He employs several young engineering students to assemble systems which he sells to customers (the right and compatible processors, modems, printers, disk storage, computer RAM memory, screen monitors and software) and to service them when repairs are needed. Thus Joseph delegates the detail and concentrates his own efforts on managing the store, especially its cash and financial records, and selling total systems to customers.

Joseph finds selling systems easy. He's college-educated, fast and smoothe with the right word at the right time, a fair engineer amateur and especially good with electronics and computer jargon (which he doesn't fully understand himself) and has an excellent memory for details such as profit margins on the host of products that ultimately constitute a total system sold to an end user (usually a small business or professional such as lawyers, doctors and consultants). Profit margins, of course, are important to Joseph. Two printers (different makers), for example, might have the same retail price to a customer but one a higher profit margin for the retailer. Joseph's success policy is to sell always the components with the highest profit margin to him so long as they are basically compatible in a system and even when they are not the most effective for the customer. "He'll never know," says Joseph.

And he's right about that. Customers, buying their first computer system, are utterly ignorant and even afraid of the technologies they are seeking (all they want is the end result such as better inventory control, financial statements or faster invoicing to reduce receivables). They tend to believe any salesman who seems believable just to relieve their anxiety and get the system "on line" and producing the results. Joseph's style of selling and profit margin policies match perfectly with his average unknowing customer. His every authoritative word or judgment or warning impels the helpless believer (customer) toward the final system Joseph wants sold, i.e. the one with the highest margins for each of its components. This is not to imply that Joseph ever sells a system that's bad or ineffective (such would be an obvious mistake he'd have to correct), only that he sells the more expensive one, when unnecessary for the customer's needs, based on the sole criterion of highest profit margin to himself -the customer never knowing the real differences in product specifications and pricing margins existing behind the scenes. And, of course, Joseph's customers pay more than really necessary for their needs (an average of $600 on each $5000-to-$8000 total system, a good part of it in software which itself greatly determines the compatible hardware required). But Joseph has never gotten any complaint from a customer. The systems work as promised. He just charges, he says, "a little extra" that "doesn't hurt anybody."

Except when a low-margin component is the only one fitting a system properly, Joseph will say things about it like "this is cheaper but we suspect serious up-coming voltage problems" (when there is no "voltage" problem and he doesn't even fully understand the term) or "this lower-priced RAM memory is a bargain -if you're a hobbiest and don't mind an occasional breakdown of the system and like fixing it" or "this is the most advanced 'state-of-the-art' word processing software, absolutely sophisticated in every detail, but a few dollars more for 'first-class' is genuine long-range economy" (when the WP disk he's pushing is ranked only in 9th place and priced higher than all the others -but with an attractive profit margin to retailers).

(a) Analyze this case carefully to:

(i) identify and state, by clear and descriptive word titles, all actions and policy decisions by Joseph which, in your opinion, are ethical issues for business (for example, his bad mouthing of products -inaccurately- for his own ends);

(ii) which of Joseph's actions are ethical and which unethical.

(b) Would you like to be Joseph's (i) customer or (ii) partner ?

(c) Is it ethical for a salesman to "exaggerate" his claims about his own product (for dramatic impact) while saying nothing bad about competitors' products? When does "exaggerating" amount to misrepresentation or lying? Give examples.

13 STATISTICS AND THE FACTS

Alice Collins has recently won a promotion to Director of Advertising and Public Relations with a mutual fund company, Growth Fund Inc. Growth Fund is relatively small ($42 million assets), only nine years old, "aggressive" in its investment strategies (mainly new high-technology firms with high risk but huge potential, "the IBMs of the future," as Alice calls them). The master strategist and founder of the fund is Don Jenkins, whose computerized approach to aggressive investing and identifying "companies on the move" made him so sought after as a financial advisor that he entered the major leagues and began his own investment fund. The fund's performance record (usually expressed as a percentage increase in dollar value of a fund's stock as compared to the Dow Jones average) has been among the top ten no-load mutual funds (no-load meaning no sales charge) over its first eight years. Its ninth year, 1981, showed virtually no gain at all, after eight successful years of average <u>annual</u> gains of 45% compared to Dow Jones' 5% (this is no reflection on Growth Fund's relative value and performance in 1981, a recession in which no funds performed well).

Don and Alice are having a meeting in her office to plan the updating of the fund's basic promotional and advertising brochure which they mail to prospective investors to "invite" them to invest money in Growth Fund. Always, in the past, the most dramatic and "selling" page of the brochure has been their color chart of rapid and steady increase over the eight years (the most recent brochure, being updated in this meeting, covered the fund's first eight years). But Don is concerned about the sharp decline that would appear on the chart when (or if) the statistics for the ninth year are entered, even though the decline was no fault of this or any other fund; but, still, the quick reader will see the plummeting last year, form a fast sceptical impression and decide <u>not</u> to invest in Growth Fund, Don fears. Finally, he makes his decision: do not do an updated brochure until about six months or a year from now, when surely our numbers will be up again; and, in the meantime, directs Alice to reprint the current brochure as is -but with reassuring comments in the Introduction about "a delay in publication but that the chart is representative of the fund's general history of performance,etc.etc." Alice is very uncomfortable about participating in this but Don just says it's an "indirect and temporary 'word-smithing' and nothing serious." Alice shrugs, says OK; after all, it's her job.

(a) Is Don's 'word-smithing' approach to the brochure deceiving potential customers? Hurting them in any way? Ethical?

(b) Are there other options Don has that are more ethical?

(c) If Don's directive to Alice involves an unethical action (or illegal) and Alice obeys despite judging the action unethical (to save her job), can she justify herself as merely following a superior's orders, that he -not she- made the unethical decision? (The classic precedent for this issue is the famous Nuremberg trials of Nazi war criminals whose main defense was that superiors ordered the actions while they only carried them out -under threat of punishment if they didn't.) In this present case, what should Alice do?

14 THE OPEC CARTEL

For over 10 years OPEC (Organization of Petroleum Exporting Nations), with Saudi-Arabia a leading nation in the organization, has operated a cartel to control the production and pricing of world oil. (A cartel is a group of companies or nations agreeing to meet regularly to set production, sales, prices for all, instead of competing and driving down each's profits; in the USA, in the last century, cartels were called "trusts" - see Chapter 2 above.) For reasons explained in Chapter 2, the USA made cartels (trusts, price-fixing, collusion) illegal about 1900 and a substantial part of the work of the Justice Department is in its Anti-trust Division investigating and halting any restraints on free trade and competition (so long as it is fair - as, for example, predatory pricing to bankrupt a competitor and then raise prices is <u>not</u>). A cartel is essentially a monopoly, except by a combination of organizations instead of by a single one (or person).

OPEC is the perfect example of a cartel in action. About a dozen organizations (nations, in this case), which account for the large bulk of oil owned and produced in the world and needed desparately by the industrial nations, agree not to compete with each other and drive down prices and profits for all but to sit down several times a year and decide on high prices all will charge equally and demand of all customers of all cartel members. American "robber barons" (Chapter 2) preferred to call it "cornering the market" (buying <u>all</u> of a critical and immediately needed commodity, such as wheat or corn, then charging any high price as the <u>only</u> source of it for those who needed it). This, of course, creates huge profits for the monopolist (or cartel member) at the expense of consumers and thus became illegal in the USA.

(a) Is a monopoly, "trust" or cartel unethical? Why?

(b) When the only three suppliers of a product or service in a city agree quietly, by phone, on prices they will all charge to avoid competing and cutting their profits ("price-fixing"), is this kind of planning unethical? Why?

15 TARGET: IBM AND JAPAN INC.

In February 1982, William Norris, chairman of Control Data Corp. organized a meeting of 15 chief executive officers of major US computer and semiconductor companies (Xerox, Rockwell, Sperry, NCR, Honeywell, Motorola, Digital Equipment etc., except IBM) to join forces for developing jointly-financed research programs for future products able to compete with giant IBM and the Japanese consortium of computer manufacturers. A research and development "cartel," one might call it,* aimed at sharing the huge costs of creating new computer products to compete with IBM and Japan Inc. (both of whom are fully capable, with their financial might, to maintain huge research programs to dominate markets of the future).

According to the Washington Post (5/30/82, p.F1), this is a joint effort of American computer companies (except IBM) to stand up to, rather than be dominated by, the giants in modern electronics and computer technologies (Japan Inc. and America's IBM). They want to compete with IBM and Japan by combining resources to do so when, as individuals, no one of them would have a chance against the might of IBM or Japan Inc.

The spokesman for Control Data said that all companies represented in the meeting enthusiastically agreed on a "need to maximize the value of their research and development dollars and, given current availability of capital and talent and the pressure to shorten development cycles -and the exploding range of individual technologies, joint R & D can save time, money and recruiting expense." IBM, he noted, with last year world sales of $29 billion, is stronger alone than all of the rest of us together, except Japan Inc.- waiting and working to dominate the computer industry of the future as they do the automobile industry of the present.

Technically, however, in terms of the Justice Department's strict prohibition of companies (in the same industry) meeting and "making mutual agreements" to "optimize each others' profits," Norris' meeting comes close to violating anti-trust laws. But, it seems a good idea, if America's companies are to band together as forms of "America Inc" to compete successfully with Japan Inc.

(a) Is Norris' meeting unethical?

(b) Should such meetings be illegal? Under what conditions?

---

* The reader might wish to read or re-read Case #14 where the term "cartel" is defined fully as related to OPEC and American trusts and monopolies of the latter's past century history. Norris has, of course, as a prudent man, reported his meeting to Anti-trust division (Justice Dept.), hoping for no interference from 'trust-busters' there and, in fact, getting none so far - but they'll watch!

16 TESTING FOR MARIJUANA

The Wall Street Journal (6/1/82,p.1) noted that the sales of Syva Co. (Palo Alto,CA) have increased 40% annually for its urinalysis testing kits that easily test for and detect marijuana use by workers somewhat the same as blood and breath tests reveal alcohol use. Ford Motor Co. has used the marijuana tests in several of its plants as has Washington Gas Light (D.C.). An ACLU (American Civil Liberties Union) spokesman says such testing is an invasion of privacy and violates a worker's rights, at least under most workplace circumstances. Some companies are using the test to screen applicants for jobs. The ACLU spokesman remarked: "....if job performance is satisfactory, it's nobody's business what you do on the weekend or who you do it with." However, such testing, at least in the private sector, is not illegal.

(a) Is it ethical? Should it be made illegal?

(b) The ACLU spokesman mentioned some conditions that might justify limited use of the majijuana test. Can you think of any such conditions?

17 THE SPECIAL TRASH COLLECTOR

Dr.James Miller, a prominent research chemist specializing in poison gas development in a private research firm -but exclusively for the U.S. Defense Department, is, except for his esoteric intellectual specialty, the average American husband of middle-age with two teenage children (in private schools), a fine ranch-style home near Los Angeles (paid for and no mortgage), financially secure with the usual investments in tax-exempt bonds, IRAs, Keoghs, T-bills and many mutual funds of conservative rather than aggressive strategies. (He has neither the patience nor time to "play the market" in individual stocks and justifies this disinterest with a vague caution about possible "conflicts of interest," although such seem unlikely. He doesn't even have a stock broker or an account with one. "Let the Mutual Fund managers pick the stocks," he says.) Naturally, he has a top-secret security clearance from DOD (Department of Defense).

Although Dr.Miller has never given DOD any reason for doubting his loyalty or suspicion that he might be inclined for some reason to pass defense secrets to the Soviets, he is periodically "spot-checked" (without his knowledge) in a variety of ways. His home and office telephones are tapped and monitored for weeks at a time by DOD security units (DOD intelligence services); his bank and other accounts are routinely audited in search of possible irregularities and changes in pattern that might have significance; and his trash is periodically collected by

DOD security units (conveniently for them, the city trash trucks come early in Miller's neighborhood so he puts the trash out the night before and DOD can easily pick it up about mid-night under protection of darkness -and later root through it for anything suspicious). Dr. Miller occasionally comments on how, sometimes, the trash truck whisks away his trash so early that it's already gone when he leaves at 7:00 AM for work. "What a fast-moving team they are," he says -with no knowledge at all of how special team it indeed is.

(a) Is DOD's monitoring of Dr. Miller unethical? Should it be illegal? Contrast DOD's and Miller's rights in the issue.
(b) Should police have the right to search a home or car suspected of possessing illegal drugs, weapons etc., without prior notice or a search warrant (the latter delay permitting criminals to conceal or dispose of such incriminating items before search)?

18 ARE CEOs OVERPAID?

Business Week reported in 1982 that many top executives of private sector firms are paid salaries (including bonus, etc.) approaching or even exceeding $1 million. Top engineers and other professionals in the same firms have annual salaries of $30,000 to $50,000 and skilled technicians (electricians, programmers, etc.) $20,000 to $30,000.

(a) What factors should be considered in determining a fair wage?
(b) Are CEOs (chief executive officers) and other top executives overpaid? Is the disparity of salaries from top levels to the operating levels ethical?

19 WEAR AND RETURN

Susan, a middle-aged wife of a well-known local surgeon and mother of three, enjoys a reasonably secure and even luxurious life. She and her children can afford anything they want within reason. But, still, Susan likes occasionally, not too often, to buy a new dress from one of the large local department stores, wear it just once for a social evening and then immediately return it to the store for a full refund. Her standard explanations: "the color clashes with our living room," "my husband says we can't afford it" or "my neighbor has one exactly like it." The stores always accept the return with no questions (she's a very good customer in terms of annual purchases which she keeps). This is just a game with Susan, no harm meant; but is it ethical?

20 THE 24% LOAN

Fidelity Finance Company is a consumer credit firm, like Household Finance Co., etc., which makes loans to individuals and families unable to get a bank loan for a car or other reason such as consolidating debts. Fidelity's customers are often people new in town, with little credit history or a history of debt problems solved or being solved. For one reason or another they are regarded as higher credit risks than the well-known bank customer, with a documented sound credit record, applying to a bank for a car or other personal loan. And even these bank customers can't get a low-interest bank loan during periods when money is tight and demand for it is high.

At a period in the early 1980s, when banks were routinely charging 10% interest on car and other personal loans (annual rate), Fidelity Finance was, quite legally, charging 20%. To appreciate the cost difference to a customer, a $3000 loan (net amount to customer) at 10% interest paid off monthly over 24 months at $ 138 monthly will cost $322 in interest charges over and above the $3000 actually received (that's enough to buy a fine TV set! -instead of paying it for interest charges); Fidelity's 20% charge on the same $3000 received over 24 months (at $153) costs $665 in interest charge and some inner-city finance firms charge 24% costing $807 to finance (as compared to the bank's 322 -quite a difference). Most consumers, unfortunately, do not calculate the dollar differences in interest charges at different interest rates; and never realize how much hard cash is involved (like enough to buy a TV set or a New York vacation trip).

(a) Is it ethical for Fidelity Finance to charge twice the interest rate banks charge for a loan? What about 24%?

(b) Why is it ethical for a bank to charge <u>any</u> interest at all for money loaned? (In medieval times, this was called usury and condemned by the church -see p.34 above). What's involved?

21 THE EASY PROFESSOR

Professor Lawrence Mulcahy is a full professor in the chemistry department of a large and prestigious (private) metropolitan university. And he's the department's "star," recognized world-wide as a great researcher and authority in the field of amino acids and routinely attracting large and profitable research grants for the university. His salary matches his "star" status. Because of his involvement in research and management of grants, he teaches only one course per semester, a graduate course of a seminar type with a typical enrollment of 30 and meeting for 3 hours on Tuesday evenings over the 16-week semester. (Each student pays a tuition fee of $500 for the course or $30 for each evening session with the professor.) But Mulcahy's heart is really in his research and grant activities, not teaching; although, when he actually finds himself in the classroom environment and with 30 interested listeners and questioners before him, something (maybe his ego) fires him into a usually exciting performance.

That is, when he attends. Mulcahy gets so engrossed in research and grants-type work that he sometimes sends a graduate assistant to the classroom on Tuesday evenings to write some reading assignments on the blackboard and then cancel the class (this happens about four times per semester and none of the classes are made up, i.e. rescheduled). This is irritating to students who traveled to class, paid for the difficult-to-find parking on campus, prepared carefully for class, anticipated important new learnings and, of course, paid an average $30 of their money for each of the cancelled classes. The professor seems unaware of these student perceptions of an occasional cancelled class and justifies it, when it crosses his mind briefly, as a necessary trade-off among his ever-pressing research, grants-management and other responsibilities. "I keep them all balanced properly," he says.

(a) What about Mulcahy's responsibility to his students? Is his "cutting classes" ethical? Legal?
(b) And, what about students who cut classes? Is that ethical?
(c) And, what about lawyers, doctors, dentists and others who leave their offices, cancel appointments without notifying clients who arrive only to be informed of the cancelation?

22 WATCH THOSE DEATH NOTICES

Len Wallace, top salesman for years with Apex Realty (a large metropolitan real estate firm) claims that the secret of his success is in listing homes for sale from the right seller at the right psychological moment and at a very attractive selling price; this done, it's easy to find a buyer who will jump at and sign off on it (followed by good and consistent commission money to the brokerage house and the salesman). The real selling is to get the right listing; then selling a buyer is almost automatic. (In real estate, a 'listing' is a firm contract a home owner signs agreeing to sell the home at a stipulated price through a named agent exclusively within usually a 2 to 4 month period.) If an agent, a real estate salesman like Len, can persuade the home owner to agree by the listing contract to a low or below-the-market contract price, the actual sale of the home is quick, easy, little hard work, good pay -but, often, at the expense of a home owner who could or should have gotten a higher price with the harder work and agent's time required for it. But, Len claims, this is not the way to "top salesman" status.

One of Len's main tactics is to study every day's newspaper death notices. Most of them inform him of the address of a widower or, more usually, a widow (women statistically outlive men by seven years) with whom he succeeds more frequently ("women appreciate my style more than men," he says). Len does his homework, checks out recent home sales and prices, drives by the home often to evaluate it (he can tell you almost every detail of the interior from just driving by and studying the home's exterior shape, windows, etc.), and, soon, a day at most after the funeral –or often even before the funeral, arrives at the door of the address, talks his way into an interview with the surviving spouse –and now exclusive home owner, explains how he can help with a quick sale for funds needed in the survivor's new and uncertain future and the importance of a "right" price to insure these benefits. Given the emotional state and feelings of uncertainty of the survivor, Len usually gets his listing at the right price for an easy later sale.

(a) Are any of Len's actions unethical? Why?

(b) What about investment advisors and others (who carefully read death notices) and phone for appointment to visit a surviving spouse soon after a funeral? Is this alert business or unethical?

23 SENIORITY OR MERIT

Jeff Norris is a young engineer with a government agency still at very low levels of pay, despite the fact that he has demonstrated in his first two years knowledge of the field and performance results far exceeding the other four engineers in his section. However, they are senior to him, making many thousands of dollars annually more than him and having 5 to 22 years more seniority in the section than him.

(a) Why should seniority be a basis for salary level, if it should?

(b) Why should merit be a basis for salary level, if it should?

(c) Is it fair or ethical to pay Jeff less for more and better work?

24 SELLING ONESELF AND ONE'S SECRETS

From a semantics point of view (p. 159 above), the word and meanings of "prostitution" are interesting. Prostitution most frequently produces in Christian nations the image of a woman selling her body (sex) for pay and is regarded as evil and generally even illegal (prostitutes, not their customers, go to jail often). But the term, in its generic meaning, means any act by which one offers himself or any of his assets for pay. Although we now confine the term to sexual trades, a witness who testifies falsely for money is selling his "word" and his honor. Anyone who sells his mind, skill or knowledge for crass reasons can be termed a prostitute.

An example is Ken Shelton, a veteran systems engineer with a major computer manufacturer, who has been a key participant in new research and a major break-through in computer chip design. The resulting new technology is basically sound now but will require many modifications and tests before it is patented and protected from copiers. Another and competing computer manufacturer, through trade rumors, has vague knowledge that the new technology exists and desparately wants to find out specifically what it is, ideally exact technical detail and specifications on progress so far. Its personnel recruiters approach Shelton, many times, little by little persuading him to resign his present position, join their company at the same salary and fringe benefits <u>plus</u> an immediate $100,000 cash bonus (to compensate for his relocation and inconvenience problems) -with the understanding, of course, that he share with his new company <u>everything</u> he knows about the new chip technology, lead the effort to perfect it and get it to market, and fully patented, before all of its competitors. Part of the arrangement is that Shelton resign for "reasons of temporary ill health" and say nothing of his new position -in order to avoid arousing suspicion of the real reason for his action. Shelton accepts the proposition and his new company does succeed in getting to market (and to the patent office) first.

(a) Identify and distinguish among the several actions Shelton did; are any of them unethical? illegal? Why?

(b) Specifically, is Shelton's decision (to sell secret knowledge in his possession to a highest bidder) ethical? Why?

(c) Are the recruiters, paying him $100,000 for his cooperation (considering their and their firm's real intent), ethical? Why?

(d) Is a woman, who "prostitutes" herself -i.e. provides sexual services for pay, acting <u>unethically</u> (as distinct from illegally) given the following two conditions:

  (i) she has two kids, no business skills, no money? Why?

  (ii) she can earn $1000 @ night with wealthy men and live a life of rare luxury (furs, big car, investments, etc) ?

(e) Analyze the human act called "selling" and several conditions comprising (i) ethical selling and (ii) unethical selling.

(f) Can you think of ways in which executive or professional people "prostitute" themselves in their careers (indicate whether <u>ethically</u> or <u>unethically</u> -and <u>why</u>) -such as lawyers, doctors, judges, politicians, professors, consultants, wives, husbands, religious ministers and priests, scientists, managers?

(g) Define the term "conflict of interest" as used in America today and relate it to "selling" and "prostitution" (as above, both ethical and unethical), using examples to explain.

25 THREE VERSIONS OF COMPANY "BOOKS"

Apex Enterprises Inc., like most American corporations, keeps three distinct versions of financial statements based on its actual day-to-day transactions as recorded in its general ledger (a general ledger is a double-entry listing of every transaction every day, such as a sale or a payment for goods, and the raw data for preparing financial statements such as Profit-and-Loss, Financial Condition, Cash Flow, etc.). But, when all this raw data is assembled into, say, a Profit-and-Loss operating statement, it usually tells three very different stories about how the company is doing -depending on how the raw data is interpreted, evaluated and arranged, a matter of subjective human judgment. For example, reported cost of merchandise in a statement might be based on actual cost of the item when bought or the average cost of the item over many different purchases of it over time as the cost varies or the lowest (or highest) price paid for it as a continuously ordered and stored item in inventory. Depending on which method of evaluating the cost of the item when sold to a company customer, the reported profit will be higher (if a lower inventory cost is used) or lower (if a higher cost is used). Another example is the varying methods of charging off (depreciating) the cost of equipment, buildings, etc.

Thus Apex Enterprises, in its Profit-and-Loss statements, reports out three different versions each quarter and annually: one showing the lowest possible profit (for IRS and to minimize income taxes), one showing highest possible profit (for annual reports to stockholders and prospective investors to retain them and attract more of them), and a hard actual version of current realities as they really are (for the use and planning of operating executives).

This practice of issuing different P & L statements for different recipients is legal -provided that evaluation methods remain the same and consistent over the years and that a certified public accountant audits and approves the statements as within the minimum legal requirements of "generally accepted standards" of accounting. But, government tax officials, banks loaning money to companies, stockholders with life savings invested in them and investors trying to evaluate a company as a good or poor investment are confused and suspicious about three versions of a company's performance when they need the actual and real one.

(a) Is the corporate practice of three versions of financial statements ethical? Should the law require just one version?

(b) What should be the main ethical purposes of financial statements (as sent to tax officials, banks, stockholders, etc.)?

(c) Do you fully understand and trust the information in the average corporation Annual Report you read? Why?

26 THE VALUE OF A SIGNATURE

Albert Jones & Associates is a CPA firm (Certified Public Accountants) whose main function is auditing company records and then certifying by signature in the Annual Report that company records, statements and accounting procedures fully satisfy "generally accepted accounting standards" (provided, of course, that they do -if not they must be corrected until they do and before the approving CPA signature which assures the integrity and credibility of the statements). But a CPA's judgment about when or whether to sign and certify an annual statement is ultimately a subjective one, based on as much objective information as is or should be made available. The CPA can range from strict to lenient interpretations. Sometimes, a very lenient, if not an almost fraudulent, interpretation serves the best practical interests of the CPA (or anyone else whose business is auditing).

A recent audit of a major and long-standing customer company was handled by Al personally and illustrates the tension between strict auditing integrity and "bending the rules" to avoid being fired by the client when he is dissatisfied with the results of an audit or reluctance of an auditor to sign off and certify his statements. (After all, the customer company or client is a revenue source to the accounting firm and losing the client's business directly affects and reduces the profits of the firm.) The company Al was auditing (Maxicomputers, Inc.) had had one very bad quarter over the year, because of a quality problem in a new series of computers (a minor problem and now fully corrected) and unusual repair costs to fix the faulty machines, which temporarily increased company costs and reduced profits. To avoid the impression of any kind of "trouble" signaled to the financial community by just one bad quarter and that for superficial correctible reasons, Tom Knox (the president of Maxicomputer and now a close friend of Al's) asked Al to do him a favor -just this one time: sign and certify his drafted annual report which, by unusual accounting procedures, treated repair costs (incurred during the bad quarter) as a strange kind of deferred and depreciable asset to be paid off over five years rather than as a current operating expense which, of course, it was by any accepted standards. Tom's accountant had done a clever job of moving these current costs subtly into deferred categories so as to be easily unnoticed by an auditor (and, therefore, no legal problem for him), especially if the auditor had some incentive to avoid noticing the subtle switches of current to deferred accounts. Al certainly had such incentive insofar as Tom was a steady and profitable customer as well as a dear friend. So he signed and certified the Annual Report exactly as drafted by Tom's accountants.

(a) Did Al's action deceive anyone? Was it ethical?

(b) Is friendship more important than honesty?

27 DUTIES, LOYALTIES AND OPPORTUNITIES

Joe knows (and has proof) that Jack is cheating IRS (Internal Revenue Service) by arranging to receive 40% of his income in cash "off the books" and then not reporting it to IRS as taxable income. Jack is one of millions who operate at least partially off the books to evade taxes which is, of course, illegal (see Case # 5). Joe approaches IRS informing an official about what he knows but without naming names, to determine how much IRS would pay for more specific information including the name. Satisfied with IRS's offer of cash, Joe says he will think about it and decide what to do later. Then Joe goes to Jack, threatens to reveal what he knows to IRS, unless Jack pays him an amount of money that is twice IRS's offer. Although angry at Joe, Jack pays him the cash. And Joe keeps his word.

(a) List and analyze every major action or decision by Joe, Jack and IRS to determine whether it is ethical or unethical.

(b) Except for Jack's tax evasion, are any of the actions illegal?

28 "RETIRED" BUT ON THE JOB

Jake, age 61, with an outstanding performance record over the past 22 years with his present employer, a competent engineer who has always kept current in his field, has no health problems and indeed works energetically at his favorite activities (programming his home computer, chairing the Condo committee in the condominium where he and his wife live and working at his new parttime real estate job). He is charged with energy on everything he does -except on his (fulltime) job. After years of outstanding performance and beginning about a year ago, Jack "coasts" through his average day on the job doing as little as possible, socializing a lot, sometimes reading real estate or home computer literature and is generally "retired" on the job. His boss says little about this, being of a non-assertive nature and disliking any sort of unpleasantness. Jake's attitude is that he's worked hard for the company a long time, "paid his dues" as he often says, and has a right now to coast a bit. With his seniority, his salary is the highest in the engineering department. He plans to retire (officially) at 65.

(a) Is Jake's attitude and performance on the job ethical? Why?

(b) Is his boss's inaction ethical? What should Jake's boss do?

29 QUOTAS OR MERIT

Abrams University has a generally good minority hiring record except in its business school which is under heavy pressure to hire more minority people, especially women and blacks. Of a fulltime faculty of 60 there are now only one black and two female professors.

The university has a considerable number of government grants and other contracts which are threatened unless it meets certain quotas of minority faculty members over a stipulated number of years in each of its schools. The business school, in its hiring over the years, is far below its quota -and the school's dean is pressured about it constantly. His explanation, quite sincere and factual, is that highly qualified women and blacks have been given firm offers often but do not accept them; insofar as they are in great demand (far greater than the supply) among a hundred or so university business schools more prestigious and financially able to offer higher salaries for women and blacks, they reject Abrams and take the higher-paying positions.

At this moment, six candidates have been interviewed for a vacant faculty position in the business school's marketing department, at the assistant professor level, five of them highly qualified white males and one a black whose qualifications are average, probably just adequate but certainly not highly qualified level. Under pressure from the university's vice presidents for academic affairs and for government grants management, the business school dean hires the black candidate.

(a) Is this decision ethical (apart from its being legally required)?
(b) Are such laws (requiring quotas of minority members) ethical?

30 SELL THE PACKAGE, NOT THE PRODUCT

Fitzhugh Smith, always called Fitz by his friends, is marketing director of Acme Cereals Inc. and has been successfully selling corn flakes for Acme for over 20 years. Fitz operates by his motto that well-processed corn flakes, no matter who makes them, are the same as anybody's corn flakes, just as good salt is good salt. Put milk and fruit on a bowl of good corn flakes and they're all the same. Fitz attributes his successful record of selling corn flakes not to the product but to his skills in selling the package containing the flakes, especially the shape of the package, the wording on it and the way it's advertised. "Sell the package, not the product," Fitz says, like the old adage "Sell the sizzle, not the steak." His years of evaluating the results of market research convince him that consumers are emotional, not rational, in purchasing, that they buy "image," what they think a product is, not what it really is. His current tactic is a box clearly larger than what the competition uses for the same quantity of flakes, made larger by virtue of a one-inch cardboard compartment in the middle of the box separating two sections of cellophane-enclosed flakes and advertised as "two boxes of corn flakes in one -for sure freshness and always sure to keep the kids always eating the good breakfast they need, etc." This ad message, on TV and modified for radio and magazines, is joined by the usual kids pictured as enthusiastic about eating their flakes and prominently displaying the competition's smaller boxes next to Fitz's larger one, suggesting, but never saying, that mother gets more flakes for her money too. The right "image," Fitz says, can be created by powerful suggestion as well as by explicit statements.

(a) Is Fitz's sales tactic clever selling or is it unethical?

(b) Can you think of any examples of unethical packaging or advertising going on now or used in the past?

31 A PRIVATE AFFAIR

Jackson Lawler, the most veteran and competent engineer in your department of a large aerospace corporation, is having a torrid affair with one of your department's word processing staff, Vivian Land. The affair, first rumored throughout the department, then known as a fact by most, is now obvious to all. Everyone grins knowingly and watches as Jackson finds new and more frequent occasions to visit the word processing section. While there, the eye contact and smiles exchanged between Vivian and Jackson satisfy the curiosity of the department watchers. You have come to realize that a lot of department time is devoted to the lovers' socializing while everyone else watches and waste time as well. Some, however, find it offensive, "adultery on the job," as one engineer put it to you and "when are you going to do something about it?" Even Jackson's wife came to your office one day (what a show that was for the department watchers!) to ask that you make them stop the affair. You have talked to Jackson once, briefly and evasively, about the affair but he quickly became irritated and left saying "as long as my work performance in this department is outstanding, as it has always been, my private life is none of anybody's business." Vivian's performance record is not changed either, not outstanding but average. You decide to fire Vivian, to at least remove the affair from the department, call her in and, with no mention of the affair, explain her termination to her in broad unintelligible bureaucratic terms and assure her of a fine recommendation to her next employer. You never discuss this decision with Jackson before or after acting on it. And, after Vivian leaves, there seems to be less wasted time.

(a) List and analyze every major action or decision by Jackson, Vivian, Jackson's wife, his boss (you), and determine which are ethical or unethical —and why.

(b) Under what conditions (please be specific), if any, is it right and ethical for a manager to inquire into the "private life" of employees, interfere in it or make decisions affecting it? Please use examples to explain answers to this question.

32 TIT FOR TAT

You are driving through a country area of a southern state on a trip from New York to Miami and your car radiator springs a leak. In this area there are few service stations but you finally come across one with the encouraging, although backward, sign above it "WE HANDLE YOUR PROBLEMS GOOD" and drive in for service. The middle-aged station owner puts on quite a performance, with his wife and kids all around watching and giggling in agreement with his every word, explaining the dangers of the car's condition and the difficulty of the work needed to be done. (You, and he, know, of course, that it is a simple radiator repair job routinely costing in any city about $40 and taking about an hour to complete.) But he's the only service station in the area and, if you want to get fixed and move on, you must pay his price ($210, he says). So you agree, he fixes the radiator, and write a check for the $210. He wanted cash but you tell him that nobody carries that kind of cash but you'll "certify" the check so that it's the <u>same</u> as cash -and you slowly and almost ceremoniously, with him so entranced in the process he doesn't understand at all, write in the low left corner of your check the impressive word (to him) "CERTIFIED." "Now," you say to him, "that's cash, and thank you for your help." Several hours later, from your Miami hotel room, you phone your bank and order the $210 check stopped and cancelled. But, you did write down the address of the service station and mail to it a good check for $40. (a) Identify and analyze any unethical actions in this case. (b) Is the country station owner acting like a monopoly?

33 GET THEM TO EAT CAKE

Kidscake Inc. is one of the largest national bakery companies in the country, making and distributing several dozen varieties of cake, cookies, candy and sweet (sugared) snacks to virtually every food and drug store in the land.* Kidscake's TV advertising is huge and directed mainly at kids who, according to market research, consume by far the greatest proportion of the firm's snacks. A group of nutritionists, angered at the aggressive ads luring kids into bad eating habits ("junk food" addicts) buy just enough Kidscake stock to attend and demonstrate their point at the annual meeting. Although the group's "ban the junk food ads" demonstrating amuses most stockholders and takes little time on the agenda, the group has carefully alerted the media and the FTC (Federal Trade Commission) which view it as a serious issue "to be

---

* The idea for this case, not the detail, is drawn from D.N.Dickson's Sugar Babies articles in <u>Across the Board</u> (Jan.&June,1982). Dickson's case is based on a <u>Harvard Business School</u> file case.

investigated."

(a) Is Kidscake's advertising aimed at kids unethical?

(b) Is it ethical to advertise beer and wine on TV (ads for other alcoholic beverages, like whisky or scotch, are illegal)?

(c) Can you think of any current ads, in magazines or TV etc., which raise questions about their ethical propriety?

34 EVERYBODY SATISFACTORY

Apex Industries, like most companies, has a performance evaluation program whereby supervisors rate the performance of their subordinates. A typical scale, and the one used by Apex, ranges from scores of 1 to 5 in which "1" means "unsatisfactory," "2" "barely satisfactory," "3" "satisfactory," "4" "highly satisfactory" and "5" "outstanding." Supervisory evaluations of "1" or "5" require considerable time-consuming written documentation and a "1" often leads to angry claims of discrimination or other inequity forcing the supervisory into huge piles of paperwork and appeal hearings; thus supervisors tend to avoid the "1" and the "5" ratings as too much trouble. Two of Apex's line supervisors, supervising similar work sections doing similar work, have different personal problems with the ratings. One of them, Sam, has a clearly outstanding female worker but routinely gives her a "4" to avoid the time-consuming paperwork involved in a "5;" he also has a black male worker who is clearly –almost blatantly– unsatisfactory but always gives him a "2" to avoid discrimination charges by the worker (the worker, with a slight grin, so threatens if he ever gets a "1"). The other supervisor, Tom, has average workers, no "outstandings" or "unsats," and rates all as honestly as he can; his problem is that, except for Sam's "outstanding" female worker, Sam "inflates" his ratings of the others giving a "4" to all who clearly deserve only a "3" when Tom is giving his similarly average workers a true "3." The salaries and pay raises of workers in both sections are closely related to the performance ratings received and Tom's people feel he is giving Sam's people an unfair advantage by <u>not</u> inflating ratings as Sam does. Tom wonders whether he should give dishonest ratings because Sam does.

(a) List and analyze every major action or decision by Sam, Tom, Sam's black male worker and Apex top management– and determine which are ethical or unethical. And <u>why</u>.

(b) Should Tom "inflate" his ratings to match "Sam's?"

(c) Many elementary and high school teachers (under pressure from administrators, politicians and parents) "pass" students into a next grade when they clearly "failed" to master needed skills of their current grade. So, today, millions of high school graduates can't read addresses well enough to qualify for and perform even simple delivery and transportation jobs such as delivering mail or packages with UPS or the Postal Service. Is it ethical for a teacher to "pass" a student who has clearly "failed?"

(d) Many college professors give most students A's or B's to avoid unpleasant sessions in the professor's office with angry "C" or "D" or "F" students (when these very difficult sessions are the ideal way to counsel and help a student improve and become a genuine "B" or better student!) and to retain his popularity with students so as to have enough of them each term to justify his retention on the faculty and receive high rating on student course evaluations which also determine his future with the college as well as his annual salary increases. Is it ethical for a professor to give a true "D" student a "C" or a true "C" student a "B" grade? Suppose the professor needs enthusiastic popularity with students, reflected in high enrollments in his courses, in order to keep his job?

35 THE COLLEGE NEWS EDITOR

Linda Saylor, now a senior with consistent "A" grades throughout her three years at a prestigious New England university, was elected for the third year in a row as editor of the university's student newspaper, the College News. Instead of the usual trite and amateurish pieces found in most college newspapers, Linda and her staff researched and wrote consistently professional-type articles. One of them was based on a survey of college drug users who volunteered hard, honest information provided they were guaranteed anonymity and thus protection from the editor. Linda promised this as a sacred oath, learned information -especially about how a drug habit starts- which would probably help readers avoid the tragedy of drugs. An interesting, well written, useful and helpful article (she received a national award for it later). Soon after the article appeared in the College News, Linda was called to a meeting of top officials of the university and ordered to reveal the names of her sources (those surveyed) as students subject to discipline for violating university rules against drug use (she was promised that the information would be held confidential and not given to state police authorities). Linda refused to name her sources and was expelled from the university with a "not recommended" note in her file.

(a) List and analyze every major action or decision by Linda, the drug users in her survey and university officials - and state which in your opinion are ethical or unethical. And why.

(b) Suppose the police insist university officals reveal the names?

36 JUST SAYING NOTHING

Alex and Joyce are section heads, respectively, of the accounts receivable section and the accounts payable section of a large firm's accounting department. The department director, Chuck Morton, will retire in about a year and everyone expects that either Alex or Joyce, both excellent managers and about equally competent, will be promoted as the new director. Which one of the two gets the promotion will probably depend on some slight edge or error by either -it's that close. Several weeks before Morton's resignation, Alex notices an unusual opportunity to secure that edge by means of an error Joyce is about to make - if he just says nothing. He accidentally overhears at a coffee break that one of Joyce's best bookkeepers, in charge of paying big suppliers in time to get important trade discounts, plans to leave for another job but <u>without notice</u> (for her own reasons). Without advance knowledge of this, Joyce would have no way of retraining someone to get big payables out fast enough to get the critical discounts -Joyce would answer for the error for months as it appeared in every operating statement used by top management to monitor profits and costs, especially avoidable ones. If Alex immediately told Joyce what he knew, she would have plenty of time to retrain someone and meet the discount deadlines. But Alex goes on just saying nothing. And gets the promotion.

(a) It was only by accident that Alex learned of a key worker's intention to leave her job. Is his <u>silence</u> about it ethical?

(b) The reason the key worker had for not giving Joyce notice was a general dislike of Joyce, the "fun" of seeing her "stumble" a bit and miss her discounts and realize how "important" that "unappreciated" key worker had been. Was her act ethical?

37 SLOWING DOWN

As a consistently effective executive with Jochlin Industries Inc. for 28 years, in almost every key area of their business, Glenn Peirce has regularly worked 50- and 60-hour weeks energetically without even noticing the hours and effort - he just wanted and got results for the company and his own career success. He was virtually pirated into the company, as a brilliant 27-year-old miracle-worker for a competitor, and has since worked many minor and greater miracles for Jochlin. Now 55, Glenn can't maintain that pace. He's not sick, his health is basically good, but his high-energy and miracle-working days are over. He knows it and so does the company. In a delicate, subtle, but clear, conversation with a company top manager, Glenn is told to take "early retirement" or be "let go."

(a) Is the company decision about Glenn ethical?

38 LUDLOW'S PROFITABILITY

Ludlow Inc. was one of five large producers of a staple food product.* These five giants accounted for virtually the entire national production of the product and competition among them was such that survival of each depended upon extremely tight cost control, especially in manpower costs. The industry was unionized and pay scales were standardized throughout the industry. One principal key to survival and profitability was manpower productivity which required careful recruiting and hiring of efficient people. Ludlow's main processing plant happened to be in a large and old eastern city which had recently begun to enforce strong policies regarding minority hiring and the creation of opportunities for the hard-core unemployed.

Ludlow's corporate management could no longer avoid the issue and was debating it in terms of the objectives of the company. Most Ludlow vice presidents stressed the highly competitive nature of the industry and hiring inefficient (hard-core unemployed) people who needed expensive training as a cost handicap threatening their basic ability to compete and survive (the resulting increase in price due to higher costs would simply drive all their customers to competitors).

Ludlow's president, although sympathetic to the help needed by hard-core unemployed people, lamented that "if all the companies in the industry got together and agreed on an equal proportion of such new training costs, we could help these people and all remain competitive." But such "getting together" among competitors is a violation of anti-trust laws. So, the president rejected the proposed policy of hiring low-efficiency workers.

(a) Was Ludlow's president's decision ethical?

(b) Should anti-trust laws be changed to permit the kind of agreements the president would like?

39 NERVOUS MANUFACTURERS

Consumerism (the American consumer-protection political movement) has grown for two decades and reached a pitch of fervor in 1982 when Congress was forced to consider <u>federal</u> consumer-protection and product-liability laws to standardize or replace the maze of state laws that vary radically from state to state. The California State Supreme court in 1980 ruled that women contracting cancer probably because decades ago their <u>mothers</u> had used the drug diethylstilbestrol (DES)

---

* This case is adapted from one of the same title in this author's <u>The Theory and Practice of Managing</u>, 1982, page 529.

could hold and sue as liable all six companies that manufactured DES in proportion to their market share, even though the women could not name which company made the DES which was legal at the time. The companies were all liable unless any could prove that the mothers had not taken the actual doses made by a particular company (how can that ever be proved?). This law now applies in California but not in most other states. If a manufacturer improves a product and increases its safety, based on prior experience with the product's use, three states (California, New York and Alaska) have laws permitting suits based on the presumption that the earlier product was negligently unsafe and required safety improvements (the other 47 states have no such laws). Makers of rotary lawn mowers have been under threat of liability suits for years, no matter what they do.

A Washington product-liability expert, who headed a government task force to reform the system of compensating victims of product failures, says "The crisis is worse than ever - how many warnings can you put on a product or guards on a lawnmower; it's a matter of fairness." (All quotes are from U.S. News and World Report, June 14, 1982, p.62). "It is the unpredictability of the current system that upsets business," says a NYU Law School professor. "Manufacturers are fearful because they don't know what to do. They don't know what standards to follow when they make their goods."

So, just as doctors practice "defensive" medicine (ordering every costly test imaginable -and beyond any reasonable need- to "cover" themselves later in a court, if necessary), so America is becoming a land of "defensive" manufacturers paying high-cost legal fees and compensations to consumers, driving up costs and prices (and cutting into the kind of productivity Japan is noted for). Lawyers are the big gainers from product-liability suits, receiving 30% to 40% of awards made while much of the rest goes for court and other costs. (Japan has just a fraction of the number of lawyers compared to America's.)

(a) Is the California law (about DES) ethical?
(b) Is the law cited in three states (Ca., NY, Alaska) ethical?
(c) Should uniform federal product-liability laws replace state laws or should the issue be handled locally as at present?

40 HAMMERS CAN BE DANGEROUS

Midland Trade Co. is a national mail order supply firm, smaller but similar to Sears Roebuck and Montgomery Ward, selling direct to consumers by mail. Their ads are in many magazines and they sell all sorts of consumer products, including hand guns. The company has a well-deserved reputation for reliability, fair prices and fair dealing.

Their problem is their sales of handguns. Consumer groups and other opponents of handguns are publicly attacking Midland Trade Co. for selling handguns and thus contributing to street crime and murders. The company's position is that it sells reliable products at a fair price and guarantees them. That's its only function and it does it well, as do Sears and Wards. Any product can be used properly –or abused, which marketing companies cannot and should not control in a free land. A handgun purchase is a legitimate one for personal safety, especially with home break-ins on the rise and older people physically no match for strong young hoodlums unless the homeowner has an "equalizer." As Midland's president puts it: "We sell knives, rope, axes, hammers and other products (including handguns and rifles) people need to do constructive human functions. Should we refuse, or be prevented from selling such products because someone might abuse the product, stab his wife with one of our hunting knives, strangle her with our rope or shoot her with a handgun or hit her over the head with a Midland Trade Co. hammer?"

(a) Do you agree with Midland's president's position? Ethical?

(b) Should cigaret sales (or candy sales) be made illegal because they cause cancer (or heart disease from obesity)? Why?

41 EXPENSE ACCOUNTS

Joel Jones, a new salesman with Armtrek Instruments Inc., soon learns from his fellow salesmen, all of whom must travel a lot, that part of your income –an important part – is what they call "indirect expense account compensation." That is, reporting higher, but not too much higher, travel expenses over amounts actually spent and, of course, pocketing the difference. Joel feels uncomfortable about this but the salesmen assure him that the sales managers (and top management) all know about the practice, accept it as a motivating incentive for salesmen and just "charge it off" against taxes. Joel finally agrees.

(a) List and analyze every major action or decision by Joel, his fellow salesmen, the sales managers and top management and determine which are ethical or unethical –and why.

(b) Are trips to foreign lands by congressmen, all expenses paid by taxpayers, ever unethical? Under what conditions?

42 WORKING AND "WELFARING"

Marty Kelly, a strong, healthy, young, white, smart high school graduate (with high grades), learns quickly how to work a comfortable 20-hour-a-week parttime job (paid in cash "off the books") and, at the same time, collect additional and substantial money regularly from unemployment compensation, food stamps and other welfare programs by just avoiding a fulltime job (of record and "on the books") and reporting, with his certifying signature, that he's unemployed, unable to get a job (although he's "looking hard" for one), submitting such reports regularly to the various government welfare agencies and then just collecting the government money. As Marty puts it: "only a fool, too dumb to figure out and 'work' the system, needs a regular, fulltime job."*

(a) Are Marty's actions smart or unethical, both or neither? Why?
(b) Under what conditions should a person (ethically) get welfare?

43 THE INSIDER

Ann Flynn, an assistant manager in the large public relations department of a Fortune 500 firm, routinely has access to company plans and information long before it is released to the public and the company's shareholders. Indeed, she is the one who, along with an army of typists and word processors, prepares the copy and handles the huge mechanical job of printing and distributing such information. As an "insider," she is directed, one day, to prepare an information release, to be dated one week later, informing the public and shareholders of a dramatic two-for-one stock split and a doubling of dividends payable to all stockholders. Anyone would know that the moment this information becomes known on Wall Street, the relative price of the company stock will rise quickly to a new and stable level. Anyone buying the stock now would enjoy a quick profit when the new information was released to the public. After the quick rise in relative price, just sell and pocket the profits. Which is exactly what Ann did. She withdrew $4000 from her savings, borrowed $5000 more (to buy a car, she told the bank), bought her company's stock, waited a week for it to soar up and then sold it for a quick profit of several thousand dollars. No one would ever know what she did or why because her "manipulation" of the market was too small for anyone to notice. A lucky break for Ann.

(a) Was Ann's action ethical or unethical? Why? Legal?
(b) Suppose Ann were a major shareholder with 40% of the stock?
(c) Why is it illegal in the U.S. for "insiders" to use inside information about mergers, stock splits, etc. to make a profit?

---

* Many states have discovered, upon investigation, millions of dollars claimed fraudulently and paid from unemployment compensation funds. "Double-dippers" (working but also claiming government compensation) are common. (Wall Street Journal, 2/9/82, p.33) Taxpayers are becoming cynical about what happens to their hard-earned money and how it's "ripped off."

44 WOULD YOU BUY A USED CAR FROM....?

Walter Hunt, a veteran used car salesman with Machlin Ford Co., a new and used car dealership in an eastern metropolitan city area for 30 years and with a generally good -or at least untainted- reputation, is hurting from drastically reduced sales and personal income because of the unprecedented "auto sales depression" of 1981-82. His sales commissions are only half of what they were a year ago, he is two months late on the home mortgage (with a warning note on foreclosure), his refrigerator has essential but not much food in it, several doctor's bills are still unpaid from six months ago, not a cent for months for a much needed 'night out' or even a dinner out. He's always been fully honest with customers about the former owner of a car, any repairs that probably will be needed after purchase, especially any repairs needed almost immediately -such as a battery or radiator about to die. Recently, under the pressure of his financial problems, he has made sales based on eloquent personal predictions (not guaranteed, of course) about the excellent condition of car parts he knows will fail soon after purchase. For example, yesterday, he sold a used Ford (1978), not old and with low mileage but with a bad transmission due to a rear-end collision, all exterior re-welded and repainted -the car was in appearance a beauty- and only he and the former owner knew about the soon upcoming $400 transmission job when the transmission finally collapsed. But, Walter reasoned, the city's used car salesmen have been using these tactics forever; he abhors such tactics, has never used deception, never will again, but now, in his financial emergency, he sells the 1978 Ford to a customer, utterly naive about car mechanics, without a word about the big transmission problem about to happen.

(a) Walter seems a generally honest man. But was he unethical?

(b) Would you buy a used car from a congressman? a professor?

45 GOODBYE, BARNSVILLE

Textiles Inc., with five major mills throughout the nation, each employing an average of 3000 workers, has been considering closing its largest mill in Barnsville (a small town where virtually everyone works in that Textile mill) to relocate to a different southern state for state tax relief. Barnsville and its local and state taxes are cutting profit margins dangerously - and, in the competitive textile business, prices cannot be raised to absorb such above average state taxes. Textile executives have pleaded with state government for adjustments in taxes to enable the plant to remain in Barnsville, but to no avail. Despite the inevitable unemployment of 3700 of its workers, Textile sees no choice but to close down at Barnsville and relocate its plant. Wishing to avoid a panic among employees which would cut productivity to low margins, Textile, after making its final decision to relocate, is careful to say nothing -until three days before closing down. Neither the town nor the workers had any time to prepare for the disaster.

(a) Did Textile executives have any ethical obligation to forewarn the town and the workers so they could make alternative plans? Even at the cost of damaged productivity in the last weeks of Barnsville operations?

(b) Does Textile have any ethical obligation to help the workers find new jobs? (If so, how and by what means?)

(c) Are any ethical questions raised related to the level of state taxes which, in a tightly competitive industry, drove Textile executives to their decision to relocate the plant?

46 CHEATING IN THE LABS*

Dr. George Wells, in his mid-forties, with growing financial problems, but still the top biochemist in the main laboratory of a large and prestigious pharmaceutical manufacturer, lives and succeeds by new-product research and publishing regularly about his successful results. Always, in the past, his research plans have worked steadily and surely toward a new product (usually predictably and "right on deadlines"), with all the data and documentation to get rapid new-drug approval by FDA (Food and Drug Administration). His company depends on such sure work, and so does his income and future with the company.

But, in his most recent research for a drug to mitigate the lumps and disfigurement of psoriasis (a skin disease), his long months of animal research are only partially successful. He "feels" sure the product will work, but his data and documentation would never pass FDA approval, which is equivalent to a complete failure from a marketing and profit point of view for his company. The company has made it most clear that it needs "results" soon, satisfactory to FDA and sufficient to begin the aggressive marketing campaign to doctors (before a competitor gets in first with their newly-developing and similar product). Dr. Wells 'knows' his new product is effective, safe and sound; all that would be needed is a few months of new tests and several minor adjustments in dosages, routinely documented in the test result records, and FDA approval, as usual for his work, would be almost automatic. But, he doesn't <u>have</u>

---

* This case material is drawn from J. Silberner's article of this title, in <u>Science Digest</u>, August, 1982, pp. 38-41. Some of the cases reported in the article are not only questionable compromises with "truth in research," but blatantly illegal and unbelievably evil by any and all ethical tests.

several months to prove it; he needs proof now. In his view, the whole matter is purely technical: he 'knows' the product works, but the usual bureaucratic documentation is required by the "bureaucrats." So, Dr. Wells decides to alter a few recorded test results (by simply, alone and late at night, erasing certain numbers from the test records and substituting others). He submits his 'final' data through his company's and FDA's usual channels; approval is relatively prompt, the new product is marketed "right on schedule," company management is delighted and Dr. Wells receives his usual substantial cash bonus for his usual good performance and delivery of results needed. An absolutely reliable man and scientist, says the company president of Dr. Wells, as he again congratulates Dr. Wells on a "job well done."

(a) Assuming that, later, Dr. Well's tests prove to all that he was right about the product's effectiveness, was it ethical for him to juggle test numbers of earlier tests in order to meet company and government (FDA) deadlines?

(b) Any comment on top management's "pressure" upon Dr. Wells for test results "by deadline" and "favorable," of course?

47 PUSHING BONDS

Della Quincy, recent college graduate and lucky to land a job with a big firm (in Summer 1982, with the recession hanging on for a full year, interest rates still soaring and nobody recruiting or hiring). She was thanking her lucky stars for having switched to a business core and major in marketing in her junior year of college (her sales tactics and sales management courses impressed the job interviewers she was able to meet with). So, here she was, with a fine career-type job (not a college-educated partly-secretary and mainly-typist and usually-sex object, like her roommates in her four-girl group apartment). But, to be expected, she supposed, there were hard demands on her time, energy and her routine ways of thinking about what was (ethically) right vs wrong. Her job was mainly sales of stocks and bonds in the large brokerage firm, which she enjoyed as she was becoming virtually a financial adviser to her customers (based on recommendations and help from the research department which analyzed stocks and bonds). Her single reservation was the several occasions when she was pressured into selling some bonds to customers which were not on the research department's recommended list (her boss was obviously pressuring her to "push" the bonds under orders from his boss to reduce inventory). She felt she had to be a team-player, and cooperated, but felt uncomfortable about it.

(a) Is Della acting ethically? Her boss? His boss? Why?

48 THE CHAIR

Laura King, a clerical worker, fortyish, just making it financially with a teenage son to support after her divorce, was unable to get credit but saved the $250 for a plush lounge chair to relax in after her tiring work schedule. Although, for her, this was a lot of money for a chair, the store had guaranteed its quality, comfort and appearance as worth the money. About two months after the purchase, the seat of the chair began to show a tear at the seam which quickly expanded until she decided to stop sitting in it. It was guaranteed, so she visited the store (she had no phone) only to find it was out of business and bankrupt. Her store guarantee was worthless and she had neither her $250 nor a sound chair. So, she wrote the manufacturer to ask what, if anything, could be done.

(a) Ethically, what should the manufacturer do, if anything?

(b) If the store owner knew he was going bankrupt, was he ethical in selling the chair and guaranteeing it?

49 IT'S NOT MY RIVER, IT'S YOURS

Warrenton Chemical Company has a single, but large, processing plant just upriver from a small town, most of whose residents work for the company, the major employer in the area. Cost control is critical for the company in order to keep its prices competitive with others marketing the products nationally to buyers at lowest prices. Thus the company is in constant tension with the town's officials who want more control of pollutants being dumped into the river, which would add greatly to company product costs ("such control equipment is just overhead adding to product costs, and prices, without improving the product at all," says the company president). The company, of course, already has operating pollution-control equipment, meeting minimum state and federal standards, so that other towns further downriver from the plant suffer no unacceptable effects from waste discharges at the Warrenton plant. But the pollution concentration in the river for the plant's immediate neighbors, the townspeople who get their drinking water from the river, is high enough to create an offensive taste in the water and some rumors about possible health dangers (although this latter has never been proved). The company president says: "we provide good jobs for these townspeople, if they want more water treatment they can raise taxes and upgrade their water treatment system; it's their river, not mine."

(a) To what extent, if any, is the company president right?

(b) To what extent, if any, are the town officials right?

50 FOREIGN "CONSULTING" FEES

Just prior to the passage of several laws in the U.S., barring payoffs by American firms to foreign officials in order to secure contracts for business, Martin Pipelines Inc., an American construction company, found itself in the following situation in a foreign country: a German firm, a French firm and Martin Pipelines were all bidding on a giant project for a nationwide oil pipeline in the country, payment to be made in cash in periodic installments as the work progressed and payment in full at its completion. Because of its expertise in the field, especially its cost efficiencies based on new equipment technology, Martin Pipelines was certain it could outbid its rivals, get the contract and still make a fine profit while, also, providing good jobs to many Americans (American unemployment was high in this, a recession, year). The only problem in securing the contract was the typical "fee" expected by the key foreign officials, a substantial one, for their "consulting services" in handling the bids. Although really just a payoff, Martin Pipelines on-the-scene executives knew that, without the expected payoff, one of the other companies would surely get the contract (both had already made their payoffs). So, Martin Pipelines made their payoff, too. Later, they won the contract.

(a) Using any or all of the major ethical tests (p.155), what, if anything, is unethical about the American firm's actions?
(b) What about the ethics of the German and French companies?
(c) What about the ethics of the foreign recipients of a payoff?

51 CANCER PREVENTION AN OVERHEAD COST

"One in five cancer cases in the U.S. is related to one's job," reported The Miami Herald (9/12/78,p.9-A) along with the following statistics: of about 4 million workers exposed to asbestos for long periods, 1.6 million will probably die of asbestos-related cancer, about 67,000 people per year for the next thirty years; of about 1.5 million workers exposed to arsenic, about 5000 excess cancer deaths are expected every year; of some 2 million workers exposed to benzene, about a thousand excess cancer deaths are anticipated every year. And so on. The workplace can, indeed, be dangerous to your health. And quite a dilemma: to develop and install pollution-control devices significantly reducing the above rates of death, company managements would incur considerably higher costs which, as overhead, must be passed on into higher prices, which lose sales and jobs. Ironically, a firm,installing such devices and accepting the higher costs and prices, would find its own workers, in their role as purchasers, buying from the competition at its lower prices (due to lower pollution-control costs and higher pollution affecting their workers). The laws of the marketplace create harsh realities for the workplace. Cancer prevention devices in the workplace raise costs, and prices, while consumers in the marketplace generally buy the products of that workplace with the lowest prices.

(a) Would you, as a consumer, pay a somewhat higher price and buy from a company whose higher price is caused by higher cancer prevention costs in its workplace? Would others?

(b) Suppose the five major producers of a product met in a hotel, agreed to install high-cost pollution controls equally and therefore raise prices equally, so that none would lose competitive position by doing it alone. Is this ethical? Is it illegal? Should it be? What do you recommend? What about international competition, their costs & prices?

52 KNOWING WHERE TO BUY

Sid Wheeling, a board director of a large land development firm specializing in development of shopping malls, learns at a board meeting of a final decision as to the location of a new and huge mall, to be developed over the next two years. Adjacent homes in the area are run-down and sell cheap (but their prices will soar as soon as the news of the new mall becomes public). The next day, he buys ten of these old homes at cheap prices. Later, when news of the new mall becomes generally known throughout the community, land prices in the new mall area double (apartment builders particularly anxious to buy and build near the new mall). Sid sells the ten properties at a huge profit. "Insider" information can be very profitable.

(a) Has Sid, in any way, acted unethically?

(b) Is there any unethical conflict of interest involved?

(c) Has Sid violated any of his ethical obligations as a director?

(d) Would you have acted as Sid did if you were in his place?

SELECT
BIBLIOGRAPHY

Ackerman, R. W., The Social Challenge to Business, Harvard, 1975
Anshen, M., (ed.), Managing the Socially Responsible Corporation, 1974
Arrow, K., Social Choice & Individual Values, Wiley, 1963
Backman, J., Advertising and Competition, New York University, 1967
Bailey, E., Economic Theory of Regulatory Constraint, Heath, 1973
Bakewell, C. M., Source Book in Ancient Philosophy, Scribners, 1907
Barry, V., Moral Issues in Business, Wadsworth, 1979
Bartels, R., Ethics in Business, Ohio State University, 1963
Baumhart, R., Ethics in Business, Rinehart, 1968
Beard, M., A History of Business (2 vols.), University of Michigan, 1962
Beauchamp, T. & N. E. Bowie, Ethical Theory and Business, Prentice, 1979
Becker, G., The Economics of Discrimination, University of Chicago, 1971
Behrman, J., Ethics and Business, Oelguschlager Press, 1981
Berle, A., et. al., The Modern Corporation & Private Property, Harcourt, 1968
Bernfield, S., The Foundations of Jewish Ethics, KTAV Publishers, 1968
Blondel, J., Comparing Political Systems, Praeger Co., 1972
Blum, J., et. al., The National Experience (2 vols), Harcourt, 1973
Boorstin, D., The Americans (3-vol. history), 1973
Bowie, N, Business Ethics, Prentice-Hall, 1982
Bradshaw, T. & D. Vogel (ed.), Corporations & Their Critics, McGraw, 1981
Brinton, C., A History of Western Morals, Harcourt, 1959
Broad, C. D., Five Types of Ethical Theory, Littlefield, 1959
Brooks, J. (ed.), The Autobiography of American Business, Doubleday, 1974
Burnham, J., Suicide of the West, Arlington House, 1964
Burr, J. R. & M. Goldinger, Philosophy & Contemporary Issues, Macmillan, '72
Bursk, E., (ed.), The World of Business (4 vols), Simon & Schuster, 1962
Campbell, A., et. al., The Quality of American Life, Sage, NY, 1976
Chamberlain, J., The Enterprising Americans: A History, Time Inc., 1962
Cherrington, D. J., The Work Ethic, American Mgmt. Assn., 1980
Childs, M. W. & D. Cater, Ethics in a Business Society, Mentor, 1954
Clark, J. W., Religion & the Moral Standards of American Businessmen, 1966
Cochran, T., Business in American Life, McGraw-Hill, 1972 (A History)
Comanor, W. & T. Wilson, Advertising and Market Power, Harvard, 1974
Cooke, D., Marvels of American Industry, Hamand Inc., 1962
Cox, E., et. al., The Nader Report on the FTC, 1969
Darlington, C. D., The Evolution of Man and Society, 1969
Davis, J., Earlier History of American Corporations (2 vols.), 1965
Davis, K. & R. L. Blomstrom, Business, Society & Environment, McGraw, 1971
DeGeorge, R. T., Business Ethics, Macmillan, 1981
Demsetz, H., The Market Concentration Doctrine, Amer. Enterprise, 1973
Derber, M., The American Idea of Industrial Democracy, U. of Illinois, 1970

Donaldson, T., *Ethical Issues in Business*, 1979
------------, *Corporations and Morality*, 1982
Dorfman, R. & N., *Economics of the Environment*, Norton Press, 1972
Drucker, P.F., *The Age of Discontinuity*, Harper, 1968
Edmunds, S.W., *Alternative U.S. Futures*, Goodyear, 1978
Ehler, S. & J. Morrall, *Church and State Through the Centuries*, Burns, 1954
Eichner, A.S., *The Emergence of Oligopoly*, Johns Hopkins, 1969
-----------, *The Megacorp and Oligopoly*, Cambridge U. Press, 1976
Elbing, A. & C., *The Value Issue of Business*, McGraw, 1967
Evans, W.A., *Management Ethics*, Nijhoff Publishers, 1981
Feather, N.T., *Values in Education and Society*, Free Press, 1975
Ferguson, J.M., *Advertising and Competition*, Cambridge, 1974
Ferm, V., *The History of Philosophical Systems*, Philosophical Lib., 1950
Fleishman, J. & B. Payne, *Ethical Dilemmas and the Education of Policy-makers*, Hastings Center, 1980
Fletcher, J., *Situation Ethics: The New Morality*, Westminster, 1966
Foot, P. (ed.), *Theories of Ethics*, Oxford Press, 1967
Frankena, W., *Ethics*, Prentice-Hall, 1963
Friedman, L., *A History of American Law*, Simon & Schuster, 1973
Friedman, M., *Capitalism and Freedom*, U. of Chicago, 1962
Fuller, J., *The Gentlemen Conspirators*, Grove Press, 1962
Galbraith, J.K., *The New Industrial State*, Houghton-Mifflin, 1967
Garrett, T., *Business Ethics*, Appleton-Century, 1966
---------, *Cases in Business Ethics*, Appleton-Century, 1968
George, C.S., *History of Management Thought*, Prentice-Hall, 1968
Golembiewski, R., *Men, Management and Morality*, McGraw-Hill, 1965
Gothie, D.L., *Business Ethics and Social Responsibilities*, U. of Va., 1974
Gouinlock, J., *John Dewey's Philosophy of Values*, Humanities Press, 1972
Gould, J., *Classic Philosophical Questions*, Merrill, 1975
Grant, R.M., *Early Christianity and Society*, Harper, 1977
Greenwood, W.T., *Issues in Business and Society*, Houghton, 1964
Gunderson, G., *A New Economic History of America*, McGraw, 1976
Gustafson, J., *Protestant and Roman Catholic Ethics*, U. of Chicago, 1978
Hancock, R.N., *Twentieth Century Ethics*, Columbia, 1974
Hardin, G., *Exploring New Ethics for Survival*, Penguin, 1973
Hastings Center, *The Teaching of Ethics in Higher Education*, 1980
Hay, R.D. & E.R. Gray, *Business and Society*, Southwestern, 1981
Hazlitt, H., *The Failure of the New Economics*, Arlington House, 1959
---------, *The Foundations of Morality*, Van Nostrand, 1964
Heilbroner, R. & L. Thurow, *Economics Explained*, Prentice-Hall, 1982
-----------, *The Worldly Philosophers*, Simon & Schuster, 1961
Heyne, P.T., *Private Keepers of the Public Interest*, McGraw-Hill, 1968
Hill, I., *The Ethical basis of Economic Freedom*, Wash. D.C., 1976

Hoffman, W. (ed.), The Work Ethic in Business, Oelguschlager Press, 1981
Hopper, R. J., The Early Greeks, Harper, 1976
Hudson, W. D., Modern Moral Philosophy, Doubleday, 1970
Hutchinson, D., The Foundations of the Constitution, Univ. Books, 1975
Jaeger, W., Aristotle, 1948
---------, Paideia: Ideals of Greek Culture (3 vols.), Oxford Press, 1944
Jay, A., Management and Machiavelli, Holt, 1967
Johnson, B., The Attack on Corporate America, McGraw-Hill, 1978
Kuhn, J. & I. Berg, Values in a Business Society, Harcourt, 1968
Kurtz, P., (ed.), Moral Problems in Contemporary Society, Prentice, 1969
Kneese, A. V., Pollution, Prices and Public Policy, Brookings Inst., 1975
LaCroix, W. L., Principles for Ethics in Business, 1978
Ladd, J., Ethical Relativism, Wadsworth, 1973
Larson, J., (ed.), The Responsible Businessman, Holt, 1966
Larson, M. A., The Religion of the Occident, Philosophical Library, 1959
Lewis, G. H., Biographical History of Philosophy, n.d.
Litschert, R. J. & E. A. Nicholson, The Corporate Role & Ethical Behavior, Petrocelli Publishing, 1977
Lodge, R., The Great Thinkers, Ungar Press, 1964
Long, E. L., A Survey of Christian Ethics, Oxford Press, 1967
Luthans, F., et. al., Social Issues in Business, Macmillan, 1980
Maccoby, M., The Gamesman, Simon & Schuster, 1976
McGee, J. S., The Defense of Industrial Concentration, Praeger, 1971
Manne, H. G., et. al., The Modern Corporation & Social Responsibility, 1972
Merrill, H. F., (ed.), Classics in Management, Amer. Mgmt. Assn., 1960
Morgan, T. D., Economic Regulation of Business, West, St. Paul, 1976
Nader, R., et. al., (ed.), Corporate Power in America, Grossman, 1973
Nagel, J., The Descriptive Analysis of Power, Yale University, 1975
Orr, D., Property, Markets and Government Intervention, Goodyear, 1976
Owens, J., The Theory and Practice of Managing, Mgmt. Educ., D.C., 1982
Packard, V., The Waste Makers (1963) and The Hidden Persuaders (1957)
Pascale, R. T. & A. G. Athos, The Art of Japanese Management, Simon, 1981
Perkins, E. J. (ed.), Men and Organizations, Putnams, 1977
Petit, T., The Moral Crisis in Management, McGraw-Hill, 1967
Powers, C, et. al., Ethics in the Education of Business Managers, Hastings, 1980
Rawls, J., A Theory of Justice, Harvard U. Press, 1971
Reischauer, E. O., The Japanese, Harvard U. Press, 1977
Rembar, C., The Law of the Land, Simon & Schuster, 1980
Roche, G., The Bewildered Society, Arlington House, 1972
Rodman, I., The Executive Jungle, Warner Books, 1973
Roll, E., The World After Keynes, Praeger, 1968
Rosen, S., Future Facts, Simon & Schuster, 1976
Ross, J. & M. Kami, Corporate Management in Crisis, Prentice-Hall, 1973

Ross, S.D., Moral Decision: An Introduction to Ethics, Freeman Press, 1972
Ross, W.D., Aristotle, 1949
Russell, B., History of Western Philosophy, Simon & Schuster, 1945
--------, Human Society in Ethics and Politics, Simon & Schuster, 1952
Russell, R., A History of the American Economic System, Appleton, 1964
Sahakian, W.&M., Ideas of the Great Philosophers, Barnes & Noble, 1966
Sayles, L.R., Individualism and Big Business, McGraw, 1963
Schumpeter, J., Capitalism, Socialism and Democracy, Harper, 1947
Sealey, R., A History of the Greek City States, Univ. of Ca. Press, 1976
Sellars, W.S. (ed.), Readings in Ethical Theory, Appleton, 1970
Shepherd, W.G., (ed.), Public Policies Toward Business, Irwin, 1979
Sherman, R., The Economics of Industry, Little Brown, 1974
Shorey, P., What Plato Said, 1958
Silk, L. & D. Vogel, Ethics and Profits, Simon & Schuster, 1976
Simon, J., Issues in the Economics of Advertising, U. of Illinois, 1970
Smart, J., et. al, Utilitarianism: For and Against, Cambridge Press, 1973
Smith, A., Wealth of Nations, Modern Library, 1937
Smith, R.A., Corporations in Crisis, Doubleday, 1963
Sneath, E.H., The Evolution of Ethics, Yale U. Press, 1927
Starling, G., The Changing Environment of Business, Wadsworth, 1980
Steiner, G.A., Business and Society, Random House, 1971
Steiner, P.O., Mergers: Motives, Effects and Policies, U. of Michigan, 1975
Stevens, E., Business Ethics, Paulist Press, 1979
Strickland, A.D., Government Regulation and Business, Houghton, 1980
Sufrin, S.C., Management of Business Ethics, Kennikat, 1980
Taylor, A.E., Plato, 1957
Taylor, P., Problems of Moral Philosophy, Dickerson, 1972
Taylor, P.W., Principles of Ethics, Dickerson, 1975
Tawney, R.H., Religion and the Rise of Capitalism, Mentor, 1947
Terkel, Studs, Working, Avon, 1974
Toffler, A., Future Shock, Bantam, 1971
Towle, J., Ethics and Standards in American Business, 1967
Tucker, R., Philosophy and Myth in Karl Marx, Cambridge Press, 1961
Vernon, R., Sovereignty at Bay: The Multinational Spread, Basic Books, 1971
Walton, C.C., Business and Social Progress, Praeger, 1970
-----------, The Ethics of Corporate Conduct, Prentice-Hall, 1977
Weber, A., History of Philosophy, Scribner, 1908
Weber, Max, Protestant Ethic and the Spirit of Capitalism
Wellman, C., Morals and Ethics, 1975
Williams, B., Morality: An Introduction to Ethics, Harper, 1972
Yaeger, L.B. & D.G. Tuerck, Foreign Trade & U.S. Policy, Praeger, 1976

INDEX